SHOLEM ASCH

EAST RIVER

A NOVEL

Translation by A. H. Gross

G. P. Putnam's Sons, New York

Fifth Impression

Designed by Robert Josephy

Manufactured in the United States of America

PART I

CHAPTER ONE

BROKEN DOLLS were strewn all about the room. The long-suffering teddy bear had lost its tail, what with the children having dragged it over the rooms and hallways, the courtyards, and the sidewalks. But it still lived, though its tail was gone, its head shapeless, and the rip in its belly clumsily sewn together with halting needle and thread. Standing on three legs—the way little Goldie had thrown it down—with its head cocked to one side, it looked like a living animal which, clumsily but adequately, performed the sum of the movements ordained for it.

The basement room seemed unusually quiet, so quiet that the footsteps of the people outside passing the window could be distinctly heard; in the customary noise and confusion, they would neither have been heard nor noticed. Door and windows were open. In spite of the sounds which carried in from outside, the basement room seemed to be bathed in a dead stillness.

Stillness is a relative term. It was only in comparison with the sounds which were ordinarily carried into the room that it now seemed quiet. The silence had even put the little two-year-old to sleep on the bed in the corner of the room, a lollipop in her mouth, her hand clutching the stick.

Man and beast—of the latter the room had more than its share —gave no sign of life, were congealed in the hot and oppressive air which filled the basement room. The two dogs, Snake, the German dachshund, and Killer, the enormous police dog, lay sprawled on the floor. They even lacked the energy to protest against the bites of the flies which, grown impudent in the heat, filled the room. Snow White, the cat, lay unashamed on the bed, her forepaws over the edge.

Goldie's mother, like a crumpled ruin, was sprawled full length on the bed, her arms flung straight out, as though all the life had

3

been drained out of her body. The heat, heavy with the smell of meat from the slaughterhouse and butcher shops near by, enveloped the senses with a deep fatigue. It was as though someone had pumped the air out of space and filled it with a vapor of humidity and oppressiveness which lay heavy as lead and paralyzed all movement. But the leaden air was able to paralyze only the living beings; the life which the child's hands had brought into being in her world of toys went on. The toys seemed to carry on their adventurous life which had only been interrupted when Goldie fell asleep.

The silence was suddenly broken by the sound of heavy footsteps clattering down the basement steps, and a nasal voice rent the sleeping quietness of the room. There was a torrent of words, in a sort of mongrel English.

"Missus... *Ola Boga!* ... the *golombia* from 57th Street... over the roofs ... and the pigeon ... the Japanese... hurry, Missus, let ours out ..."

The words came from Antoni Choleva, whose nickname was "Ola Boga," the Polish knacker and butcher's apprentice who worked in one of the slaughterhouses. Dressed in his Sunday shirt, soaked with sweat, which dripped, too, from the bushy head of hair above his short, thick neck, he ecstatically shouted out the news which, rendered into English, was intended to mean: "Missus! May God be in your heart! The 57th Street pigeons are flying over the roofs, and the rare Japanese pigeon is among them. Hurry up, Missus, and let ours out!"

In the neighborhood of the East River, from 48th Street to the sixties, there were two amateur pigeon breeders who were constantly staging pigeon fights. One was the millionaire Kassman on 57th Street; the other was Harry Greenstock, known simply as Harry to the entire neighborhood. There was constant competition between the two breeders as to which one's female birds would entice the other's males to their cages. Anyone who knows anything about pigeon breeding will understand the importance of the issue; for the unfortunate outsider its dramatic significance will be obscure.

Not very long before, the millionaire Kassman had imported from Japan a rare male specimen, known to pigeon fanciers as "dove," because of the rainbow colors on its throat and pinfeathers. For this specimen Harry Greenstock lusted; he would have given anything to pair it with one of his females. Whenever

4

Kassman flew his pigeons over the roofs near the East River, Harry would let out his birds, too.

In the wink of an eye, as though someone had waved a magic wand, every living thing in the room was up and out into the yard, the young Polack in the lead, his fat wife trailing after him, after them the awakened dogs and the crying child, all of them running to the pigeon cages in a corner of the long yard. A hurried opening of the cage doors and at once the beating of wings stirred the air and the birds rose high. The Polack waved a sheet attached to a pole, urging the pigeons on, and soon the silver wings of a host of birds gleamed in the high sunlight, wheeling in a circle above the roofs of the tall houses.

On the street the Sunday stillness spread its Sabbath calm over the sidewalks and houses. Most of the people in the houses of the East River neighborhood were held fast in the heat and laziness which the Sunday day of rest had brought to them. Lulled by the heat into a sleepless coma, the husbands and fathers sprawled on the beds in their stifling rooms and took the edge off the heat with the cans of beer or the containers of ice cream their wives sent up to them from the sidewalk below by means of strings dropped down from the open windows. Few children were in the houses, nor could they be seen on the streets. Kind neighbors had taken them along to a picnic which the Tammany Hall boss was giving this Sunday to the people of the neighborhood, starting with a boat ride up the Hudson. Of course, only members of Tammany in good standing had the right to attend; it was among these that the district captain had distributed the tickets. But practically all the children of the district went along, escorted by neighbors who passed them off as their own. Everyone was eager for the ice cream and the bottles of milk which the boss had promised to distribute among the younger ones.

It was for this reason that the streets seemed dead. Only a few of the women, whom the heat had driven out of their rooms, sat about on the steps of the buildings, or leaned on the window sills over which bedclothes, sheets, and worn mattresses had been thrust.

Through the open windows came the odors of Sunday cooking. The sharp tang of gefüllte fish or boiled beef from a Jewish household joined with odors of a stew from an Irish home or the spaghetti and meat balls of an Italian family. The sour smell of

5

damp mattresses and drying wash engulfed the thousand and one odors into one uniform smell.

As soon as the wings of the pigeons began to show in the sky above the roofs a stir began in all the houses. Heads showed through open windows, eyes following the weaving flight of the birds. It was astonishing how the common interest in Harry's pigeons knit together the motley population of the neighborhood.

Grownups, like children, are greedy for play. It might be said that practically all the inhabitants of 48th Street were interested in Harry's pigeons. Old and young, people of different nationalities and faiths, all creeds and races found a common level. To the neighborhood the birds were not "Harry's pigeons"; they were "the 48th Street pigeons." The millionaire's flock was "the 57th Street pigeons." And everyone knew of the competition between them.

It took hardly a moment for the news to spread that the 57th Street flock was flying, and that the Japanese dove was in it. Every heart in the neighborhood beat fast with hope that a 48th Street female bird would decoy the 57th Street prize to Harry's cages. And everyone in the neighborhood lent a helping hand.

At last Uncle Maloney put in an appearance.

Mike Maloney was the actual "captain" of the block. He was close to the Tammany boss of the district, and one of the leaders of the local Elks club. Although it was he who had handed out the invitations and tickets to the neighborhood for the day's picnic in the name of the big boss, himself he hadn't gone along. In his private life he was a lonely and undemonstrative type of man. He hated noise and excitement and the presence of a lot of people. For this reason he never attended the picnics which the boss gave, finding objectionable the crowded boats, the men reeking of beer, the women odorous with the sour smell of spoiled milk, and the children smeared with melting ice cream. He was a man with a delicate nature; what he liked above all was to spend his time alone in his bachelor quarters. His only real friend— apart from the appearance of friendship he had to put up for the party members in good standing—was Harry Greenstock. He looked on Harry's home as his own, and when Harry was away he considered himself responsible for everything that happened there.

So that now, when the event eagerly awaited for weeks was at

6

last taking place, Uncle Maloney showed up. He was dressed—
as was his custom even on the hottest days—in his traditional
severe suit, buttoned up to the last button, an Elks emblem gleaming in his lapel, and with a stiff straw hat on his head. Quietly and
with dignity he took over the command of the pigeon cages.

He dispatched Antoni, "Ola Boga," to the roof of the adjoining
slaughterhouse armed with a stick to keep the pigeons from
perching there. The Italian Tony of 48th Street, who had come
running, half dressed and out of breath, he sent off to the super-
intendent of the new skyscraper on 52nd Street with a message
from "the boss" to post himself on the roof with a flag so as to
maneuver the pigeons farther north. Soon there were watchers
posted on most of the high roofs between 48th Street and 57th
Street, armed with sticks and sheets—most of them volunteers,
come of their own initiative to lend a hand. They maneuvered
the wheeling pigeons so that they swung in broad circles ten blocks
wide, the circles gradually approaching each other.

Moshe Wolf Davidowsky, owner of the grocery store on
48th Street, had carried his paralyzed nineteen-year-old son
from the sultry air of the flat on the first floor and seated him
on the wheel chair in front of the store. The store was open on
Sunday; it was closed on Saturday, the Jewish Sabbath. The
boy, whom the infantile paralysis epidemic had crippled during
his first year at college, had a book spread open on his knees. He
sat in the shadow of the street's solitary tree and read while the
beating of the pigeons' wings awoke the street from its Sunday
semi-sleep. His father, alarmed by the noise that came in from
the street, left two customers waiting and went out to his son.
Shading his dark eyes with his hands, he peered at the sky where
the pigeons circled, and turned to his son. On the youth's face,
with its faint traces of beard, there was a smile of cynicism over
the antics of the grownups.

"Our holy writings call such people 'pigeon-flyers,'" Moshe
Wolf said. "They are considered unfit to be witnesses. They are
too frivolous." With a handkerchief he wiped the perspiration
from his son's forehead.

"Why?" the boy asked.

"I don't know why. But that's what the holy writings say. In
the old country we looked down on them, too."

7

"Those holy writings of yours..." The boy shrugged his shoulders.

"And what do your books say?" his father asked with an indulgent smile.

"My books say that play is a necessity for people, just as necessary as food and air. Pigeon flying is play for grownups, like any other kind of play."

"Is that so?" Moshe Wolf made a gesture. "Play is necessary for people, just like food and air? I didn't know that." He adjusted the awning that was attached to the wheel chair. "Does the sun bother you?"

"No," the boy answered. He turned back to his book.

"If you need anything, call me," Moshe Wolf said, and went into the store to attend to the waiting customers.

In the tranquil Sunday air the pigeons wheeled in two great circles over the roofs. Faces from below were turned up to them; hearts beat in eagerness waiting for the moment when the two flocks, their circles coming nearer to each other, would intermingle.

The moment came. One flock entered the congruent circle, cut a path through it, and again began to wheel over a wide circumference. This happened several times until the watchers saw a single pigeon from the 57th Street flock leave its own circle and join the 48th Streeters.

The excitement of the onlookers was intense. Uncle Maloney's face turned a beet red. By a series of prearranged signals he gave his watchers to understand that they were not to disturb the birds but were to refrain from any kind of movement. Harry's flock, circling in the air, gradually began to careen toward 48th Street, the lone 57th Street pigeon with it, until all the birds were back in their home grounds. Some went directly into the cages; others perched on roofs near by, in a little while returning one by one to their perches in Harry's yard.

Only two pigeons remained out, one a female from Harry's flock, the other, wheeling after her, a male from the 57th Street flock. For a while they perched on the wall of the Greenstock yard, one a little distance from the other. It seemed as though the male couldn't make up his mind about leaving his home cage and letting himself be seduced into a strange nest by the attractive female who had so suddenly captured his heart. He perched, his

8

head on his breast, and the sunlight shone on his throat feathers that bloomed with all the colors of the rainbow. The female tried all her wiles to seduce the male stranger into her nest. She circled about him, soft cooings burbling from her throat, as though she was trying to entice him with the special magic of her voice. She spread her feathers, white to ashen gray, to the brown feathers of her tail. She beat her wings violently as though she wanted to show the timorous male the vigor of her muscles, the promise of the strength of her femaleness. The male, as though aware of his rarity, his aristocratic breed, and his exotic Japanese ancestry—officially attested by the badge affixed to one of his scarlet legs—allowed himself to be persuaded, and as though he had decided that the adventure was worth trying, he hopped over nearer to the female, spreading his feathers and showing their glorious colors to the enthusiastic watchers. The pair began to whisper secrets, putting their heads together and murmuring to one another, for all the world like an engaged couple, until they seemed to reach an understanding, each accepting the other's conditions, and the male, modestly but with dignity, flew after the female and entered the door of the cage.

It was this that the young Polack, Choleva, was waiting for. Pulling down a central lever, he closed all the windows to the cage. Uncle Maloney, his severe black Sunday suit covered with feathers, straw, and corn, was seated inside the cage. Now he crawled out of the lower door, gently holding in his hand the rare prize, the Japanese pigeon which the millionaire Kassman had imported from the Orient at so much cost and care—the prize for which all of 48th Street had been waiting.

Nothing had ever exceeded the excitement and enthusiasm that the affair of the pigeons stirred up in the block. The street was a city in itself, in a world of its own. The people who lived in it knew each other and were interested in each other. All of them took part in the block's affairs: not only the "official" assistants who helped Harry with his pigeons, watched out for the cats and dogs and fowl in his yard during his absence, and were his closest associates, such as Uncle Maloney, the young Polish butcher, and the Italian bricklayer, Tony; but even, for instance, the Hungarian restaurant owner, Mr. Neufeld.

Neufeld was the aristocrat of 48th Street and had little to do with the Russian and Polish Jews on the block, or with the Irish

9

and Italians. He had a small restaurant on First Avenue and was very proud of his Hungarian background. His favorite remark was: "I'm not one of those Russians; I'm a Hungarian." Nevertheless, at a time like this, with the others—Donato and Pasquale, the Italian bakers on First Avenue—he came running to Harry's pigeon cage to take a look at the unexampled phenomenon, the Japanese rarity that all had talked about but none had yet seen. Although Neufeld considered himself a pitch above the others and kept himself aloof from them, he had been enthusiastic about pigeons ever since his youth in the little Carpathian village where he was born, and he was unable to resist the temptation of gloating over the prize the 48th Street flock had captured. He stood among the others in his custom-made silk shirt, with his initials embroidered in enormous letters just above his round belly, an amber cigar holder stuck in his mouth below his black-dyed mustache, and gazed in astonishment at the frightened pigeon in Maloney's hand. He was unable to resist the temptation of pouring a little cold water over the enthusiasm of the triumphant amateurs.

"He'll never be a good mixer," Mr. Neufeld remarked, with a shake of his head. He waved his cigar holder in the air, accompanying it with a long "No-o-o!"

"Why not?" asked one of the others belligerently.

"Can't you see that his breed is too delicate to have anything to do with your two-for-a-nickel birds? He won't mate with your female."

"But he went after her! Who got him here if not our female?"

"He'll never mate," Neufeld repeated, shaking his head. "Too delicate."

"He'll mate all right," said Uncle Maloney. "Wait till you see one of our grays with a rainbow-colored throat and tail feathers. We'll start a new breed."

But Neufeld kept shaking his head and waving his cigar holder pessimistically. He left the yard, the baleful glares of the others following him.

From outside on the street there came a confused clatter as though a regiment of troops was approaching. Through the basement door into the courtyard charged Harry Greenstock. After him trooped a crowd of children of all ages, boys and girls, but mostly girls. They made way for him, and Uncle Maloney came toward him with the Japanese pigeon in his outstretched hand.

For all his eagerness and excitement, Harry took the pigeon in his hand with experienced care. As though he would protect it with his own body he nestled it carefully under his shirt, against his chest, holding it there gently while Uncle Maloney gave him all the details of what had taken place.

"It was me who stood on the roof of the slaughterhouse, not Tony," the young Polack interrupted Maloney's report. It was clear he didn't mean to be cheated out of the credit that was due him for his part in the capture. Uncle Maloney looked sternly at the Polack who had the impudence to interrupt him, and Harry held up his hand as a warning to Choleva to be quiet.

The children back from the picnic stood around breathlessly listening to Uncle Maloney. They were all neighborhood children. Harry's daughters, the two older ones, were among them. Rachel, with her flashing black eyes, her black hair bound in a ribbon over her oval face, her well-rounded young breasts and her tall figure, looked herself like a specimen of a delicate breed from a strange world, like a character stepped right out of the pages of the Bible. She was sixteen years old. Although her hand-embroidered white batiste dress was wrinkled and her hair tumbling out of the ribbon around it, the delicate cream color of her skin, the proud lines of her cheeks, nose, and chin, and the long throat, gave her a holiday appearance which compensated for the wrinkles of her dress and the disorder of her hair. She was her father's favorite, and she knew it. She was the only one who dared to put out her hand to caress the frightened pigeon's head, which peered out in terror from her father's shirt front. She even persuaded her father to allow her to take the precious bird in her hands. As she held the exotic bird to her own breast she seemed herself like an exotic princess who had blundered from a storybook into the courtyard on 48th Street.

Her younger sister, Bertha, in a similar white batiste dress that was even more wrinkled, and with her hair even more disordered, was jealous. She, too, wanted to hold the pigeon. Harry allowed each of them to hold it for a while, protecting it all the time with his own hands. He even allowed Rachel's friend and schoolmate, the dark and winsome Mary McCarthy, to hold it for a moment. Mary was the oldest daughter of the Greenstocks' Irish neighbor who lived in the adjoining house and whose windows overlooked Harry's yard. As she took the pigeon in her delicate, graceful hands, she bent her head down to the bird's head. The bow on the green ribbon that encircled her hair covered the bird, throwing a new and strange color on its feathers. She closed her eyes, and her sensitive face took on the same tender and pathetic appearance as the head of the pigeon. With her eyes closed she kept repeating:

"Oh, my lovely little birdie..."

When she opened her eyes and carefully gave the pigeon back to Harry, there was a tear on her cheek.

"How about you, young fellow?" Harry turned to a short, stout youngster, Irving Davidowsky, the younger son of the owner of the grocery store. "Would you like to hold him?"

Irving was only a year older than Rachel and Mary and was always around them. He was one of those Harry had taken to the picnic.

"I don't care." He gave a noncommittal shrug of his shoulders, a gesture he had copied from his crippled brother.

"Why?"

"It's all right for girls." He pointed to the cages. "What's the good of raising pigeons anyway? It doesn't pay to breed them to sell for food."

"Who told you that?" Harry asked.

"Mr. Shmulevitch told me. He says it's too much work and not enough meat."

It was an attitude the grownups hadn't expected. It seemed to make them children in the boy's eyes.

"And don't you think they're worth anything besides the meat on their bones?" Uncle Maloney asked him with a smile.

"They're all right to play with. But that's for kids, not for grownups," Irving answered.

The grownups burst into laughter.

"Stick around us, young man," Harry said. "You'll amount to something. Come around to the clubhouse during election. You'll be able to give us a hand. Politics is the kind of game you've got to learn when you're young."

"I'm not interested," said Irving, and shrugged his shoulders again.

"What are you interested in? In socialism? Like your brother Nathan?"

"Socialism don't mean anything to me."

"What does mean anything to you?" asked Uncle Maloney.

"This!" Irving rubbed his thumb over the first two fingers of his hand. "Money. When you've got money in your pocket, you've got politics in your pocket too. If, you haven't got it, you've got nothing. Rachel! Mary! See you later." Irving turned and ran out of the yard.

"A practical youngster," Maloney commented.

"You know what that kid does?" Harry said. "When other kids get out of school they sell newspapers. Not Irving. He buys damaged remnants of piece goods and peddles them among the pushcarts on First Avenue. He brings his mother about five dollars a week."

"A practical youngster," Maloney repeated. "The new generation. He'll get on."

CHAPTER TWO

HARRY GREENSTOCK loved nature. He had been born and brought up in Lenchiz, a little town in Poland, surrounded by forests, fields, and pasture land on which roved flocks of sheep. Barges and rafts floated on the river that passed near the town. His father, a cattle dealer, traveled through the villages with horse and wagon. Harry, from his childhood, had loved horses, cattle, dogs.

In America, to which his "uncle" Silberberg, a distant kinsman, had brought him, together with other of the townspeople, Harry had never let himself be harnessed to a factory sewing machine. He brought with him from the old country his trade of house painting and found work in America in the very houses his "uncle" owned. He had married a poor relative of Uncle Silberberg, and his first job had been to take care of a row of Silberberg's tenements on 48th Street, near the East River. This job he administered together with Yossel Shmulevitch, another of his "uncle's" relatives. To no one but his relatives would Silberberg entrust the care of his houses and business affairs.

Harry soon got acquainted with the Gentiles in the neighborhood, learned English—helped by his Americanized wife—and became a member of the Elks. Soon politics began to interest him; he quickly enough found out that without political influence you couldn't go far in New York. You had to have influential friends or you'd go under.

Tammany soon began to take notice of him. Mike Maloney became his intimate, and with Tammany influence Harry got some contracts to paint the slaughterhouses in the neighborhood. In this way he became independent of his "uncle," not like the others from the old country who couldn't manage without Silberberg's help and who were scared to death of offending him.

Harry was all right. Harry was a good mixer. Harry was

Harry. He made it his business to get along peacefully with every-body, with his kinsfolk from the old country as well as with the Gentiles in the neighborhood. His reputation in Tammany circles was good. Even Judge Greenberg, the district leader, who was Harry's god as well as his political boss, trusted him implicitly. He helped Tammany in the elections, and Tammany knew how to reward him. If anyone needed a favor—when a peddler got a summons for operating his pushcart without a license, or if there was any trouble with the police, or if it was a question of bail, or if some family got put out on the sidewalk with their scraps of furniture piled beside them—Harry was the one to do some-thing about it. He could fix anything through his friend Maloney ... or even through the district boss, Judge Greenberg himself, if necessary. The Judge would take his word for anything. Harry Greenstock was definitely the most influential person in the neighborhood.

Harry and Mike Maloney shared the administration of the block between them. Nothing could be done on 48th Street near the East River without their knowledge or permission. If there was trouble, they were the ones to adjust it; if there was a flare-up between the Irish and the Jews, they were the ones to straighten things out. Harry took care of the Jews; Mike took care of the Irish. But for Harry and Mike, the block would more than once have blazed out in a bloody riot that might have spread over the entire East River neighborhood.

The people in the block were Tammany's children, and Tam-many gave them a father's care. The neighborhood gathered under Tammany's wings like frightened chicks around the mother hen when it rains. And not only at election time but all the year round; not only when there was trouble, or when a favor was wanted; Tammany took care of its own on 48th Street at work and at play.

Harry Greenstock's house on the block had a yard. As to how he got the house, it's best not to ask too many questions. The yard didn't belong to him; he merely occupied it. It belonged to an estate that was deep in a complicated lawsuit. In the mean-while, with Tammany's help, Harry had managed to get the use of it, not only for his own affairs—raising pigeons and the like—but for all the neighbors on the block.

Harry's yard was not merely a yard. It was a paradise for

man and beast. He put up his pigeon cages there, and raised all kinds of animals and fowl. In one enclosure were rabbits; the Polack, Choleva, took care of them. In another was a pair of unique Chinese hens, which Harry kept as a curiosity. He had somehow or other acquired a small fox, taken from its mother when it was a cub; Harry's ambition was to domesticate the animal and give it the freedom of the house. Next to the fox he kept a lamb and a goat. It was as though he wanted to realize Isaiah's vision of the lion and the lamb lying down side by side. In a special stall in the yard, Zelig the junk dealer kept his nag.

So far as being a good Jew was concerned, Harry was by no means an indifferent member of his faith. Whenever a dispute broke out between the Jews and the Irish—"the Ikes and the Mikes"—that even Tammany couldn't control and that had to be fought out with fists, there was no doubt where Harry's sympathies lay. There was no question mark after the term Jew as applied to Harry, as was witnessed by his participation in the religious services arranged by Yossel Shmulevitch, the chicken dealer, and Moshe Wolf Davidowsky in a private house in the neighborhood. Nevertheless the neighborhood smelled something of the "goy" in him, as Shmulevitch expressed it.

His most intimate friends on the block were not the Jews but the Gentiles. Hundreds of mutual interests bound them together. His manner of life and his habits, which brought him close to the Christians in the neighborhood, separated and alienated the Jewish population from him. The mere fact that a Jew raised pigeons, and rabbits—whose flesh was not kosher and was banned from Jewish tables—and other "Gentile" animals, not to speak of his interest in such matters, was enough to attract the Christians in the neighborhood, of whatever nationality, to him. They were brothers under the skin; they had the same tastes. They were his comrades and his assistants. It was as though the animals and birds in Harry's yard in the middle of Manhattan had bewitched the Gentiles.

In time the yard became transformed into a literal garden of nations. Everyone tried to plant some flower or vegetable from the old country in the yard. In one corner Choleva started a Polish garden. He had somewhere or other managed to get some sunflower seeds and a couple of the cabbage plants without which no Polish garden would be complete. He worked on it every hour

16

of his free time, evenings and Sundays, and planted geraniums and morning-glories besides.

In the same way Tony, the Italian bricklayer, as soon as spring came around, spent his time in the yard to care for the bushes and fig tree he had planted in the autumn and covered with a mat of rushes. The fig tree, so carefully tended in a foreign clime, came to be a sort of shrine for the Italians around First Avenue, who would visit the yard each Sunday to gaze in ecstasy at this reminder of the old country.

Even Schultz, the German butcher from across the street, who was to be classed not as a friend of Harry's but rather as a distant friend of the pigeons, asked for and received Harry's permission to put a few potato hills in the yard; not that he needed the potatoes for his table; he just wanted to feast his eyes on the flowering plants.

In this way Harry's yard was the meeting place for the flowers, the vegetables, and the fruits of the nations—wine grapes from southern Italy, German potatoes and Polish morning-glories and nasturtiums and sunflowers, Italian artichokes that almost reached ripeness, and the barren branch that Tony optimistically called a fig tree.

On Sunday afternoons, when the summer heat drove the people of the block out of their flats to the scorching fire escapes, Harry's friends would gather in the yard. It was the link that bound them with their past. They recaptured their youth there. There they got a reminder of the smells of the old country's fields, the green valleys, the dewy meadows, the ponds and streams, the horses and dogs and fowl that they had left behind them. In Harry's yard pigeons flew over their heads with beating wings.

There was one feature of Harry's yard that attracted the entire block. That was Zelig the junk dealer's half-lame nag, which all of 48th Street—no one knew why—called "Long Anthony." Horses were by no means strangers to 48th Street. All along its length the East River was one extended stable for Manhattan's horses; automobiles were just beginning to make their appearance, but they were luxuries confined to the wealthy; the day of the automobile for mass use and mass transportation was still to come. Along the East River the air was thick with the smell of horses mingled with the fumes of raw whisky and noisy with the shouts and curses of truckmen and stable hands.

17

Long Anthony was not strictly a horse. He was an intimate member of every family on the block, without regard to religion, race, or color. It is unnecessary to report that every house on 48th Street had its household animals, dogs and cats, that were petted and kicked indiscriminately and were often the causes of violent disputes among the neighbors. But Long Anthony united the block into one family and was their common interest. Long Anthony was the kind of horse you couldn't help loving, mostly because of the sympathy he awakened in every heart. He was an unfortunate creature. Whatever disease there was to get, Long Anthony was the first to get it. Everyone on the block, big and little, worried about Anthony's health and gave advice to Zelig the junk dealer about what was to be done—how to feed him, how to groom him, even how to harness him. They plagued Zelig to death. There wasn't a one who didn't bitterly berate the miserable Zelig for the way he tended the nag. As soon as Zelig made his morning appearance, reins in hand, on the seat of the wagon, and his junk dealer's bells started jingling, everyone would begin to gather around. It wasn't that they had any junk to sell; they simply wanted to see how Long Anthony was getting along.

"Look at the way he's got the collar on him! Rubbing all the skin off his neck!"

"Look at the way he's got the bit in his mouth!"

And when Zelig would come back from his day's route, the wagon loaded with junk, and the sweat pouring from Long Anthony's flanks—surely no wonder on the hot, sultry summer days—then men, women, and children would really let him have it.

"Look at the way he's working the life out of the poor animal. He can hardly get his breath. Hey, Irishman, if they harnessed you up like that on a day like this..." The Italian bricklayer called Zelig "Irishman" in a spirit of gay nonsense.

"They ought to tell the S.P.C.A. the way that Jew takes care of the horse," one of the women yelled out of a third floor window. From her perch it was impossible to tell that Long Anthony was all of a lather and panting, but making complaints was taken for granted.

Poor Zelig was at last driven to some sort of reply. "What do you think he is, a horse for a circus?" he shouted back. "I've got to make a living out of him, haven't I?"

As was customary in such cases, the block divided into two

18

factions, each with contrasting philosophies—a Jewish party and Christian party.

"They should show as much pity, dear God, for human beings as they do for animals," a Jewish housewife said. She was standing at the door of Moshe Wolf's store and watching the scene. "They can see how the horse is sweating, but not poor Zelig. Let Zelig sweat for all they care, but not the horse."

"The prophet Hosea said it long ago. They sacrifice human beings, and they kiss calves." Moshe Wolf recited the phrase in a synagogue chant.

"Let them say what they like. They don't feed him; I feed him," Zelig commented in Yiddish. He completely ignored the Christian scoffers. "What do they think I've got him for? A circus horse? I've got him to drag junk, the way I drag plenty of it, God help me."

But the truth was that Zelig did not make a beast of burden out of Long Anthony all the time; sometimes he really was a "circus horse." The transformation took place on Sunday. Every Italian, Irish, or Jewish girl on the block would have her photograph taken sitting on Long Anthony's back, or sitting in a carriage to which the horse was harnessed, and holding the reins with both hands. Long Anthony appeared in the photographs well groomed, his hide well brushed, trimmed with all sorts of Sunday decorations, just like the girls with their bright ribbons braided into their well-combed hair. The photographs decorated the walls of the houses of numberless relatives and kinsfolk in the old countries.

Some time before, Harry had conceived the bright idea of teaching the children on the block to ride horseback. And who was to be the steed to carry the boys and girls of the block on his back for a ride around 48th Street if not Long Anthony? Harry had special claims on the horse. First of all he gave him quarters in his yard, more out of kindness than out of the hope of profit. He and his friends watched out for the horse and attended to his needs more than Zelig did. On the occasions when Zelig forgot to fill Long Anthony's trough with oats, or to clean out the stable, or to water him, Harry or one of the others—the Polack, or the bricklayer, or even Uncle Maloney himself—would attend to the chores. It is true they didn't spare curses on Zelig's head—but Long Anthony got what he was entitled to at the proper time.

And who but Harry and his pals tended Long Anthony through the thousand and one ailments that he always managed to contract? Harry was an expert in such matters from the old days back in the old country. In the house of his father, the cattle dealer, there were always horses, and Harry knew all about them. His first assistant, the Polack, was an expert, too, and so were the Italian bricklayer and the Italian baker. True, they knew more about mules than they knew about horses; it was mules who did the work in the Italian fields. But mules or horses, what difference did it make? They both stemmed from the same stock, didn't they? What would cure one would cure the other.

On one occasion there was a dispute between Harry and the Polack on the one hand, and the Italians on the other, as to the best way of burning out a "rose" on the horse's hide. It was a miracle that the argument didn't cost Long Anthony his life, for both sides insisted on trying their own remedies. The swelling on Long Anthony's hide was constantly exuding pus and blood. Zelig said that the horse had too delicate a hide. The trouble had come from a scratch from a rusty iron rail protruding over the front of the wagon; Zelig had backed up the horse suddenly with a violent tug of the reins.

"Any other horse would have laughed at a scratch like that. Many's the time I get a piece of rusty iron right in my guts, and nothing happens," Zelig complained to Harry. "Any other horse would have had a scratch, and that would have been the end of it! But not this—this—apology for a horse."

On the question of the diagnosis both sides to the dispute were in full agreement. The trouble was definitely an infection. Nor was there any difference of opinion over the necessity for burning it out. The only question was the method to be used. Harry and the Polack insisted that in Poland, in the old country, when a horse got an infection it was taken to the blacksmith, who would take a red-hot bar of iron, burn out the infected spot, and that would be the end of it. The Italians maintained that in Italy the practice was to apply hot compresses soaked in turpentine mixed with salt. The compress was kept on until the infected spot cleared up.

On the long-suffering horse both methods were tried. He bore

20

it all with patience and recovered, though it was never sure which treatment had cured him. If he could endure the Sunday "parade" in Harry's yard with the children of the block on his back, he could certainly endure anything.

On week days he was Zelig's horse. On Sundays he belonged to the block.

No Sunday summer afternoon was complete without a ride on Long Anthony's back for young and old; for it was not only the children of the block who were learning to ride. The older folks, too, would climb onto Long Anthony's patient back to show off the horsemanship they remembered from their youth in the old country. And although this Sunday the block was aquiver with excitement over the great pigeon battle and the name of the Japanese pigeon was on everyone's lips, it would have been unimaginable to let the day go by without putting Long Anthony through his paces.

As soon as the Japanese pigeon was safely stowed away in the cage, the crowd strolled over to the garden patches. Plants were watered, there were earnest discussions about the progress of the blooms since the previous Sunday, and there was friendly rivalry about the respective merits of the agricultural products of the old home countries, all of them represented in Harry's yard.

"There's a new leaf on the fig tree," Tony yelled out in excitement. "It wasn't there last Sunday."

Everyone went over to observe the phenomenon.

"Look at the morning-glory! Just like at home in Poland!" Choleva, the Polack, beamed in delight at the blossom growing near the pigeon cages.

"What do you know about morning-glories? The only thing that is grown in Poland is cabbage. Italy, that's where morning-glories grow!"

"Everything grows in Italy! Figs, grapes, roses, morning-glories! Maybe spaghetti, too," said Maloney, coming to the Polack's help.

"Yes, everything grows in Italy. In Napoli. Figs, roses, grapes, everything. . . ."

In the meanwhile Long Anthony stood near the fence trying to gnaw at the withered twigs of a clump of bushes. Zelig lay stretched out on the ground near him. Man and beast knew that they wouldn't be allowed to rest long, that soon enough it would be time for Long Anthony to go through his chores. Soon enough they both emitted painful sighs.... The time of torture was beginning.

This time, because of the stifling heat, the grownups didn't show off with their fancy horsemanship—how they "rode like Cossacks" in Poland, or how in Italy they trained the horse to pick up a handkerchief from the ground with its mouth; it had taken Tony two months to teach Long Anthony that one. Instead they turned Long Anthony over to the children. The horse stood there, his big intelligent head drooped down, and patiently allowed one child after another to mount him, just as patiently allowing the fathers of the children to lead him around the yard.

Harry's daughters, Mary McCarthy, the bricklayer's two children, and Jimmy, Mary's younger brother, had already had their ride on Long Anthony's back. At the opening in the low fence leading into the yard a woman appeared. In her arms she carried a crippled seven-year-old girl whose contorted mouth made unintelligible sounds, like the mewings of a cat in pain.

Everyone knew the mother and child. They belonged to the Russian, Stachovitch, who had a laundry in the cellar under Shmulevitch's chicken store. That spring an epidemic of infantile paralysis had swept over lower Manhattan. The disease, like an impenetrable Sphinx, hovered over the houses and glared at the young children. From time to time it spared its victims, but this spring it left its mark on homes and families. In many houses of the East River district there was a crippled child; at Moshe Wolf's house it was his older son; at the house of Silverman, the music teacher, his six-year-old son died. Among the Italian families of the neighborhood it was like a slaughter.

The little Stachovitch girl looked about with her eager young eyes, smiling at everyone, stammering her unintelligible sounds.

"She'd like a ride," her mother said with a pleading, half apologetic smile.

"Sure," said Harry. He took the child from the mother's arms, carried her as tenderly as though she were one of his pigeons, and put her on Long Anthony's back. The paralysis made it impossible for her to sit. Harry laid her gently on the old green blanket that lay across the horse's back.

Long Anthony bent down his wise old head to make it as easy as possible for the child and with careful steps began to walk the

22

well-trodden path in the yard, seeming to seek out the softest spots to plant his hoofs, as though he knew he carried a crippled child on his back.

"Let me take her picture," Maloney called out. "I'll go and get my camera. It'll only take a minute."

While Maloney was gone the mother, helped by the other children, freshened and fussed over the little girl. The children took the ribbons from their hair and offered them to be braided in the child's locks. When Maloney, bedewed with perspiration, came back with his camera, he found her, neat, polished, and furbelowed, lying ready on Long Anthony's back.

"Lift up your head. Otherwise they won't be able to see you," one of the children called out.

The child smiled.

The mother supported the child so that her little face, the ribbons braided into her blonde hair, would show up well, and so that everyone who saw the photograph would simply see the picture of a normal child riding the horse.

Long Anthony made his contribution, too. He disposed himself so that the child might be able easily to lie on his back and rest her head against her mother's arms. He didn't move or give a single flick of his tail. He stood frozen; it wouldn't be his fault if the photograph was not a success.

CHAPTER THREE

THE INHABITANTS of 48th Street fell into two categories. There were those who came and went, occupying for a short period the usually empty flats in one of the buildings of the long uniform row of three-story houses that lined part of both sides of the street. These were mostly down-at-the-heel theater folk, small-bit actors, musicians, and stage hands, who worked in the theatrical section farther west in Manhattan and whom poverty had driven to the cheaper neighborhood of the East River. Their places of residence changed with their "engagements." They weren't looked on as properly part of the local population; Uncle Maloney didn't even bother to try to get them to become members of the local Tammany club, or Harry to get them to vote correctly at election. Most of them were unnaturalized foreigners, but even the natives and naturalized citizens among them gave little thought to their voting rights. They were here today and gone tomorrow.

To the same category belonged the residents who were waiters in the elegant restaurants in the swanky sections of the city, and all of those who had jobs around the city's night life, over toward Broadway.

The other category was represented by the "old settlers," the permanent residents, the backbone of the block, who knew one another, loved or hated one another, but belonged together.

Mrs. Kranz's "apartment hotel" was in the middle of the block. The patrons kept constantly changing—but not the hotel nor Mrs. Kranz. Clara Kranz was a European; and she stayed one. Did she come from Vienna, from Slovakia, from Hungary? No one knew. She seemed to be the type that might belong to any of those countries, a characteristic type from the Austria of the Hapsburgs. She had the seductive figure and blonde hair of the Viennese, the good nature of Prague, and the easy acquiescence and friendliness of Budapest. Whether she was a widow, or a divorcee, or maybe an old maid, no one was quite sure. It was known that in her bedroom there was an enlarged colored photograph of a man with long, curled mustaches, dressed in a mountain-climbing costume, knee-length deerskin breeches, leather suspenders, a green hunting jacket, with a gun in his hand. Some said it was a picture of her husband, others of her sweetheart. But everyone believed he was a baron, of the Hungarian or Czech nobility. And everyone knew that he had fallen, dressed as he was in the picture, and gun in hand, from a mountain peak, and had been killed on the spot. At any rate that had all happened in the old country. In America there was nothing more of him than this handsomely colored photograph, enlarged from a small European original.

Mrs. Kranz was an independent woman, running her rooming house, which she graced with the name of apartment hotel, in two adjoining buildings which she had rented and furnished, for artists, musicians, and singers, most of them Central Europeans who had come from Austria to seek their fortunes in the world of the theater in America. Her clientele, needless to say, consisted of the type of artists who had either not yet begun or long since ended their careers on Broadway.

The musicians and singers lent color to the block, taking away the weekday bleakness of similar neighborhoods. There was always to be heard the scraping of fiddles and the tinkling of pianos through the rooming house windows. The block was bathed in the blue Danube waters of the Strauss waltzes which kept pouring through the windows into the street. In the early evenings the children of the block would dance to the rhythm of the music.

In front of the house one could see men of various ages, with long, wavy hair, in artistic knotted ties, unfamiliar European clothes, pastel-colored jackets, trousers narrow at the knees; women with unusual hair arrangements and gaily colored dresses and shawls. To the street they were "Bohemians."

It would seem that Mrs. Kranz was much attached to this sort of people, and she was said to be very good to them. She herself loved to sing and make music. It was told of her that she was once on the stage in the old country. From her appearance it would not be difficult to believe that she was once a "Bohemian" herself.

For as long as people could remember on 48th Street—and

that was a matter of six or eight years—Mrs. Kranz hadn't changed so much as a hair. It was difficult to tell her age. There are natures which seem to resist the passing of the years; time seems to have no effect on them, as though they live in a sphere beyond its sway. Mrs. Kranz looked as though her appearance had remained permanently fixed in her middle thirties.

Her figure was tall, and her unlined face was carefully and heavily powdered. At all times her blonde hair was carefully braided about her head and three little curls clung close to her forehead. In a short gypsy jacket, an Indian shawl around her shoulders, and a bewildering variety of ornaments, she presented an exotic picture. Long earrings dangled from the lobes of her ears; around her throat was a coral and amber band; old European ornaments were pinned over her high breasts; on her wrists an entire arsenal of charms and amulets dangled and glittered from wide bracelets. Her fingers sparkled with rings set with imitation stones. Her whole person was surrounded with an aura of heady and heavy Oriental perfume. You could detect, too, the odor of lavender and camphor, like the faint atmosphere around an ancient wedding dress left hanging forgotten in an old wardrobe. All the cosmetics and rose waters and other feminine devices with which she sought to retain the appearance of her youth now gone could not give her tall figure and smooth cheeks the freshness of youth. There was a sort of deadly fatigue that seemed to push its way through the cosmetics. True, it gave a quality of feminine delicacy and grace to her face, but it also evoked a feeling of anxiety lest she might suddenly wither away, like a flower that has been kept in a tightly closed glass jar and is suddenly exposed to the air.

It was no secret to 48th Street—there was no secret in 48th Street about anyone on the block—that the main reason for Mrs. Kranz's heroic efforts to hold on to her youth was to entangle and hold Harry Greenstock in the net she had spread for him. Everyone knew that Harry's wife suffered from asthma and that her heart was bad—she had already had a couple of serious attacks—and that she couldn't last long. Mrs. Kranz, they were sure, was simply making preparations ahead of time. That was the reason she was such a constant visitor to Harry's house, taking care of things, washing and combing the children. It was said, too, that she was winning away the children's affections even while their mother was still alive. She was even deluding the heart of the sick woman herself with all the attentions she heaped on her, helping her during her bad days, caring for the children so generously that they loved her almost as their mother. And all in order to take over when the proper time should come.

But it wasn't altogether so. It is true that she was in love with Harry. In all the block he was the only one who reminded her of the old country. She loved his home and she loved his children, and she loved to steal away with him some evenings—when there were no prying eyes about —to sit in Neufeld's Hungarian restaurant and listen to gypsy music and watch the dancing of a Hungarian czardas. He was such a sport, was Harry Greenstock. The figure of a hussar, a Hungarian hussar. Thick black hair and black mustache. And the way he dressed. Like a count. It was a privilege and a pleasure to go out with him. You felt important sitting with Harry in a restaurant or being ushered into your theater seats. And then there were his connections with important politicians. The boss of the ward clapped him on the shoulder and the district captain was his intimate friend. He was high up in the inner circles of the lodge, and his words were listened to with respect by everyone on the block. Even the Judge, Judge Greenberg, was his friend. If there was any trouble at all, Harry was the one to come to. All Harry had to do was to call up this or that one. There wasn't a wire Harry couldn't pull.

A woman alone in the world ... and a man, lonely too ... with a wife sick for the last two years ... practically without a wife since the beginning of her sickness. ... There was really nothing to wonder at.

And therefore it was nothing to be surprised about that Mrs. Kranz, the moment she heard of the great feat of Harry's pigeons in bringing home the rare Japanese specimen, should put on one of her cinnamon-colored gypsy blouses, short-sleeved and cut low at the neck, adjust a pair of her dangling earrings, load her arms down with bracelets, pat her three blonde curls more fetchingly on her forehead, put an Indian shawl around her shoulders, and go over to Harry's yard—although she usually waited for the evening for her visits—to celebrate the unparalleled victory. Without waiting for the cover of night, she walked over in the broad daylight, with the women of the neighborhood seated on the doorsteps or the balcony fire escapes. Pairs of scornful eyes followed

27

her, and the women, too exhausted with the heat to summon enough energy for anything else, found the strength to toss remarks to one another.

"The slut . . ."

". . . and while his wife is still alive . . ."

"It's no wonder that God sends a blistering heat like this," a Jewish woman said.

". . . and all the sicknesses the children get . . ."

Mrs. Kranz ignored the remarks. Trailing a heavy perfume after her she walked along with a coquettish swing, and even had the impudence to stop at Davidowsky's grocery store to buy corned beef, smoked tongue, a couple of loaves of bread, some sour pickles, and a laxative for the children.

"They stuffed themselves with ice cream and stale milk on the excursion. They'll probably all be sick," she said, as though she owed an explanation to Moshe Wolf, who waited on her.

Moshe Wolf made no answer. He served her without a word.

When Mrs. Kranz reached the dark basement apartment, she could hear from the yard the familiar noises of the men—the children had already left. The men were passing a flask of whisky from hand to hand, drinking from the bottle, to celebrate the victory over the captured Japanese from the 57th Street flock. The raucous, rumbling male noise was refreshing to Mrs. Kranz after the delicate sentimentality of the music and singing with which she had been surrounded all day. She didn't go directly out into the yard, but paused at Mrs. Greenstock's rocking chair, with her sympathetic and patient smile, while Mrs. Greenstock swayed back and forth, trying to take a deep breath and fanning herself.

"It's all the fault of the noise out there," Mrs. Kranz said. "Here." She took some rock candy out of a bag. "Mr. Davidowsky says it's the best thing for asthma. Even the doctors haven't been able to find anything better."

Mrs. Greenstock—she was known simply as "the Missus" in the neighborhood—took the rock candy, and like a man grasping at a straw or anything that might save him from imminent disaster, put it in her mouth without a word or a glance. With the self-centeredness characteristic of sick people, she seemed not to have any interest in anything outside her.

Mrs. Kranz turned around to see Rachel picking at her finger-

28

nails. She slapped her hand fondly, and gave her a nail file. "This is what ladies use," she scolded her. "I don't know where you learn such habits. Go and put on a clean dress, and put some water to boil. And Goldie—see the way she looks!" She lifted the youngest child onto a chair and wiped her perspiring face with a towel. "The poor child probably hasn't had anything to eat all day. And in all this heat! What are you standing there for, Rachel? Don't you see that your mother can't help herself? You out there," she called to the men in the yard, "one of you come in and help!"

"What's the trouble?" asked Harry, coming in from the yard.

"What's the trouble? Your wife can hardly catch her breath and you sit outside and have a good time! There's no one to give her a glass of water. And look at the way this room looks! And the children! They haven't had a bit of warm food all day—and all of you stay outside with your Tammany and your pigeons. You're a pack of animals. . . ."

"All right, Clara, all right. . . ." Harry turned to his wife. "What's the matter, Sara? Don't you feel well?" He called out to the yard. "Ola Boga! Run over to Davidowsky's. Tell him I asked him to come over right away."

Moshe Wolf Davidowsky was the emergency first aid for everyone on 48th Street. Whatever the sickness, the patient would first of all go over to the grocery store to take counsel with Davidowsky. Whether it was a splinter in the finger or a cinder in the eye or a painful belly ache, it was to Davidowsky that they went. In his store could be found cures for everything. He had brought them with him from the old country, and he knew all about mixing herbs and applying ointments—all the old home remedies.

But it wasn't only for physical ailments that Davidowsky was consulted. Most of all he was the one to come to for advice in time of trouble—whether it was necessary or not to call in a doctor, whether the case called for a lawyer. He was, so to say, the first haven of refuge, in case of a family fight, or trouble with the landlord, or when it was just a person feeling lonesome and needing someone to pour out his heart to. Harry was no exception. Like everyone else in the block, he sent for Davidowsky before he sent for the doctor.

"Maybe you can do something to help her," he said to Moshe Wolf, standing over his wife's chair like a helpless child.

"I see, I see," said Moshe Wolf, stroking his beard. "I see what she needs. She needs a husband. . . ."

"What have I done now?" asked Harry angrily, but with a note of apology in his tone.

"It's what you haven't done. A woman with a bad asthma shouldn't be in New York in the summer. In America they have blue mountains, green mountains, black mountains, white mountains, all kinds of mountains. That's where a woman with asthma should be in the summer. And you keep her caged in here. And you're supposed to be such a big shot, such a politician. . . ."

"Didn't I do everything I could? Didn't I run over to the Committee? Didn't I plead with them? Judge Greenberg gave me a letter of recommendation. 'No vacancies,' they told me, 'till after Labor Day.' "

"Listen to what I'm telling you. For your pigeons and your animals you'd find a summer place if they needed mountain air. Don't forget she's your wife, the mother of your children."

"Moshe Wolf, believe me . . . may I drop dead . . ." Harry was white with anger. He bit his lip in rage.

"Who cares for your oaths! Get her to bed first, then go back to your friends. We'll manage without you. You were no good in the old country and you're no good here. Get me a glass of water. . . . Here, Sara, take this. . . ."—he took a spill of powder and poured it into the glass—"it'll make you feel better; it'll calm you. There's been too much noise and excitement. . . . What heroes! What great pigeon heroes! You'd think they'd captured the eagle of King Solomon. . . . You ought to be ashamed of yourself! You, a grown man, a Jew, a father! . . ."

Moshe Wolf was the only one who would dare talk that way to Harry, and it was only from Moshe Wolf that Harry would take it. Pale with anger and biting his lip he did everything that Moshe Wolf asked him, brought the water for the powder, dragged the bed over to the open window. The powder actually worked—probably more as a result of the sick woman's satisfaction at hearing her husband raked over the coals in the very presence of his mistress. Her coughing subsided. Moshe Wolf was able to return to his store—and Harry to the yard where his cronies were waiting for the provisions Mrs. Kranz had brought.

The ones in the yard were Harry's closest intimates. Mike

30

Maloney, Tony the bricklayer, Maczikowicz the Polack, and Harry's errand boy Choleva—and of course, Mrs. Kranz, sitting in the doorway leading to the yard. They talked about familiar things, about horses and dogs, holdups, about the fights they had had, about policemen and politicians. Choleva was constantly occupied in running over to the saloon, where the saloonkeeper would hand him out cans of beer through the side door. He was in and out the yard a dozen times.

For Mrs. Kranz it was paradise. She loved to listen to the talk about horses, bandits, policemen, politicians. She loved the smell of whisky and beer, the sour smell of male sweat.

She sat quietly, half in and half out of the house, careful not to move, so as not to arouse the jealousy of the sick woman, who, lying on the bed near the window, kept her eyes closed and made no sound, but was aware of everything going on. Mrs. Kranz didn't say a word. She sat there in blissful satisfaction at being near real men, listening to real men's talk. She sat in the shadows, wrapped in her gypsy scarf, in silence except for the occasional tinkling of the charms and amulets dangling from her bracelets as though she wanted to give a gentle reminder of her presence. She could feel the eyes of the men peering at her. With her languid eyes she looked up at the stars in the sky. "The stars are coming out," she said, unaffectedly.

"The stars are coming out," Maloney repeated after her.

Harry was silent. He just looked at her with his keen, black sparkling eyes. Mrs. Kranz's breast heaved in a sigh. She fanned herself with her hand.

Choleva took his harmonica out of his pocket and began to play a Polish mazurka. The harmonica—like the flask of whisky and the beer can—began to pass from mouth to mouth, each of them piping out his national songs.

From the second-story windows overlooking the yard came the sounds of weeping. They were not shrieks, they were muffled, painful sobs. They all knew what it was. Patrick McCarthy, the Irishman on the second floor, was beating his daughter Mary.

"Bastard!" Harry shouted. He shook his fist in the direction of the windows.

"Sunday is McCarthy's day for handing out a beating. If it isn't his wife, it's his daughter," Maloney said.

33

"The bastard! He's beating Mary because she went with Rachel and Irving on the picnic," Harry shouted angrily.

Harry was right. McCarthy, with his small job in a shipping agency, was the block's official anti-Semite. He hated Jews—and, as though some weird spell had been cast over him, he couldn't bring himself to move away from them. There were plenty of places in the neighborhood where most of the people were Italian Catholics and German Protestants; but as though the devil drove him to it, he stayed on 48th Street, where most of the inhabitants were Jews. He never thought of moving away. On the contrary, he not only insisted on living in the Jewish section but in the Jewish tenements themselves, to get a whiff every Friday of the Jewish gefüllte fish and other Sabbath delicacies—and to curse and pick fights and parade his hatred. His children, like his wife, didn't share his spleen. His older daughter, Mary, had for several years been the schoolmate of Rachel Greenstock and Irving Davidowsky, and had become so accustomed to Jewish families that she spent more time in the Davidowsky home or the Greenstock home than she did in her own. Many a time she would hide from her father at Harry's house. Her own home life was unhappy. She would see her father come home drunk, his wages spent, and let out his shame and bitterness on her mother. She suffered a great deal. Her family troubles had awakened a deep religious emotion in her; it was a way of escape for her. But her piety, encouraged by the old priest of the Church of St. Boniface over on Second Avenue, did not estrange her from Jews. It seemed to give her a closer feeling of sympathy with the Jewish customs and traditions she saw practiced in Davidowsky's house. Driven out by her father's brutality, the child was grateful for the warmth and kindliness she found in the homes of her friends.

"The best thing would be to haul the bastard once for all to court," said Harry. "Judge Greenberg would fix him."

"They'll only send him to jail, and in the meantime his wife and kids will starve," commented Maloney. "The thing to do is to beat him up."

"A beating won't do that kind of guy any good," said Harry.

"It'll help for a couple of weeks, and that'll be all to the good," Maloney said quietly.

"Yes, it'll have to be done one of these days," Harry agreed.

32

CHAPTER FOUR

THE EVENING brought no relief from the oppressive heat. On the contrary, the walls of the buildings, having absorbed the heat all day, now began to throw it back into the street. The air was so humid that the people of the . neighborhood had the feeling they were wrapped in a damp sheet which hampered their movements and from which they were unable to free themselves. It was impossible to stay indoors. The walls, the ceilings, the floors sweated with the heat; the dampness filled the rooms and made it impossible to breathe. The heavy smells of food, sweat, and clothing, and the stale smell of mattresses and bedclothes added to the oppressiveness. The heat seemed to make bodies enormous and cumbersome. It sapped the energy and tortured the limbs.

The block dwellers swarmed out of their rooms, searching for a relieving gust of air. They crowded the fire escapes, the steps in front of doors, and the sidewalks.

Most of all they sought relief in the cool winds that came once in a while over the East River. But direct approach to the river shore was blocked to them. The streets ended in "dead ends" hemmed in by fences erected by the owners of the feed storehouses and stables. In a couple of places, however, there was an old unused dock, the planks water-soaked and rotted. From these docks one could hear the splashing of children swimming close to the shore, driven to find relief from the overpowering heat, disregarding the perils of the holes and falling timbers of the dock.

Other entrances to the waterfront were provided by the stables on the river shore. By climbing over fences and scrambling over the stable roofs it was possible to get down to the water's edge.

But 48th Street had two yards that opened on the river, and of these the people of the adjoining blocks were properly jealous. One of them was Harry's, to which, naturally, only his intimate

33

friends, the people of his own block, who were interested in his pigeons, had admission. The other belonged to a private real-estate firm. Tammany had taken over the use of it so that the legitimate dwellers on 48th Street could come there to take their ease on the hot summer nights. With Judge Greenberg's help Uncle Maloney had managed to get permission to keep the property open to the Tammany members in the block. There was a lot of competition for the privilege among the inhabitants of the street. The yard stretched to the river shore, and the general belief was that cool winds blew there. Everyone in the neighborhood besieged the office of the Tammany captain for tickets of admission. The first tickets, naturally enough, went to the members in good standing of the local Tammany club; Maloney knew all of them. But in time everyone on the block came to feel that he or she had special rights to the place, even Heimowitz, the socialist, who had little enough to do with Tammany in other matters.

The yard was full of people; men, women, and children of the neighborhood. They had brought with them mattresses, blankets, pillows, cans of cold tea or beer or ice water, ready to spend half the night there, until the tenement rooms got cool enough to return to.

The river lay motionless in its broad bed, its dark patches of oily scum reflecting the star-studded sky. Now and then a light blinked from a slowly moving coal barge. A heavy silence lay over the river.

From time to time the hoarse blast of a freight boat cut through the air. The morbid prison shadows of Blackwell's Island in the middle of the river pressed on the water's surface. The dimly lighted mist that hung over the island seemed to oppress the spirit and burden the heart more than it served to lighten the darkness. Involuntarily, everyone who saw the lights gleaming through the island's mist would think of the poor devils sent "across the river." The melancholy which the sight of the island brought to every one of Manhattan's dwellers fell like a pall on the group gathered in the Tammany yard to escape the unbearable heat. How could anyone of them know what the morrow might bring? Poverty ruled their lives and—who could know?—might drive them relentlessly to a similar fate. The same melancholy drove them to find escape in sleep, to find a rest from all the cares and worries cf the day.

34

Some of them sprawled out on blankets they had brought with them from their homes. Others, the Slavs, for instance, talked with animation about the old country, about the boats that floated down its rivers; the nearness of the East River had brought it to their minds. Yes, along the Vistula, the Bug, and the Volga enormous rafts of logs floated; people would live on them all summer. They talked about horses being led in the night to graze on the green plains.

"Another year's work in the slaughterhouse, and I'll save enough, and then back home, back to Czezov. I'll buy my brother's share and take over my father's farm, eight acres and ten head of cattle." Choleva let his fantasy roam. His speech was a mixture of Polish, Russian, and English.

"It'll be no good. You'll use up your few dollars in the old country and then you'll come back to America. Everybody comes back. One smell of the American air, and it draws you back. There's some kind of magic in it," someone said.

"Yes, I've heard about things like that. Once the Dombrowskis went home . . . and then they came back. America's the only place. You can earn money. . . . Only the weather's no good. Too hot in the summer and too cold in the winter."

"And the potatoes are no good here. In the old country the potatoes have something to them. Here they're too big . . . they have too much water. . . ." one of the other Slavs remarked.

"You're not satisfied? Why don't you go back? Go ahead, and be a servant for the landowner, with your hat in your hand and down on your knees to him! Otherwise you'll have the butt of his whip in your face. Go on, go home!" This was from Harry, who was always to be found among the Slavs. "Believe me, I'm glad I've got no one to go back to. America's good enough for me."

"That's right. What's true is true. . . ."

Among the Italians a hot dispute was going on between Tony, who was a Neapolitan, and Donato and Pasquale, the pastry bakers, who came from Sicily, about the wines of the two districts. They talked with violent gestures, smacking their lips to give an idea of the quality of their native wines, waving their arms, shouting at the top of their voices, loud enough to wake up Schultz the butcher who was snoring in a corner of the yard. The fat German lay on his back, waving off the noise of the

35

Italians as though he were brushing off a swarm of troublesome flies, till he finally sat up and shouted: *"Donnerwetter,* it'll soon be time to get up and go to work!"

A group of Jews were gathered around the consumptive Chaim Melamed. Chaim was the accepted "victim of the capitalist system." Abram Heimowitz had given him the title, and it had stuck. By trade he had been a presser in the sweatshops, and it was there that he had contracted "the proletarian sickness." The charity organizations found his case impossible. His needs seemed to be so great that there wasn't enough money in all of New York to satisfy them. First of all he had to be sent to a sanitorium every couple of months, and then brought home again, because he would get homesick for 48th Street. He had a large family, which kept increasing year by year throughout his illness. Somehow or other the block managed to provide what the charity organizations couldn't; that was only fitting for the block's official consumptive. Chaim paid no rent, although Shmulevitch, the rent collector, threatened time and again to throw him out on the sidewalk, family, children, furniture, and all. But if he had ever dared try it, his life wouldn't have been safe. From time to time the block ran a benefit in a Jewish theater and sold tickets to everybody "for the benefit of the victim of the capitalist system." There wasn't a single person with the fear of God in his heart who didn't in one way or another watch out for the sick man. Every household would supply him with some comfort or other; a rich chicken broth, a warm woolen muffler, anything to warm his insides or to protect him from the cold. At election time there was a regular battle between Tammany and the block's lone socialist over the sick man, each one wanting to use him as the touching Exhibit A to advance his party interests. He became practically the only issue during the election campaign between Tammany and the socialists on 48th Street. Heimowitz would point to the consumptive as a victim of the vicious capitalist system whose pillar was Tammany. Tammany would point to him as an example of its constant attention to social needs. He would be set up as a living proof that Tammany was the only organization to care for the sick and the poor on the block and to see to it that they weren't dispossessed from their homes.

"Who is it that sees to it that our sick brother gets the fresh

36

milk he needs?" the Tammany speaker would declaim to the listening crowd at election time. And he would answer his own question. "Tammany."

Chaim Melamed, with his sputum cup and his bottle of milk— these he carried around with him wherever he went—would spend the hot nights in the Tammany yard. His wife would bring him there, make him comfortable on a chair with blankets behind him and over him, his shoulders wrapped in a woolen shawl, all in spite of the heat. Near him was always to be found Abram Heimowitz, who assumed the role of protector and comforter for the sick man.

The block had its official anti-Semite, Patrick McCarthy, but it also had its official radical—that was Heimowitz.

Tammany had plenty of trouble with Heimowitz. At election time, when Tammany swarmed over the entire block, every window plastered with posters of Tammany candidates so that not a ray of light came into the houses, Heimowitz had to be the lone exception. From his window stared the faces of the socialist candidates. He well knew that it wouldn't do any good, that the socialist candidates didn't stand a chance against the Tammany stalwarts, but Heimowitz stuck to his colors.

Each night the socialist posters were torn down, and when they were pasted inside the windows the panes of glass were smashed. But Heimowitz was stubborn. In the morning the holes in the windows were covered over with socialist posters again.

And the morning after election, when the block celebrated the election of the Tammany ticket, doors and windows would be plastered with enormous signs—"I told you so"—although no one had thought for a minute that the outcome would be different. It seemed as though the demonstration had no other purpose than to taunt poor Heimowitz. But, undaunted by defeat, the next election would find Heimowitz bravely displaying his socialist candidates, lost and alone among the Tammany posters.

Someone had had the happy idea of bringing a gramophone out to the yard, and the air resounded with the wailings of old Hebrew liturgical chants. Everyone listened. Even Heimowitz, who had never stuck his nose in a synagogue and considered religion "a relic of the Middle Ages," was entranced by the music. He tried to stay at a distance, so that no one would notice his enjoyment and twit him about it. He couldn't help himself; the

37

mournful voice of the famous cantor on the record awakened in him a deep nostalgia. Memories of his young years aroused his Jewish blood. Sometimes he would come closer to the gramophone and join the circle of Jews listening to the music. He would even forget his official radicalism and would call out for records particularly dear to him.

"You, Heimowitz?" someone would say to him in mock astonishment.

"It's reactionary darkness, a relic of the Middle Ages; but what can I do if I enjoy the cantor's singing?" Heimowitz would reply apologetically.

In the meantime the wailing music would awaken the sleepers and interfere with the loud disputes of the Italians. Voices would be heard.

"Stop it!"

"Hey, you Jews, let me sleep," would come Schultz's angry grumble.

"Quiet! It's Yossele Rosenblatt, the great cantor!"

Everyone would heed the commanding voice and would remain silent. There was no mistaking it when Michael Maloney spoke.

Moshe Wolf Davidowsky had his own corner in the yard, near a chimney wall, where he would bring his son in the wheel chair and turn him to face the river. Himself he sat down on a rock, leaning his head against the wall.

"Close your eyes and try to sleep, my son. There's a good breeze."

"I can't sleep with that sky and all those stars. I don't get a chance to see them often."

Moshe Wolf felt a wave of humility sweep over him. He said in a voice of deep pathos: "It's good to look into the heavens, my son. It's a reminder that there's a dear God in the world. As in the sacred Psalms—the heavens proclaim the glory of the Lord."

"There are no heavens, Papa. It's just an optical illusion."

"What do you mean there are no heavens? We can see it right above our heads."

"What we see is clouds and some stars above the clouds. That's all we see, and that's all there is to see."

"What do you mean?"

"I mean that there's an enormous expanse, the universe. And

38

there are lots of constellations wheeling around each other, and all of them put together don't amount to more than a couple of peas rattling around in a vast bowl."

"But what about what I can see with my own eyes, right above my head?"

"That's just an illusion of space, a trick of the senses."

"And if what you say is true—that there's no heaven—then where does God dwell?"

"God—God . . . ? If there is anything like a God, then He lives in our hearts. Outside of our hearts there is no God."

Moshe Wolf sighed heavily. Inside him he was thinking: "Who needs God's grace more than you, my son?" Aloud he said: "God watches out for all His creatures."

"Do you think God has nothing else to do but to watch over us to see what we're going to have for lunch? What is man, after all? A worm among worms. . . ." There was bitterness in the boy's voice, the same bitterness that had colored all his thinking.

"That is only an evidence of God's greatness. Of course man is nothing but dust. As it says in our Bible—What is man that Thou art mindful of him? But still the Heavenly Father is concerned over him, watches over him every minute of his life, guards his every footstep. Not only mankind but every individual man and woman is under His watchful care. And every animal, every blade of grass. Our sages have said that under every blade of grass there is an angel, who tends it to make it grow. Thus it is that all creation gives thanks to God. The grass that grows fulfills God's commandment, and the bird that sings, sings only for God. The great and the small, the stars in the sky and the drops of water in the ocean, are all in God's care. There is not a leaf on a tree which does not tremble at God's will, for everything which God has created belongs to God. There is not and there cannot be anything in existence without God. It cannot be otherwise; everything is of God and in God . . . as our sages have said."

The crippled boy listened to his father's impassioned words but did not answer. He only smiled to himself.

"Yes, my son. There is nothing in the world, nothing at all, in philosophy or in science—in a word, nothing—that doesn't have its source in our holy writings. Believe me, Nathan, if you'd

39

steep yourself in the Jewish books, it would help you, it would be useful to you."

"Useful—for what? To become a rabbi, maybe?"

"Is it only to be a rabbi that one should have faith? Faith is the only pillar that gives hope. And who needs it more than you, my son?"

The crippled boy was silent, gazing up at the sky. The light of the stars threw their reflection on his pale, sensitive features; his eyes shone unnaturally with a dead whiteness.

Suddenly a low, hysterical laugh broke out of the boy's twisted lips.

"Hope?" He repeated the words with scorn. "In what?"

"In God, my son."

"There is no God," the boy stammered.

"There is! There is! There is!" Moshe Wolf insisted vehemently.

"If there is a God, he is no friend to me."

"My son, my son, don't speak such words."

"Why not?"

Moshe Wolf fell silent.

When he wheeled his son back to the house the street was still alive with people, although it was very late. Some sat dozing on the doorway steps, others talked in subdued voices, still others wove back and forth on the sidewalks. From First Avenue came the echo of the traffic and the bustle that still went on in the late hours.

From the building across the way, where Shmulevitch kept his poultry, came the stirrings of the chickens in their crates, letting the neighborhood know that dawn was not far off.

Later, when Moshe Wolf lay down on the cot which he set up near his son's bed, he closed his eyes, and while his lips were murmuring the prescribed prayer before sleep, there was a prayer in his heart for his son.

"Dear Father in Heaven. Take pity on my son. And if in Your grace You do not restore him, then put a yearning for You in his heart, so that he may have a pillar and a comfort in his misfortune."

On the following day, Monday, the heat continued unbroken. Exhausted with the stifling heaviness that had plagued them all

40

night long, man and beast, dripping with sweat, panted in the sultry air.

From early in the morning, before the full light of day had emerged, there came through the open tenement windows the clatter of truck wheels and the pounding of heavily shod horses' hoofs on the cobblestones of the street. Wagons laden with slabs of meat made a constant procession from the slaughterhouses. Wagons jammed with milk cans, beer wagons drawn by powerful brewery horses, grain wagons, wagons heaped high with vegetables and fruits, crowded the East River streets and belabored the air with the deafening sounds of clanking iron and creaking wood. To this was added the scraping and clattering of garbage cans and the pleasant sound of swishing water turned on the sidewalk flagstones to cool them against the oncoming heat, together with the smell of the garbage and rotting food. But ears and noses were used to these sounds and smells; no one heard them or paid any attention to them.

No one took his ease on 48th Street. Moshe Wolf Davidowsky carried boxes of groceries from the cellar, afterward sweeping the sidewalk in front of his store. He still wore the skullcap which he had forgotten to take off after his quick morning prayers, Deborah, his wife, was busy at the ice box in the store. Irving, the younger son, had long since gone off to the pushcarts on First Avenue with a bolt of piece goods he had had stored in the cellar.

From every house on the block came streams of people, young and old, all of them hurrying, the men unshaven, with three-day beards on their faces, all of them with red, swollen eyes after the sleepless night. They scurried at the same pace with which they had swallowed their morning meals. Girls with swollen lips and puffy faces sped along, with hasty dabs of powder on their cheeks and noses, lunch packages under their arms. All the trolleys on First Avenue were packed with human freight, the passengers pushed together, one holding onto the other to avoid falling off the car which raced along in the morning rush hour with a special confusion, noise, and clanging.

There seemed to be no end to the hordes pouring out toward First Avenue, no beginning or end to the long line of trolleycars, all crowded to the running boards. The street leading to the Second Avenue El station was thick with people. But they were

41

there only for a while; soon they had disappeared as though the pavement had opened up and swallowed them. New throngs appeared, a riot of black-red-white-gray dots, to be swallowed in their turn by the open steps of the El station. Above, on the tracks, one El train after another raced along like an iron monster, splitting the ears with the deafening clatter of iron wheels on iron rails. Trains stopped at the station with a grinding and creaking of brakes, the passengers squeezed together in a tight mass. The structure covered the avenue like an iron roof, shutting out the light of day.

With the passing of the Sunday, even some of the children of the neighborhood were at work. During the summer vacation days they made artificial flowers at home. It was "easy work," their parents thought, and the children could do it without much effort.

Even manufacturers of women's clothing and shirts provided the city's poor children with homework in the hot summer vacation days. The families, driven by need, yoked their children to the task. The sound of children at play almost disappeared from the streets.

Sunday play and Sunday leisure were over on 48th Street. Long Anthony's day as a circus horse was over. No longer did his patient back carry laughing princesses with beribboned hair. Now, harnessed to the junk wagon and with a worn and frayed collar, he pulled rusty iron bed frames, tin cans, iron rails, pots and pans, discarded stoves. Like his boss, Zelig, he panted heavily—not so much from the heavy load as from the heavy heat which seemed more unmerciful now in the blazing day.

Tony the bricklayer swayed on an iron lift which carried him up to the twenty-fourth floor of a skyscraper under construction. He maneuvered the beam he carried so as to fit it into its proper spot. His head swam when his gaze caught a glimpse of the street far below; the horses and people looked like ants hurrying to their ant hills. He tried to keep his gaze away. As he hung suspended between heaven and earth he would mutter, without thinking, his customary phrase: "Jesu Maria."

Harry Greenstock, brush and paint in hand, was sliding over the scalding, sloping tin roof of the slaughterhouse. Wearing a leather safety belt he hung below the roof edge and daubed the gutters. One careless move and his body would follow his dangling legs to the pavement below. Like Tony, he tried not to look down

42

toward the sidewalk. Like Tony he was scared of becoming dizzy. Concentrating on his work, his lips tight, his shirt drenched with the sweat induced by his precarious perch and the stifling heat, out of custom—again like Tony—he kept on muttering the prayer of his fathers in his old home. "Dear Father in Heaven! Do not forsake me."

In a puddle of blood, Choleva, the Polish butcher, stood with other half-naked men, who, in their blood-drenched nakedness, looked like destroying angels from some Gehenna. They were occupied in stripping the hide off the slaughtered animals hanging from the hooks of racks. Other half-naked figures, dressed only in bloodstained pants, carried on their bare backs sides of beef from the slaughterhouse to the ice chambers. The sweat on their bodies would congeal in the icy temperature, but they gave no sign that it bothered them.

Most of the Jews on 48th Street were connected with the garment sweatshops; operators at machines, pressers at the long ironing tables, hand finishers working with the needle. The steaming heat sapped the last drop of strength from their exhausted nerves.

The block itself was empty. The children who were not busy making artificial flowers in the houses had been driven out early by the heat. These happy ones were finding some relief and pleasure in the river, scummy with the oil waste of the freight boats and coal barges cutting over the river from Long Island to Manhattan.

CHAPTER FIVE

YOUTH HAS the resilience to absorb disaster and weave it into the pattern of its life, no matter how anguishing the thorn that penetrates its flesh.

This was the case with Nathan Davidowsky. In his early youth when he was thinking his young thoughts of the love and joy which life would open up to him, he had found himself in the clutches of the beast of prey that hovered over the young of New York—infantile paralysis. The claws of the monster dug deep into him, the promising nineteen-year-old boy who had just entered college. The monster had crippled his limbs and made him dependent on others for all his needs. Nathan had protested bitterly against his evil fate, cursing God, justice, and all the accepted moralities, hysterically protesting against the crime committed on his body. He refused to accept his fate; he begged for death; he even had thoughts of suicide. Gradually, however, the poison of the disease deadened his will—even the will to die. He made peace with his destiny.

His paralysis confined him to the scant space between the door of the house and the entrance to his father's store. But he had built an entire world for himself. He lived in an unending universe of books and imagination. In this world he was free, for in this world he was the victor over the greatest destroyer of freedom—fear. The gods had done their worst to him. He was no longer afraid of them.

It was not so much that he had made peace with his destiny as that he had accepted his crippled limbs as a natural condition, a condition which freed him from all obligations, cut him off from all the strings and roots which bound men to each other and to the world in which they lived, and set him apart uniquely, himself alone, Nathan Davidowsky, in a physical existence dependent on others, but spiritually independent of everything in the world. He could not wholly drown his bitterness, but he was not envious of anyone. He felt ennobled in his circumstance and, like every invalid, privileged, and he used his privileges against the very ones who were most devoted to him and most ready to sacrifice themselves for him. That meant most of all his father, Moshe Wolf Davidowsky.

Moshe Wolf himself had once had ambitions to become a learned man. An "enlightened" Jew, emancipated from the ghetto traditions, he had secretly studied wordly subjects, hiding the secular books under the heavy volumes of the sacred writings in the prayer house. He had gone so far as to take the examination at the secondary school in his native town preparatory to studying pharmacy, in itself a violent departure, if not a heretical revolution, in the pious Jewish life of his village. But the match which his father arranged for him with a miller's daughter put an end to all such dreams. His father-in-law's promised riches had come to nothing, and Moshe Wolf, after many trials and tribulations, had joined the stream of emigrants to America, with a wife and two children—and had ended up as the proprietor of a grocery store on Manhattan's 48th Street.

But in his son Nathan, Moshe Wolf had seen the realization of his own dreams. Not only was the boy a good student, but he had shown a fever for learning from his early childhood. While other children were playing in the street, building bonfires, playing ball, young Nathan sat over the books which he borrowed from the public library and consumed them voraciously.

Nathan had spent his childhood in one of the rawest sections of Manhattan. The hidden cellar holes around the East River bred a tough youth. Around the yards and crooked alleys of the neighborhood which led to the East River, bands of children roamed, engaging in warfare with other neighborhood gangs. In the living quarters above the grocery store young Nathan would sit, summer and winter, constantly reading. The other youngsters would try to draw him into all sorts of activities, playing games, selling newspapers, but Nathan continued to live his own secluded life. There was many an occasion when he came home from school black and blue from the beatings the tough kids administered to the "bookworm." He offered no resistance. He took all the blows and jeerings and ran into the house. He showed no feeling of shame at being called "sissy"

45

and "kike" by the Irish kids. He kept on the path he had laid out for himself—from the school to the public library, and from the library home. He had no interest in play; books were his solace and his life. He lived in a dreamworld. Even his mother, who had seized on America and American life with a voracious eagerness to assimilate it and be assimiliated by it in one gulp, would be driven to complain.

"Did you ever in your life hear anything like it?" she would say. "Who ever heard of a boy in America sitting over books all day? In America boys run around in the streets, do what other boys do, sell newspapers, build fires. Take Irving, two years younger than you, and sells newspapers every evening. He'll be a businessman. Remember, my genius, there's lots of room in America for business; for book learning there's no room."

Moshe Wolfe enjoyed his son's perseverance; not only enjoyed it, but when he saw his son at his books he beamed with pride. If he could find a minute's time in the evening, he would leave the store and come to the living quarters, and the first thing he would do was to engage in conversation with Nathan about the books he was reading. After he washed his hands before sitting down to the food his wife had set for him on the table, while she went down to take his place in the store, and after reciting the prescribed prayer before meals, he would come over to take a look at his son's book.

"What are you studying today, my son? Hmm...the triangle...." He glanced at the homework in geometry his boy was doing. "I didn't get as far as that. We didn't study about the triangle until after the fourth class. And here they study it in the early classes! Very good. It's good exercise for the brain."

How great the abyss that yawned between father and son in the first immigrant generation in America depended a good deal on the length of time that the youth had spent with his father in the old country. Children who remembered their parents from the old home could remember them in the dignity of the traditional Sabbaths and Holy Days; they had respect for their fathers despite seeing them as greenhorns in a new country, were more closely bound to them and understood them better than did the youth who had been born in America or who had left the old country at a tender age. Among the latter the chasm between parent and child was great indeed.

Although Nathan had no comprehension of his father's exaggerated Jewish patriotism and pride and was certainly free of any feeling of Jewish "chosenness"—a conviction with which the old man comforted his spirit and found consolation for the injustices heaped upon the Jews—the youth still felt a deep respect for his father and an overwhelming love which he himself could not understand and which he was often ashamed to demonstrate.

On many occasions Nathan would see his father, after a hard day of work, or on a Saturday when the store was closed, dig out an old and tattered volume from the pack of books he had brought with him from the old country, and sit down and pore over the printed pages. Fatigue would soon close his eyes. However much the boy tried to hide his deep love, he felt in his heart a boundless affection and a profound reverence for his father.

Moshe Wolf, finding no satisfaction for his spirit in the lectures of the radicals and socialists he attended now and then, had dropped all his ideas of worldly "enlightenment" and had returned to the Hasidic pattern of his youth. He wanted something to lean on. In order to escape, even for a little while, from the swamp of hard work and poverty which sucked him in deeper and deeper, he would travel down to the East Side to spend a Sabbath at the Hasidic prayer house. Although he lived a distance from the lower East Side and could not manage to attend the regular Sabbath and holiday services of these townsfolk of his, he was a member of their congregation, paid his dues, and helped to maintain it.

He would spend Friday night at the home of a kinsman and the Saturday at the prayer house, filling himself with prayer and piety, joining in discussions of the Torah, conversing with his old comrades, recalling old Hasidic days, and the old Hasidic songs, and then return to the store and fall into the round of work for another week, or two or three, until the fever would seize him again and he would again make the pilgrimage to the East Side, to drink again at the well of his old Jewishness and Hasidism.

But since his son had shown such eagerness for learning,

47

Moshe Wolf had become interested in the books the boy studied, and he would inquire into their contents. Nathan, although without too much enthusiasm, would tell his father about them, and in Moshe Wolf the old yearning for knowledge would stir again. What he had not been able to realize in his own life was being realized in his son. And his ambitions for Nathan took on more resplendent hues than he had ever dared imagine for himself. His son would not only finish college, he would be a professor of mathematics in a university.... This, to Moshe Wolf's mind, was the highest rung on the ladder of learning. His son would write books; he would be famous.

And then suddenly it had come: the secret destroyer which pounced like a fiend on the youth of the city. It threw itself upon his child. In a few weeks the pride, the joy, the heart of Moshe Wolf's life lay crippled on his bed, his limbs dead and lifeless.

"The compassion of a father for his son." A father's compassion wells up from deeper sources than the pity of a mother. The pity of the mother has in it the maternal dynamism toward one's own flesh and blood; it is a part of the mother's self-love, it is a continuation of her own blood. It has in it the birth element, the elemental animal element, and it is therefore hysterical, passionate, and furious. But the compassion of a father stems from the feeling of relationship to Man; it has in it the Adam element, the father-son continuum down to the first man. It wells up not from self-love, but from self-preservation. Thus it is not compounded of hysteria. It is not fitful, it is solid and enduring.

When the disaster struck in Moshe Wolf's home—as it struck in other homes—he did not weep nor crouch at the door of the hospital in spasms of anguish. He stood for hours and days with the patience of a dog at the hospital gates. And when at last they delivered to him his crippled son, he took him in his arms, brought him home, put him into the large room whose two windows opened on to the street, put him in his own bed, set up a cot for himself next to it—and gave the boy his own limbs for the rest of his life.

From then on Moshe Wolf no longer lived his own life. His hands served his son more than they served himself. He walked for him; he saw for him. He knew by instinct when Nathan needed him. He would be down in the store serving a customer; suddenly, with an inscrutable smile on his face, he would leave the customer standing and run upstairs to attend to his son, then he would return to resume serving the customers. He was jealous of everyone else; no one else could attend to the boy, not even the boy's mother.

From the day the catastrophe struck, Nathan's room became the Hasidic prayer house for Moshe Wolf. It was the sanctuary to which he came to pray to his God.

For generations the Jewish wife was traditionally the provider of the family's livelihood. It was her task to keep her husband and sons free from all care of material needs in order that they might be able to dedicate their lives to God, to His Torah and His service. Her shoulders carried the yoke of providing the daily bread. She it was who traveled to the market place, often at great danger, among drunken peasants and lecherous gentry. It was not only on occasion necessary for her to defend herself against assault but actually to save her life. This assumption of the economic responsibility, in addition to her boundless devotion to her family, bred a dominating type of mother, a reminder of the matriarchal type of family institution.

Deborah, Moshe Wolf's wife, had no time to nurse the feeling of pity for her crippled son which possessed the father. But she comprehended with even more concern and anxiety the tragic meaning of the boy's illness, not only for himself but for the whole family. She knew that for his whole lifetime the boy would be a dead weight on their backs. And Deborah, on whose shoulders lay the responsibility for the household, had to weigh and measure the situation in the light of their material circumstances and come to the harsh conclusion that it would be better for Nathan, whom the doctors had already pronounced permanently crippled, to find release in death from the sufferings to which he was doomed for life, and thus for them all to be released from the burden which his illness had placed on them.

She was not able to conceal her thoughts even when she was with him. No matter how much she tried in the beginning to show him the same selfless devotion as did Moshe Wolf, the realities of life pressed too strongly. The boy's helplessness was a chain that shackled their feet at every step. The attentions that

49

had to be performed for him, the services that had to be given, ate away at the hours that the store—the family's livelihood—exacted from them. Hardened by the struggle for existence, Deborah could not spare for the boy a pity she begrudged even for herself.

Besides, she had never really loved her first-born; he was too much like her husband, too deeply steeped in books and learning.

It may be that she had been jealous of the boy. From the day the boy had shown such promise, he had completely captured Moshe Wolf's heart. The old man showed no interest in anything but his first-born son's career. He seemed to be utterly uninterested in his wife and Irving, the younger boy. Since Nathan's illness and Moshe Wolf's complete absorption in him, Deborah had begun to show openly her impatience, even her contempt of the cripple.

She hated books and everything about them. They had stolen her husband away from her in the first years of their married life. Instead of spending his free time with her, instead of showing her some companionship and affection, Moshe Wolf, directly after their wedding, had turned to his books . . . always those books. And it had been the same way with her first-born. From his earliest childhood, it might be said, only one thing interested him—books. Deborah had developed an unbelievable hatred of books. To books she ascribed everything that was evil. Every bit of bad luck that had happened to the family was due to books. Moshe Wolf's head was always buried in them. Because of them the burden of a livelihood lay on her shoulders. It was she who had to order the supplies, worry about the bills, watch the credits. She had to worry about everything. And on top of everything else, Moshe Wolf was more concerned about giving other people advice than in handing some out to himself. She would always be upbraiding him. "Do you think this is the old country, where there's time to stick your nose in other people's troubles? This is America! Here it's 'hurry up' and 'mind your own business.' . . . " And then in the evenings it was the books again; father and son, bending over the books. It was the books that had brought disaster to her son. If Nathan had played around in the streets like other children, the cursed plague would never have engulfed him. . . .

It was for these reasons—or their precise opposites—that her younger son, Irving, was completely to her liking. From his earliest years young Irving had shown a practical sense which filled Deborah with joy and hope. He was bringing pennies into the house to his mother when other children were begging pennies from their mothers. After he had finished public school he immediately began to help his mother in the store. Not only did he know the business thoroughly from the after-school hours he spent there, not only did he help her get merchandise and keep her accounts in order, he also knew the tricks of finding goods cheap. He hunted out dealers who dealt in bankrupt stocks, cigars and cigarettes from firms that had failed, and grocery supplies from forced sales. And in addition to helping in the store he had his own private affairs. He bought remnants of piece goods and sold them among the pushcarts on First Avenue. Recently he had become interested in garments; somewhere he had bought a lot of rejected, damaged dresses, aprons, children's wearing apparel, and he had sold them piece by piece over on First Avenue. Deborah glowed with pleasure over her son's business career. Moshe Wolf's household was split into two camps: himself and his invalid son against his wife and Irving.

Whenever Moshe Wolf would hold up Nathan's industry in learning as an example to the younger, Deborah's blood would boil. She took it as an affront to what was closest to her. "You see what your books lead to," she would say, pointing to the cripple. "If he had run around, done what other boys do, he wouldn't have come to this pass. But if a boy keeps his nose buried in books all the time ... "

On one such occasion Moshe Wolf went over to Nathan, put his hand on his shoulder and said to him half in jest: "Our sages have said that women have feeble brains. What do they understand about the benefits of books, eh, Nathan?"

Of late Moshe Wolf had found someone to help him in attending to the boy. His assistant was Mary, Patrick McCarthy's daughter.

In spite of her father's violent hatred of Jews, Mary made friends with the Jewish children on the block. Through Irving she had come to know Nathan and to admire his astonishing knowledge. Since his illness there was something of awe in her feelings toward him.

Mary had plenty of free time. She had been promised a few

weeks' vacation in the summer at a camp, but her father had been unable to accumulate the necessary registration money to pay to the Catholic charitable organization which maintained the camp and it was still doubtful that she could go.

Only once in her life, when she was twelve years old, had Mary been to the country. It had been to a Catholic camp for poor and sick children. She had been bothered by a persistent cough, and the doctor had advised that she be sent to the country. Since then she had never been out of the city. But this summer she was glad to stay.

She had little ways of making Nathan feel he was still a college student, that there was nothing unusual about him. On this occasion, when she brought him his library books, she made a pretense of having looked all over the block for him, although she knew very well that the boy could not move about.

"Where are you? I've brought your books," her voice called from the stairs; she well knew that he was in the house.

"Come up," Nathan called back.

"I've brought your library books for you. Do you know what the librarian said? She said that these books are too deep. She asked me who was going to read them. Whether they were for an author!"

"More books," Mrs. Davidowsky observed, bringing in some food for Nathan. "What does he need them all for? I can understand that if a person is studying to be a doctor he needs books, but . . . " She put down the tray of food. "Here, your father is busy in the store. No, my son, you'll never be a doctor, so what's the use of all these books?" She began to feed him, lifting a spoonful of soup to his lips.

"Mrs. Davidowsky, please let me. I'll gladly help," said Mary, trying to take the spoon.

"You better go home. If your father finds out that you've been in a Jewish house he'll disgrace you, as he did last Sunday."

"It's not true, Mrs. Davidowsky. My father didn't do anything to me. My father's not a bad man."

"I suppose he just patted your cheeks. Everybody on the block could hear you scream!"

"Ma!" Nathan twisted his lips into a grimace of protest.

"Isn't it the truth? Am I lying?"

52

"Ma!" The boy turned his face away from the spoon.

From the stairs came the sound of hurried footsteps. Moshe Wolf burst into the room.

"Here, give it to me. I'll take care of him." He practically tore the spoon out of his wife's hand.

"The store's full of customers. What did you come rushing up here for?"

"This is more important. Let them wait."

"You'd think I was starving him. I can give him his food without you. Go back to the customers."

"Let them wait, I told you. Give me the spoon."

"Here, here, take it! See if that will make you a living." Deborah went out of the room angrily.

"Please, Mr. Davidowsky, let me," Mary asked.

"You? Why?"

"I'll be careful, Mr. Davidowsky. Please, let me."

Moshe Wolf looked at her with surprise.

"You're McCarthy's daughter. What are you doing here?"

"I brought Nathan's books from the library. Let me give Nathan his lunch, Mr. Davidowsky. I'd be so glad to do it. I always feed my own brother. I know how to do it."

"Of course you know how ... but why should you? You're not Nathan's sister."

"But we're neighbors. Irving and I went to school together."

Moshe Wolf looked at the girl. There was pleading in her face. Her eyes begged.

"But why should you do it?" he repeated.

"Because I want to! Can't you understand, Mr. Davidowsky?"

Moshe Wolf looked at his son. There was a look of consent in Nathan's eyes.

Hesitantly Moshe Wolf handed over the spoon to Mary.

With elaborate care she spooned up the soup and brought it to Nathan's lips.

"I see that you do it very well," Moshe Wolf said. "I can go back to the store."

He stood in indecision for a while, as though he were not sure of his next step, then his wife's voice came up from the store:

"Moshe Wolf, are you coming down?"

"I'm coming," he answered. He looked again at Mary feeding Nathan as though he were a small child. Then with quick steps he left the room and went down the stairs.

Beginning with that day Moshe Wolf had someone to help him take care of his son.

CHAPTER SIX

MANHATTAN COULD also be kind and comforting. In the middle of the unbearable spell of heat a day stole in which bore on its wings all the fresh and salty odors of the winds sweeping across the Atlantic. In the very heart of Manhattan, among the tenement houses and garbage cans, among the restaurants, factories, storage houses, horses and wagons, trucks and gas storage tanks, came a day redolent with the odors of hidden forests of cedar, of distant wooded mountains. The air was filled with the sweet fragrance of jasmine and acacia, the tart smell of ripe apples, and the tang of pine trees. Manhattan sprouted wings. It seemed that the people did not walk over its sidewalks; they soared.

Such a blessed day descended on 48th Street after the tropical onslaughts it had so long endured. The block caught its breath. Children appeared again on the sidewalks, filling the street with quick movement, play, and laughter.

No child in the world knows as well as the child of Manhattan how to overcome the obstacles with which the city street bars its attempt at play. Imprisoned between the walls of the tenement houses lining both sides of the block, under the feet of horses and the wheels of wagons and automobiles, Manhattan's child knows how to bend the street to his uses. He throws his ball over the heads of pedestrians, rides among cars and trucks with his play wagon, and, putting a torch to the paper in unemptied garbage cans, transforms them into fiery beacons.

The block came alive. It was a new Zelig the junk dealer who drove into the street. Long Anthony trotted along with high steps, as though he trod the sawdust of a circus. The wagon bells jangled merrily, and Zelig called out in a voice that carried to the upper stories: "Junk! Junk!" The cry seemed to have in it the clash and clang of cymbals.

From one of the upper windows came the voice of an Irish housewife. She emptied a dust pan over the heads of the passers-by, singing out a popular tune—"Oh, Kelly with the green necktie!" From the window of a Jewish flat came the sound of a synagogue chant being played on a gramophone while the woman of the house was doing the week's wash. A hand organ on the street played "Alexander's Ragtime Band." Girls held hands and danced to the tune. A passing plumber took up the refrain—the song was sweeping the city. Women and girls looked out of windows. Some of them hummed, others sang the melody. Even the milkman, driving up to deposit his cans of milk in front of Moshe Wolf's store, clattered his cans to the rhythm. Schultz, the fat German butcher, stood at the door of his store, his bloodstained apron over his big belly, and made a try at whistling the tune. The young Negro who helped the Italian iceman make his deliveries to the tenement flats halted in the middle of the street, a block of ice resting on his back between the hooks of his ice tongs, and started to do a ragtime dance to the ecstatic glee of the ring of children which immediately formed around him.

In Abram Heimowitz' cleaning shop sat a customer, Professor Oppenheimer. The professor boarded at Mrs. Kranz's "apartment hotel." In the old country he had been a renowned musician, a virtuoso, a pupil of Liszt and Taussig, and of who knows whom else. But America had not been kind to him. He had started out by giving concerts, then playing in orchestras, and he had ended up a boarder at Mrs. Kranz's hotel, that haven for musicians and actors who had fallen behind in the race.

Now Professor Oppenheimer gave music lessons to the children of the poor Irish, Jewish, and Italian families in the neighborhood. Every Italian father and mother had dreams about a son emerging as a second Caruso, and every Jewish mother nursed the illusion of producing a second Mischa Elman. The pennies that were needed for food would be spent to expose the children to music and singing lessons. Through the open windows of the block could constantly be heard the scraping of violins, the tinkling of piano keys, and the high sweet sound of young soprano voices.

Professor Oppenheimer was a tall, robust man, with a leonine head and a shock of long gray hair. He had plenty of work but little money. For the lessons he gave he frequently had to take

56

payment in "services." Every mother wanted to do his laundry in payment for her child's lessons, but the professor had nowhere enough laundry to match the number of lessons he gave. The couple of stiff shirts and high collars which had remained to him from the good old days were worn thin with years of laundering. The same was true of his good black suit, which he was always bringing to Heimowitz to be cleaned and pressed. Now he was sitting comfortably in his underwear, a sheet over his lap; his trousers were at the sewing machine in the process of repair.

"Ai, there's not much more life left in these pants of yours," Heimowitz sighed, looking skeptically at the professor's shiny, threadbare garment. "They'll not last much longer. I'm afraid, Professor, you're going to need another pair."

"And where do you think I'm going to get the money for them? You hear the kind of music they want—Alexander's Ragtime Band! America doesn't want Beethoven, or Bach, or my old teacher Liszt. America wants ragtime. Idiots!"

"That's capitalism, Professor. Under Tammany a professor of music, a man like you, has to wear shiny pants. . . . Wait until the socialists get in. . . ."

"And what'll happen then? Will the socialists give me a new pair of pants?"

"Yes, certainly, Professor. Under socialism a man like you won't have to carry his pants to a man like me every Monday and Thursday to get them patched up. The state will see to it that a man like you, a professor, will have three pairs of pants. Not only you, everyone in the whole world, everyone, will have new pants." Heimowitz' face shone with earnestness.

The professor looked at the little tailor staring so earnestly at him, his glasses pushed up on his forehead, with the confident look of a man who had the revolution in his pocket and knew clearly and in all details exactly what wonders it would accomplish. Professor Oppenheimer looked at him in surprise. Such an insignificant little Jewish tailor, a nobody, one would imagine, and there he sits at his sewing machine, planning a grandiose world in which everyone would have a new pair of pants. . . !

"Maybe it'll be the way you say, but it's too long to wait," he sighed in answer.

On the sidewalk in front of Shmulevitch's poultry store sat the "victim of the capitalist class." His wife had brought the consumptive downstairs to get a breath of fresh air. He sat on an armchair, made secure by pillows all around him, and provided with his customary sputum cups. Everything else he needed would be supplied by the goodhearted neighbors.

"I have no time to stay here," his wife told him. "I have to go and cook something for the children." She knew she could depend on the neighbors.

The first woman to come out of Moshe Wolf's store, when she saw the sick man sitting on his chair, went over to ask him about his health.

"How are you today, Chaim? A little better?"

"A little," the sick man answered and coughed weakly.

"Maybe you'll drink a glass of milk. Moshe Wolf just got in some fresh milk from the farm. Practically cream. Chaia, Chaia," she called to Shmulevitch's wife, who sat in the doorway of the store plucking the feathers off a chicken. "Bring me a cup. Chaim would like some fresh milk."

Chaia handed out the cup and the neighbor filled it with milk from the jug she carried. The sick man drank it down and coughed.

Another woman appeared in the doorway of the adjoining tenement.

"Chaim, I just made some delicious beet soup. Take some. It's good for you."

"Here, Chaim, take this orange. It's good to suck at when your throat is dry."

Chaim Melamed drank the milk, tasted the soup, sucked at the orange, chewed rock candy, taking everything the goodhearted neighbors brought him, answering all who inquired if he was feeling any better in the same way.

"A little."

Moshe Wolf's grocery was directly across the street from the poultry store. In front of it Nathan sat on his wheel chair watching the life of the street. His eyes were the only medium that bound him to the life around him. He sucked in the sights with his eyes, like roots sucking in the moisture from the earth. For him his eyes were fingers with which he could grasp things and events. His eyes led him where his feet could not carry him. They penetrated everywhere, into the rooms where people lived, looking at and listening to everything that took place. He remembered the days before the paralysis had laid him low. It seemed to him that everything that had happened then belonged to another life. A thought came to him which reminded him of those days. He remembered how he used to think of ways of saving himself and the family from the net of poverty which had snared them. He lived on 48th Street, but his life and his friends belonged to an altogether different world. He was often with the Hirsches, who lived uptown. They weren't wealthy, but there was a special atmosphere about them. Robert, Nathan's friend, was unusually gifted, a brilliant student of German poetry, philosophy, and music. Through him Nathan had made the acquaintance of a whole circle of intelligent youths, most of them of German-Jewish families. They talked of Spinoza and Kant, and regaled themselves with readings of German poetry.

The Hirsches had many musical evenings. On Mondays a few people would gather, and there would be chamber music—Haydn and Mozart and Bach. Nathan loved music. Sometimes, on a Saturday afternoon, he would stand in line for hours at the Metropolitan and climb to the gallery to hear a Wagnèrian opera. Sometimes he would go with the Hirsches to Carnegie Hall, to sit on the gallery steps and hear an all-Beethoven program.

Everything that was beautiful and elevated came from Germany. American music simply did not exist. Nor American literature, either. If Nathan should timidly mention Edgar Allan Poe or Walt Whitman, or even Hawthorne or Emerson, they would laugh at him. Provincial, backwoods literature and philosophy! World literature, world poetry, and world culture could be found only among the Germans! Russia? Dostoevsky, Gogol, Tolstoi, when Nathan timidly ventured to mention them, were disposed of as minor talents, Asiatics; European culture was German culture. Nathan swallowed everything, drinking with a deep spiritual thirst the heady drafts which flowed at the Hirsches'. What had he to do with 48th Street, that confusion of people and customs, that world without culture, into which he had fallen only by chance! They were immigrants, driven out of their native countries. In their baggage they had brought no literature, no spiritual values, nothing but a mixture of jargons and dialects. They were just pieces and fragments of the European masses, all thrown together into the melting pot called New York.

And that only temporarily, provisionally, for a little while and accidentally. Each group lived on with the memories of their old homes, and all of them longed and hoped for the day when they would have enough money saved to return—money saved through sweat and labor—and be able to establish themselves in their old homes with the gold scraped from the American streets. The Italians spoke of the vineyards they would buy in Naples or in Sicily; the Slavs talked of Poland, of Slovakia and Ruthenia; the Germans sent home every penny they could spare to be saved for them in the banks of Germany, so that they could buy a farm in their native provinces. Even the Jewish intellectuals and intelligentsia, driven with knouts from the Tsarist domains, waited only for the miracle which would release them from the American exile. The Messiah had different forms. For the intelligentsia it wore the face of a revolution in Russia; for the Jewish nationalists the Messiah was Zion.

There was no America in New York. Maybe there was an America in the distant hinterland, in Oklahoma, Nebraska, in the far-flung farms, on the blue fields of Kentucky. But in the New York that was Nathan's world there was no America. Everyone lived on a separate island, with the exception, maybe, of a few isolated individuals who had been torn away from their native countries, remembered little about them, and were not bound to them with any ties. These were the homeless ones. They had lost their old home and had not yet found a new one. He was such a homeless one, Nathan, and he must therefore warm himself at the hearth of a strange culture. That hearth had been opened up to him in kindness by a circle of German Jewish intellectuals.

But the more he learned at the Hirsches' about German culture, the more he heard in Jewish intelligentsia circles about the coming Russian revolution, the more he yearned for a country that would be his own. He had no other country but the land to which his father had brought him. He had been cast upon the New York streets like a child whose mother lets him roam on a free meadow. Not Germany, not Russia, not Palestine even, was ever his home. His home was America; it was New York, and he was ready to give it all his love.

He began to study American history and to bury himself in American literature. He sought his salvation in America, among the people with whom he lived, in the country which was his home.

But that was in another life.

Now he sat imprisoned on the wheel chair his father had placed

60

in front of the store, and looked about him. The blades of his thoughts raced around like a swiftly rotating windmill. He thought that all these people he saw in the street, gathered from the four corners of the world in this small space between the East River and First Avenue, were, like himself, spewed out of their old homes like some superfluous matter. Superfluous people, whom no one wanted. They had been torn out by the roots from a soil which no longer was willing to harbor them, and here they were, on an island, on a small patch of ground, and they were swallowed up like tiny fishes in the maws of the leviathan called New York. All of them tried to live their own unique, individual lives, to hold on to what they had brought with them from the old country. And those who had nothing to hold on to grasped like beggars at the skirts of foreign cultures to which they had never belonged. As he, Nathan, had clung to the circle of the Hirsches; or others to the Russian revolution. They sought to root themselves in alien soil; to be received into an alien home.

Why could they not—these superfluous people who had been spewed out of their native countries—share their common fate; accept a common destiny; plant themselves in the new soil?

"What have these things to do with me? Why do I think these thoughts? What interest have I in this life?" Nathan thought to himself when he became conscious again of his wheel chair and the people of the block around him. "It all means nothing to me."

He could sense someone coming. He felt her presence before he heard the sound of her voice. Her smile, her joyfulness and sympathy preceded her like a sentinel.

"Nat, would you like me to take you to the East River? There's such a cool breeze." Mary McCarthy spoke in a cheerful voice, as though she were suggesting taking his arm and setting off with him for a stroll.

"Have you got the time?"

"Oh, sure. I've always got time. You know very well I'm on vacation. I have nothing to do."

"I thought you were going to camp."

"I don't know yet. Wait, I'll tell your father. Mr. Davidowsky, may I go with Nathan to the river?" She said "go with Nathan," not "take Nathan."

"Who is that?" Moshe Wolf put his head through the doorway

61

of the store. "Oh, it's you. You have the time? Don't you have to be home?"

"I've got all the time I want, Mr. Davidowsky. Honest! I've got nothing else to do."

"And what'll your father and mother say? They'll scold you."

"Oh, they know. My mother suggested it herself. And my grandmother, too."

"You're a good girl, Mary. Wait a minute." Moshe Wolf brought a package of cookies out of the store, and some almond chocolate. "Here. Take this with you. And here's a bottle of milk. Maybe Nathan will get thirsty."

"Fine, Mr. Davidowsky. Thanks."

"But you're sure you've got time? You're sure you don't have to go home to help your mother?"

"I've got all day for myself."

"We'll pay her for it," Deborah's voice shouted out of the store.

"It isn't necessary." Mary smiled and began to wheel Nathan toward the river.

The swollen river rocked in its comfortable bed. Overhead the sun shone in a clear sky. Everything around and on the river seemed to be in constant movement. Chains of barges, heavily laden with all kinds of freight, nosed along by tugs, snaked over the swelling surface of the river.

The Long Island side of the river was an unending line of somber factory buildings, their tall chimneys belching black clouds of smoke, but their windows were reflected gold in the sunlight. Barges laden with coal, bricks, and iron rails moved toward them. Flat-decked boats left the factory piers heaped with crates of manufactured products. Boats with building material, the salvage of razed buildings, bricks, sand, corrugated sheeting and lumber for building and cords of wood for fuel made a continuous procession on the river. They all left behind them thick, writhing columns of blue smoke which dispersed lazily in the sky. The hoarse sounds of sirens split the air.

The Manhattan shore was lined with storehouses, granaries, and warehouses. Gangs of laborers, naked to the waist, their sweat-drenched torsos seemingly molded of bronze, hauled loaded sacks from ship to dock and from dock to ship. Others, busy as ants, were hidden in clouds of black dust as they shoveled powdered coal through wide iron funnels into trucks. Teams of broad-flanked, powerful horses pawed impatiently on the pavement cobbles. Trucks came and went. One gang of longshoremen after another unloaded sand, rolled iron drums filled with gasoline, or beer casks bound with iron hoops, carried bricks, or hauled sacks of sugar and salt and other provisions for the local markets.

Amid the medley of noises naked youngsters darted among the legs of the laborers and dived from the pier ends into the foul waters of the river edge. Others dropped lines in a futile attempt to catch fish in the oily waters.

Through the clouds of smoke flocks of seagulls flew, their hoarse, piercing call heralding the capture of some toothsome morsel in the river. They landed on the pier, hopping among the feet of the laborers, flying above their heads, filling the air with their restless commotion.

Everything on the shore was alive with movement. Everything but Nathan. His eyes were buried in the book which Mary had placed on his lap. He drank in the printed page with his thirsty eyes and it seemed to Mary that he was far away, somewhere in another world, where he could move as freely as did the life about him.

"You know, Nat," Mary said, "when I see you so absorbed in the book, I imagine that it isn't us who can move about freely, but you. We stay in one place, but you go forward . . . and on and on . . ."

Nathan smiled. "When you haven't got feet you have to travel with your eyes."

"Eyes can take you much farther than feet," Mary commented.

"Who told you that?"

"Nobody. But that's what I think when I look at you."

"You're a smart girl, Mary," said Nathan.

Mary's eyes grew bigger. Her face glowed with pride.

CHAPTER SEVEN

THE TWO MONTHS of summer vacation Mary devoted to Nathan Davidowsky. Everybody in the block wondered about it—most of all her own parents. Her father, when he came home from his work in the evening, yelled that she was becoming nothing but a servant to Jews. Once or twice he beat her and threatened to throw her out of the house. She neglected her own duties at home; she rarely took her young brother to the river front where the children of the neighborhood gathered to play.

As soon as Mary got up in the morning she went out of the house and over to the Davidowskys' to help Moshe Wolf bathe and feed the crippled boy. Later she helped Moshe Wolf or Irving carry the wheel chair down into the street. Then she wheeled Nathan to the river and sat with him all day. She ran to the library to get books for him, read aloud to him, engaged in lengthy conversations with him, and rushed to get Moshe Wolf whenever he was needed.

Moshe Wolf grew to rely on her more and more; he was free to spend more time in the store. She got to be such a help to the Davidowskys that Moshe Wolf thought of paying her a few dollars. Even Deborah voiced her agreement. "Let her have a chance to save a few dollars for a dress."

When he broached the suggestion to Mary, however, the girl's eyes filled with tears.

"I'm not doing it to be paid," she said, ashamed.

"We know that," Moshe Wolf said. "But we can't take your help for nothing."

"If you're going to pay me, then I won't do it," Mary insisted.

"Are you so rich, you silly girl? It's a chance to save a few dollars. They'll come in handy, maybe for a dress or something when you're ready to go to work," said Deborah. "And maybe your father won't yell at you so much."

"If I'm going to be paid, then I won't do it," Mary insisted stubbornly.

"Why not?"

"For no reason," Mary mumbled, her face red, and she ran out of the room.

For a few days she stayed away. Then she came back.

"You better not talk to her about it any more," said Deborah to her husband. "She's proud and she'll get insulted. At the end of the vacation we'll give her a present."

There was no more talk about money, and Mary kept on taking care of Nathan.

Most of the youngsters of the block went to work as soon as they got through with public school. Patrick McCarthy's ambition was to see Mary through high school, but she knew that now that her sixteenth birthday had come around, her school life would have to be over. After the summer she would have to go to work.

Some of her Catholic friends had gone away for the summer to a camp run by Catholic charity. The old priest of St. Boniface's, to which Mary's family belonged, had seen to it that Mary received an invitation to spend the last three weeks of the summer vacation at the camp in New Jersey. To the astonishment of everyone in the family Mary refused to go. Her careworn mother, beaten down by the years of poverty and endless battles with a violent and irresponsible husband, tried to conceal Mary's refusal from him. Mary herself attempted to find all sorts of excuses to justify her unwillingness to go.

But everyone in the block knew that Mary's refusal to go to camp was so that she could continue to take care of Davidowsky's cripple. Mary's devotion was an admirable but at the same time a puzzling thing. The Davidowskys were already so used to her that they allowed her to tend the cripple as though she were a member of the family. Even Nathan, who at first was resentful and embarrassed by the helplessness he had to reveal before Mary, accepted her help and let her minister to him. It was not only necessity which made him accept it; it was also the kindness and warmth which Mary extended to him. He became accustomed to her and gradually he lost all his feelings of embarrass-

65

ment. He couldn't understand her devotion to him, nor did he seek to understand it. He accepted it as something that was destined to be that way.

Like everyone else he had heard that Mary had had the chance to go to camp and he wondered why she had refused. One day, as they sat near the river, he asked her about it.

"Oh, I don't like it," Mary answered. "I was there once, the year I was confirmed. I know what it's like." Her tone seemed to convey that the whole subject had no interest for her. She passed her hand over her flushed face.

"I thought that you loved to be in the country. I remember how you always used to talk about the fields and the birch trees and about the brook and the lawn in front of the house. And now you suddenly don't care for it?"

"Oh, they make you pray all day."

"But I thought you liked to pray. You go to church all the time."

"Yes, I like to pray, but only when I feel like it. Not when I don't feel like it and I'm made to."

"Naturally, you oughtn't to pray when you don't feel like it. Do you pray often?"

"Yes, when I've got some special reason. And God hears me, too."

"He does?"

"Yes. Every time I ask God for something He listens to me. Even now I'm praying to Him for something, and I'm sure He'll hear me."

"I don't see you praying just now."

"You don't have to pray so that people can see you. You can pray in your heart, and always keep your prayer in your heart, until God grants it."

"And does God always grant it?"

"Not always. But that means I haven't wanted it hard enough. It's only when I want it hard enough and keep on praying for it in my heart that God grants it. It happened that way only a little while ago, on my mother's birthday. You see, Nat, it was like this. You all think that my father is a bad, cruel man. I know that's what everybody believes. But it isn't so, Nat. My father's not a bad man. He's only unhappy because he never got what he wanted—to get to be a lawyer. You see, Nat, my

66

mother's not well, and she can't work hard...she gets dizzy spells. So my grandma has to do all the work in the house. Grandma doesn't complain about it; when we want to help her, she doesn't let us. But when my father comes home and finds her working so hard, he feels bad and he yells at us. And do you know what else? He doesn't know that Mother gets those dizzy spells. If he knew about it, he would only make things worse. That's his nature. When things are bad with him and he can't improve them, he starts to yell and blame everybody for his bad luck. He can't control himself. He says that my mother is to blame that he didn't become a lawyer. He doesn't mean it —but he says it."

Nathan looked at her timidly. Surely it must be embarrassing for her to pour out these intimate family secrets. But her face was calm, as though the situation she was talking about had nothing to do with her personal life. It filled him with wonder. "You don't have things so easy, Mary," he said.

"Oh, it isn't always that way. Only once in a while. Very seldom, even." She looked at him with her soft, brown eyes. "When my father's good—and my father's good very often—he's the best father in the world. And he takes us on picnics lots of times. Once he took us all the way to Bronx Park to show us the zoo. He knows so much about the animals; where they come from and about their life. My father told us that in Ireland he used to have pigeons...and he knows more about breeding them than Harry. He says that a Jew has no right to breed pigeons or to have anything to do with animals. He says the law oughtn't to allow Jews to have pigeons or animals in the house."

"For what reason?" Nathan asked, amused.

"My father"—Mary suddenly seemed a little subdued—"doesn't like your people. He says it's the fault of the Jews that he has such a bad job, and that it's the Jews' fault that he didn't finish studying law."

"I thought you said he blamed your mother for that."

Mary smiled helplessly. "Yes, he blames mother—and he blames the Jews too. You see, it's like this. I wouldn't want to repeat what my father says—but I ought to tell you. My father says the Jews tortured Jesus Christ and crucified Him. He's not the only one; lots of our people say it. Even the priest and the sisters. Once, when I was younger, I went to a Passion play and I saw Judas—he was a Jew with a black beard, and a big fat belly and a golden chain over it, and I saw how he betrayed Jesus for thirty pieces of silver. And I saw two Jews—one of them a tall, stout one—he looked like Shmulevitch—and the other a short one, with a yellow beard, and they beat poor Jesus. They tore His clothes and they put the Cross on His shoulders. From that time I hated the Jews. I really thought that all Jews were wicked, and that all of them had tortured and beaten the sweet Jesus. . . . "

Tears began to fill Mary's eyes and she turned her face aside.

"I hated the Jews so much that I wasn't able to look a Jew straight in the face. I used to push the Jewish kids off the side-walk, and—you know what?—I used to spit at them. Do you know what I used to do at school? We used to write dirty words about the Jews on the Jewish children's schoolbooks. That's the way I was until . . . until . . . I'll tell you the whole truth, Nat . . . until I got to know you people. . . . "

"What people do you mean?" asked Nathan.

"I mean the Jews in the neighborhood. I'll tell you how it was. When we moved here—we used to live on 83rd Street, but it was too expensive for us—we met Jewish people for the first time really. Over on 83rd Street there were very few of your people; they were mostly German or Irish. When we moved here my father warned us to buy only at the Christian grocery store on First Avenue, where the man was an Italian Catholic, and that we shouldn't dare to go into your father's store. So we did as he said. We always paid cash, but once mother had no money and she sent me to buy some spaghetti and some bread and butter. I told Mr. Marsini we wanted the groceries on credit and that on Saturday, when my father brought home his wages, my mother would pay him. Mr. Marsini asked me who my father was, where he worked, whether he went to Kelly's saloon, and things like that—and he wouldn't give me the grocer-ies. It was late and there was nothing in the house for supper.

"At that time we used to eat only spaghetti, like the Italians. We never had enough money to buy meat at the butcher's. So I was standing in the street and I didn't know what to do. My father would be home soon and I knew what would happen when he came and didn't find supper ready. So I stood there praying in my heart to Jesus.

"I told you before that when I want something—not when I want something, but when I need something that we just have to have—I always pray to Jesus. And Jesus always hears me ...always! I closed my eyes right on the street where I was standing, crossed myself, and I said in my mind: 'Sweet Jesus, You know that I have to bring food home. My father will soon come home, and if he doesn't find supper ready he'll make things miserable for us. Dear, sweet Jesus, help us.' And then I opened my eyes and saw that I was standing in front of your father's store. And I saw all the good things through the window— corned beef and sausages and other things—different from the other store. I went inside; I felt as though Jesus had guided me there. And I saw your father standing behind the counter waiting on a customer and smiling. I was afraid to look at him. I stood near the door and didn't know what to do. I was ashamed to ask him to give us credit. After all, he knew we lived on the block; so I guess he understood that when we had money we went to another store but when we needed credit we were coming to him. That's what I was thinking and I was ready to run out of the store without saying a word to your father. But your father noticed me and started smiling at me with those soft eyes he has.... You have the same kind of eyes as your father, Nat...."

"Thanks, Mary. But go on, tell me the rest. What happened?"

"Your father smiled at me and said: 'I think you're the new neighbor's daughter. It's nice to have you for a neighbor. Tell me, what can I do for you?' He spoke so kindly and he gave me so much courage...and he looked at me with those soft eyes. And, you know, when I saw his eyes I got the feeling that I'd seen them somewhere before. And then I wasn't scared any more. I told him that I wanted to get some spaghetti and a can of tomato sauce on credit, because we had no money in the house and we'd pay at the end of the week, and your father said 'Sure, sure,' and kept on looking at me with such a kind face that I began to feel good all over. And do you know what he said? 'What kind of a meal can you have out of spaghetti and tomato sauce?' he said. 'Your father works hard; he needs strengthening food. And your mother, too. She doesn't look too strong.

She needs to drink milk, a lot of it. Here, my child,' he said, 'take this bottle of milk—for your mother—and a quarter of a pound of butter—your mother ought to eat plenty of butter. And here's corned beef. All the Irish like corned beef. It's good rich food, and this is kosher also.' And he cut off a great big piece of corned beef and weighed it. My heart was beating like anything and I said to him: 'Mr. Davidowsky, we haven't got enough money for all that. I don't know if I ought to take all that home. My mother will scold me.'

" 'You're a very good girl,' he said, and gave me a great big piece of chocolate with almonds. 'Here,' he told me, 'share it with your brothers and sisters. It's free. This is a present from me, from Davidowsky's grocery store. No charge. And tell your mother not to worry about the groceries. I'm glad to have her for a customer and she can always have credit. If she can't pay this week, then she'll pay next week. I know how it is when you move into a new flat; there's always extra expense. None of us around here is a Rockefeller—or even a Jacob Schiff,' he said to me, and he gave me a little poke with his finger."

Nat smiled broadly at Mary's unconscious imitation of his father. "You're a perfect mimic, Mary," he said jokingly. "What a hit you'd make in the movies."

"Please don't laugh at me," Mary begged. "I want you to believe me, Nat—when your father talked that way to me and looked at me with those eyes of his, I knew it wasn't true about the Jews killing Christ. No, I said to myself, a man like your father couldn't have killed Christ; why, Jesus Himself sent me to him. And from that time on ... from then ... from then on ..." She put her head on Nathan's shoulder and began to weep.

"What's the matter, Mary?" Nathan asked helplessly.

She lifted her head from his shoulder, shook her head vigorously so that her dark braids swung back and forth, and dried her eyes, smiling timidly.

Mary wasn't exactly pretty, but everything about her was lively, fresh, and sensitive. Her small forehead had a tendency to wrinkle. Her eyes, bright and brown, had a clear, sympathetic gaze. Her nose, a little too short and small for her too-small face, was the sensitive nose of a little animal that seemed to detect scents hidden from others. It was the index to her likes and dislikes, wrinkling in distaste when anything displeased her. Her

70

mouth was wide and the lips thin, with a certain abandon in their expression that belied the modesty and piety of her eyes.

"It doesn't matter," she said, and ran her hand over her disordered hair. Do you know what happened that evening, Nat?" She smiled bitterly. "Father came home and saw the food on the table—Grandmother had prepared the corned beef with some cabbage left over from the night before. It was like a Sunday meal. Father could tell from the Jewish bread on the table that the food had come from your father's store, and he pushed his plate away even before he sat down, and he asked where the food came from. Every one of us was scared, no one wanted to answer him, but he insisted on knowing where the corned beef came from, and the butter, and the milk—but most of all the Jewish bread. He wanted to know if it came from your father's store. But I wasn't afraid of him. I told him right to his face that that's where it came from! And do you know what else I told him? I told him that I took it on credit. That I did it myself, without mother knowing anything about it. And I told him that the Jewish grocer was a thousand times better to us than the Italian grocer and that from now on I was only going to buy at the Jewish store.

"My father got very angry and he said to me: 'Do you know where this food comes from? From the Devil! The Jew is setting a trap for you! He gives you credit so he can have you in his power! The Jew is the Devil!' And I said to him: 'Oh, no, he's not the Devil. He didn't set any trap for me. And from now on I'm always going to buy there, because Jesus Himself sent me to him.' And when my father heard that he began hitting me. And when mother tried to protect me he shoved her aside so that she fell down. And grandmother shouted at him and the kids began to cry. . . . It was awful!

"My father just stood there and I could tell from his face that he was feeling terrible. I told him that he hadn't hurt me, that it was nothing. And I went over to him and took hold of his sleeve to quiet him, because I was sorrier for him than for us. And then he got real mad and pushed me aside and took the plate of corned beef and cabbage and threw it all on the floor. Then he took all the rent money from the cupboard—every penny of it—and went out of the house.

"But since that happened he doesn't start any trouble even

though he knows we buy at your father's. He doesn't say a word. Sometimes he scolds me because I visit Jews and because most of my school friends are Jews. He says that I'm a servant for the Jews, and sometimes when I come home late—because I like to be over at Harry's, with the pigeons—he starts trouble. He's given me plenty of beatings, but I never cry. When he beats me for associating with Jews I don't care! I don't mind it! I'm even glad!"

"What sort of talk is that?" Nat interrupted. "You're glad that your crazy father beats you?" Little beads of froth formed at the corners of his mouth.

"Don't you understand what I mean, Nat? Don't you understand? If my father beat me for something I did that was wrong I would fight him back; I would scratch at him with my nails. Sometimes I feel like doing it—and one day I will! But if my father—or anyone else—wants to beat me for doing something good, something that was right—I don't mind. I want to suffer for doing good . . . for doing something that I ought to do . . . that it is right to do."

She spoke slowly and earnestly, as though she wanted to make it easy for Nathan to comprehend exactly how she felt.

"Do you understand me, Nat?"

"No, Mary, I can't understand."

"Look, Nat, it's this way. I know—I am sure—that Jesus Himself sent me into your father's store so that I could get to know you people . . . so that I could get to know the people I could really love . . . I mean so that I could get to know your father . . . and your brother Irving . . . and Rachel . . . and Harry. . . . Jesus Himself wanted to open my eyes and He sent me into your father's store . . . as I told you before . . . when I was standing on the street and didn't know where to turn. Jesus wanted me to go in! He told me to go in! And I know that it's good. . . . Oh, it's good to suffer a little for Jesus' sake. . . ."

"What sort of ideas have you got in your head, Mary? Jesus had nothing to do with it. You're a human being, aren't you? You've got self-respect, haven't you? You're an American girl! You live in a free country. So what sort of talk is that about suffering for Jesus' sake?"

"Yes, Nat! Yes! I'm telling you it's good . . . it's good . . . I'm content with my whole heart, with my whole soul. . . . It's good to suffer for Jesus' sake...." Mary closed her eyes in ecstasy.

"Look, Mary," Nat said after a pause. "That's no life for you, in that house! It's a hell. You're young. Your life is just beginning. Christ doesn't want any person to suffer. Run away, Mary, and save yourself. You're sixteen years old. Go and get a job, any kind of a job, and get out of this neighborhood. Go far away, among strangers. Begin to live your own life. Live for yourself. Forget about your home. You have no home. Your home is a hell. And get this idea of suffering for Jesus out of your head. You haven't planned to become a nun, Mary, to go into a convent, have you?"

"Oh, no, Nat. I want to stay here, here in 48th Street... not for my parents' sake, no! Not for my mother's sake, or my brother's and sister's. No... it's for something else... for something altogether different...."

"But what is it? What is it that holds you here?"

"It's because... because I'm in love, Nat." Mary looked at the boy with pleading, devoted eyes. Her lips quivered.

Nathan breathed heavily and his face flushed.

"In love? That's good, that's good, Mary," he stammered.

"Don't you want to know who it is?" Mary asked after a short silence.

"That isn't any of my business," Nathan answered with a wry smile.

"I'm in love with you, Nathan."

"With me!" Nathan burst into a spasm of laughter.

"Yes, Nat, with you. I love you and I'll always love you. I worship you, Nat." She bent her head to his crippled hand and began to kiss it, wetting it with her tears.

"Don't, Mary, don't!" Nathan stammered, helplessly trying to draw away his crippled hand from the girl's burning lips.

That night Nathan dreamed that he walked. He had dreamed before that he could walk, but this time it was different. In his earlier dreams there had always been someone who commanded him to walk; sometimes it was Dr. Chazanowitch, or his father; once it was one of his high school teachers. They would stand over him and tell him—sometimes with kindness, at other times harshly—that he could walk. He would be aware that his legs

73

were simply useless appendages, doll's legs, without motion, stuffed with straw. They only dangled from his body; if he should try to stand on them they would collapse under him. And yet these people wanted him to stand on them, on these useless doll's legs, and they didn't put out a hand to help him—and he could feel his legs giving way under him—and in the act of falling he would awake.

In these dreams he always fell when others made him try to stand on his legs. And it was good to fall; he wanted to fall. This time he did not fall; he stood on his feet and he did not fall.

And the most wonderful part of it was that he wasn't surprised that he could stand. In his dream he had completely forgotten that his legs were useless, that he could neither stand nor walk. He forgot to fall; he *wanted* to walk.

He dreamed that he was in a field, near a river... or maybe it was on the shore of the ocean. What was extraordinary was that the river... or the ocean shore... was in his own room above the store. His father and mother were downstairs in the store and he was alone with Mary at the edge of the ocean. He was naked, entirely naked, but he wasn't ashamed, because he was like a child, for all that he was a grownup at the same time. He wasn't surprised at all that Mary was not embarrassed at his nakedness. "She thinks that I'm a helpless child who can't walk," he thought in his dream. "She doesn't know that I'm an adult, that I'm Nathan, and she isn't embarrassed by my nakedness because she sees me as a small child."

Suddenly in his dream he felt humiliated and ashamed that she thought him a small helpless child. He looked for something to hide his nakedness. Although his clothes were lying near him on the ground he couldn't reach them. But he had to cover his nakedness and he had to prove to her that he wasn't a helpless child; he was Nathan, Nathan, Nathan! And then he began to walk—how strange that he had forgotten that he *could* not walk —and he took a few steps away from her. No, not away from her—only to show her that he could walk, that he was a grownup. So he stood up and he walked. But what was most astonishing was that she was not surprised that he was grownup and that he could walk. She looked at him with her warm eyes and smiled to him and said: "Nat, you're my little brother and I must take

74

care of you. Why should I be ashamed to see you naked? You're a little child, Nat; you're my little Nat, and I love you." He could have hit her for it. He became full of anger and went toward her just as he was, all naked, and said to her: "Don't you see, I'm Nathan, I'm a grownup." But still she wasn't ashamed of his nakedness. She put her arms around him and lifted him to her lap, just as though he were a child—yet just as though he were a grownup. And in his dream he felt content. . . .

He woke up in fright. His first reaction to the dream was fear. A mountain of fear weighed him down. The knowledge of his helplessness suddenly burst on his mind, as though until this moment he hadn't been aware of it. And at the same time, together with his fear and anxiety, there was a faint, thin intimation of . . . what it was he did not know. The dream had been so real . . . as though his legs had really moved on the bed where he lay. It even seemed to him that he had changed his position, that his body was over on the other side of the bed, not where his father had placed him . . . as though he had actually turned on his side.

He fled in fright from the very thought. But the remembrance of the events of his dream, echoing with the resonances of actuality, vibrated in him like the sound of distant, fading music.

But the real throat-gripping fright was to come later, when his father came into the room to dress him. Moshe Wolf started back in panic when he came over to the bed.

"Who moved you, Nat? You're not lying the way I put you to bed."

"You're imagining it, Pa," Nathan whispered.

"But I know how. I put you in bed . . . over at the other side . . . like every night. . . . Deborah! Deborah!" he called his wife.

"What happened!" Deborah came to the door "Tell me what happened! You scared the life out of me!"

"Call Dr. Chazanowitch! Nat moved over in the bed!"

"Pa, leave me alone! You're only imagining it! You put me in bed this way!"

"But I remember, I remember!"

"Don't be an old fool," Deborah said. "How could he move himself? Could a stone move itself? What foolishness are you talking yourself into? This curse is on us for the rest of our lives!"

Nathan looked at his father with pleading eyes. In his gaze was the heartbreaking, helpless, begging look of a dumb animal. It was in his voice, too.

"Pa, please, please..."

"Why do you torture him?" Deborah said in a loud voice. "Have some pity."

His heart constricted with pain, Moshe Wolf silently began to attend to his son.

Later, when Mary came into the room with her fresh morning smile, Nathan wouldn't look at her. He simply said: "Please, Mary, let me be...."

"Why?"

"Let me be! Please, please, let me be...."

There was such urgent pleading in his voice that the tears rushed to Mary's eyes and she went out of the room.

She stood aimlessly on the sidewalk in front of the store, waiting for them to call her upstairs. She was only a little distance away when Moshe Wolf brought Nathan out in his wheel chair. She came up to him, but Nathan closed his eyes and moved his lips, showing his young white teeth.

Mary could hear his unspoken "Please, please!" and she walked away from him.

CHAPTER EIGHT

MOSHE WOLF'S store and living quarters were in a typical New York tenement. Behind the shop was a storeroom which held a large icebox, a long table on which Moshe Wolf prepared his homemade jars of salves and ointments, and a small stove on which simmered the home-cooked foods he sold in the store. A cellar under the store held barrels of sour pickled cucumbers, and crates and cases and boxes of packaged merchandise. It also served Irving as a storeroom for his piece goods and remnants.

The living quarters were on the floor above the store. Two separate stairways led to them; besides the common stairway opening from the dark hallway—which served all the tenants of the house and which Moshe Wolf and his family seldom used—there was a flight of steps which led directly from the store.

The two windows of the front room looked out over the street. That was the room Moshe Wolf and Deborah had slept in until his son's illness. Then they had moved Nathan in there, and Deborah made her bed in the "blind" room that had neither window nor ventilation. This room lay between the front room and the back room, the latter having a window looking out on a courtyard, facing the wall of another tenement. The tenement windows looked into one another; into all of them were wafted the smells of the food cooking in all the flats. In addition to the symphony of smells, the windows admitted the squeals of children and the quarrelings of husbands and wives. Without intending it, every householder was the witness of everything happening in the opposite flat. But all the tenants were used to the noises and the goings-on of their neighbors; they were as oblivious to domestic scenes as they were to the underwear and wash drying on the lines which stretched from window to window.

The back room of Moshe Wolf's flat, a little smaller than the front room and a little larger than the "blind" room, was not only the kitchen; it was the family sitting room. Its washtub served as the family bathtub on Fridays. There were a stove, a gas meter, an icebox, and a kitchen table with chairs around it. Against the wall, hidden behind a curtain, was a folding bed on which Irving slept. Here the family would gather on winter evenings near the stove. Here the family ate. Here sat visitors and friends.

For Moshe Wolf the kitchen was also a room for prayer. Here in the gray of the early morning he kept his rendezvous with his Maker, and devoutly recited his daily prayers. It was here on Friday evening that the Sabbath eve table was set.

Under the Sabbath candles in the brass holders the Davidowsky family would gather to partake of the Sabbath meal. There were just the four of them, Moshe Wolf, his wife, and the two boys. Never during the week days did they all meet at the table; instead they would eat on the run whenever there was time and of whatever food was at hand. Apart from Nathan, for whom his mother prepared warm cooked food, they would make their meals of whatever cold cuts there were in the store, maybe a sandwich of smoked salmon or corned beef on heavy corn bread, with sour pickles. Irving was hardly ever in the house. He spent most of the day and early evening marketing his remnants and other merchandise. Friday evening was like a gathering of the clan, the only evening when the family ate together from a linen-bedecked table, with the Sabbath candles burning, and the ritual washing before eating, and the blessing over the wine, and the quiet chanting of Sabbath songs.

On this Friday evening Irving was missing. Moshe Wolf had said the blessing, had already greeted the gentle angel who had entered his humble home on the wings of the Sabbath. He had already filled the cup of Sabbath wine, the silver beaker which he had brought with him from the old country. Never before had Irving been away from the table on the Sabbath eve.

Moshe Wolf deliberately prolonged the ritual opening prayer in the hope that Irving would arrive in time. But he could draw it out no longer. With an impatient rap on the table, as though the matter had to be brought to an end, he pronounced the final blessing before eating. Deborah brought the fish to the table and, in the usual Friday evening calm but with a good deal of sighing, the family began to eat the Sabbath meal.

It was not until the steaming chicken soup with noodles was on the table that the door leading from the outside hallway opened hurriedly and Irving, his face covered with perspiration and a package under his arm, burst into the room. He threw the package down in a corner, and without the usual Sabbath · greeting he called out: "Mama, come here!"

With a sigh and a tolerant look Deborah left the table and went over to him.

"Here's something toward the rent," said Irving, holding out a handful of bills.

"Where did you get all this money?"

"I didn't hold anybody up," Irving said with a self-conscious laugh. "I sold all the children's dresses I had. Every last one. It was fine stuff. They went like hot cakes. On Monday I'm going over to Goldberg and Goldberg's and buy out their entire stock."

Without a glance at his father he went over to the sink, hurriedly washed his hands and called out to his brother:

"Hello, Nat! I brought you a lot of books. I found them on a pushcart. They cost practically nothing. I thought you'd like to have them. There's a Webster's dictionary, too. I knew you wanted one. It's over there in the package." Irving sat down at the table and started on the fish and noodle soup his mother put before him.

"Without saying grace? Without reciting a blessing? Right from the street to the table! This is the Sabbath!" said Moshe Wolf, unable to control his anger.

"What about it? For other people the Sabbath is the best day for business!"

"I don't want to hear about other people and what other people do! In this family the Sabbath is the Sabbath, and we're going to observe it like God-fearing Jews!"

"Who's stopping you from observing it?" Irving asked, looking at his father, his spoon halfway up to his mouth.

"You're stopping me! My own son is stopping me! My own son brings the pagan street up to the Sabbath table."

"Well, what do you want me to do? Do you want me to move out of the house?" Irving looked straight at his father's face.

"What do you want, Moshe Wolf?" Deborah chimed in. "Do

you want to make America over? The boy has just brought fifteen dollars home! Fifteen dollars!" Deborah held out the bills for Moshe Wolf to see.

"I don't want his money! I don't need it!" Moshe Wolf fumed.

"You don't want it, eh? And how will you pay the bills? You're the good-natured kind; you give credit to every good-for-nothing who asks for it. If it weren't for the money Irving brings home we'd not be able to make ends meet."

"I won't sell the holy Sabbath for a few dollars, do you hear! If he wants to live in this house he's got to be home on Friday night in time for the Sabbath!"

"Look, Pa," Irving said earnestly. "People like us, living in all this poverty, without enough money to pay the rent, haven't any right to neglect such a good time for business as Friday evening and Saturday. First let's make a living, then we can celebrate the Sabbath."

"Are you teaching me how to live my life?" Moshe Wolf demanded sternly.

"I'm not teaching you, but don't you teach me. I pay for my board and lodging," Irving replied. "And from now on I'm going to do as I please. And if it doesn't suit you, Pa, maybe it would be better for me to move out. I'm sorry, but I can't help it. I want to be my own boss."

The determined words, from his seventeen-year-old son, left Moshe Wolf speechless. He suddenly realized how helpless he was against the brashness of America as typified by this young son of his. His wife broke in.

"Moshe Wolf," she said. "It's time you forgot about the old country and the old ways. In America children have rights, just like their parents. And especially when a child brings home money. Do you understand?"

"So I'm no longer a father, and you're no longer a mother, and the home is no longer a home. It's only a boarding house!"

Nathan, who had kept silent during the argument, suddenly broke into an unrestrained, uncontrollable stammering. Although normally his speech was distinct and clear, in moments of excitement he would find it difficult to enunciate his words.

"Wh-wh-why are p-p-people so cr-cr-cr-cruel to each other?" he half sobbed.

Moshe Wolf forgot his anger. He got up from his chair and

went over to Nathan, "Do you want to go into your room, my son?" he asked tenderly, his voice barely concealing his tears.

Nathan nodded his head.

Moshe Wolf carried the boy into the front room.

"I guess it'll be better if I move out, Ma," Irving said. "We'll only have the same arguments again."

Deborah began to weep. "How can I manage without you?" she sobbed. "You're the only one . . ."

"All right, all right, Ma," Irving consoled her. "Don't cry, Ma. I'll stay."

When Moshe Wolf returned to the kitchen the table was cleared, the Sabbath candles standing alone in the center of the table like forlorn orphans. Deborah began energetically to wash the dishes. She didn't say a word, but her mood was evident in the angry clatter she made at the sink. Like a beaten dog Moshe Wolf sat down at the table. It was in his mind to read the week's Portion in the Bible as he was used to do every Friday after the Sabbath meal, but instead he opened up the old volume at the Book of Psalms. He began to shake his head and shoulders back and forth with a quick motion as his broken voice chanted the words: "Hear my prayer, O Lord, and let my cry come unto Thee . . ."

On the sidewalk in front of the house Irving saw Mary. She was leaning against the iron railing in front of the store.

"Hello, Mary," Irving greeted her.

"Hello, Irving."

"Are you waiting for someone?"

"Not exactly. I'm just standing here."

"Would you like to come to a movie?"

"I'm afraid to come home late . . . on account of my father."

"The same old story. He's still got you terrorized. I put my father in his place tonight. I told him where he gets off."

"I wish I had a father like yours. Your father's a fine man."

"Yes, they're all fine. The only trouble is they mix in other people's business too much. They brought their old ideas with them from the old country and they want to force them on us. Believe me, Mary, it's time for people like us to live our own lives, and not live their lives all over again. I'm through with that stuff."

81

"Gee, Irving. What is it you're going to do?"

"The first thing any person has to do is earn some money. I want to make a living and be independent. When a person makes a living for himself and his family he has an entirely different outlook on life. He lives and lets live. He isn't jealous of anybody and doesn't need to ask help from anybody. And he's got no time for any of that nonsense—religion, Irish, Jewish—that only keeps people apart. It's only when things go bad with people that they're jealous of each other. The rich aren't jealous of each other. Let your father make a decent living and you'd see how quick he'd stop being an anti-Semite. I'm telling you, Mary, there's nothing in the world more important than making a living. When a man's got money, he's got everything."

"I never want to be rich. I always want to be poor ... poor!" Mary answered with fervor.

"What's the idea?"

"Because when you're rich you simply oppress the poor."

"You must have heard that from Nat. I know his talk. I want to be rich—not to oppress the poor, but so that the rich won't oppress me. I want to be the equal of anyone. Understand? Why should Rachel's uncle be able to live in a swell house in Flatbush and we have to live in these dirty tenement houses with the rats all over the place, and with that Shmulevitch always standing over us and eating our hearts out the first of every month? You ought to see the way my mother shivers when the first of the month comes around. She hardly closes an eye the whole week before."

"You're telling me. You ought to see my mother," said Mary.

"You see, that's why I want money. So that I can support my mother in a decent house and not have to be afraid of the landlord. Then my father can be as orthodox as he likes. That's the whole reason I want to be rich. And believe me, Mary, in a couple of years I'll be on top with the best of them. I know how it's done."

"Gee, you're smart all right, Irving, and I'm sure you'll get along. You'll be able to get your family out of this neighborhood, but I guess we'll stay here as long as they let us."

"Say—let's go to the movies, Mary. How about it? I did all right today. I gave my mother fifteen dollars ... and I've got plenty left. If you like, I'll bring you home before ten. Come on," Irving urged, and took Mary by the arm.

"I really don't know whether I ought to go. After all, Irving, you belong to Rachel, everybody knows that. Everybody even thinks you're engaged. If she finds out you took me to the movies she'll scratch my eyes out."

"She won't scratch your eyes out; I'll take care of that," Irving said, laughing. They walked toward First Avenue. "And besides I'm not Rachel's steady friend. I belong to nobody. And you're all right, Mary, you're okay. You take care of my brother Nat, don't you? You're fine, Mary. I've wanted to tell you that for a long time. All the things you do for him, and the way he allows you to! Why it's just as though you were his sister. You're all right, Mary. My parents are crazy about you. They think you're swell. I'll tell you the truth, since you've been taking care of Nat he's changed entirely. I can see it. It's as though something happened to him."

In the dim light of the street Irving could not see that Mary was blushing to the roots of her hair. He didn't even notice the trembling in her voice as she asked:

"What do you think made him change?"

"I don't know, but there's certainly a change in him."

"What do you mean?"

"He's not the same person. He used to be quiet . . . you know . . . indifferent . . . as though nothing made any difference to him. He always had that cynical smile on his face. It used to hurt me, sort of. It was a kind of smile . . . as if . . . you know . . . as if he didn't care about going on living. I used to hate it. I used to think it would be better if he yelled out and complained at the top of his voice . . . do you see what I mean? It would have been better than always smiling. I was afraid of that smile. Now, for the last few days, he doesn't smile that way any more. He seems more restless and nervous, gets excited over the least thing. I don't know if it's better that way. He seems to understand his condition better. . . ."

Mary interrupted him:

"Irving, do you love your brother?"

"Love him? I wish it had happened to me, not to him!"

Mary involuntarily seized his hand. Irving continued talking earnestly.

"That's one of the reasons I want to make money. I want to be

83

able to give him everything he needs. A nurse day and night to take care of him, and a decent apartment, and to send him to Florida. Since Nathan got sick I lost all interest in going to school. The only thing I want now is to make money, a lot of money."

"Gee, you're wonderful, Irving. I always knew it."

"You're all right yourself, Mary, to be so devoted to Nat. What made you do it?"

"Oh . . . I like to help him."

"That's fine of you, Mary. When I see Nat lying in bed waiting patiently for someone to come to take him out or to do something for him, I could scream. Why did God do that to him? What did He have against him?"

"Oh, Irving, don't talk that way. God loves those who suffer. The more a person suffers, the closer he is to God. God Himself suffered. Didn't Jesus hang on the Cross?"

"I don't believe in all that stuff. I don't see why God should want people to suffer. If God was good, He'd want people to be happy and not suffer. Let's not talk about that, Mary. Tell me what your plans are. What are you thinking of doing? Will your parents send you back to high school, or are you going to go to work?"

"I don't know yet. My parents talk about my taking a commercial course. But it costs fifty dollars. Where are they going to get it? I guess I'll get a job in a factory. They can use the few dollars I'll be able to earn."

"Don't do it, Mary. If you get into a factory, you're lost. Keep away from the factory as long as you can. Do what I tell you; anything in the world, but not a factory. Don't take a steady job. Get some sort of temporary work, helping in a store, or even taking care of children, but not a factory. And then you can take an evening course in stenography. Keep away from a factory, I'm telling you. It's a graveyard; you'll never get out of it, once you're in."

They walked along First Avenue. In the August evening the avenue was as bright as daylight. Along the sidewalks stood pushcarts loaded with fruit and illuminated with naked, flaming torches or with oil lamps. Some of the pushcarts displayed pots and pans, ironware, secondhand shoes, piece goods, remnants, artisan's tools. But it was the electric lights in the ice-cream parlor windows that lighted up the avenue. Inside they were crowded with women, girls, and children. The men filled the saloons.

In front of the window of a pastry shop a group of women stood, carrying children in their arms, other children holding on to their skirts, gazing in admiration at the enormous wedding cakes, baked tier on tier, with a little bride and bridegroom on the topmost turret. There were birthday cakes and butter cakes and cookies, a wealth of good things. A big crowd stood in front of the brilliantly lighted movie theater, the Scala, where multicolored posters covered the sides of the entrance. Ragged children begged for the return checks from the customers leaving the theater. The manager and his assistant were engaged in chasing the children away, and carefully examining every entrance ticket. There was constant quarreling between the eager children and the irritable manager.

Mary and Irving managed to push through the crowd and enter the theater, passing through the lobby draped with Italian flags. They went into the darkened hall.

There was a hair-raising murder scene being enacted in the picture, but neither Irving nor Mary paid much attention. Irving was thinking of the girl sitting beside him. She was so close to him, yet so strange. His own girl was Rachel. Everyone in the neighborhood knew that young Davidowsky, who was turning out to be such a good businessman, was interested in Harry Greenstock's daughter, the good-looking Rachel. The two were always seen together. Irving felt that he was in love with her. He was always astonished at her beauty, her proud gait, her poise, her lovely throat, her big eyes, and her classical features. He hadn't given much thought to the little Irish girl, Rachel's friend, who always seemed to be around them. Mary was nothing to look at or notice, not much more than an appendage to the beautiful Rachel. Everyone in the neighborhood knew that McCarthy beat his wife and children regularly; it was natural that no one should have much respect for the McCarthys. No one could understand why Rachel Greenstock should be friendly with Mary—unless it was that Rachel saw in her the contrast that would make her own good looks stand out more distinctly. The women in the neighborhood used to say: "That Rachel knows what she's doing, all right, when she lets that McCarthy girl drag around with her." Irving, like the others, paid her little attention, but sometimes the warmth that welled from the little Irish girl's personality startled him out of his indifference.

On Sundays the McCarthys would go to church, the whole family washed and scrubbed and dressed in their best. The girls wore ribbons in their hair, and the family walked along with dignity, their prayer books in their hands. It was hard to fit the week-day McCarthys into the picture of this respectable Sunday parade.

Once Irving had met Mary standing on the street, all dressed up. She was wearing her confirmation dress. It wasn't on a Sunday; Irving was used to seeing her neat and clean on Sunday; it was in the middle of the week. In her finery, with the green ribbon in her hair, a green band across her breast, with white shoes and stockings and a bouquet of flowers in her hand, Mary shone with a new radiance. It wasn't so much the finery that changed Mary in Irving's eyes; it was her whole bearing. A certain dignity looked out of her sparkling eyes; there was pride in her posture. She carried her head high. Irving had gone up to her, looked her over, and said:

"Gee, you look beautiful, kid! What's the special occasion?"

"Sure," she had answered proudly, "this is Saint Patrick's Day."

Irving was discomfited for a minute. But he had quickly recovered his poise and said: "Just you wait till Saint Moses' Day comes around. Then you'll see me dressed up too." He had turned and gone away.

Mary's eyes were unusually luminous. The light in them was warming; her glance was so attractive; there was a sincerity and goodness in her which did the heart good.

Irving was glad to be sitting beside her. Not that there was anything special in his mind. His girl, after all, was Rachel. But each time he met Mary, without knowing why, he felt good. She excited him with the strangeness and the challenge of the unknown, with the fascination even of the enmity which her father bore toward the Jews, in the knowledge of the Catholic pictures on the walls of her home, in the Sunday parade to church. Sometimes, when she came back from church on Sunday, she seemed to be an entirely different person; there was a strange aura about her, as though she were still under the spell of the incense which the priest had waved about in the church. The incense was not only in her clothing, it was in all her person. Her eyes were luminous and moist, her cheeks flushed, and there was a curious pathos and melancholy about her. Deborah, his mother, did not like it when Mary came into their house directly from the church. "It gives me the creeps. It makes me feel the house is alien, that it's not a kosher home," his mother would say. Even his father would turn his head away when Mary came in on Sunday. But it was the incense in her clothes and the mystery she carried about with her that so strongly drew Irving; not because he loved it, but because it was so strange, so unknown, so . . . forbidden. Besides, since Mary had begun to pay so much attention to Nat and spend so much time with him, the younger brother had begun to feel a deep gratitude toward her and a new friendliness.

Irving worshiped his brother, but he could find no way to show his deep suffering and his love to his brother as his father could —he was too inhibited for that. Nor could he give him the attention and service his father gave; he lacked the patience and the gentleness. Sometimes the sight of his helpless brother drove him into the street. He blamed their poverty for the tragedy of his brother; it gnawed at him constantly and made his young mind see life only from the single, concrete point of view of money. Money became for him the only way out of all of the difficulties and tribulations of his family's life. It was this feeling which drew him closer to his mother, who felt as he did.

Although Mary's devotion to Nat aroused his gratitude, he could not understand the motive behind her devotion to Nathan. She would have been able to work and earn some money during the time she spent with Nat. Her family was poverty-stricken, yet she wouldn't take the money that his mother had offered her. And now Nat was used to her. What would he do when she was no longer there? She was wonderful for Nat, with her friendliness and goodness—but she paid for it at her own home.

"She's all right," Irving thought to himself, and he reached over and took her hand as she sat beside him in the dark theater auditorium. The warmth of her hand crept through his fingers. Her skin was smooth and her fingers trembled. A deep satisfaction permeated him. He glanced at her glowing eyes and bent over to whisper into her ear—she could feel the warmth of his breath on her cheek.

"You're all right, Mary. I mean it. You're all right."

The tone of his voice aroused her. She looked at him with open mouth, her wide open eyes smiling. She whispered back:

"I thought Rachel was the one who was all right."

"Rachel, too," Irving answered, again putting his lips close to her ear. She felt the warmth of his nearness, and she sensed the smell of his skin—like the familiar scent of Nathan's skin when she tended to him. She was suddenly frightened. She started up out of the seat.

"It's getting late, Irving. I have to go."

"All right, Mary, let's go. I don't care for the picture anyway."

On the way home he wanted to stop at the ice-cream parlor for a soda. "It'll only take a minute, Mary." And while she ate the tutti-frutti ice cream, eating it slowly and enjoying each spoonful, she looked at Irving shyly. He noticed how she closed her eyes each time she brought a spoonful of the ice cream to her lips, then opened them after each swallow, and licked her lips with the tip of her tongue. Irving felt himself flushing. When they were walking through the dark street, he took her hand and again whispered into her ear:

"You're more than all right, Mary. You're swell. And you're pretty, too."

Mary stopped still and looked at him. It seemed to him that in the darkness her eyes shone even more luminously. There were little points of fire in them, such as he had never seen before. Then he heard her say:

"Do you really mean it?"

"I really mean it."

Without a word Mary turned and ran off toward her house, her feet moving swiftly over the sidewalk.

"Mary! What's the matter?" Irving called after her, but Mary didn't answer.

CHAPTER NINE

SPACE WAS A wilderness of empty blackness. Walls and boundaries had disappeared. Nathan lay in the center of the universe, an unmoving immovable body, immobile in space. Yet, though he was himself helpless to make the slightest move, he was the focus from which the dimensions of space radiated. He was the center of the vast nothingness. In him alone nothingness had its existence. He embraced nothingness to become nothingness, to possess it. Only through nonbeing would the nothingness within him reach its foredoomed destiny.

Why not obliterate this meaningless point in space—just as one might erase a meaningless symbol in a mathematical equation! But in his helplessness even the act of self-annihilation would require another's help. There was no way for him to end his life except by a negative act. Many times he had made up his mind to refuse to take food, but he wasn't able to summon up the determination to reach the yearned-for goal. He lacked even the will to desire death. He would need to find the strength, gather the energy and revive the will which his sickness had dried up and crushed within him.

But now he knew that the will to die was strong within him; now he could carry out his desire; now he had the will he had hitherto lacked. It was Mary's confession that she loved him which had given him the strength to will death.

Now the will was strong enough within him to keep her at a distance from him. He did not let her approach him even though her confession that she loved him had awakened another desire which he tried with all his strength to banish and destroy. He had never dared dream that a feeling such as this would possess him. It was a physical feeling which uplifted and terrified him at the same time, a feeling which gave him new hope and destroyed all hope, which lifted him up to the heights of the most

89

unattainable fantasies—and threw him down deeper into the abyss.

The glimmer of physical desire recalled to him—no, not recalled—realized in him...brought to fulfillment in him...a prophecy which Dr. Chazanowitch had often made. Dr. Chazanowitch had explained to him the entire nature of his illness. He was the family doctor, and he violently disagreed with the eminent specialists at Bellevue Hospital—where Nathan had lain for two months—who believed that the boy's central nervous system was paralyzed, and that he would never be able to move his limbs. Dr. Chazanowitch had interested himself in Nathan's case and had spent days and nights beside the boy's bedside. It was his firm conviction that the paralysis was localized in the limb muscles, but that the shock of the illness had temporarily paralyzed the central nerves and thrown them into a coma. What was needed, according to Dr. Chazanowitch, was for Nathan to be shocked out of his apathy so that he might regain his temporarily lost power of will. The doctor believed there was life in the leg muscles, and if he could succeed in awakening the boy's confidence that his muscles were alive, there would be a simultaneous awakening of his will. He had searched for a way to give the boy the impetus which would stir his dormant will to life. He hoped to find this impetus in the most irresistible of all physical drives—sex. So he tried to awaken in the boy an active sexual drive by telling him over and over that such a feeling was within his grasp.

He tried to persuade him that he was able to move his knees. "If your legs were dead, the flesh would be entirely atrophied. Your legs would be only skin and bone. The fact that the flesh of your legs is firm is evidence that there is life in them, and that you can move them. Try, my boy, with all the strength of your will, to move your legs, even the least little bit under the blanket. Try to feel pain in your effort to move. You've got to help nature. When you can move your limbs, there's no reason why you can't have a normal sex life." Dr. Chazanowitch spoke to him with the utmost earnestness. "Use your imagination! Try to arouse a physical desire. It'll help you gain control of your leg muscles."

He told Moshe Wolf and Deborah to give the boy an alcohol rub every morning. For some time Moshe Wolf massaged the boy regularly, but later the thousand and one details in connection with the store made him neglect it.

Mary had often heard Mr. Davidowsky complain that he had again forgotten to give Nathan an alcohol massage. She heard so much about the importance of the treatment that she began to administer it herself, in haste and secretly, so that no one should know about it. It became so natural a procedure that Nathan couldn't summon enough spirit to protest. He felt like a small child under her ministrations; the sensation of her warm hands on his flesh and the vibrations they awoke in his nerves did him good.

For a time he had tolerated the alcohol massages. He took it as another kindness from her hands—just as he accepted her attentions at mealtimes. Not knowing the real reason for her devotion to him, he had ascribed her attentions to nothing more than the warm human sympathy which so many in the neighborhood showed him. The sensation of the contact of her hands was no more than a secret spur for his fantasies, serving to strengthen the hope that he would one day be able to move his legs. He would actually try to move them, in order to see what weight there was in Dr. Chazanowitch's theory. On a few occasions he actually felt that he had moved them. At such times his hopes would soar to unimaginable heights. But since the day Mary had fallen on his lap and kissed his hands and bathed them in her tears and told him that she loved him, his will was no longer stimulated to move his limbs; the sequel was completely the opposite. He suddenly saw, as with a flash of illumination, all the hopelessness of his situation. All his life long he would be dependent on others for the meanest physical functions. Another's life would have to be chained to his own so that he could live out his miserable cripple's existence.

"What's the difference! Permanent paralysis or a temporary coma! I'll never be able to use my hands anyway," Nathan thought bitterly to himself. "Even a blind man can be master of a world of his own. But what's the good of the world my eyes can see when I'm a cripple in my own world?"

It was the will to death, not to life, that the awakening of his physical feeling had created in him.

When Moshe Wolf brought Nathan's breakfast to him the following morning he found Nathan lying motionless, like a living corpse. His eyes stared at the ceiling, his pale features rigid. He breathed deeply through his open mouth. He neither looked at his father nor answered his greeting. When a spoonful of food was lifted to his mouth he locked his strong teeth tight.

Moshe Wolf's patient pleading was of no avail. Of no avail were his arguments about the sanctity of human life, or of his repeating the objurgations of the sages of Israel. Nor was there any answer to his heartbroken prayer—"Dear Father in Heaven, help me!" Nathan neither looked at his father nor made any answer. He kept his eyes fixed on the ceiling.

"A man's got to have a heart of stone...." Moshe Wolf began to lose his self-control.

"Don't break your head about it! Wait till later. When he gets hungry enough he'll eat," Deborah said harshly.

Moshe Wolf left Nathan to Irving and went out of the room.

But Irving had no more success than his father. His "What's the matter, Nat?" brought no reply. When Mary appeared at the door Nathan's eyes were still fixed on the ceiling. She came close to him and tried to give him some food. A terrified cry broke from his lips: "Don't touch me!" And then even louder: "Leave me alone!"

Later in the day Moshe Wolf put on his coat and went to the corner drugstore to telephone to Dr. Chazanowitch, although he felt ashamed to bother him, especially since the doctor would never accept a fee for his visits.

Dr. Chazanowitch was known all over the East Side as a "dynamic anarchist." He was a typical Jewish radical. For him his anarchism was not a repudiation of social discipline. It was rather an assumption of humanitarian responsibility. Like his father, the pious Hasid in Poland, consumed with his devout belief in his rabbi, so Dr. Chazanowitch had surrendered to the new Bible given to him by his masters, Bakhunin and Kropotkin, with his father's Hasidic zeal and fervor. Atheism had become his religion, a faith which imposed its own obligations and discipline upon him.

His career was a typical one among the East Side intelligentsia. He had come from Russian Poland, a fugitive from the persecutions of the Russian gendarmerie. He had brought with him some education, a disciplined mind, and a wealth of social and economic knowledge. He was well versed in all the various socialist and anarchist theories, and a firm believer in the freedom of the individual from the restraints of all civil and religious laws. He had supported himself by working in a cigar factory, studying at night in evening school. He had been active in radical circles, and had had innumerable quarrels with the official leaders of the radical movement. Abandoning the labor movement, he had begun to study medicine, managing to get through college with the help of a factory girl who later became his common-law wife. Unlike many of the other radicals who entered the profession and sought to advance their personal careers, he dedicated himself solely to working among the poor.

Like hungry crows, the poor and the needy scented at once the prey that was ready to be served up to them, and like birds of prey they crowded around him. Dr. Chazanowitch was soon up to his eyes in an ocean of need and suffering. He set up his office in a midtown section, hoping to find a practice among the theatrical folk. The more practical and business-minded doctors got the richer patients; to Dr. Chazanowitch were left the low-grade, down-at-the-heel actors, the singers without engagements, the unemployed comedians, the out-of-work vaudevillians, the kind who lived at Mrs. Kranz's apartment hotel, the kind of patients to whom it was necessary to give free medical treatment or try to get them a free bed in a hospital ward. His practice among these theater folk, together with the patients who came to him from the mixed Irish and Jewish population of the neighborhood, made him a bare living, hardly any improvement over his years in the cigar factory. The only difference was that he now spent his time in a large, ugly and dark office crowded with dusty journals and newspapers. There he received his patients. His common-law wife, in addition to her duties as cook and housekeeper, had to be a nurse, too; she helped Dr. Chazanowitch in his work, receiving and registering patients, and often helping him with his examinations. The doctor's office became a haven of refuge. The poverty-stricken neighborhood knocked at his door in its need—just as Moshe Wolf had knocked in his time of need.

Dr. Chazanowitch had been interested in Nathan's case from the very beginning and had thrown himself into the task of helping the youth with all his fervor and enthusiasm. He was convinced that there was hope for the boy. At the hospital Na-

93

than hadn't received the necessary attention; the doctors and specialists were too busy with the hundreds of cases that the outbreak of the epidemic had caused among the poverty-stricken population of the neighborhood to give special attention to any individual case. But Dr. Chazanowitch studied Nathan intently and devoted to him all the time he could spare from his ill-paying practice and his radical activities. With the typical application which had enabled him to complete his medical course at college in record time, and with all the restlessness of his nature, he threw himself into the most minute study of the boy's affliction. He sat until late at night reading every medical work he could find on the subject. He read through every new piece of research in the medical journals, and tried every method and technique he thought might work some improvement in the boy's condition.

When Moshe Wolf called him on the telephone and told him what had happened, Dr. Chazanowitch left the patients who crowded his office, took his bag, and went over to 48th Street. Moshe Wolf was waiting for him in the doorway of the store and led him upstairs.

He sat down and looked at the patient. Nathan lay as he had lain all day, motionless and with his gaze fixed on the ceiling, as though he were noticing nothing around him, and answering no word to anything said to him.

Dr. Chazanowitch looked at him intently, his high scholar's forehead furrowed beneath his gray hair, his eyes in the wide sockets peering behind the heavy lids, his thin lips drawn tight, his face absorbing like a sponge every detail of the boy's appearance. He examined Nathan, listening to his heart, noting his expression, all the while muttering "lazybones . . . shirker . . ." Nathan made no answer.

"How long has he been acting this way?" the doctor asked Moshe Wolf.

"Ever since this morning."

"How about last night?"

"Last night he ate and talked and joked as usual. But a few days ago I noticed—at least that's how it seemed to me—that he moved by himself on the bed."

"What!" The doctor jumped up from his chair.

Deborah, who had come into the room, interrupted. "Don't

94

pay any attention to him! He talked himself into it. He wants to believe it, so he talked himself into it."

"But that's the way it seemed to me," Moshe Wolf repeated.

"And you didn't call me? You didn't let me know? Who is that . . . ?" Dr. Chazanowitch interrupted himself, noticing Mary at the door.

"That's a neighbor's daughter. She went to the same school as my boys. She's very good to Nat; she brings him books from the library and reads to him and helps to take care of him."

"How long has she been doing it?"

"For some time already."

The doctor addressed Mary but kept his eyes fixed on Nat, noting every change of expression on the boy's face.

"Are you ever with him alone?" he asked her.

"Yes," she answered.

"How does he act?"

"Like himself, like Nat."

The doctor turned to Moshe Wolf and Deborah. "Both of you go out," he said. And to Mary: "You stay here."

When they had left the room, Dr. Chazanowitch turned to Mary.

"Now tell me," he said, "what happens when you're alone together?"

There was a change in Nathan's expression. His lips opened as though he were going to speak . . . then they closed again.

"I read to him and I give him his food, and we talk."

"What do you usually talk about?" the doctor asked.

"Oh, about different things."

Dr. Chazanowitch didn't notice the color that rose in the girl's face, but he could see the mounting expression on Nathan's pale features.

"Tell me," he said to Mary. "Do you give him his alcohol rubs?"

Before Mary could answer, a frantic, broken cry came from Nathan.

"Stop! Stop! Leave me alone!" His eyes blazed.

"Good!" Dr. Chazanowitch said to Mary. "Now you can go!"

He turned to Nathan. "You little mule, you!" he said. "If you can summon enough will power to die, you can also find enough will power to live." He rubbed his hands in satisfaction.

95

"I don't want to live; I want to die!" Nathan sobbed.

"Get hold of yourself, you good-for-nothing. That'll be enough for today. I'll come to see you again."

Outside the room, Moshe Wolf was waiting for him anxiously. "Well, Doctor?"

"What did they say, those wise men of yours? 'No one can withstand human desire. . . .' Sometimes they weren't so stupid!"

Later Dr. Chazanowitch sat beside Nathan and talked to him.

"Do you know, you mule, what the secret of life is? The secret is that nature has planted into every living creature the subconscious feeling that he is the center of all life; that everything was created for him. That's what we call the will to existence, the most important factor in our beings. The seed of the will to existence is woven into our cells. Did you ever see the determination with which birds swoop down to the peasant's arduously plowed soil to dig with their beaks among the seeds he has sown? So far as the bird is concerned, it was for him that the seeds were placed there. It's the same all through life. To the strong, the weak is his natural prey. That's the will to existence. And that's the strength you have to win back. The world was made for you. You have a right to it."

"I'm not an animal," Nathan answered.

"So far as biological laws are concerned, man is an animal like all animals. We're governed by the same laws. There are no other laws no matter what the clericals try to talk into us about the spiritual factors of existence. We scientists know nothing of them and don't depend on them. We recognize only the laws of nature. If you want to live you've got to abide by those laws— like any animal. You have a right to your share of existence because it's the center of all existence for you. You have a right to enjoy everything you're entitled to. Do you understand what I'm telling you, you stupid young idiot?"

"You mean I have the right to live the normal life of a cripple!" Nathan said ironically.

"In one sense there's no such thing as a normal person. We're all cripples in one way or another. Our nerves and organs carry out their functions, but even those functions are limited. Who can say that only people with limbs have a right to exist, and that those without limbs are denied the right?"

96

"What's my existence worth?" asked Nathan. "It only means enslaving someone else."

"Listen here, lazybones. Apart from your limbs—and I'm by no means sure that their nerves are entirely dead—you're a normal, healthy male. Your body is sound; your mind functions. That your nerve centers are sound I have no doubt at all—and that's what's most important for a normal, functioning life. Of course, your legs have to function for you to live a normal life, but I'm sure that regular massage will give them the power to move again. I don't say you'll be a track sprinter, but you'll be able to get around, even in a limited way. We're all limited in our activities in one way or another. And so far as your arms are concerned, I'm convinced that there's life in them. Maybe, in time... just leave it to science. If you can't use your own limb muscles, there are mechanical contrivances. There are plenty of people in the world living with artificial aids. You'll not be the only one. The principal thing is that your physical functioning has been retarded; do you understand me? You can function physically. You can even have children!"

Nathan laughed.

"I don't see why not. I've just told you, your vitality is sound —although I don't know why anyone should want to spawn more brats into this kind of world. You can be active, if not in one field, then in another. I once saw an essay you wrote—your father showed it to me. It had to do, I think, with the causes of economic crises and unemployment. It had a good economic basis—a little too Marxist for my taste; you've all been snared in Karl Marx's beard—but the essay was alive and fresh. It was written with conviction. You said something about the exploitation of labor's energies to produce more goods than could be consumed, and that that was what caused hunger and poverty among millions of workers at a time when the country was overflowing with abundance. I even remember one of your phrases. 'The living standard of the worker must advance at the same progress and tempo as the process of production.' You have a head and you have a heart, my fine young man, and eyes to see and mouth to speak. What else does a man need to function? Here you are in the pit of poverty! Look at the way people live around you! The tenement houses and the fire traps they live in; and the filth and neglect that allows children's diseases to flourish in the heart of the richest city in the world! The landlords and the rent collectors and the sweatshops—the whole sacrosanct capitalist system busy filling the jaws of the Moloch of disease with living bodies—and the clericals hand in hand with whoever holds the purse strings. Look around you and see what's going on. If you can't write yourself, you can dictate. Maybe you want to join the radical movement. You've got a mouth to talk with. We can bring you to meetings. Somebody else will be your hands and feet for a while; in the meantime, you can make use of the gifts nature has given you. Join the movement. We need young intellects to educate the masses and open their eyes. You could write for our magazines. There are plenty of ways you could be useful, and you, you idiot, talk about death. Oh, no, my boy! Not now! Not when things are coming out the way I said they would—not the way those professors in the hospital decided they would. They were ready to throw you in the wastepaper basket, like a piece of scrap."

Moshe Wolf had been standing behind the door all the while, trembling and muttering prayers. He could no longer restrain himself. Carefully, he opened the door and asked:

"Well, Doctor? How is it?"

"Everything'll be all right, Moshe Wolf; all right. Nature knows what to do!" The doctor rubbed his hands with satisfaction; his eyes sparkled with pleasure as he looked at Nathan.

"Thank You and praise You, dear God," Moshe Wolf said piously.

"What's God got to do with it?"

"Who am I to enter into a disputation with you, dear Doctor," said Moshe Wolf humbly. "You're a doctor. But if God wills it, Nature can work; if God wills otherwise, Nature won't work. ... The principal thing is: will my boy eat now?"

"He will eat! He will eat! Bring him a glass of milk."

But the doctor was mistaken; Nat refused to take it. Dr. Chazanowitch indicated with a glance that Moshe Wolf was not to press the boy. As though he wanted to change the subject, he suddenly turned to Moshe Wolf with one of his eternal attacks on the clericals.

"But what will the end be? He hasn't eaten all day! He'll not survive it!" pleaded Moshe Wolf.

"Don't worry. One day's fast won't hurt him. Just imagine

it's a fast day. Just imagine it's Yom Kippur for him. You come with me, Moshe Wolf. Leave him alone. He's got something to think about. Don't disturb him." He led Moshe Wolf out of Nathan's room.

All day Nathan remained as he was. He touched no food, but he no longer had his gaze fixed on the ceiling. His eyes had come alive, as had his face. He was buried in thought, completely engrossed in his own searchings. He answered none of his father's questions, but it was easy to tell that he heard them and reacted to them.

Moshe Wolf stayed up all night to watch by his son's bed. He could see how restless he was, tossing his head from side to side and sighing deeply. An immense pity welled up in Moshe Wolf's heart. He sat by the boy's bedside and spoke to him in the tone he had used when Nathan was a small child.

"My dear child... is there anything you want?"

Nathan didn't answer.

"Does something hurt you?"

There was no answer.

"Tell me, I beg of you. Have pity on me! Can you hear what I say to you?"

Nathan made no sound.

"Have pity on me! Give me a sign to let me know you hear me."

Nathan nodded his head.

The affirmative sign gave new life to Moshe Wolf. He bent over the boy and said in a trembling voice:

"My dear son, I'm not a doctor and I'm not an educated man. I don't know what the doctor told you. I only know what our wise men have said and what they taught, and what our ancient faith tells us. Our faith tells us to guard our souls, to treasure the life within us. Everybody in the world, no matter what his circumstances, is God's vessel, God's messenger, sent on the earth to make something of himself. Every life is holy. Nobody can ever tell how important his life is for all mankind, and not only for mankind but for God's purpose. Man is God's noblest creation. Our holy books say that man is so great that it is only man who can call down the divine mercy from Heaven. That is the real meaning of prayer, because a man prays not for himself

99

but for the whole of creation, so that God's pity might descend from Heaven. Nathan, my son, don't throw away your life. You don't know God's purpose for you. Even without hands and without feet, God has provided a destiny for you and it is your sacred obligation to carry out the will of God. Nathan, my son..." Moshe Wolf put his face on his hands and wept.

He heard Nathan's voice, gentle and clear: "Papa!"

"Yes, my son."

"'Give me a glass of water."

"Yes! Yes! Yes!" Moshe Wolf hurried with quick steps to the kitchen, his lips murmuring, "I thank You, dear Father in Heaven! Thank You for hearing my prayer! Thank You, dear Father! Thank you!"

As he lifted the glass to the boy's lips, Nathan said: "Go to sleep, Pa. I'll go to sleep too."

"Thank You, dear Father in Heaven," Moshe Wolf repeated over and over.

When Dr. Chazanowitch arrived in the morning, he found a new Nathan. The boy smiled at him from the wheel chair in front of the store.

"Hello, Doctor!"

"What did I tell you, Moshe Wolf! Leave it to nature. And you, you young idiot, get ready! In an hour from now the ambulance is coming for you. I've arranged everything with Dr. Foster."

Moshe Wolf began to stammer in alarm.

"Nathan's going back to the hospital for a new examination. Dr. Foster's interested in his case. We're going to make it a test case."

"But, Doctor, what does it mean! Deborah, Deborah, come here! Hear what the doctor's saying!"

Deborah came to the front of the store.

"Deborah," Moshe Wolf said, "there's a great Father in Heaven...."

"There's a great nature in the world...." Dr. Chazanowitch corrected him, "but she needs a little help now and then. You'll see, Moshe Wolf, we'll bring your son home walking on his own feet."

"What are you saying? What are you saying? Dear Father in Heaven...."

CHAPTER TEN

IT WAS IN any case high time to look around and make provision for the future. Rachel was getting ready to take a civil service examination so as to be able, with Mike Maloney's help, to get a job in one of the city bureaus. Mary was to have done the same. A Catholic charity organization was to have helped by paying the school fees and helping out with a little money for winter clothing. But nothing came of it. Poverty ruled the McCarthy household. Every penny was needed. The father's meager wages dwindled even more on the way home; anyway, they were nowhere near enough to provide for the six mouths that had to be fed in the dark tenement flat on 48th Street. But for Grandma McCarthy, the family would never have survived.

Grandma McCarthy waged a constant fight against the wolf of hunger. No one knew how she managed. She was a silent woman; she hardly ever said a word. In all of the shoutings and hysteria and quarrels that raged in the house she rarely broke her silence. She went about her work calmly. She was never seen walking on the street or sitting at the fire escape. Winter and summer she spent in the kitchen. She seemed to be a part of the room. She was always cooking, cleaning, scrubbing, polishing, washing dishes or clothes. Not for a moment did she sit idle.

No matter how empty the larder, Grandma McCarthy was somehow or other always able to provide a meal. No one knew how she did it. The secret was that she knew that the poor must never dare lick the pot clean at a single meal; she would steal bits of the weekday dinners and the Sunday repasts, thieving them away from the hungry mouths of the family to save for a rainy day. She had her own secret hiding places where she concealed a piece of corned beef, a cut of sausage, or a few strands of spaghetti. When it seemed there wasn't another bit of food in the house, and everybody began to tremble because it looked as though there would be no food for Patrick McCarthy when he came home from work, somehow or other the table was all set and ready for him, with sparkling plates and freshly polished knives and forks.

Grandma McCarthy, in a clean white blouse, would welcome her son with a broad smile on her heavy, flushed face. His mother's smile, like music, was a soothing influence on McCarthy. No matter how ugly his mood, no matter how ready he was to make everyone but himself responsible for the poverty and misery of the household, so that he could afterward vent his anger by emptying the rent money out of the china bowl where it was hoarded, and go to Kelly's saloon—when he was greeted by his mother's broad smile, he would be calmed.

"We've something special for you tonight, McCarthy," she would say to him—she always called him by his last name, as she had been accustomed to call her husband—"something you like. I suppose you had a hard day at the office."

It was only late in the evening when she had washed and put away the dishes and pots and pans, and cleaned the kitchen so that everything sparkled, that she permitted herself to sit on the rocking chair. Her son had bought it for her long before, so that she might ease her tired, swollen feet. She would rock back and forth for a half an hour or so before going to bed. Sometimes—mostly on the fast days—she would take from the cupboard in which she concealed her bits of provisions a book of stories of the Holy Martyrs she had brought with her from the old country. This she would read, but mostly she would sit idle, lost in thoughts which no one could guess—maybe about her youth, so far in the past, in Ireland, or about the days soon to come when she would be leaving this world of sorrow for a better world. Or maybe she thought of nothing at all.

The half hour's rest on the rocking chair was a great comfort for her. When everybody had gone to bed, Grandmother McCarthy would draw back the curtain behind which her folding bed stood and wheel it over to the corner below the picture of the Madonna and Child. She would set the bed up, straighten the bedclothes, then kneel painfully and say her prayers—first for Ireland, then for her family, and last for herself, praying that she might have an easy death.

But despite the valiant efforts of the old woman, the wolf came closer and closer to their door. Now the scratching of his claws could be heard.

Her daughter-in-law was losing her energy rapidly. Ever since she had had a hemorrhage—a closely guarded secret from McCarthy—she had stopped bringing home the sewing she used to get from a contractor's shop. Now the few dollars her sewing earned were missing. The only thing left was for Mary to put an end to her vacation and take her mother's place as a breadwinner for the family.

The shop where Mary found work was in a long, large cellar in the neighborhood of 34th Street and Second Avenue. The cellar opened on a large yard full of grain stores and warehouses for merchandise, with a cheap restaurant for the truckmen who worked in the vicinity. The cellar, formerly used as a laundry, was under the restaurant, and the stench of decayed food and greasy cooking permeated the cellar workroom. There was no ventilation; only a single window, always closed, which faced a blank wall, grimy with cobwebs. There was no daylight, except for the light that came in through the open door to the cellar together with the waves of heat of the summer and the cold blasts of the winter. The cellar was illuminated by electric bulbs which hung naked from the low ceiling, without covering of any kind. In the summer, when the heat scorched the walls of the warehouses, the fetid smell of meat, cheese, fish, and other foods kept in them would be borne into the workroom. Piles of garbage were strewn about the yard. Stray cats and bedraggled beggars dug into the garbage cans outside the restaurant kitchen and the warehouses.

Wagons laden with merchandise rattled in and out of the yard all day. The heavy creaking of truck wheels, the noise and shouts of the truckmen and porters poured in through the workroom door. Overhead, through the ceiling, came the noise of footsteps and the clatter of dishes from the restaurant above.

In this cellar Mendel Greenspan, the owner of the workroom, had placed a row of sewing machines purchased on time payments. The machines were so constructed that they could be operated by foot pedals or by electric power. For the present, until Greenspan had enough money to equip a real shop and get enough orders, they were operated by foot pedals.

Before the twelve machines, each of them set below a naked

103

electric bulb hanging from the low ceiling, sat twelve girls—Irish, Jewish, Italian—of whom Mary was now one. In addition to the machines there were long tables at which sat seven or eight finishers, hand workers. These were all middle-aged Jews, with grizzled beards and orthodox ear curls. Two sad-faced youths stood at ironing boards, in the midst of clouds of vapor raised by the hot irons on damp cloth.

Greenspan was a man in his thirties, with a carefully trimmed beard, artfully cropped so as to avoid the impression that he was one of the modern "pagan" Jews addicted to the use of the razor; in the trim of his sidelocks there was even the slight suggestion of the ear curls. He wore a skullcap. He stood at a long table and from paper patterns cut piles of cheap printed fabrics to be made into dresses. His meek-eyed wife, about the same age as himself and wearing a smock, worked on a bundle of garments at the head of the row of sewing machines and kept an eye on the girls to see that they labored with proper diligence.

The Greenspans, with their two children and Mrs. Greenspan's mother, lived in the two rooms that shut off the front end of the factory, thus blocking off the only windows leading onto the street below the restaurant.

Greenspan and his wife hardly slept or ate. He worked at the bench himself, and even found jobs to do for his old mother-in-law, and his two children, for all their tender years. He was acquainted with some pious Jews who frequented the same synagogue on the East Side. He talked it into them that at his shop they would be able to gather for the afternoon prayers without interruption—and on his time, too; that they would be able to wear their cherished skullcaps, and even be able to chant from the sacred Psalms as they worked—something they certainly wouldn't be able to do in a union shop. In this way, he exploited their piety by working them long hours and paying them starvation wages. He hired young, inexperienced girls forced by the desperate poverty in their homes to help contribute to the family larder. He convinced the girls that the union shops wouldn't take them in, and that, to get into the union, they'd have to pay enormous initiation fees.

He worked side by side with them, his wife, too, at one of the machines, and speeded up their work by putting before them the example of his own industry. He got up at dawn to prepare the work for the hands, and he sat at the bench until late at night—

104

he, his wife, and often his mother-in-law—to finish the work the hands hadn't completed during the long day. He begrudged himself a single minute's rest, hastily gulping the food his mother-in-law would set beside him at the cutting table. It was as though he were saying to his employees: "How can you have the heart to take time off to eat your lunch in peace when I, the boss, work until I'm ready to drop!"

When Mary came to the factory early on Monday morning, Greenspan welcomed her with a broad smile.

"You're a good girl," he said, "to help out your family. I know your mother; she worked for us. Homework. Come, sit down here. They'll show you how it goes."

He had his own system for breaking in green hands. He sat Mary between two experienced operators, old employees in the shop, who knew how to make the foot pedals fly. One of them sewed one edge of a dress and handed it over to Mary to complete the other side. The operations had to dovetail so that the dress could be handed over to the finishers to complete.

"You'll catch on! You'll learn! In the beginning it's a little bit hard. You'll get used to it," Greenspan said to the embarrassed girl who in her inexperience was not able to drive the pedal as fast as the other two.

Mary was swimming in perspiration; her cheeks flushed with embarrassment, and although she had been used to operating a sewing machine at home at a fair speed, now her limbs seemed to be made of lead. She began to make clumsy blunders; the thread came out of the needle time after time. But Greenspan was patient.

"Don't worry! You'll do it! You'll be all right!"

And she did do it. She managed to catch up with the fast tempo and keep abreast of the others.

"You see!" Greenspan said. "I told you you could do it! You're a smart girl."

Greenspan left her side and went back to the cutting table.

But no sooner had Greenspan left them than the two girls at either side of Mary began to slow down. Now it was Mary who was finished with her part of the garment first. She caught a wink from the bright black eyes of the girl who sat at her right, and heard the quiet whisper: "Take it easy!"

Mary caught on and answered with a smile from her own dark eyes.

Now she found the tempo of the machine much easier and as natural as her handling of it at home.

Her feet were getting tired and her hands weary. The heavy footsteps and clatter from the restaurant above the shop hammered into her head. Her throat was suffocating from the smell of the fumes of frying lard which came down from the restaurant kitchen. But she stuck to the work. Gradually she got used to the constant thump of footsteps and the kitchen smells. Then at last it was time for lunch.

The old Jews in the shop had their lunch indoors. The girls went out into the courtyard, where some of them found seats on the tailboard of a truck, and opened up the packages of sandwiches they had brought along with them.

For Mary's first day at the factory, Grandma McCarthy had prepared a corned beef sandwich, of meat she had managed to save from the Sunday meal, with a bit of lettuce and spread with mayonnaise, the way Mary liked it. She had also given her a nickel for a cup of coffee, but Mary preferred to invest it in some ice cream.

On the way out of the shop, the girl who had advised Mary to take it easy came over.

"This is your first day here, isn't it?" she said. "Where do you come from?"

"I live on 48th Street. We know the boss. He used to give my mother work to take home."

"You know that this isn't a union shop."

"I couldn't help myself. This is the first place I ever worked. My family needs my wages."

"My parents, too. My father's in the hospital for two months already. They say that he needs an operation. Something to do with his stomach. I looked for work in a union shop, but I couldn't find a job. Besides, you have to work on Saturday in a union shop, and my parents are orthodox; they wouldn't let me work on Saturday. They said it's better to work even for less wages as long as you don't have to work on the Sabbath. That's why I'm working here. I had no choice. It's only for a while, anyway. I know the boss is taking advantage of us. He uses green hands— old orthodox Jews and inexperienced girls. We ought to get the union to organize the place. What's your name?"

Mary told her.

106

"My name is Sarah Lifschitz. Look, Mary, we ought to stick together. I already talked to the other girls. Some are willing, but the others are afraid. Will you stick with us?"

"Sure."

"Fine, Mary! Gee, I'd like to have you for a friend."

"Why not?" Mary said. Their eyes met in a warm glance. They broke into spontaneous laughter.

Sarah's friendliness lightened Mary's first day. Though her legs ached and her back was weary, the moment she left the shop at the end of the day and took a deep breath of the fresh air, all her youthful elasticity was restored.

At home the table was set. From the pots on the kitchen stove came a bubbling and a seething and a fragrant steam of vapor which half hid Grandma McCarthy, a promise that something specially good was being prepared.

Mary's mother greeted her with the half apologetic, pitying smile she had adopted ever since the red blotches had appeared in her sunken cheeks. The cords in her thin neck stood out like swollen blue veins.

"How was it in the shop?" she asked.

"All right," Mary answered with a self-conscious smile.

Grandma McCarthy, although she was occupied in the kitchen like a priestess before an altar, peered out of the cloud of steam, and without saying a word took Mary by the hand and led her to the sink, handed her a clean towel, and indicated with a gesture that she was to wash her hands and face. Then she returned to the stove. When she was back over the pots, her voice was heard: "The first thing a person ought to do after a day of work is to wash!"

The rest of the McCarthy children came up from the street: Mary's twelve-year-old brother, Jimmy, with a sack full of metal scrap he had collected along the East River to sell to Zelig the junk dealer; and Sylvia, the youngest, who had helped Jimmy collect his booty. Both of them gathered about Mary, staring at her as though she had just come from a long journey.

"How was it?" they asked eagerly.

"All right," Mary said again.

"You ought to help me collect junk, instead," Jimmy remarked. "You'd make more money than you can in the factory."

Grandma McCarthy again appeared out of the clouds of steam,

grabbed Jimmy and Sylvia by the arms, and—just as she had done before with Mary, and without saying a word—marched them to the sink, and returned to her pots.

Everything was now ready. Everything was fine and satisfactory. Now there was only one mountain to cross, but it was a prospect which heavily oppressed the timorous spirit of Mrs. McCarthy, weighed heavily on Grandma McCarthy, and even bothered Mary. How to tell the father and head of the family? How would he take the news that Mary was working in a factory?

The door was opened violently, an indication that Patrick McCarthy was in a bad mood.

A tense silence fell on the room.

Patrick McCarthy was a tall and unnaturally thin man. His eyes were blue, watery, and sad. His hair was brown and he wore a narrow mustache, waxed at the ends. He had a high forehead, long cheekbones, and a long, thin, regular nose. His lower jaw was long, his neck was long and thin. So were his hands. Everything about him was long, thin, and mournful. Only his mouth was small, but his thin lips gave the impression of overwhelming sadness.

He was dressed in a well-worn, tight-fitting checked suit. It looked like a second skin, an outer covering, that had grown on to his body like a protective hide. It seemed something of a miracle when he took off his coat, revealing the blue shirt he wore. He washed his hands and combed his hair, without a word. Everyone was quiet. Jimmy was already seated at the table; he kept winking at Mary and Sylvia.

All the time that McCarthy stood at the sink, his wife stood near him, handing him towel and comb. Her lips were silent, but her eyes were eloquent. She had the same eyes as Mary, with the same color and the same sparkle. All the pathos of her life was lodged in her eyes; although they smiled, there was sadness in them. With a half smiling, half tearful look and closed lips, she seemed to be pleading with her husband that he control his temper and let the dinner pass in peace. But his wife's gaze simply served to exacerbate McCarthy's frayed nerves. He knew, or rather suspected, that Mary had gone to work in a shop. He preferred not to know it, and the family acted out the farce of concealing from him the unconcealable fact that Mary was now a factory hand. Although he had seen all the preparations and well

108

knew what they were for, he didn't want to know about it officially; the move hadn't been given his parental approval.

"What are you staring at me for?" he growled as he twisted the ends of his mustache.

"I wasn't staring," Mrs. McCarthy said with an apologetic smile.

"What the man needs is some hot food. Come on, McCarthy, here it is!" Grandma McCarthy brought the steaming bowl of food to the table and set it at her son's place.

McCarthy sat down quietly, without a word. His lips were closed tight. He began to fill the plates and to hand them around the table.

Reciting the customary grace helped somewhat to relieve the tension which, like an electric current, radiated from McCarthy's charged mood. The children ate lustily, none of them but Mary noticing McCarthy's angry glances at his wife during the entire meal.

Katherine McCarthy kept her gaze fixed on her husband. She knew those yellow specks that showed in his eyeballs. There was a yellow tinge all over his eyes now. She knew what they were due to—the outpouring of bile that followed each spell of anger, and which came especially when he had taken a drink too much. She could sense all the bitterness that had gathered in him because he could not afford to keep Mary in high school. He gave no expression to his bitterness; it boiled inside him. She pitied him for his sufferings, and her eyes sent him rays of pleading, sympathy, and trust.

The fixed gaze of his wife unnerved him, and again he said to her angrily: "What are you staring at me for?"

"I'm not staring at you. I'm looking at your shirt collar. It's too big for you again. You're losing weight, Patrick."

"The man's eating himself up all the time," Grandma McCarthy said.

McCarthy pushed his plate away. He didn't look at his mother; he was afraid of her.

"I know all about it. You've made Mary stop school and sent her to work in a factory for the Jews. You didn't waste a minute. You enslaved her to the Jews the minute you could."

"Mother didn't send me there. She didn't even want me to go

109

there. I went there myself and I found work," Mary interrupted boldly.

"I know you! You enjoy being a servant for Jews!"

"Mary'll go to evening school and learn to be a stenographer, the way lots of others girls do," Mrs. McCarthy said.

"She go to evening school! She'll end up scrubbing floors for Jews. That's what you want to turn her into!"

"It isn't me who's doing it!"

"Yes, it's you. Why did you send her to a Jew's factory without my knowledge?"

Mrs. McCarthy was quiet. She only looked at her husband with her pleading eyes, her lips quivering.

Mary looked at her mother and her eyes filled with tears.

"Mother!"

Grandma McCarthy was unable to restrain herself any longer. She broke her customary silence.

"Listen to me, McCarthy. Is there anything else you've got to suggest? Someone's got to help pay the rent. Katherine can't always go on doing all this sewing at home. Who're you yelling at! Who're you blaming! You ought to be yelling at yourself! What have you got against her?"

McCarthy was quiet. He closed his mouth tight, breathed heavily through his nose, and glared. His eyes were like points of flame. He didn't dare to look at his mother with those furious eyes of his; it was his wife who would have to take the brunt of his helpless rage and bitterness. She felt his angry eyes on her. She didn't say a word, but there was heartbreaking appeal in her eyes, a plea not for herself but for his sufferings.

McCarthy felt an urge to grab the plates from the table and smash them to the floor. He fought against the impulse.

Mary could no longer stand to see her mother's suffering. She broke into an uncontrollable fit of sobbing. The other children followed her example. It seemed to calm McCarthy's rage. He got up from the chair and walked over to the closet where the rent money was hidden, and with the same deliberate calm with which he had portioned out the family's food at the table, he poked his fingers into the bowl, took out some coins and looked at them, as though considering how much to take. The others watched the performance with beating hearts and bated breath.

When McCarthy put most of the money back into the cup, keeping only a couple of coins, they breathed easier.

Still without saying a word, McCarthy put on his coat and went to the door.

"So that's the suggestion you've got to make, is it, McCarthy?" his mother called after him.

McCarthy didn't answer.

Katherine called after him with her pleading voice: "Please, Patrick! Don't drink too much. You know it's bad for your liver."

Quarrel or no quarrel, whether Patrick McCarthy liked it or not, when the end of the week came, Mary had managed to earn all of five dollars at the shop, not counting some small change. She got her pay on Saturday afternoon. It was only the pious Jews who didn't work on the Jewish Sabbath—they worked on Sunday instead. The girls, however, worked on Saturdays. After all, how could a factory be allowed to stand idle for two days a week, Saturday and Sunday? The Christian girls, too, had to have a chance for a day of rest! Greenspan reconciled his conscience by letting only the Christian girls work on Saturday, like every other day. Officially it was not he, but the Christian girls who were desecrating the Jewish Sabbath—although there were some Jewish girls among them. The pay was handed out by one of the trusted girls, according to the pay slips which had been prepared on the Friday.

Mary had never before had a sum of money like the five dollars and change she had earned from her own labor. She had never even seen such a sum of money.

Two yearnings possessed her; they had always seemed unattainable—she had only dared to dream of them. The first longing was to buy for the children—and even for herself—a cake filled with raisins which she and Jimmy and her sister had often seen and wondered at in the show windows of the Italian pastry shop on First Avenue. True enough, Grandma McCarthy—although only on special occasions—baked a raisin cake, but it wasn't the same as the cake at the Italian bakery, of which they had never tasted. Besides, Grandma McCarthy's cake was only for Sundays or holidays; there'd only be a little for each child at the table. Mary had dreamed of some day having enough money to buy one of those Italian cakes and dividing it among the children, so that they could eat and eat. . . .

The other thing she wanted was to be able to pay for the pair of elastic stockings for Grandma McCarthy which she and Jimmy had ordered the year before in the small orthopedic store which a German craftsman operated on Second Avenue. Grandma McCarthy used to wrap bandages around her swollen legs. Every night, before she went to sleep, she would be busy cleaning, darning, and repairing the tears in the bandages. She had two sets which she had made out of old shirts, and she was always changing them. Hours of each day went into keeping the bandages in order. Although she never complained, the children knew that she had trouble with her legs. Mary and Jimmy and little Sylvia had decided to surprise Grandma and get her a pair of elastic stockings. They had ordered them from the German—they cost two and a half dollars—hoping to pay for them out of the money Jimmy and Sylvia got from Zelig the junk dealer for the metal scrap they collected in the yards. But they never seemed to be able to accumulate the last dollar that remained to be paid, and the stockings kept on gathering dust among the rupture belts, garters, and other articles in the orthopedic store. Now Mary could pay for them and give them to Jimmy and Sylvia to present to Grandma.

She went to Second Avenue to satisfy the two deep longings of her heart.

On the cake she spent all of fifteen cents. It wasn't as big as her fancy had imagined it, but still it was close to the raisin cake of her dreams. For ten cents she bought a bag of rock candy for her mother, a delicacy renowned all over the neighborhood as a tried and tested remedy for asthma and consumption.

On the way from the bakery to the orthopedic store, she passed a flower stand which an Italian peddler had set up on the sidewalk among the pushcarts. She wanted to buy a bouquet of roses, but she was afraid of spending so much out of her first pay. Grandma's stockings had to be paid for, whatever else happened! No, she wouldn't spend another penny until the stockings were settled for.

Suddenly the thought of Nathan in the hospital came to her mind. She hadn't seen him since he had been taken there. His parents had told her that no visitors would be allowed until the

Sunday—tomorrow. She knew that his parents would be going to see him then. She hoped to go with them, but if she couldn't go, she would send some flowers to him through Irving; how could she let the first visiting day at the hospital go by for Nat with no reminder of her! For ten cents she bought a small sprig of tiny pale buds which were just beginning to fade and wither. She asked the Italian to wrap them well in paper. She would keep them in water overnight so that they would be fresh in the morning.

Then she went to the orthopedic store and with a beating heart paid the German the whole dollar that was still due on the stockings.

Now she had all her packages and was ready to go home to find the children before she got into the house and to divide the cake among them and give them Grandma's stockings. If only everything went along all right! If only her father would be in a decent mood.

She knew that her father planned to take the family to Central Park the next day, Sunday. There was to be a gathering of one of his Irish societies. On such occasions, her father got hold of himself and behaved soberly and with dignity. She knew, too, that her grandmother was preparing a special meal for Sunday dinner. If only everything went well at home tonight! About Sunday, she was fairly sure.

Her worried thoughts passed through her mind as she came near the church. Mary would often go into the church on weekdays, too, when she felt a special need for prayer. She did not pray at the great altar, but knelt in one of the dark niches under the high vault where there was a small chapel and a large carved wooden crucifix which the Italian congregants of the neighborhood had had made by an Italian craftsman and had presented to the church. The chapel was almost always deserted; most of the worshipers were kneeling at the large altar which held the Sacred Host, or at the picture of the Madonna before which the congregants lighted their candles.

In the nave in which the wooden crucifix stood, a pair of candles burned in an iron stand; there were only a few worshipers. Mary loved to pray in front of the wooden crucifix in the dim nave. No matter how often she had been told at Sunday school that she

113

must pray to one of the Saints or to the Holy Mary, who would intercede for her, Mary felt the need to bring her prayers to the feet of Jesus Himself.

On this Saturday she did not pray. She only knelt quietly, her lips still. The packages—grandma's stockings, the rock candy, the cake, and the sprig of flowers—lay beside her on the floor. Her eyes were fixed on the carved figure suspended on the cross. No word of prayer passed her lips. Her arms hung limply beside her as she looked at the figure of the crucified Jesus. She was thinking her own thoughts. She was thinking of her mother. She could see the pity and love in her mother's eyes as she looked at Patrick McCarthy when he was in one of his rages. She could hear her pleading with him to be calm. She thought of her father, too. She saw the yellow flecks in his eyeballs, his long thin throat which grew thinner day by day. She could feel all his bitterness and the pain of his life. She knew that her father suffered a thousand times more than anyone else in the family for the misery he brought to them all. She thought of him with a newly awakened love; in her fantasy she kissed his hands, comforted him, calmed him. "You'll see, Papa, everything will come out all right. I'll go to evening school; I'll finish the course in record time. I'll be working in an office, Papa! But, Papa, the shop isn't so bad! Honest, Papa, it isn't so bad! The work isn't hard, and look, Papa, I'm earning five dollars a week already! It'll be such a help for us all."

So went Mary's thoughts as she gazed at the crucified figure. "My father isn't a bad man. It's all on account of his love for us. If he could only understand that my wages will help us to live better and let mother do the things that the doctor told her—not to work but to get plenty of fresh air and drink lots of milk—he would feel more secure. And when he isn't excited, he's so good . . . so good! He's such a loving father when he's calm. . . . ."

She thought of her grandmother. "Dear sweet Grandma . . . now she can have her elastic stockings. . . . Thank you, dear Lord. . . . She'll feel so good, like a newborn person. Now she'll be able to stand without her legs killing her. . . ."

She thought of Jimmy and Sylvia. Then the thought of them vanished from her mind—and she could see only the helpless Nat and his lamed and crippled limbs. She saw him in her thoughts as she had seen him so often in reality in the days when she tended and cared for him. There he lay like one enchained, like a helpless baby, a body with twisted and thin limbs, like a child's, and thin, helpless hands lying lifeless on his lap. It was only his eyes that were alive, kind eyes that saw and heard and spoke. Nat spoke with his eyes when he smiled. His smile was so full of pathos and his eyes were so full of gratitude when even the tiniest thing was done for him. . . .

She thought of Nat's crippled body, and she looked at the feet of the crucified Jesus. Christ's feet, too, rested one on the other, nailed together into the wood of the Cross.

It seemed to Mary that what she was seeing was not lifeless wood. The figure which hung on the Cross was alive! It was the living Jesus, the Jesus of flesh and blood, hung there on the cross. Those were Christ's living hands and feet which the nails pierced; the crown of thorns pricked and pierced the skin and flesh of Christ's living head. And the wound in His side was a living, running wound. Jesus was not a figure carved in wood! Jesus lived on the cross! He hung on the crucifix, He suffered, He felt the pain and anguish of the rusty nails that pierced His hands and feet, the pricking of the crown of thorns, the gnawing of the open wound in His side. Yet He smiled at her with a smile of grace and pity and love. And now she felt that Nat's suffering was Christ's suffering; that the body of Jesus bore the sufferings of everyone; Jesus suffered her mother's sickness, her father's misery, her grandmother's swollen legs. . . . Christ's body hanging crucified before her was a sponge which had sucked into itself all the sufferings of man. It was not a strange god carved in wood that was crucified here before her. It was her intimate and personal life, everything that was dear and close to her, everything that filled her mind . . . Nat's lameness . . . her mother's sickness, her father's bitterness. . . .

She bent her body toward the floor, her arms folded over her breast, and it seemed to her that she was taking into her arms all those near to her who suffered, those she knew and those she did not know. Her lips murmured: "Oh, dear Jesus, oh, dear Jesus." She knelt with her mouth and eyes open, bowing to the naked stone floor on which she had been kneeling for so long before the figure of the crucified Christ, and she whispered to herself: "Oh, dear Jesus, please let my father be good!"

The children were waiting for her on the street near the door to the house. They knew that Mary was bringing home her first wages, and they knew there would be something for themselves. When she gave them the cake, they decided not to eat it on the spot but to take it upstairs and make a real Sunday treat out of it. They would each have small pieces—and Grandma would save most of it for the next day.

What excited the children most of all was the elastic stockings for Grandma. They at once planned an elaborate ceremony with which to present them to her. They made Grandma McCarthy and Mrs. McCarthy sit down, blindfolded, at the table. And then when the blindfolds were removed, there on the table were Grandma's elastic stockings, the Italian cake, the rock candy, and several dollars in bills, together with some small coins.

Everything was all right. There was only one cloud in the sky. How would Patrick McCarthy behave?

The cloud passed. McCarthy was having one of his good days. He came home whistling. When they heard his whistling on the steps, they knew that everything was going to be all right.

Grandma McCarthy had prepared an Irish stew for the family supper. That was the usual Saturday night meal; they ate it warmed over the next day so as to save Grandma the job of cooking on Sunday.

McCarthy knew how to be good to his family when the worm of rage was not gnawing at him. On this Saturday night he didn't go to Kelly's saloon—that was what they had all been afraid of. He spent the evening cleaning and brushing his Sunday clothes. He polished his shoes and helped the others to prepare for the morrow's celebration. The entire McCarthy household bustled with washing, pressing, polishing, repairing rips in clothing, sewing on buttons, and cleaning away soiled spots.

Early on Sunday morning, scrubbed, polished, combed, and dressed in their best Sunday clothes, they paraded down the street to church. For the first time in a long time, Grandma Mc-Carthy went along with them; the new elastic stockings made it easier for her to walk.

McCarthy himself, tall and distinguished-looking, wearing a green tie and the pin of the organization "For a Free Ireland" in his lapel, escorted his family with a pride and dignity which made

48th Street immediately forget his sins. Now they saw in him the head of an Irish family proudly escorting his brood to early Sunday mass. They greeted him as he walked along, and the neighbors winked to each other.

"What's the matter with the McCarthys?" one of the neighbors asked Deborah Davidowsky, who was standing in front of the grocery store.

"Mary brought home her first week's pay," Mrs. Davidowsky replied.

After the midday Sunday meal, Irving saw Mary come out of the house. He had been waiting for her.

"Where have you been all week, Mary?"

"I'm a working girl now," Mary answered with a show of pride.

"I heard about it, but that's no kind of work for you."

"Why?"

"Once you fall into a factory, you're through. But soon I'll have something to offer you."

"Oh!"

"Yes, I've been thinking about it. Tell me, Mary, are you coming out later?"

"I don't know. My father's taking us to an Irish affair in Central Park."

"How about a movie this evening?"

"I'll have to see later. How's Nat? Have you heard anything from him?"

"Yes. They're trying some experiments on him. They say that he'll be able to walk."

"What?"

"That's what I said."

"Wait a minute, Irving. Are you going to see him today?"

"No, not me. They won't allow us to. The only one who'll be allowed to see him is my father."

"Would you do me a favor?"

"Sure."

"Just wait here a minute."

Mary ran upstairs and came down with the sprig of buds wrapped in paper.

"Please, Irving, ask your father to give these to Nat."

"Sure."

117

"And tell him that this is out of my first wages," Mary said with a smile.

"Sure."

Later when Moshe Wolf opened up the paper wrappings from the flowers which Mary had sent to Nathan, the blooms were beginning to fade. From among the drooping petals a small metal crucifix fell on the blanket of Nathan's bed.

Moshe Wolf felt a sharp pang in his heart.

"A foolish thing. . . a foolish Christian girl . . . to send a crucifix to a Jew."

"She meant no harm, Pa. It's something that's close to her, and she sent it to me," Nathan said.

CHAPTER ELEVEN

NATHAN HAD been in the hospital for more than two months. They were all interested in his case, from the most important doctor to the humblest orderly. All of them were busy paying him attentions—necessary and unnecessary—that might add to his comfort or contribute toward his cure. The newest techniques, electrical therapy and physical exercise, were tried on him; these had only recently been adopted by the medical profession for the treatment of muscular paralysis. He was the focus of interest in the hospital, the guinea pig in a new series of experiments. His days were a constant round of exposures to electric radiations, bakings in electric ovens, physical exercise, and massage.

He let them do anything they pleased with him and gave himself to all their experimentation, although he himself had little faith in the outcome. The experiments might some day be of use to other sufferers, but as for the guinea pig, it was doomed. Never for a moment did he think that any of these innovations would help him, even though the doctors seemed to be encouraged with the results, beaming with pleasure and assuring him that he would soon be able to move his legs. He could not deny that he was beginning to feel some responsiveness in his leg muscles. In the warm chemical baths in which they kept him for hours at a time, he was actually able to move his legs. The first time it happened he almost fainted with the almost unbearable excitement; a torch of hope flamed up in his heart. But the deeply ingrained habit of analytical introspection served to throw a pall on his hopes.

His father's efforts to convince him that his life was important brought little response. It was only his profound pity and reverence for his father—even though he rarely gave it expression—that moved him to try to ease Moshe Wolf's feelings.

But even this desire was fading, as was his will to live. There was only one thin thread which bound him to life, a thread which was at the same time a noose round his neck, inviting him to annihilation, to the denial of life.

This thread was the desire toward Mary that was beginning to flame up inside him. He did not love her—of that he was sure. The thought often occupied his mind, and he strove to lift his purely physical desire up to the plane of idyllic love. But that he was unable to do.

He felt within him the urge to commit an act of revenge against life itself. He hated life; it was only its cruelty that he knew. In the days and nights that had passed, as the urge to deny life had strengthened inside his soul, he had begun to mock at truth, honor, and justice in life—they were only empty words! However much he felt drawn to Mary, however much he idealized her in his fantasies, he was too much the whipped dog of fate to be concerned for her—or for anyone. For the warmth and loyalty of her affection to him he felt toward her—as toward his father—a deep gratitude which under normal circumstances might have blossomed into love. But, like a vandal, he tore to shreds the net of deliverance which might save him from falling into the abyss of his own making. Life was so generous in its gifts to others and so miserly to him! He hated it. But he hated himself even more for his helplessness and uselessness. He was a used-up rag, thrown into life's gutter.

"What rights has a cripple like me?" he asked himself. "What right have I to thoughts and feelings which are only for the normal and healthy of the world!"

Nevertheless he was powerless to free himself from the physical lusts which had awakened in him; the urge of his body was stronger than all the introspective brooding into which his circumstances had plunged him.

The remembrance of the touch of her sensitive fingers, and the host of associated ideas they brought to him, robbed him of sleep at night in his bed. These fantasies were the intimate and personal hiding place in which he concealed himself from the beast of life. There, in this secret nook, he was a normal youth and she was the girl of his desire. Forgotten was his helplessness. The blow that had struck him down had never fallen.

The unconscious urge to fulfillment fought like a lion against his will to death and created for Nathan a world of real-seeming substantiality in which he could find the illusion of highest physical delight. To his bewildered mind illusions became transformed into reality, feeding his hopes, promising him continuance. But, stronger than himself and beyond the reach of his control, another force arose within him, canceling out the release which his normal young desire had brought him. Deeply rooted fears and inhibitions asserted themselves, the legacy of countless years and generations, curbing the stream of primitive desire. But shame and regret brought no absolution to him; he felt fouled and dirtied. Each time the lust of his flesh broke over the dam of his inhibitions, each time his illusions awakened his desire, Nathan felt degraded. To his physical helplessness there was added a moral paralysis which plunged him into an abyss of despair from which he saw no escape. No ray of light glowed in the darkness. He seemed to himself rejected spiritually as well as physically; his soul was as crippled as the physical body which contained it.

There could be no escape for him except through death and extinction. The quicker it happened the better it would be for him. He began to be afraid of himself. He began to fear that his lacks were not so much in his physical condition as in his warped soul, which was seeking to befoul, together with itself, the only pure emotion he had left—his feeling for Mary. He must save himself—and salvation lay only in death. There was no help for it. A wild animal was hot on his heels, seeking to tear him apart, and he was running for his life, from one ditch to another. Now he had come to the last ditch. There was no other hiding place. Before him spread the foul waters of the East River, swelling in its banks. The beast was not outside him; it was within him. He must save himself from himself.

Such tortuous thoughts filled his mind for days. Night after night as he lay in bed he thought of how he might carry out the suicide plan which had been interrupted by his being shifted to the hospital.

Late one night, as he lay awake staring out into the dimly lighted and silent room, he heard the voice of an old alcoholic who was a patient in the next bed.

"Hey, buddy," his neighbor said, "do you believe in God?"

Nathan did not answer. He was occupied with his own

thoughts; the problems of others meant nothing to him. He had the feeling that in the wing of the hospital in which he had been placed the other patients were his enemies. In this general ward at Bellevue most of the patients were derelicts, living on the charity of the city. The patients came and went; the nurses and orderlies paid little attention to them. Nathan's privileged position in the hospital, and the special attention which was shown him, aroused a good deal of resentment on the part of the other patients. They had a sarcastic nickname for him—"the prince of Bellevue." Every time a nurse performed a service for him, or brought him some food, or whenever he was wheeled out of the ward for one of the therapy treatments, he would hear their sneering remarks—"The prince of Bellevue can have anything he wants, but they don't give a damn for us!"

Nathan returned their contempt. He spoke to none of them. Least of all did he want to have anything to do with the alcoholic they had put in the adjoining bed.

This new patient, Nathan learned from the remarks of the nurses, was a chronic drunkard whom they had picked up in the gutter down on the Bowery. He had made several attempts to start a conversation with Nathan, but Nathan hadn't bothered to answer. This time, too, he was silent.

The old drunkard kept after him. Over and over again he repeated the question: "Hey, buddy, do you believe in God?"

At last Nathan answered. "What's the difference?"

"What's the difference?" the other repeated, cackling in his hoarse, cracked voice. "When a man gets old he's got to know whether there's a God or not. Ain't that right?"

"Well, I'm not old, so it doesn't make any difference to me," Nathan replied. He spoke abruptly, hoping it would shut the drunkard up.

"You're old, brother! You're older than me! A sick man is an old man. And the way you're sick, you're a mighty old man."

Nathan let the phrase revolve in his mind. "A mighty old man." No one had made a remark like that to him before. And yet the old drunkard was right. He was an old man. He was at the threshold of death. Did the drunkard know that he was at the threshold of death?

"So what about it! So I'm an old man! What difference does it make?" Nathan said curtly.

"An old man's got to know where he belongs. He's got to know who'll take care of him. That's what I'm trying to tell you. An old man has to know who'll take him in when he's thrown out on the street. Take me! I hang around the Bowery and I only think of one thing. Who'll take me in now that I'm old? Who'll watch out for me in the last years of my life? What'll I do with myself? Who'll lift me out of the gutter and give me a decent home? So I keep on getting drunk, do you understand? No matter what I did to take care of my old age, everything went to pieces. My daughter ran away with some dirty dog and took away the last bit of money I had saved up—two hundred dollars. So I hang around the Bowery. It's a good thing the Salvation Army hands out a meal and a bed to sleep on. Good Christian people. I even sold the cemetery plot I'd been paying on every month. 'Buddy,' I said to the agent, 'I can't pay any more. Give me five dollars and we'll be even.' What's the difference what they do with my carcass when I kick off? If I pass out in the street, they won't let me lay there—they have to sweep the garbage away. That's the way I figured when I was strong enough to pick up a job as a dishwasher now and then for a dollar and a half a day. But when my strength ran out of me, that's when the thought began to gnaw at me. 'Charlie,' I said to myself, 'Who's going to take you in now?' They say that the Jews have some sort of institutions for old men, but I'm no Jew. The Salvation Army takes care of a man with a hot meal and a night's lodging and prayers, but I can't join in their prayer services because I'm a Catholic. The Catholics don't have anything like that. The priest I went to was even scared to give me the price of a cup of coffee. 'You'll spend it on drink,' he said to me. Well, what else should a man do who's got no home to go to in his old age? And you can feel your strength leaving you from day to day, and the Devil keeps on whispering at you— 'What'll you do if you collapse in the gutter?' All right, so I collapsed in the gutter. And they brought me here to the hospital. . . . The orderly who brings the bed pan said to me, 'I can tell from your water that it won't take long. You're getting closer.' He thought he'd scare me, but the truth of it is I suddenly felt good. Here I'd been all the time thinking—'Who'll take care of you in your old age?'—when I should have known all the time that the good Jesus will take me unto Himself when

I die in the street. Now do you understand why a man has to know where he belongs when he gets old? And you, buddy, you're an old man. A mighty old man."

Nathan listened with a strange fascination. This illiterate plea for faith by a sodden drunkard made a stronger impression on him than the reasoned eloquence of his own father. Moshe Wolf had tried so tirelessly to make him see that he, more than anyone else, desperately needed faith; he had tried to lead him into belief by appealing to his reason, by quoting to him from the Holy Writings. Yet, with all the strength of his love for his son, Nathan's father had been unable to exert such an influence over him as had the rambling, disjointed words of the drunkard in the next bed. But this was a trap, too. He would not allow himself to be snared by the ignorant vaporings of a drunkard. He answered him contemptuously:

"Maybe you're right. But before you get to the arms of your Jesus you'll have to go through the penance of purgatory."

"So what about it! What have I to be afraid of? Will I be the only man who's gone through it? My whole life has been a hell from the day I was born. And if I've sinned I deserve to be punished. I'm ready to be punished. . . . But I don't believe the good Jesus will let them torture me too much . . . although the priests always kept me scared of it. Jesus knows I've taken enough of a beating right here, and He'll have pity on me. I'm telling you, buddy, a man can stand any suffering as long as he knows where he belongs and that he's got a home to go to, that he's got a Jesus in Heaven. A couple of beatings more or less, what's the difference? The whole point is that you know that the sweet Jesus will take you home."

The night nurse looked around, although the old Irishman was talking in a low voice. She came over to the bed.

"Keep quiet. You're waking up the patients," she ordered.

"Listen, sister. You got a drink? Give me a drink. I'm allowed to have it. The doctor himself'll prescribe it for me."

"What makes you think you're allowed to have it?" the nurse asked.

"Because nothing can do me any harm now. I belong to the kind Jesus. He's going to take me home when I leave the hospital. What's the difference whether I go to Him a day earlier or later? He's got a palace waiting for me, and there's all kinds

124

of drinks there, whatever kind I want. The priest'll tell you to-morrow—if I last until tomorrow—that after I take the holy sacrament nothing can do me any harm. You'll hear the priest tell it to you himself."

The nurse laughed and went over to Nathan's bed.

"You'd better get to sleep, Nat. The patients are beginning to complain. Quiet!" She went back to her post at the end of the room.

But Nathan couldn't fall asleep; the drunkard's ramblings at least helped the night to pass. He lowered his voice and asked him:

"Will there be a palace waiting for me, too? With any kind of drink I want?"

"Are you a Catholic?" the drunkard asked.

"No. A Jew."

"That's bad. Looks like it won't be so good for you. Too bad. But you got time to get it fixed up."

Nat laughed.

"How about the ones who believe their own religion is good enough for them?"

"They're cursed. They'll suffer in Hell's torments. It's too bad, buddy, but that's way it is."

Nathan no longer listened. He sank back into his own brood-ings.

"The way the Christians think about the Jews," he thought to himself, "is the way the pious Jews think about the Christians. And it's the way one Christian sect thinks about the other—the Catholics about the Protestants and the Protestants about the Catholics. Not a single one of them has thought to spread the mantle of God's mercy wide enough to cover all people. How strange it is," his thoughts ran, "that I, created by God, can conceive of a universal salvation, whereas God—according to the conception of the religious sects—lacks the tolerance to offer salvation to all men."

Yet for all its narrowness the drunkard's implicit faith made a profound impression on Nathan. This primitive and elemental trust which was so real an anchor for the foundering drunkard, this greedy, clamoring clinging, this "Sweet Jesus, take me to you," drove Nathan to search deep into his own soul. He was "a mighty old man." And if he should succeed in carrying out his determination to end his life, he would soon be face to face with the dilemma of faith which the drunkard's words had made real to him. It was as though the drunkard's simple and unquestioning relationship to God had opened a window for him through which he could see clearly his way to God, a road which was open to every man of faith, whatever his circumstance in life. The realization made Nathan search deep into his own soul. How was it with him in relation to God?

He let himself come to grips with the problem. He meditated over it in the long night. Each night was an endless and impenetrable forest. He had to fight with all his strength to force his way through the heavy growths; he fell into deep abysses, he climbed over precipitous mountains. In the black and unending night, as he writhed in the infinite, formless nonexistence to which the paralysis had doomed him, he sought with all his mind and heart for something concrete and eternal on which he might base his life. He searched for the "why," the reason for his crippled body—but he could go no further than the final answer which his father and all the other good people had given him— God. His mind came to a stop at the vague conception of an incomprehensible power functioning and creating without a "reason." His was the rationalist's image of God, a blind Samson, bound to the millwheel, treading its path forever and ever, driven by the irrevocable urge of his being. What difference whether it was the Philistine who had chained him to the wheel, or whether it was the irresistible urge within him? His was not the choice to stop the wheel's turning, nor in his blindness could he know that he was part of the endless round. Whether the millwheel moved the axis of the universe or the miller's millstone—what difference did it make! The measure of time may be eternity or a breath, the revolutions of the circle millenia or a split moment. The miller could not see the single kernel under the millstone; how could the blind Sampson, turning the axis of the universe, perceive the fate of one miserable soul fallen between those mammoth stones?

What was the sense of praying to this unseeing one, of pouring out one's anguish and bitterness? What help could be hoped for from one who was his own slave, who could not find release for himself?

126

Nathan's father had tried untiringly and earnestly to implant in him a belief in special providence. Nathan had not accepted it. His failure to accept it or comprehend it now saved him from directing his bitterness toward God. To him it was blind destiny that was responsible for his condition. Thus his attitude toward God was one of neutrality; he could neither have grievances toward him nor anticipate favors from him. Yet while this neutrality permitted him to be "nonpartisan," it did not close his eyes to the divine wonder which had been unveiled for him.

Here was this derelict, he thought to himself, thrown out on the street like a mongrel dog grown old and sick and useless. And the respectable of the earth had established institutions to give a shelter to these outcasts—not so much out of regard for the outcasts as out of regard for themselves. On the very brink of death, the stream of life drying up, the worthless and discarded human flotsam suddenly finds a new life. A birth in death, as the child in the womb finds birth in life. And what was the force with which he grasped his salvation? It was the force of the conviction that made him believe that there is a divine power which makes him the object of its special concern. What it had not done for the miserable outcast in life, it would do for him in death. It was ready for him, waiting for him, like a mother, to give him a new birth...a birth in death....

No adopted or even accustomed faith could create for a man, in the hour of his bitterest need, so real, so substantial, so comforting a conviction of a haven after death. However strong the accustomed faith within him, it could not accept the miracle of the real haven which the drunkard saw so clearly, were it not so basic, so deeply implanted into the very embryo of his being that it could blossom into a convincing reality in the hour of his need. This feeling, this conviction of a personal belonging to God, must therefore be a basic instinct, a human need. The instinct in its origin had to be the common possession of all men; it was only that the rationalists had deadened it within them, seeking to replace it with their false standards of matter and form with which the mind seeks to measure and weigh that which cannot be measured and weighed. It was a concept which could not be comprehended through the mind; it could be understood only through the magic of intuition. Thus apperceived it had crowned with grace this drunkard lifted up from the gutter.

127

It had transformed his befouled body into the clean purity of an eternal child of heaven.

Why should he not awaken and bring to life within himself this sense of divinity? Of what avail up to now had been his hopeless rationalizations? Involuntarily he compared his own attitude toward his condition with that of his father. To his father suffering was a sacred trial visited on man so that he might fulfill a divine mission; his father accepted it without complaint or questioning, with the sole desire and yearning to serve his God through love. It was a source of joy for him; it created for him an island of comfort in a sea of trouble and pain. His father had said to him: "Who needs faith as much as you do, my son?" Now he understood his father's words. Faith had ennobled and transformed his father's suffering into a lofty and tranquil joy, while for Nathan his sufferings were a foul swamp of despair, a contempt for himself and the world, a bitterness toward friend and stranger, a disgust for his own helplessness.

This ship which carried him over the stormy sea of life—it was rudderless and unmanned, it was beyond his control. Why not abandon it? Or why not let it be guided by a hand stronger than his own? Why not deliver himself over, like a trusting child, to the guidance of a higher power? You are not able to guide your own life, Nathan—surrender yourself into the hands of Him who gave you life. He understands the shifting tides; He knows the goal of your existence. Make Him responsible for your life, only so that you can best fulfill the task He has assigned you. It was He who brought you to this hospital; it who He who, in the hour of your deepest doubts, brought to you this meanest of His creatures to show you how faith can bring the miracle to pass. His was the quiet voice that whispered to the men of science so that they might try on you the experiments which might bring help and healing to thousands as unfortunate as you. Yield with all your heart and all your willingness to them. Maybe it was for this you were chosen; maybe you have been called to be the vicar for the sufferings of others. . . .

An infinite range of reasons and possibilities opened up before Nathan's mind. New vistas presented themselves to him of which he had never before dreamed. Even his thoughts of suicide found a new justification. "God," he said to himself—he could use the word now without the fear that he was insulting his intelligence—"God intentionally brought me to the brink of the abyss so that I need no longer care for my own life. I have already died; I am no longer here. 'Nothing can happen to me now,' " he repeated the drunkard's words. Why not try to tread this new path?

No, not try, step firmly, surely, with confidence! Now he saw the road clearly. Now he knew where he stood.

He saw a long, thin rope suspended between widely separated posts. He was an acrobat, balancing himself on the tightrope. But nothing could happen to him. There was a net spread underneath him; it would catch him and hold him if he should fall.

In the two months he had been in the hospital they had tried a wide variety of experiments on him. Dr. Bennet, a pioneer in the use of the ultraviolet rays, had experimented with the application of heat treatments to Nathan's limbs. Although there had been no definite results, he was unwilling to abandon the treatment.

The doctor, a New Englander, emotionless as a fish, quiet as a mouse, and with the quick movements of a moth, showed all these characteristics in the patience and confidence with which he treated the boy. He had faith in his methods, and there was enough evidence to indicate to him that a cure could be effected. He noticed the increase in the firmness of the texture of Nathan's leg muscles, and even of his arms. To Dr. Bennet this was evidence that the local nerve centers were not permanently paralyzed. What was missing was the patient's will to co-operate; of this Nathan had given no sign. At frequent intervals he would be exposed for long periods to ultraviolet rays, or would be placed in warm baths. After such treatments the nurses would try to make him stand unaided. None of the attempts succeeded.

For as long as the experiments went on, the improvement in the muscles of his limbs could be clearly seen; for permanent results the patient's co-operation and will were essential. But it was precisely these missing ingredients which Nathan could not or would not supply.

Dr. Bennet called in Dr. Chazanowitch; it had been the anarchist doctor who had pointed out to the Bellevue staff the error they had made in abandoning the case. He asked Chazanowitch to stand by during the treatments and try to influence Nathan to co-operate.

Each time Nathan resisted, Dr. Chazanowitch scolded him roundly.

"You little mule," he shouted. "We can't do anything for you unless you're willing to help. Don't be so stubborn."

"I'm not being stubborn, Doctor. I can't stand, I just can't," Nathan pleaded.

"You can. You don't want to."

Nor was his father's pleading of any avail. How could it be, when what they required of Nathan was the impossible—that he stand upright on those—those—appendages to his body? The growing firmness of the flesh was only an illusion. His legs were useless parasites attached to his body; they would collapse under his weight like matchsticks if he should try to stand on them. And it wasn't only his legs; he himself, his very "I," was powerless to dictate to his physical body. The communication between his ego and his physical self had been destroyed by the paralysis of the nerves. What was the good of his will when its demands could not be dispatched over the shattered lines of communication? It was this conviction of Nathan's that blocked any real progress.

But since the belief had come to Nathan that he was the instrument of a divine mission, he began to feel the conviction—although at first timorously—that God had reunited, even if by the thinnest of threads, his will to his body. It was over this wire-fine thread that his impulses, like an electric current, traveled from his will to his nerve centers. And from the nerve centers to the tangled network of his paralyzed nerves God had opened a channel through which his will could reach the muscles of his legs. With all the strength of his new conviction he made an effort to move his legs under the blankets as he lay in bed. Over and over he tried. He clenched his lips and gritted his teeth so as to resist the pain. The expectation of pain was sweet, like the premonitions of birth. He closed his eyes and told himself that what he was doing was not for himself alone but for hundreds, thousands, of the victims of the epidemic; for youths like himself, and for those younger, for children and infants.

He could see these children, thousands of them, all over the country, in poor hovels and rich homes, lying crippled in their beds, looking at him with begging eyes. They were all looking at him. In their eyes was the plea: "Our lives depend on you. Move your legs for us. If you can walk...then we, too, will walk. Save us! For our sake!"

And he moved!

Once, twice, and a third time. His lips tightly pressed together and his eyes close shut, he forced his fingers to clench into a fist... with the eyes of the crippled thousands fixed on him... he moved his legs, he extended them to their length and drew them up at the knees... extended them... drew them up... once and again and again... in the deepness of the night... in the bright light of the day....

Now he knew that what he felt was not a snare, an illusion. It was a reality. God had reunited his spirit with his body. Now he could order—and his legs would obey.

He said nothing to the doctors or the nurses. The most important test of all still remained. He would try to stand.

When, the next day, the nurses took him out of the warm bath, he closed his eyes. He thought of himself as an acrobat. Yes, he was an acrobat before God. He was on a high tightrope; he was giving a performance for God. He was undergoing a test before God. His life and the lives of the thousands of others depended on it. There they were, all of them, gathered all about in the vast arena and watching him. He could not fail them.

He stood up.

He stood up, clumsily, like a young calf nosed away from its mother's side, on thin, stiff, unsure legs. He swayed toward the right, then toward the left. A nurse ran to him to support him, but he found his balance and remained standing. He began to move his legs, halting movements, one step... another.... Then he collapsed on the floor.

But the net into which he fell was soft and elastic, warm with beneficent love, as though he had fallen into his father's arms.

And he did fall into his father's arms. He saw his father's joyful face, the warm love in his father's eyes.

Nathan smiled at him. He smiled at the nurses. He smiled at the white-bearded Dr. Bennet, at Dr. Chazanowitch. He smiled to his mother, to his brother, to Mary, to everyone on 48th Street. He smiled to the tens of thousands of crippled children. He smiled to Charlie, the drunkard. But his secret smile was directed to Him whom he had denied . . . Him who he knew was around him and within him in his heart. . . . He smiled to God.

There they were, all of them, crowded into the arena in which Nathan had taken his test before God. And his smile was at the same time a smile of anxiety and a smile of contentment. It asked their pardon for his helplessness. It was filled with grace and joy and contentment of soul. Most of all there was thankfulness in his smile.

They stood around him with open-mouthed astonishment, too moved to speak. Dr. Bennet said: "This is God's work."

Nathan, as he lay helpless on the floor, looked with an understanding smile at Dr. Bennet and nodded his head.

CHAPTER TWELVE

LIKE A song bursting forth from a young heart, like the
dawn of a new day in spring, so did a new life begin to
blossom for Nathan.

From the windows of the hospital corridor into which the
nurses wheeled him in his invalid chair he could see women sitting and children playing in the square below. It was a typical
Indian summer day. The copper-red leaves on the few trees in
the square were falling from the branches. The tops of the trees
glistened in the sunlight. The air was full of the fragrance of
apples and grapes. Children ran about among the red and gold
autumn leaves; infants slept in their carriages. Their mothers
sat in small groups, intent on their sewing, knitting or darning.
Older children darted along on roller skates, or ran up and down
pushing wagons made of boxes and crates mounted on roller-
skate wheels. The sound of the wheels clattering over the cobblestones, and young voices calling, came through the hospital
windows. Nathan looked out of the window at the mothers
and their children, and he smiled.

He smiled joyfully and lightheartedly. He no longer felt that
he was separated from the life about him, like an outsider in a
strange world. He was united with the life there below him; he
was one of them; he would strap wheels to his feet and skate
along after them.

"Dear God, I can walk! I can move!"

He thought of how powerful and strong and mighty he was.
He could walk! He could place one foot before the other! Even
if it was only a couple of steps, the glorious truth remained that
he could walk—unaided—from one place to another. How in-
conceivably rich, how mighty were the treasures he had found!
He could move!

It occurred to him that all those who moved about so freely

133

—the children, their parents, even the nurses and doctors and the other patients in the hospital—were foolish and ignorant and blind. They did not realize the infinity of riches with which they were blessed. They could walk, they could see, they could speak, they could move! They were sound of limb and body, but they failed to comprehend that astonishing phenomenon. They thought that they were entitled to all these riches; that these riches were all of their own making; that they could take them for granted. It was only when a man lost one of his functions that he could know how priceless was the soundness of his body; such an understanding was beyond the normal man. To some extent Nathan could feel grateful to God for the misfortune that had overtaken him; through it he had learned of the countless blessings and privileges God lavished on his creatures. It was only now that he was able to see that man himself was nothing more than a lump of matter, no different from the meanest substance. That he was above and beyond the common clay was the work of God, who had endowed him with limbs and organs. He was grateful to God not only that his legs could move, but that he could breathe, and see, and speak.

"Nothing is mine of right. Everything has been given to me. For every moment of my life, and in every function of my body, I must be grateful for the blessings which have been given to me by God. Let me always remember that just as they have been given, so can they be taken away; let me remember that they have been given to me only so that I may use them in the service of God and man."

Children crippled by the infantile paralysis epidemic were brought to see him. There were girls and boys, with fair blond heads and dark curly ringlets. There were children with the prematurely wizened faces of the aged and long-suffering, children with angelic faces, looking in open-eyed astonishment at everything about them, rejoicing in every new sight, in every new discovery. There were others who were abstracted and thoughtful, as though they were still strangers to the real world; they seemed to gaze into unknown distances where mortal eyes could not follow them. Others rested their heads against their mothers' breasts in resignation and despair, as though they could find truth and justice only in their mothers' compassionate arms. There were yet others who fought violently against their fate,

134

grimacing, weeping, striving vainly to escape. There were those whose eyes were like strange, calm lakes, hidden among thickly growing trees in dim forests. There were eyes like stormy, tempestuous seas; and tears, despairing protests to God and man.

Nathan "performed" for them. To him his clumsy attempts at walking were still "performances." When he performed for these crippled children, he felt that he was simultaneously the acrobat cavorting before them and their champion before the throne of grace. He dare not fail. With a smile on his face, as though it was all so easy and effortless, he performed for the crippled children about him. He walked the few steps as though he were performing a holy rite. He placed his feet with earnestness and concentration, and yet with reckless bravery, as though the very life of his onlookers, for whom he was demonstrating this miracle of God, depended on it. He dare not fail! He must not fail! With a determined shake of his head he refused the nurse's offers of help, and took stiff-legged steps, one after the other. When he finished, his body was bathed in perspiration, his clothing sticking to him, but there was a glow on his face, his eyes were shining with the joy of achievement, his teeth sparkling behind his open, smiling lips. He had given his "performance"! He had not failed!

There came the great moment when Nathan's father could see with his own eyes the miracle God had wrought.

When he saw Nathan standing alone and unsupported, Moshe Wolf raised his arms and said in a choking voice: "My son! I'm afraid..."

"What is there to be afraid of, Pa?" Nathan answered with an eager smile. He took a few steps.

"I am afraid of God," Moshe Wolf said. He shuddered, then sobbed like a child.

"Don't cry, Pa," Nathan pleaded.

"No, I won't cry," Moshe Wolf stammered. He wiped his eyes with the back of his hand. "And now, my son, you must become a pious Jew. You must hold fast to our Jewish faith."

"What has the Jewish faith, or the Christian faith, to do with God? Judaism or Christianity... they're only rituals. I don't believe in rituals; I believe in God. God is all I have; I'll not be robbed of Him by a ritual," Nathan said earnestly.

"A ritual? What do you mean, my son?"

135

"What you're telling me to do—to go to synagogue—that is ritual."

"But what is the harm in it?"

"Ritual makes a prisoner out of God. It declares that God is only in the synagogue or in the church."

"I understand you, my son, yet I don't understand you. But what difference, as long as you believe in God. For now that is enough. The rest can wait."

Nathan lay in his hospital bed. His wide eyes shone out of his unshaven face, his parted lips moved inaudibly. He was studying from the book that lay open before him on a board rest. Tensely, eagerly and persistently he strove to overcome the handicaps which his paralysis set between him and his desire. Like the hidden roots of the tree turning and twisting in the depths of the soil to outwit the obstacles between them and the life-giving moisture, Nathan, fortified by his newly found will to live, sought to find ways to drink at the wells of learning from which his condition had barred him.

He bent his head, and with his lips and tongue turned the pages—an act which his hands were powerless to accomplish. In the chambers of his brain he stored and memorized the figures, names, dates, facts, which he was powerless to write down. In his imagination he conjured up an enormous blackboard, on which his mind wrote down the data he needed for his studies. It was as though all his energy and will for life, deadened and crushed during his illness, had now reawakened, drawing new strength from unsuspected springs. On the blackboard in his imagination he inscribed mathematical formulas and equations. He saw an entire library before his eyes, and from his memory he drew the knowledge which he had stored within himself as a bee stores honey.

It did not take long until he overcame the problem of his useless hands. He fashioned new ways of doing what they could not do for him.

The "crazy doctor," as the nurses called Dr. Chazanowitch, watched over Nathan as a mother over a child. Nathan *was* his child; it was he who had brought him to life. It was as though the doctor, who had been swimming, naked and lost, in a universe to which he did not belong, had found an anchor from which he could plot his life's course. Nathan had awakened emotions with-in him that Dr. Chazanowitch had thought long dead. Every improvement which Nathan showed meant joy and deep satisfaction for the older man. No father rejoiced more over the first stumbling steps of his own child than did Dr. Chazanowitch over Nathan's progress. He wanted to speed him on faster and faster to the goal of recovery. He invented all sorts of suggestions and ideas to further stimulate Nathan's will to use his paralyzed limbs. The doctor was now absolutely convinced that not only would Nathan be able to move his legs, but that he would be able to regain the use of at least one of his arms. The muscles of the right arm, the doctor knew, were not atrophied by the paralysis. The increasing firmness of the flesh was clear proof that the veins were carrying healthy blood to the tissues.

Dr. Chazanowitch tried ardently to persuade Nathan to move his arms. He spent every moment he could spare at Nathan's bedside. The hospital bed took the place of the Bohemian café on the East Side where Dr. Chazanowitch spent his evenings with his anarchist cronies. It was a delight to him to sit beside the hospital bed, discussing world affairs, reading aloud, trying to interest Nathan in the life around him, trying to arouse in him an even greater yearning for an active life.

"You're not a cripple any more, Nat. It's time you started to do some studying. What were you studying at college? Law?"

"Yes."

"Well, what are you wasting time for? Do you want to spend your whole life here in the hospital?"

"I certainly can't go back to college."

"Why not? You want to do something in the world, don't you? You say you're interested in social problems. You don't want to leave the world to the mercies of Tammany Hall!"

"How can I do anything about it?"

"That's easy. Tomorrow I'll bring you the books you need. I've got a friend, a young lawyer without a practice. He'll help you. I'll find out the details about the course. Didn't you have any friends at Columbia taking the course with you?"

"There was Robert Hirsch. . . . "

"Where is he? Why doesn't he come to visit you? He can bring you his notebooks, and you can study from them."

"Please, Dr. Chazanowitch, I don't want to see him."

137

"Why not? What are you ashamed of? Because you're not on a baseball team?"

"But, Doctor, what's the use, when I can't move my hands?"

"You didn't think you could move your legs either! Your right arm shows plenty of life. The muscles have taken on flesh; that's a good sign. As long as the blood circulation is normal there's no reason why the nerve system shouldn't be able to function. All that's necessary is for you to give it a bit of help."

"Doctor!"

"Yes, yes, I mean it. Here, let's try something! Take this pencil"—Dr. Chazanowitch took a pencil out of his pocket—"I'm going to tie it to your right hand. Naturally, I don't expect you'll be an expert penman, but when you want to make a note of something special in the book you're studying, try to move the pencil over the page."

"I'll never be able to do it, Doctor."

"We'll see. In the meantime let the pencil stay tied to your hand. It won't bite you."

Dr. Chazanowitch tied the pencil to Nathan's hand and left him with an open book before him.

The days went by. Nathan went to sleep and awakened with the pencil still tied to his hand. Dr. Chazanowitch saw no sign of a penciled scrawl on the book's pages. But after a week's time, during which Nathan had tried with all his will to move his arm, the doctor noticed an uneven, wavering line on a page of the volume on Roman law which Nathan had been studying with Robert Hirsch, whom Dr. Chazanowitch had located and who paid daily visits to the hospital to help Nathan in his studies.

By now almost everyone in the neighborhood had been in to visit Nathan. He had "performed" for all of them. He had shown them how he could stand, how he could move about on his legs, how he could even raise his right arm. Everyone had seen him; everyone but Mary. Of all of 48th Street she was almost the only one who hadn't paid a visit. It was not her fault; Nathan didn't want to see her. He had asked his brother Irving to tell her not to come to visit him; to wait until he returned home.

Nathan had his reasons. It was Mary who, more than anyone else, was responsible for rekindling in him the will to live. Because of her he had sought death; because of her he wanted to live. When, with clenched, tight lips, he had strained to move his paralyzed legs under the bedcovers, it was her face he saw in the white flashes of pain that tortured his nerves. It was the fresh moistness of her sensitive lips that cooled his fever. And now when he had achieved the impossible, when by the irresistible force of his will he had moved his lifeless arm, so long only a mocking appendage to his body, he had been able to do it only because the compensation for his pain lay in the warm glance of those dark eyes under the full eyebrows, in the trembling of her sensitive lips, in the softness of her breath, in the tenderness of her nut brown skin for which he yearned in a thirst of love and desire as he lay in bed at night.

He remembered her in the ways he had seen her so many times. He filled the emptiness of his night with sweet fantasies and dreams. Her piquant strangeness had always stirred him, but never as it did now in his recollection. Once he had seen her in the half-nakedness which was more naked than complete nudity. On hot summer days Harry Greenstock would herd the children of the block into his yard and turn on the "fountain," an improvised fire pump he had found in Zelig's junk yard. The children would dash in and out of the spray of water to get some relief from the heat of the day. Mary and Rachel, for all that they were much older than the other children, would often join them. Lying on his wheel chair Nathan had stared at her eagerly. Mary's bathing suit—her mother had made it for her out of some remnants of satin—clung to her slender, shapely body. His eyes lingered over her swelling hips, her firm, graceful legs, her round belly, her budding breasts. He avidly searched out every curve of her young body. He took the sight of her with him into the dark jungle of his lonesomeness, feeding his sensuality with her image. All his unnameable yearnings would be concentrated in his memory of her. He sated his hunger with the conjurings of his fantasy.

There were times when he despised himself for the riot of his imagination. He heaped contempt on himself for his dreams. It was not only his body that was crippled, he thought to himself, even his soul was warped. His despair over his uncleanness culminated in his frantic yearning for death.

But the victory over his limbs had brought soundness to his thoughts. Now he found the moral strength to accept his physical as well as his spiritual self. "I am entitled to life's joys," he thought to himself. "It is not only others I must serve; I must serve myself. I have a just right to find the measure of joy which life can offer me. But I must earn it honestly. I must make myself better, more able. I must live a useful life, like a normal person. I have a right to think of marriage, too, like everybody else. And if Mary has picked me out—whatever her reason, even if it is out of pity—then it means there is something worth-while for her in me. I can give, not only receive, but I must see to it that my giving is generous enough to make up for what I lack."

Like a drowning man who struggles with desperate energy to reach the shore his eyes can see, so did Nathan struggle to reach his own shore of safety. He saw Mary on the shore, with all the bounty and treasure she had to offer. How worthy she was of the struggle!

No, she must not see him until he could leave the hospital, walking on his own legs, alone and unaided. She must not see him until he was again admitted to college. She must not see him until he could use his hands and take care of his own needs. She must not see him until his body vibrated with the same energy and health for her as did her own body for him.

And until that day should come, he could have his fantasies; he could substitute the illusion for the reality.

With this conviction his fantasies became normal and healthy, the fantasies of any normal youth when dreaming of the girl he loves.

Now he saw his happiness in his warped limbs. She had fallen in love with his helplessness and desolation; he was content to remain so for the rest of his days. He imagined himself in his wheel chair, Mary guiding it. She brought him into the park— did not every mother take her child to the park?—so that he might rest in the warmth of the sun. She took him to a concert at Carnegie Hall, to a meeting where he addressed workers, to a lecture hall where he delivered an address. She fed him with her own hands, she held the glass to his lips. She helped him to bed at night and tended him in the morning. She bathed him and dressed him. She would let no one else attend him, even though they could well afford servants and special nurses—of course they could afford it; in his fantasy Nathan was not only a defender of the poor, he was a successful lawyer as well. Just as he found joy in eating from her hands, just as his body trembled with delight when she touched him, so did she find delight in serving him. The two of them were one, united by intimate unseen cords. They were two bodies, but they were bound together as one, like a mother and child... even more, like a mother and child and the child still in the mother's womb. Mary functioned for him, just as the mother functions for the child in her body before it is separated from her at birth. They were one and the same. Her hands were his hands, for her hands served his needs. They were not two separate entities fulfilling one another, like husband and wife. No, in Nathan's fantasy Mary was an integral part of him, created to carry out for him the functions which he could not carry out for himself.

As a young boy he had often dreamed of being able some day to travel to Europe. For hours at a time he had stood on the bank of the East River and watched the ships cutting through its broad, billowy surface. With a hiss of steam and the blowing of sirens and the black, billowing clouds of smoke they went by, carrying coal, building material, scrap and wreckage from demolished houses, and sand from one shore of the river to the other. Farther down on the river he would sometimes see a passenger boat for which there was no room at the crowded piers along the Hudson. The sight of it would awaken in him a yearning for travel.

It was the old Europe which drew him. The cities, the museums, the centers of music and science about which he had read so much, drew him. A longing for distant lands was awakened in him by the sea gulls flying through the thick smoke of the ship funnels and alighting on the banks of the East River to join the flocks of pigeons and sparrows perched on the shore. They brought him a greeting from distant oceans, from countries which lay far away across the waters. When as a child he had stood at the shore of the East River, watching the ships and the sea gulls, he had thought of the long voyage over the ocean to Paris, the magical city. He had tried to imagine himself grown up, a man, standing at the rail of the ship on a silver, moonlit night, gazing at the foam of the ship's wake, his bride beside him. He had never been able to imagine her, but now he knew who she was.

Helpless in his wheel chair, now he saw that it was Mary who would accompany him on his journey over the ocean, who would always remain at his side. It was not hand in hand that they would walk along the banks of the Seine and roam among the old book stalls about which he had so often dreamed. He would be in his wheel chair and Mary would be guiding him. And how strange! Being an invalid in a wheel chair was not an obstacle nor a blemish to his joy. It was the very condition of his joy; it brought his joy into being.

CHAPTER THIRTEEN

MARY HAD been working at Greenspan's shop for about two months. She and Sarah Lifschitz had become close friends. One day, as the two girls sat together eating lunch, Sarah said:

"Listen to this, Mary. The Triangle Waist Company on Washington Place is looking for girls to work on blouses. It's easy work, one of the girls who works there told me, because this season's styles are simple, not much fancy stuff. It's not a union shop, but even if you're a union member you can get in—you just don't have to tell them. The pay's wonderful, ten or twelve dollars a week, if you work from half-past seven in the morning to six. With overtime some of the girls make fourteen dollars a week, even though they don't pay extra rates for overtime. It's a big shop, and the working conditions are pretty good. I'm going to try to get a job there; I wouldn't mind earning more money; they need it at home. What do you say? Do you want to come with me?"

"Twelve dollars a week!" Mary could hardly believe it. "And fourteen with overtime! Sure I'll go with you. I'm sick of this place, with all the smells of that darned restaurant. And I can't stand working with all those old men. I'd like to work among a lot of girls in a real shop for a change, even though it would take longer to get all the way down there. I get up early, anyway. I have to make breakfast for my father—my grandma hasn't been feeling well lately and my mother's supposed to stay in bed as much as she can. I could use a few extra dollars. The kids at home are in rags; my mother can't patch Jimmy's pants any more. I'd like to earn some extra money and get some new clothes for the kids as a surprise for Easter."

A few days later both girls went over to the Triangle firm on Washington Place to ask about jobs. When they satisfied the foreman that they were experienced hands and didn't belong to the union, he took them on.

That evening Mary came home radiant. At last she would be working in a real shop. Besides she would be earning at least six dollars a week more than she was getting at Greenspan's; with some overtime she might even make as much as fourteen dollars a week.

The Triangle firm was housed in a modern building, practically a skyscraper, situated on the edge of the enormous open square in the heart of the city. The factory took up several floors of the building. The offices, showrooms, and cutting rooms were on the lower floors. On the ninth floor about two hundred and thirty girls and a few men worked at sewing machines. Other hands worked on the eighth floor. The tenth floor housed the finishers, cleaners, and examiners. Besides a large number of men, cutters and pressers, Triangle employed more than seven hundred girls.

Entrance and exit to the ninth floor were furnished by two doors, one opposite the other. One of them, the one giving on the stairway on the Washington Square side, was always kept locked. The other door opened on the corridor and elevator leading to Greene Street. This door was constantly guarded by a watchman who looked the girls over each time they left the shop. His beady eyes were like exploring, impudent fingers, making sure that a girl didn't have a blouse or a stray piece of material concealed under her dress or coat. Nor did he hesitate to paw them for a more thorough inspection. There was no other way for the girls to enter or leave the shop except through the door guarded by the watchman.

March twenty-fifth fell on a Saturday. Through the wide windows overlooking Washington Place the afternoon sky was snow-laden and gloomy. The ninth floor bustled with activity. Rows of girls sat at the sewing machines, the electric bulbs gleaming over their bowed heads. The work was going on at full speed; all the girls were hurrying to get through with the day's work so as to get home as early as possible. Although Saturday was a full working day, the girls were permitted to leave an hour earlier if the day's quota was disposed of. Saturday was payday, another inducement to hurry; everyone had plans for the evening, to go visiting, to go shopping, to go to the movies or to a dance.

Mary and Sarah sat at adjoining machines. As they worked

144

they chatted of their evening plans. The electricity-driven leather belts of the machines clattered so noisily they were barely able to hear one another.

Sarah was in an elated mood. This week she had managed to earn, with overtime, all of fourteen dollars, an enormous sum. Besides, she was going to a dance in the evening; Jack Klein, who worked in the factory, had invited her. Her problem was what to wear, the new evening dress she had bought with her increased earnings at Triangle, or her black skirt and waist; the waist was a Triangle number; she might even have worked on it herself.

"Gee, Sarah," Mary commented, "I love those new waists with the ribbon at the collar that we're making now. But I guess it's really a question of how interested you are in Jack. Do you want to look gorgeous—or just attractive?"

"Well, naturally, a girl wants to look gorgeous when a fellow takes her out to a dance for the first time," Sarah replied.

"In that case you better wear your evening dress. A girl looks more—more important in an evening dress. That's what the fellows like."

As they talked above the whirr of the machines a sudden quiet fell on the shop; even the machines sounded subdued. Something seemed to be happening at the far end of the room. Sarah stood up to see what was going on. Mary scrambled up beside her. They could see nothing.

"What is it?" Mary asked in sudden alarm.

"I don't know," Sarah answered.

All at once they saw puffs of thick smoke coming up between the cracks of the floor boards near the door leading to the elevator. Forked flames of fire followed the smoke. All the fright in the world broke out in a chorus of hysterical screams.

"Fire! Fire! Fire!"

Panic swept through the room. There was the noise of running feet, the clatter of chairs and stools being thrown over. The two girls began to run with the rest.

The running mob pushed them toward the exit door on the Greene Street side. It was near the door leading to the elevator that the flames were licking through the planks of the floor. They remembered that no stairway descended from the corridor. The elevator was the only exit. They would be trapped in the corridor by the flames. The smoke and fire coming through the floor near the door terrified them. The crowd veered and dashed to the other side of the loft, where the door led to the stairway that went down to Washington Place. Mary and Sarah, holding each other by the hand, ran with the rest.

They stumbled over chairs and upended stools. They were blocked by hysterical girls who were too terrified to move. Sarah and Mary tried to drag some of them along with them. Here and there tongues of fire were coming up through the floor. Around the sewing machines the heaps of remnants of material and trimmings, silks, linings, padded cotton, the oil-soaked rags which the girls used to clean the machines after oiling them, blazed into flame. The oil-soaked rags were the first to catch fire, setting alight the piles of cuttings and feeding the flames from one machine to the next. The grease-covered machines themselves began to blaze together with the piles of material on them. The fire grew in volume by the minute. It spread like a stream overflowing its banks. The waves of living flame licked at the skirts of the fleeing, screaming, trapped girls.

Barely had they escaped through the corridor of flame between the rows of machines when they were blocked by a wall of smoke which rose up from the large stacks of finished blouses. With the smoke came a suffocating odor. The smoke arose to the ceiling, where it hung like a cloud. They began to suffocate, gagging and choking. Her eyes blinded and her throat gasping, Sarah dragged Mary along. The door, when they reached it, was blocked with a mass of bodies. Hair loosed, clothing torn, the mob pulled and tore at each other in panicked attempts to get to the door. From the packed mass of bodies came a high-pitched keening, a hysterical yammering.

Those nearest the door were jammed against it, beating at it with their fists, tearing at it with their fingers, clawing at it with their nails. Some, in an ecstasy of terror, beat against it with their heads. The door did not budge.

The press around the door grew thicker. Sarah and Mary, midway in the mob, were held immovable and helpless in the tightly pressed crush of girls' bodies.

Some of the cooler heads among them tried to shout out advice to those nearest the door. Their shouts were lost in the hysterical shrieks of the terrified girls. Someone, more resourceful, managed to pass the metal head of a sewing machine over the struggling mob to the girls at the door. One of them began to beat the door frantically with the heavy metal head. The door did not yield.

The press of bodies was now an immovable mass. Sarah and Mary saw themselves hopelessly hemmed in. Sarah kept her senses. Unless they got out of the packed crowd around the door they were lost. She could see the tongues of flame coming closer and closer. With an energy born of desperation she grabbed Mary by the arm and began to drag her after her. With heads, shoulders, feet, and arms they managed to force their way through the mass of bodies and away from the door. Biting, scratching, tearing and clawing at arms, bodies, and legs, Sarah, half crawling, pulled Mary along after her, until they reached the outer edge of the crush.

Desperately Sarah looked around. Half of the floor was in flames, and the flames were coming toward them. The space near the windows which overlooked Washington Place was still untouched. In front of the windows frantic girls were weaving, clutching at the window sills, desperately trying to find some way of escape.

Near one of the windows the flames were coming closer. Here only a few girls were gathered. If there was any escape it would have to be through this window, the thought flashed through Sarah's mind. They would have to get through it before the flames reached it. She began to drag Mary toward the window. Mary showed no resistance. She was only half conscious. She let the other do what she willed.

The window was nailed down. It resisted all Sarah's efforts to open it. There was a small, jagged break in the pane, stained with blood about the edges; others had tried to shatter the glass. Sarah banged her clenched fist against the glass again and again and made the opening larger.

When the opening was big enough she put her head through. On the street below she could see crowds of people. She could see firemen holding safety nets to catch the girls who dropped from the openings in other windows. From the crowd came frantic shouts. The wails of the girls answered them. The firemen made unavailing attempts to raise their too-short ladders to the upper floors. One girl after another dropped from the windows. Sarah looked to see if there was a ledge below the window which she might be able to reach with her toes. Outside the eighth floor window there was a small iron balcony. It might be possible to reach that, and from there to the balcony outside the seventh floor window, and so on down to safety.

She turned to Mary. "Quick, crawl through to the window ledge!"

"I'm afraid. . . ."

"Quick! Come on! Here, through the broken glass."

"I can't! I can't! What will I hold on to?"

"I'll hold your arms. Try to get your toes on the iron balcony down there. Look, the other girls are doing it."

"You go first, Sarah."

"No, I'm stronger than you. I'll be able to hold on to you. You're too weak to hold on to me. I'll come after you. Go ahead!"

The flames came closer. Urged on by Sarah and driven by the terrifying spectacle of the approaching tongues of flame, Mary scrambled onto the sill, and, with her back to the street, managed to get her legs through the hole in the window, holding on frantically to Sarah's shoulders. She gashed her knee on the jagged edges of the glass but never felt the pain. Holding tightly to Sarah, she groped for some projecting ledge to support her. Except for the balconies outside the line of windows below her, the wall fell sheer. But the balcony was too far down; she couldn't reach it. Sarah, holding Mary firmly by the arms, reached out of the window as far as she dared, trying to lower her as close as possible to the balcony. It was still too far to be reached.

Yells came up to Mary's ears from the street, but she could not understand what they were shouting. Only one thought possessed her, how to get a toehold on the iron balcony below. She still gripped Sarah's arms in an iron clutch. Sarah managed to shift her hold so as to grab Mary by both hands, thus lowering her body farther down. Mary strained to reach the balcony; still it was no use. Sarah strained even farther out of the window; she was now halfway out of the jagged opening. The sharp edges of the broken glass cut into her arms and chest. As Mary strained with her feet to find a hold, the jagged edges cut deeper and deeper into Sarah's flesh. She felt the raw edges going into her, but she felt no pain. There was only the one overwhelming urge—to lower Mary closer to the balcony. She strained farther out. Sud-

148

denly she felt a fierce wave of heat licking at her legs. The anguish was so intense, the instinct for self-preservation so compelling, that all thoughts of Mary disappeared from her mind. She couldn't withdraw her body into the room to face the enemy that was attacking her. But she knew what the enemy was. The flames were licking at her stockings. In another moment, her dress would be on fire.

"Mama!" she screamed hysterically. Her body went farther out through the window. The broken edges of the jagged glass tore at her flesh.

With the tips of her toes Mary could feel the balcony under her feet. The faint hint of safety only served to heighten her terror. Through the mist of consciousness left to her Sarah saw that Mary could now find a footing. "Just a little more. Just a little more," she thought. She could feel herself moving farther forward. She could feel the flames licking up from her shoes, climbing her legs. Then she could feel nothing. If only she could lean out a little more, Mary would reach the balcony. She dare not let go of Mary's hands. She was no longer herself. She no longer existed. She had become a part of Mary. She was only an instrument to help her reach the balcony. . . . Now she could reach it. Sarah threw the upper half of her body violently forward. Mary felt below her feet the firm surface of the balcony. Her hands, suddenly released, clutched at the bare sides of the building. Above her, out of the shattered window, a flaming body fell, like a living torch, down to the street below.

Mary knew that flaming torch. She opened her mouth to shriek Sarah's name. In her pain and terror no sound came from her lips. Now the single thought of escape obsessed her. From the window outside of which she stood, a wave of blasting heat came to her from the roaring flames inside.

She threw a terrified glance to the street below. It was so far away that it seemed to her that it must be a distant, unattainable world. The area immediately below her was an empty expanse. The crowds had been herded away by lines of police; there were only the firemen and fire-fighting apparatus. She could see safety nets held out spread by groups of firemen. She could see bodies falling from the walls of the building with hair and clothing aflame. She could hear voices calling to her; she did not know what they were shouting. She looked around her at the other windows of the building. She could see girls crawling through the windows on hands and knees, trying frantically to hold on to the bare walls. Others seemed to be hanging in mid-air, their falling bodies caught by projecting cornices.

The second that she remained crouched on the balcony seemed like an eternity. Angry flames were shooting out through the window, licking at her. She was alone now; there was no Sarah holding on to her hands. Her consciousness and resourcefulness began to function; she would have to depend on her own initiative now. Driven more by fear of the flames that licked at her from the window than by any considered design, she held on to the iron rail of the balcony and let her body down. Her feet swung in the air; she hadn't looked first to see whether she could reach the landing below. She was afraid to let go of the rail. Her feet sought for a foothold; they found none; the wall was smooth and unbroken. Again and again her toes sought out a niche in the wall, but they found only a sheer surface. Her hands were getting weak, she would have to let go the iron rail; it was hot from the flames which were shooting farther and farther through the window. The palms of her hands burned. She could feel her fingers relaxing. She would let herself go, like the others, to fall into the safety net—or to crash onto the sidewalk.

She couldn't summon up the courage to let go. But she knew if she didn't let go herself, her fingers would slip from the rail and she would fall onto the sidewalk. She must jump. She must try to jump to the nets spread below. Her lips kept murmuring "Jesus, Christ, Jesus, Mary." She closed her eyes for a second. She saw before her the carved wooden figure of Jesus to which she prayed in the Italian church. She knelt before it and prayed her familiar prayer. "Sweet Jesus, save me." As her lips murmured the words her fingers let go their clutch on the iron balcony rail and her body fell.

She did not fall to the ground. Her dress caught on the iron bar of a sign extending outside the third floor window. In the second that she remained suspended, strong arms reached out of the window and pulled her in.

For three weeks Mary was kept at the hospital. By the end of that time her gashed knee had healed. Also her shattered nerves.

More than one hundred and fifty girls had lost their lives in the fire. They were buried at mass funerals; the Jewish girls in Jewish cemeteries, the Christian girls in Christian cemeteries. The survivors soon began to search for work in other factories. The wave of excitement and anger that swept through the city and all through the country didn't last very long. A commission was appointed to investigate fire hazards in the state's garment factories. Some bills were introduced into the Assembly. There were heated debates; some measures were adopted, others were defeated. When it was all over, everything in the needle industries remained the same.

The McCarthy family had become accustomed to Mary's contributions to the household; now they found it impossible to manage on the reduced scale. Patrick McCarthy renewed his old, endless arguments. Although most of the victims were Jewish girls, only a few Gentile girls having been killed, McCarthy blamed the fire and everything about it on the Jews. He swore he would not allow Mary to go back to work, but he soon began to drown his troubles in drink—with the help of the rent money to which Mary had so substantially contributed in the weeks past. After she had been out of the hospital for about two weeks, the McCarthy larder was so empty that Mary had to go out looking for a job.

She found work in a factory whose owner assured her it was fireproof. McCarthy made a show of protesting, but, like the rest of the family, he knew well enough what Mary's earnings meant. Since she had been working he had been able to go more often to the rent money in the bowl in the cupboard with less pangs of conscience.

"Fire or no fire," Grandma McCarthy said, "the world has to go on about its business. Coal miners go back to the pit after a mine disaster."

They all had to agree with her.

One vivid vision remained in Mary's memory: Sarah's terrified eyes staring from below her flaming hair.

CHAPTER FOURTEEN

EACH YEAR, on Thanksgiving Day, the Young Men's Lenchiz Fraternal Association gave its annual ball. It was a long-standing custom—it had already become a tradition—for all the Lenchiz townsfolk in New York, whatever their political complexion or economic station, to put in an appearance for the occasion. The ball was the yearly meeting place for all the *landsleit*. It gave them a chance to renew interrupted friendships and tell each other of the things that had happened to them in the year gone by. They would talk of the old country and of the letters that came from there. They would talk of the years—black years, may they never come again—they had spent together in Uncle Silberberg's sweatshop on the Bowery, where they had been oppressed like the Jews of old under Pharoah in Egypt. They talked of their societies, the cemetery, the sick benefit fund, the relief association for the luckless ones still left in Lenchiz, and of helping to bring over some of their relatives to America's blessed shores.

The older people brought their children to the ball, proudly showing off the kind of offspring they were bringing up in the free new world. It was at the annual ball that the children of old friends and neighbors got acquainted with each other. Often for the first time they would meet their kinsfolk, aunts, uncles, nephews and nieces.

Harry Greenstock was always sure to show up at the yearly event with his family. It was the only time in the year when his asthmatic wife summoned enough energy to dress up in her best. New dresses and shoes and stockings would be bought for the children, and Harry, in a carefully pressed blue suit with his diamond lodge pin sparkling in his lapel and his shoes so highly polished that they glistened from afar, appeared in all his glory before his old townsfolk and relatives at the ball.

This year Mrs. Greenstock was too ill to go to the annual event, and Harry felt it would be unfitting to go without her. Instead, Rachel was to represent the family, escorted by Irving Davidowsky. It was the first time she'd been to the ball without her parents, and for a girl to appear at the Lenchiz annual ball with an escort was tantamount to announcing an engagement. At least so it seemed to the Lenchiz townsfolk.

Rachel was dressed up to the limit of the Greenstock family's resources. Mrs. Kranz sat up half the night sewing Rachel's ball dress according to the elegant style of her beloved Austria. The dress was made of an odd length of sky blue marquisette which they had bought on a First Avenue pushcart. It swept all the way to her toes, billowing with pleats and folds and silk ribbons. The sleeves were puffed, and the Greek neckline effectively set off Rachel's proud young head, her graceful throat, and the dark tone of her complexion.

Poor Mrs. Greenstock had to stand helplessly by as Mrs. Kranz plaited Rachel's long, thick hair into two heavy braids, which she wound in classic style over the girl's head. Her own long golden earrings dangled on Rachel's ears. She pinned a brooch on her bosom and hung an amber necklace around her throat.

But Mrs. Greenstock had asserted herself about Rachel's using powder. She refused to be convinced by Mrs. Kranz that a little powder would do no harm, but would, on the contrary, help to bring out the natural tone of the girl's complexion. From her sickbed Mrs. Greenstock insisted: "She don't need it; she don't need it. My Rachel, thank God, is beautiful without powder."

Mary, too, helped in getting Rachel ready. Mrs. McCarthy had an old mother-of-pearl fan, a cherished family heirloom, which Mary borrowed, because it went so well with Rachel's dress. Her father had bought her a pair of patent leather shoes.

When the business of dressing her up was finished, they all stood around her admiringly. Mrs. Greenstock trembled with fear lest someone cast an evil eye at her daughter. She remembered what had happened the first time Harry had taken her to a ball, when her own mother had worried about an evil eye. As her mother had done then, she called Rachel over and tied a little wad of bread and salt into a knot in the hem of her stocking. Rachel protested, but everyone seemed to feel that there was no harm in taking advantage of a sure charm against an evil eye. Even little

Bertha, who had been allowed to stay up late for the grand occasion, said: "Wear it, Rachel. It's good for you."

There was a ring at the doorbell. Irving came in, resplendent in his first tuxedo—the first tuxedo seen on 48th Street, outside of the "professional" evening clothes of the musicians and actors of Mrs. Kranz's apartment hotel. His patent leather shoes shone brightly. There was a flower in his lapel. He carried a bouquet of roses tied with a white ribbon and wrapped in green paper.

"Are you ready, Rachel?" he asked impatiently. "The cab is waiting outside."

Mrs. Kranz's deft hands pinned the bouquet of roses on Rachel's dress. Rachel, looking like a bride about to be led to the canopy, gave her mother a quick kiss.

"Good night, Mama."

Mrs. Greenstock pressed Rachel's head for a long time to her breast. She closed her eyes and sighed heavily. Her heart was filled with a single prayer, and her lips murmured: "May I live long enough to see you a bride!"

"You'll spoil my hair, Mama!" Rachel protested, and tried to pull away from her mother's embrace.

"Hurry up. The cab is waiting! Come along," Irving pleaded.

The women took another quick inventory of Rachel's appearance. There was a last straightening of a fold of the dress, a final smoothing of her hair, then the putting of a white silk scarf over her head so as to keep her hairdress in place. Irving held up her new coat with the fur collar and helped her into it.

"Bring her home early," said Harry with fatherly pride. He slapped Irving on the shoulder.

"All right, Mr. Greenstock." Irving led Rachel out of the room. "Good night, Mary! Good night, Mrs. Kranz! Good night, Mrs. Greenstock!"

"Have a good time, Rachel."

It was no secret on the block that young Davidowsky was taking his girl to the fraternal society's ball. Housewives were clustered on the steps of the tenement houses, heads were poked through windows of flats, children gathered around the cab waiting outside the Greenstock door.

As the cab started, Irving took Rachel's hand. "Gee, you look beautiful, Rachel," he said admiringly.

"Honest?"

154

"Sure! Everyone'll be jealous of me."

Rachel threw him a satisfied smile.

"You want to know something, Rachel? I'm in business for myself."

"You never told me!"

"I wanted to keep it secret for a while. I found a partner to put up the money. I'm supposed to run the shop. But he's too dead; he doesn't let me do the things I want to. Believe me, if I could only be my own boss I'd know what to do!"

"Oh, Irving, you're too young to run your own business."

"Too young? Just give me the chance and I'll show you that in a couple of years I'll have one of the most progressive factories in New York, way ahead of Granowsky and Granick and all those other big shots. I can do everything they can do—and beat them at their own game. I know the dress business from the ground up. I know what the department stores are looking for, and I know what the buyers want. The latest styles and the cheapest prices, that's what counts. I know how to get the styles before they're on the market. Just keep an eye on the department stores' first showings; then all you have to do is copy them. Just let me get started and you'll see what I can do. The only thing somebody with ambition needs is a start. Just let me get started."

Rachel was overwhelmed.

"Gee, Irving! It certainly sounds as though you've got a great future ahead of you."

"You bet!" Irving was well pleased with himself and the impression he was making. "Say, Rachel, I hear you went to see your uncle in Flatbush? You never told me."

"He asked about you. I think he'd even be ready to help you."

"Why didn't you tell me? Your uncle has a lot of influence. A word from him in the right places and I'm a made man. Do me a favor? Write and tell him that I want to see him and make him a proposition."

"Why don't you write him yourself?"

"I will. I'll say you told me he was willing to see me."

At the ball Rachel was a sensation. When the women learned that her escort was Moshe Wolf's son, opinion was sharply divided.

"Such a beauty has to go around with a grocer's boy? She's like a queen!"

"Moshe Wolf's son is a first-class businessman. Only eighteen years old, and he's got his own business."

"Who cares about a business! With a figure and a face like hers she could get a doctor!"

"The boy's good to his mother. He brings in more than half the family's living. You know how it is with the Davidowskys. Moshe Wolf and that helpless cripple..."

"All right, so he's good to his mother. When a boy's good to his mother, he's no good to his wife...."

They buzzed like bees.

The young blades all gathered around, crowding each other aside and begging her for every dance. They were plainly jealous of Irving. "You're a lucky guy, Irving," they said, pounding him on the shoulder. "Can I dance with your girl?' '

"Sure, sure, go right ahead," Irving answered generously. What he was thinking about was the letter he would write to Uncle Silberberg.

Twice a week Uncle Silberberg went downtown to his office in the building on Broadway that had once housed one of his garment factories. It was generally believed that he went down to attend to his "charities"; the truth was that Uncle's "charities" were cold, hard business affairs. When the old man had been talked into liquidating his garment factories, retiring from the "East Side" business and investing his capital in the banking business in which his son held a partnership, he had made it a condition that he be allowed to carry on the affairs of his several tenement houses, although these, too, now belonged to the banking enterprise.

In the outer room of the office "Uncle's gang," as the old-country townsfolk called the rent collectors of Silberberg's tenements, were already gathered. Most of them were orthodox, bearded Jews; even the unorthodox wore beards carefully trimmed so as to avoid the appearance of being clean-shaven—Uncle Silberberg was a stickler for orthodoxy, and a beard was to him the symbol of true piety. He was himself clean-shaven, but woe to any of his retainers who failed to wear the traditional beard. For any such rebel there was no hope for a future with Uncle Silberberg as rent collector or manager of one of his houses.

Besides the rent reports they were waiting to turn over, there were a thousand and one complaints to convey from the tenants. A roof was leaking; a new faucet was needed in a kitchen sink; water pipes had burst; the rats were getting so bold that they didn't fear to show themselves in the daytime, scurrying all over the place, even in the beds. Besides, each of the collectors had a request of his own; for a raise, or a loan, or some other financial favor. In anticipation of Silberberg's arrival they busied themselves smoothing their beards, adjusting their hats, clearing their throats. They eyed each other with jealous and suspicious glances.

At last Silberberg came in with his heavy, bearish tread, swaying his broad hips. He walked through the outer office without seeming to give them a glance. But he saw them for all that. In the old days the workers in the shop used to say of him that he had his eyes in the seat of his pants; he would walk through a long line of operators in the shop, pretending to notice nothing, buried in his own thoughts, but just the same he would be taking in everything there was to be seen.

He went into his office and lowered his enormous body onto his chair; it seemed almost to collapse under his weight. He rested his head on his hands and stared angrily about him. There was no cause for it; it was part of his strategy to put on a sullen expression for these kinsfolk of his; it might frighten them out of making any requests they had in mind.

"You look wonderful today, Uncle Silberberg, like a young man," Shmulevitch smirked; he was the first to go into the inner office.

"Say what you've got to say, Shmulevitch," Silberberg growled. "But hurry up."

"The stairways in number 318 are rotting away. There's liable to be an accident...."

"Let the insurance company worry. It isn't my business."

"And the rats, Uncle; the rats.... It's a real plague...."

"What's the matter with the rats? They won't eat the tenants up."

Uncle Silberberg knew these retainers of his from the time they'd been operators in his sweatshops. He knew that whenever they had some particular request to make, they would never come

157

straight to the point; they'd have to arrive at it by a series of detours. He knew, too, that his collectors didn't care one way or another about the rotten steps or the plague of rats; these were only the introductory steps to the important issue.

"All right, Shmulevitch. What's on your mind?" he said. "What kind of business is it this time?"

"How can anyone keep anything from you, Uncle Silberberg? You can read a person's mind. Like the great King Solomon; one look at a person and he already knew what he was thinking. . . ."

"Never mind King Solomon. Come to the point! How much!"

"It's impossible to hide anything from you, Uncle Silberberg. . . . It's a question of buying a house—not a large house—twelve tenants. . . ."

"With rats or without rats?"

"Uncle, may you live to be a hundred and twenty. You see everything. A man is only a man after all . . . he would like to make something of himself. . . . And with two daughters to marry off. . . . And I happen to have five hundred dollars saved in the bank. . . . And my daughters have a couple of hundred dollars. If I could put my hands on another thousand cash on a second mortgage . . ."

"I've got nothing against it if a relative of mine wants to get to be a landlord and comes to me for some help. I have nothing against it at all. If I decide to help you, then I'll help you. If I decide against it, I won't help you. But I don't like it, Shmulevitch, when you start to tell me about rotten steps and about rats. . . . If it's a thousand dollars you want for a second mortgage, say so! But don't tell me about rotten steps and rats. I don't like it. . . ."

"Yes, Uncle . . . I only thought . . . The tenants complain. . . ."

"The tenants complain! My tenants don't complain! If they don't like it, let them move. Let them move right away! And what's this on this rent statement? The tenant in number eight didn't pay on the first!"

"She paid part. Her husband's in the hospital for the past two months. . . ."

"I don't want to know about it, Shmulevitch. That's got nothing to do with me. If I want to give charity, that's my business. With me, tenants aren't charity."

"Yes, Uncle."

"If they don't pay on the first, out on the sidewalk, furniture and all! I don't want to know anything about it."

"Yes, Uncle."

"Tell me, Shmulevitch, how will you carry on your own business when you're a landlord? Will you take a part payment on the rent? Will you bother with rotten steps and rats?"

"Excuse me, Uncle. I only thought . . ."

"I don't need you to think."

"Yes, Uncle."

"All right, now you can go."

When Shmulevitch reached the door Uncle Silberberg called after him: "Bring the papers for the second mortgage to me at the bank."

"Yes, Uncle. Thank you, Uncle. Thank you."

"Wait a minute. Do you know Davidowsky's boy?"

"Sure I know him."

"I hear he's a good businessman."

"A businessman? The boy practically supports the whole family. You know Moshe Wolf and his craziness. He gives credit to anybody who asks him. And when it gets to the first of the month he can't pay the rent. If it wasn't for Irving . . ."

"Tell me, Shmulevitch. Is the boy engaged to Greenstock's daughter Rachel?"

"Engaged? I don't know. But they go around together. Everybody takes it they're engaged. Only lately he took her to the Lenchiz annual ball."

"I want to see the boy. Rachel told me about him. I told her I would see him. She never got in touch with me, but I got a letter from the boy. Can you bring him to me here at the office?"

"Why not? A fine boy. One in the world! What a head he has."

"I want to talk to him. I want to see if I can do anything for him. I like Rachel, and she likes him. When you come next time, bring him with you. I want to see him."

"Yes, Uncle."

Irving Davidowsky sat at the desk in Uncle Silberberg's office. "How old are you?" he asked, looking him over appraisingly.

"Eighteen."

"And at eighteen you want to go into business for yourself?"

159

"There's no time to waste, Mr. Silberberg. You've got to start early. That's the way you did, isn't it? You started early."

Silberberg thought of his own youth, when he had run away from home, stolen across the Prussian border, hidden in freight trains, and then slaved on a cattle boat.... Castle Garden.... Washing dishes in a Bowery restaurant.... His hard youth flashed through his mind. For this boy it was easier. He was brought up in America; he knew the language. The boy was as full of energy as he had been in his youth. He might have been the boy now before him, and the boy could have been he.... "If this boy had been brought up in the old country," Uncle Silberberg thought to himself, "he'd do what I did. He'd get to America on a cattle boat. I like this boy." He examined Irving's face. The energetic mouth and the determined lips could have been his own. Uncle Silberberg saw his own youth repeated in the boy. He felt a wave of sympathy flooding him.

"And what do you want to do?"

"I'm doing it already. I've started my own business. I've opened a small dress factory on Twenty-third Street. With about ten machines. I've got a fine designer. She's got good taste. We go to look at Altman's and Wanamaker's windows whenever they're showing new styles. We copy them and we reproduce them. We can do them for half the price and make plenty."

"Very smart. But don't you know it's against the law to copy someone else's designs?"

"I'm not selling to their customers. I'm not competing with them. I'm selling on Second Avenue and on Grand Street. Why shouldn't the East Side have the same dresses as Fifth Avenue? Naturally we don't use the same materials—and we make some changes in the design—so they can't do anything to us."

"How much are you producing?"

"Not enough. What I need is cash. And then there's my partner."

"What about your partner?"

"I took him because he had the plant. I couldn't do anything else. But I can't stay with him. I'd like to buy him out."

"Why?"

"I want to be my own boss. I don't want anybody to tell me what to do. I want to get big."

"How big?"

"Well, in the beginning I'd be satisfied with another ten machines with electric motors. And I'd want to get a cutter, and a real designer, not a copier. I'd like to develop my own styles for my own trade."

"What kind of styles?"

"Oh, I have ideas. I have ideas about making the style more important than the material. Our customers can't afford the expensive materials; the style has to make up for it. Then I figure on getting an exclusive lot of materials. I want to contract for all the output of some mill, in different colors and designs. Then I'll have something to sell that the other fellow hasn't got."

"That's a pretty ambitious way to begin, young man."

"If others can do it, why can't I? I'm as smart and smarter than the rest of them. If they can do it, so can I."

Uncle Silberberg closed his eyes and let young Irving's confident voice roll on. It seemed to him that he was hearing his own voice, that it was he himself who was talking.

"How much cash do you think you're going to need?"

"I think I'll be able to do it with about five thousand."

Shmulevitch, who had been in the office during the interview, thought he would faint when he heard the figure, but Uncle Silberberg seemed to be pleased.

"What do you need the cash for?"

"To buy out my partner."

"And what about material, and machines? Where'll you get them from?"

"First let me be my own boss, and then I'll know what to do."

Uncle Silberberg glowed. "What kind of guarantee can you put up? How about collateral for the money?"

"Nothing but my name—and my business."

"And do you think an eighteen-year-old boy can do all this?"

"What's the matter with eighteen? If you want to figure it right, according to my experience I'm practically thirty. I've been earning my living since I'm nine. I've had plenty of time to get experience."

"I see. When do you need the money?"

"Right away."

"All right. Give me the name of your bank. I'll see what I can do."

When all the details of the loan had been arranged, instead of telling Rachel, Irving left that for another time. He went looking for Mary; she, he decided, could be of more help to him than Rachel in getting the factory going. Deep inside him there were other reasons, too. He waited to meet her as she came home from work.

"Are you still working at a machine?" he asked her when she came along.

"What else should I be doing? Of course."

"Well, you won't be there long. I need you. I'm my own boss now. I'm opening my own shop. I want you to come to work for me. You don't want to be an operator all your life. Some fine day there'll be another fire, the same as the Triangle. I want you to quit. You're going to be a saleslady for me."

"Me, a saleslady?" Irving's confidence left her breathless.

"Sure. Why not? You're a smart girl. You've got a good figure and a pretty face. You've got good taste, too; you know how to wear clothes. There's a few things you'll have to learn. You'll have to dress smarter, and in the latest style. You'll learn quick, Mary; you've got ability. You'll see, Mary, when you put on stylish clothes you won't recognize yourself."

"Cut out the joking, Irving. You're getting me dizzy."

"I'm not joking; I'm serious. You start tomorrow morning. I've bought out my partner. I've got the money. Just keep your eye on Davidowsky, Mary. In a couple of years I'll be one of the big shots in the industry—and you'll be my chief saleslady."

"Do you really mean it?"

"Sure I mean it. Leave it all to me. I'll expect you tomorrow at eight o'clock. I need you right away to get the shop running. You're working for Davidowsky starting now. Here, take this." He handed her some bills.

"What's this for?"

"To buy yourself a new dress. Wait, I'll go with you. This is on the firm."

"Rachel will scratch my eyes out."

"Don't worry about Rachel. She'll be working for Davidowsky, too. I'll have all the 48th Street kids working for me. We'll show New York what 48th Street can do."

CHAPTER FIFTEEN

EVERY YEAR, at the first signs of spring, it was Harry Greenstock's custom to put a few of his pigeons into a portable cage and ride away with them to the outskirts of the city. There he would release the pigeons from the cage for a training flight back home after being cooped up for the long winter months. He would usually take Rachel and Bertha with him; little Goldie would be left at home with her ailing mother. Mike Maloney would also go along, and sometimes Choleva.

The trip would usually mean riding the elevated line to South Ferry and then the ferry across to Staten Island. After opening the cages and freeing the pigeons they would go home. By the time they got back to 48th Street, they would find the pigeons perched on top of the cage in the yard.

On this early spring Sunday morning Harry, Rachel and Bertha, and Mike Maloney made up the group.

They came home toward the end of the afternoon. There was a crowd gathered in front of the Greenstock house. Something bad must have happened; Harry could sense it from the awkward silence as he approached, and from the way they moved aside to make a path for him. Heavy sighs came from some of the women as they saw Rachel and Bertha. Rachel rushed into the house, her heart beating wildly. Harry turned pale. Inside his wife was stretched out on the bed, her face covered with the sheet. Little Goldie whimpered on a neighbor's lap. Out in the yard the two dogs barked restlessly.

A hand rested on Harry's shoulders. Maloney's voice said somberly: "It's God's will, Harry. Take it like a man."

Tears gathered in Harry's eyes. His lips quivered.

"The end always comes in the spring for people with asthma. ..." a neighbor's voice said.

"When did it happen?" Harry asked.

"We don't know exactly. The dogs were barking. Everybody wondered what it was—whether somebody was trying to get at the pigeons or something. My husband opened the door and went inside to see if anybody was there. He raised a yell. When I ran over I found her lying on the floor, without a breath coming out of her, and the little one was crawling around and pulling at her skirt and crying. We shouted for help and some of the neighbors came running over. We started to call a doctor, and some of us tried to bring her round by rubbing her forehead. Moshe Wolf felt her pulse and looked at her eyes and said it was too late. Then he closed her eyes, and then we put her on the bed, and covered her."

Moshe Wolf had been standing quietly at the back of the room. Now he came forward.

"There was nothing to do, Harry. She was dead before anybody came in. It was her heart."

Harry was silent; he stood as though stunned. His face was pale, his lips were drawn, and the tears rolled down his cheeks.

"God-fearing Jews have more to do than weep over the dead," Moshe Wolf said quietly. "There are things that have to be done." He went out to arrange for the funeral.

Mrs. Kranz came in and took Goldie and Bertha over to stay with her until after the funeral. Rachel and her father stayed with the dead woman.

In a few days it was all over.

Harry began to realize his loss. As long as Sara was alive the house had been home. It had been home for the children, for himself, even for the pigeons and dogs and the other creatures that Harry kept in his yard. Without Sara the house seemed empty. With her had departed the established warmth, the settled domesticity that made the house a haven for the faithful Polish youth, Choleva, for the bachelor Maloney, and all Harry's other friends who enjoyed fussing around Harry's pigeons. The empty rocking chair made the house strange to all of them—even to the dogs. The animals seemed to avoid being indoors; they preferred to stay in the yard.

With his wife always at home, Harry had grown accustomed to living the free life of a bachelor, like his friend Maloney. Now he was burdened with the responsibility of being both father and mother to his orphaned children. In trying to carry out the task, for the first time in his life he forgot about himself.

For a few weeks after Sara's death, while the shock of her sudden passing still stirred the neighborhood, goodhearted neighbors lent a hand in taking care of the children, or brought in a pot of savory food, or some other small comfort. A Negro maid was hired to come in to clean the house. And then there was always Mrs. Kranz. In spite of all her efforts to avoid neighborhood gossip, the need of the children forced her to accept a mother's responsibilities.

Rachel was grown-up enough to live her own life; if need be, she could be completely independent. Her mother's death speeded up the process by confronting her with some of the realities and hardships of life. She had been taking a course at a vocational school for a civil service job; now she switched over to a course in stenography and bookkeeping with the idea of making herself useful in Irving's business; everybody on the block was talking of the progress young Davidowsky was making. Her preoccupation with her studies helped to lighten her grief over her mother's death.

Goldie, almost three years old, was too young to feel her mother's loss. Infants find comfort more quickly than adults. For them consolation is always at hand—the God-given instinct of suckling, the child's comfort in all its emergencies, and its satisfaction for all its needs. In suckling, the child finds forgetfulness for all its sorrows.

Little Goldie found comfort in assiduously sucking her thumb as she lay in her crib, or played on the floor, or sat on someone's lap. The moment Mrs. Kranz took her in her arms Goldie would put her head against Mrs. Kranz's breast and look up at her with such an imploring, trusting, pleading smile, all the time sucking away at her thumb, that it was impossible to put the child down. But it made no difference who held her; if it was not Mrs. Kranz, she would wheedle love and attention out of the first neighbor who put her head into the Greenstock door to make sure that the children were all right.

The one who took the loss of her mother hardest was the six-year-old Bertha. The child refused to accept the fact of her mother's death. She could not comprehend why her mother was no longer there. At first she kept asking, "When will Mama come back?" There was no way of making her understand what had happened. She kept up her persistent questioning. "Where did Mama go?" And when she was told that her mother had gone up there, to heaven, and that she was now an angel, the child's yearning was only increased. "Why did Mama go to heaven? Why did she become an angel? What is she doing up there? When will she come back?" Nothing could distract her. She would take the candy and toys they offered her, and a moment or two later resume her sobs. Day after day, even in the midst of play and laughter with other children, she would call for her mother. Finally she gave up weeping, but she sighed constantly, and without warning, while they were all seated at the table, or even while she was asleep, her heavy sigh would tear their hearts.

Only Mrs. Kranz could comfort her, only when she was in the house did the child feel security and peace. It was the profound, trusting faith of Bertha more than anything else that compelled Mrs. Kranz to play the role of mother to the Greenstock children.

There is a basic axiom of nature which Harry, like all who have bred and raised household animals, knew well. "Do not take away the mother from her young." When one of his female pigeons failed to return to the cage after flying with the flock, and abandoned its day-old fledglings, Harry himself would play the protector for the helpless chicks. He would warm the tiny, helpless creatures against his own body; he would chew their food to a mash and offer it to them on the tip of his tongue, close to their little beaks just as the mother pigeon had done, until they were old enough to manage for themselves.

Now he had to play the mother to his own children. He awoke early in the morning to prepare breakfast and see that the young ones were washed and dressed for the day. Visiting neighbors would find him with an apron tied around his waist washing the children's things or hanging them out in the yard to dry. "A man can play the sport when his wife's alive to slave for him and his children, but when she dies..." the women would say and shake their heads.

But all his efforts were of no avail; he had to turn to Mrs. Kranz for help, in spite of his worry about the gossip in the neighborhood and in spite of the fact that he felt she had been holding herself aloof from him since Sara's death. There was no one else he could turn to. He couldn't go on neglecting his

166

work; he had to make up for the time he had lost, and he couldn't go on relying on the kindness of neighbors. There was nothing for him to do but to appeal to Mrs. Kranz.

"Why don't you move in with us here? You can see how the children need you," he said to her. They were all in the living room; Mike Maloney was with them.

Mrs. Kranz flushed. "What about the neighborhood? And your people—Shmulevitch, Davidowsky, and the others?"

"What's more important—for the children to have someone to take care of them, or to worry about what the neighbors say? You know how attached the children are to you."

Maloney, who was giving little Goldie a ride on his knee, remarked: "It's a shame that the kids have to suffer because of a lot of gossiping old busybodies. Harry's got to go out to make a living, hasn't he?"

Rachel added her entreaties.

"Please, Clara," she begged. "You used to take care of us even when Mama was alive. I know that poor Mama would rather have you take care of us than some stranger. And I don't know why you should all worry over what people say."

Bertha, who was playing on the floor with her dolls, came over to Mrs. Kranz. As though she understood what was going on, she stood at her knee and silently looked up at her with her solemn eyes. The child's look settled the matter. Mrs. Kranz burst into tears; Rachel followed suit. When the two young ones saw the others weeping, they wept, too.

After a little more discussion it was decided that Mrs. Kranz would stay with the children during the day while Harry was away at work; for the while, nothing was said about her moving in permanently. Maloney promised to help her out by keeping an eye on her "apartment hotel" so that she would have more time to give to the Greenstock brood.

But in spite of their decision, Mrs. Kranz became a permanent part of the Greenstock household. It happened gradually. She stayed overnight once, and then again. In a couple of weeks she moved in permanently and took Sara's place. Nor was it only in the kitchen that she carried out the obligations of her position. There was no specific talk of a legal marriage, but everyone seemed to take that as understood.

Now the good old times began again for Harry Greenstock.

On Saturday afternoons, after his morning's work, he would leave Choleva to dispose of the cans of turpentine and paint and would apply himself to cleaning out the pigeon cage, a chore he found no time for during the week. Saturday was the pigeons' day. The birds would be let out for a flight and for the weekly game of capturing a prize from some other flock. On Saturdays the sky above 48th Street was again filled with the beating of wings, and the street resounded with the shouts of the pigeon lovers of the neighborhood.

In the late afternoons, with the birds back in their cage, Harry would bathe and shave and dress in his best, put on his stiff derby hat—like the one "the big boss" wore—and wait for Maloney. Maloney would also be dressed in style. Mrs. Kranz stayed at home to attend to the household affairs, as Sara had done before her, when the two men went off.

Their first stop was the Italian shoe-shining booth at the corner of the street. Stepping down from the chairs with their brightly polished shoes sparkling in the sun, they would go over to Kelly's saloon, have a quick one, throw a silver coin on the bar and toss a word to Kelly—"How's business? Watch your step, Kelly." —and stroll down First Avenue to 42nd Street. From there they walked—or if it was getting late, they would catch the crosstown trolley—to Times Square. Planting themselves in front of the drugstore at the corner, or farther up in front of the Hotel Astor, they would "watch the crowd."

Watching the crowd followed a strict ritual. They would put a match to their big cigars and eye the people passing in an unending stream. Most of the time they were silent, but when an elaborately dressed woman would pass, with an enormous ostrich feather waving from the hat over her thick coils of hair, one would wink at the other. A young, eager-eyed pair might pass by, obviously hicks from out of town, and Harry would say: "They're from Missouri." "Sure," Maloney would answer, "they're from Missouri; they've come to have a good time."

After about an hour Harry would say: "Well, I guess it's time to be going home." "Yes, it's time to be going home," Maloney would agree, and they would wink at each other and take the trolley across to First Avenue, or walk across, if there was time. Again they would stop at Kelly's saloon for a drink, throw a half dollar on the counter and call out to Kelly: "Big crowd tonight, Kelly; watch your step, Kelly." Then they would call for Mrs. Kranz to take her to dinner at a restaurant and on to a show.

As long as Harry wore the crêpe mourning band on his coat-sleeve he avoided going to Neufeld's cellar restaurant, where a gypsy band played and a couple of professional dancers danced the Hungarian czardas; he had taken her there while Sara was alive; now it wouldn't be fitting. Instead he took her to the small Italian restaurant under the Second Avenue El. There, now and then, one could meet some of the big shots of the party; often Judge Greenberg, the big boss himself, would be there. Napoli, as they all called the fat, short, perspiring proprietor, always smelling of olive oil, was one of the boys, and kept an eye on the Italian voters in the neighborhood.

Mike Maloney was always part of the Saturday evening outing. Mike had no life of his own; he lived Harry's life.

After eating the three would go to a vaudeville show; they all preferred it to the movies; they didn't find much pleasure in those silent shadows moving about on the screen. Sometimes they'd even go down on the El to 14th Street. Or Harry would take them to a Jewish show on Grand Street or the Bowery. When Mrs. Kranz got passes for a Broadway show from one of her boarders, they would go out in style.

On their return from the Saturday afternoon trip to Times Square, Harry and Mike would find Mrs. Kranz waiting for them. Rachel would already have gone óff with Irving. Bertha and little Goldie would already have eaten their suppers and would be eagerly waiting for the lollipops which Harry always brought for them. Choleva, Harry's assistant, stayed at the Greenstock home every Saturday night to keep an eye on the pigeons; Harry wouldn't allow them to be left alone for a minute. Out of his devotion to the pigeons, which he loved as much as Harry did, Choleva was glad to give his Saturday nights to them. And as long as he was keeping an eye on the birds, he might as well watch out for Harry's kids, whom he would entertain by playing his harmonica. Mrs. Kranz thus had the opportunity of going out with "the boys."

Everything would have gone along fine if it hadn't been for the wrath of the gods, who apparently chose to descend from

169

their Olympian heights in order to shatter the domestic peace of two lonely people in a humble home on 48th Street in Manhattan. The block soon became a caldron in which boiled and bubbled a seething witch's brew compounded of the devilish poisons of jealousy and spite. Jews and Gentiles alike stopped greeting Harry and Mrs. Kranz. They pretended not to recognize them when they saw them about. For Harry it wasn't so bad; they were all a little afraid of him and needed his favors with Tammany for protection now and then. Most of their spite was let loose on Mrs. Kranz.

"It isn't his fault. What can a man do when he's left alone with three children? It's all her fault. She's the one who figured it out."

"There she goes! She was just waiting for his poor wife to die to step into her shoes!"

"Sneaks into his house without any shame in broad daylight," said Tony the bricklayer's wife to Deborah Davidowsky at the entrance to the grocery store. "Right in front of people's noses. You don't find that among the Catholics."

"Not among the Jews either," said Deborah tartly. "You don't call him a Jew. He's a Cossack—and she's a gypsy."

Chaia Hindel, Shmulevitch's wife, called across from the poultry store: "Poor Sara's body wasn't cold in the grave before she crawled into her bed."

Shmulevitch, who had his poultry place across from Moshe Wolf's store, was known on the block by the nickname of "Mr. Skullcap." He was never seen bareheaded. He always wore the traditional skullcap of the pious Jew on his head. He had a variety of them to suit his various functions; and of these he had many. First there was his kosher chicken business. He did his own slaughtering in a room back of the store where a *shochet* slit the throats of the chickens over a blood-filled bucket. Old women sat around plucking the slaughtered fowl. Shmulevitch, wearing a tall skullcap, stayed inside the store selling the fowl to butchers and restaurant keepers; only seldom to retail customers. Once in a while he might sell to a private customer, but that would only be by way of a distinct favor. The store was crowded with crates of live birds delivered by trucks during the night.

In the dirty window of the store stood an enormous sign written in crude English and Hebrew characters—the word "kosher" standing out huge and bold—and carrying at the bottom a rabbinical signature attesting to the fact that the fowl were kosher according to the strictest Jewish law and that they were slaughtered under the supervision of rabbis who had carefully inspected the knives used in the slaughtering, etc. etc. Similar signs were pasted to the walls of the store.

What Shmulevitch needed as he needed his very life was a regular synagogue in the neighborhood. Without his own synagogue he had to go for approval of the ritual cleanliness of his chickens to a rabbi somewhere downtown, and that caused him no end of trouble. The rabbi would demand that Shmulevitch bring down his slaughtering tools for inspection, or he would suddenly put in an appearance at the store, especially in the summer, when the stock had to be disposed of quickly, and examine the manner of slaughtering the fowl. On one occasion he had even declared an enormous stock of poultry unclean and caused Shmulevitch a substantial loss. With his own synagogue Shmulevitch would be able to employ his own rabbi; thus his own man would pass on the ritual cleanliness of his merchandise. The year round, the pious Jews on the block held services in a private house. For the High Holidays—Rosh Hashanah and Yom Kippur—Shmulevitch rented a dance hall on First Avenue, hired a cantor from downtown, installed a Holy Scroll and the other necessary ritual objects, and sold tickets to the Jews of the entire neighborhood.

Though he was not particularly observant in religious affairs, Harry Greenstock bought a ticket every year. Harry's relationship to his God was a simple and natural one. If he had been put to the test, he would have shown his loyalty to the God of his fathers just as staunchly as his own father and their fathers. He would without hesitation have sacrificed his life rather than change his faith. But with that remote test his responsibilities to the religion of his forebears ended. Don't bother me and I won't bother you, was his attitude.

Such an attitude sufficed for ordinary times; there were times of crisis, however. There were times when one had to give an accounting of one's self, and put in an appearance in the office of the Jewish God's "district attorney." Such occasions arose when a man found himself in unusual circumstances or when he needed the Jewish God. As for example when someone died in the family—or on the High Holidays.

171

The High Holidays, and especially Yom Kippur, were critical days in Harry's life. On those days he had the feeling that "the big boss" might have an eye on him; it would be best to show up. Therefore the safest thing would be to buy a ticket to Shmulevitch's synagogue. He would put in a couple of appearances at the dance hall and wander about with the other once-a-year congregants. He would pop his head inside and throw a glance at the white prayer shawls and the lighted candelabras. Some attendant would put a prayer book into his hand, or hand him a prayer shawl. Once he even put the *tallith* on for a while and wore it while he went outside and paraded for a few minutes before the entrance.

But this year Harry did not realize that the High Holidays had come around until he saw that the Jewish stores on the block were closed and the Jewish families were walking sedately into the dance hall. Shmulevitch had neglected to bring him his tickets.

Harry bit his lips. He was too proud to show his humiliation. At last, however, he could not help showing his resentment. On the day before Yom Kippur he walked in to see Moshe Wolf and said: "What's the matter? I'm not good enough for you any more?"

Moshe Wolf didn't understand. "What's the matter, Harry?" he asked.

"You know what's the matter all right! Why didn't they sell me a ticket for the services?"

"I have nothing to do with that; you know that very well. Shmulevitch takes care of that."

"Then Shmulevitch did it. You can tell him from me that I know what to do."

When Shmulevitch heard of Harry's anger, he was worried and frightened. He needed Harry's favor whenever he had trouble with the Health Department of the city; they were always making demands that he slaughter his fowl in a regular slaughterhouse, and not at the back of the store. Harry, or Maloney, had taken care of such matters. He saw that he had gone too far, and hurried over to see Harry, the perspiration dripping from under his skullcap over his hairy face. In an appeasing voice he said: "Moshe Wolf tells me you want to come to the Yom Kippur service."

"Sure, sure," said Harry. "What am I? A goy?"

"Of course not," Shmulevitch stammered. "I only thought . . . "

"What did you think? Just because a decent neighbor helps me out with the children, you had to start thinking ... "

"God forbid, Harry," Shmulevitch eagerly broke in. "Believe me, I wasn't thinking of anything like that."

"Well, why didn't you bring me the synagogue tickets? Never mind, I'll go to the synagogue where the Judge goes. The Judge will take me to his own synagogue on Fifth Avenue. I'll show you that I'm just as good a Jew as you."

"Harry, I beg you. Come over to our services. I'll arrange a special prayer for poor Sara. Bring the children. You'll see, I'll fix it with the rabbi. All you'll have to do will be to donate five dollars for the new synagogue."

"I'll give you ten dollars if there's a special prayer for Sara."

"All right ... It's a bargain."

On Yom Kippur, Harry dressed the children in their best clothes and put on his own best suit. Maloney brought him a white flower for his lapel, the kind the big boss wore when he went to the Temple on Fifth Avenue.

CHAPTER SIXTEEN

THERE WAS little peace on 48th Street. It seemed that the whole block was busy figuring out ways to break up the scandalous goings-on in the Greenstock house, where Mrs. Kranz was brazenly taking the place of the poor dead woman who was hardly cold in her grave. Harry still had a mother living in the old country with an older son. His contacts with her were limited to the few dollars he would send her once in a while and an annual Jewish New Year's card, usually a representation of a synagogue pulpit with a venerable, bearded Jew blowing the *shofar,* the traditional ram's horn, or a brilliantly lighted ship sailing the ocean to America.

One evening a few weeks after the High Holidays, Moshe Wolf appeared at Harry's door.

"I want to talk to you, Harry," he said. "It's for nobody else's ears; not even for the children. It's important."

"What is it?" Harry asked.

"I've received a letter from the old country: from your mother. I'll read it to you later. Come over when I close the store."

"What does she say?"

"You'll hear later."

In an hour or so Harry went to the store. Moshe Wolf put on his glasses, took the letter from his pocket, and read it aloud. The last paragraph was addressed to Harry.

"You are my son, whom I carried for nine months under my heart. How can you deliver up your innocent Jewish children to a Gentile mother? Do you think that your dead wife—may the gates of Paradise be opened to her!—will allow you to take her orphaned children away from the Jewish path? She will return and demand an accounting from you. She will clutch you by the throat at night and call you to judgment. You will see her each night while you lie in the arms of your Gentile; she will come

174

in her shrouds and demand of you: 'What have you done to my children?'"

Harry turned white as a sheet, then flushed with rage. Convulsively he banged on the counter with his fists so that the boxes of cigars in the glass case bounced.

"It's for the children! I had no one else to care for them!"

"You mean take care of your pigeons! You know that a decent Jewish girl wouldn't have anything to do with your pigeons. That's why you took her in! She's like you. You're more worried about the pigeons than you are about your children."

"Stop it! I won't listen to you!" Harry shouted.

"I'm not afraid of you. I'm not Shmulevitch. I don't need you to put in a good word for me with Tammany. I'm telling you plain, Harry, send her away."

"And what'll I do with the children? I can't send her away. She's like a mother to them. They love her. I'm not going to turn my children over to a stranger."

"If you really had the children's interests at heart, you'd realize that you have a daughter to marry off."

Harry stared at him. "What's that got to do with it?"

"It has a great deal to do with it. Do you think it will be easy to marry off Rachel when she has a Christian stepmother?"

"You can't scare me. I did the best I could. What I did was for their sake. I'm not afraid of anyone!"

"All right, Harry. Do what you please. There's nothing more for me to say."

It is true that Harry was afraid of nobody; nobody living, that is. Against the living he knew how to defend himself; he had no defense against the dead. He tossed uneasily as he lay in bed beside Mrs. Kranz, his mind a chaos of confused thoughts. The children were used to her; they felt as though she were their real mother. True, maybe they had forgotten their real mother too quickly; but should not Sara be satisfied that the children had found a comforter and protector? Was it for his sake that he had asked Mrs. Kranz to move in with them? It wasn't that he needed her as a woman. He could have as many women as he pleased; there was no lack of them. Was it his fault that Mrs. Kranz was born a Gentile? She hadn't demanded that he change his religion for her; why should he ask her to change her re-

175

ligion for him and the children? Maybe she would do it if he talked to her about it; she was indifferent about such things. But why should he ask her? It wouldn't be right, and it would only mean more trouble. No, he wouldn't ask it of her. He'd ignore what everybody thought. He had done it all for the children's sake, and if God wanted to punish him, then that was God's business. There was nothing he could do about it.

But in spite of all his reasoning, he felt crowding in on him the unsuspected terrors which dwelt in the deepest chambers of his unconscious mind; the fear of desecrating those deep-rooted religious traditions which the long chain of Jewish martyrdom had implanted in his innermost nature. He could not dismiss his mother's warning lightly—nor Moshe Wolf's. All night he brooded over what Moshe Wolf had said—that his carryings on with Mrs. Kranz would injure Rachel. Perhaps he meant that he wouldn't consent to the match between Rachel and Irving. Of course he wouldn't consent, and that would mean that Harry was shaming his own child. And here he was, expecting every day that Irving would walk in to talk over having an official engagement announced. What right had he to destroy his own daughter's chances for happiness? And maybe there was something in what his mother had written—that Sara would find no rest in the grave; that she would come back to demand justice for her orphaned children.

He groaned aloud under the weight which oppressed his conscience.

Mrs. Kranz awoke. "What's the matter, Harry? Do you feel sick?"

"It's nothing, nothing! Maybe I'd better get up."

He put on some clothes and went out into the yard. The day was beginning to dawn. He opened the gate of the pigeon cage and went inside. He looked at the little fledglings, their feathers not yet grown, fluttering their feeble wings and nestling under the warm breast of the mother bird. He took one of them into his hands. It trembled as he held it in his palm. He thought of his little Goldie. A pang tore at his heart and tears rose to his eyes. "Why did you do it, God?" he murmured. "Why did you take away their mother from my children?"

For a few days he went about his work sick in body and spirit. He could neither eat nor sleep. He walked about with his lips tight and his eyes lost. Harry had never been the weakling who refused to fight back; but how could he fight against God? In his heart he hated God for his own helplessness.

"Harry, what's the matter?" Mrs. Kranz kept asking.

"Nothing. It's nothing. I'm having business troubles."

Mrs. Kranz knew it was something deeper. So did Mike Maloney, Harry's shadow, his other self. He knew it was something more than business trouble that had Harry in its grip.

One evening the two sat in the back room of Kelly's saloon, which Kelly used as his private office, but which served also as a meeting place for the Tammany leaders of the district. The walls were covered with photographs—Kelly as a professional baseball player, a reproduction of Abraham Lincoln's bartender's license, portraits of the "big bosses," old prints of fire engines and fire fighters. Kelly knew that when "the boys" sat in the back room they were not to be disturbed.

The two friends sat at the small, oilcloth-covered table, with two glasses of whisky in front of them, while Harry told Maloney of the letter which had come from his mother.

Maloney, like Harry, was indifferent about religion. He had put his God away with his other heirlooms—his mother's photograph, her beads and crucifix, his father's gold chain, and an elk's tooth. He had put God away with the packet of love letters he had had from the only woman he had ever loved. All these mementos of a bygone life he had stored away in a wooden cigar box tied with a white silk ribbon. If anyone had attempted to rifle the box, Maloney would have torn him limb from limb, but he paid little attention to it himself. Once a year, on All Saints Day, he would open it, look at his mother's photograph, and kiss the crucifix. Once a year, on Easter Sunday, he would go to High Mass, dressed up in his best. That was all.

Maloney, too, had a grievance against God. God had been the obstacle between him and the woman he loved. She had been married to a drunken vaudeville actor who had become no better than a Bowery bum. Although he was willing to give her a divorce—for a consideration, which Maloney was willing to pay —the church refused to grant permission. Maloney had done all he could. They had made application to the Vatican, but it had all come to nothing. The years had gone by and the woman had died. Maloney had remained a bachelor.

Though his lawyer had advised them to change their faith,

in spite of his love for her Maloney could not take the step. He would rather have died than abandon the faith of his mother, whose memory he worshiped.

He could understand Harry's dilemma. He took a drink of whisky, nodded his head sympathetically, and said: "I understand, Harry. It's not an easy thing."

"Since I got the letter I'm in torment. I can't sleep."

"I can believe it," Maloney said.

"What have they got against Clara? She's a fine woman."

"You bet. She's a fine woman."

"And the children love her. Do you see the way they're attached to her?"

"Are you telling me? Can't I see it for myself?"

"What can I do now?"

"You're in a hell of a fix," Maloney said. He took another drink of whisky and wiped his mouth with the back of his hand. "Why don't you ask the Judge's advice? He's a Jew. He'll tell you what to do."

"That's what I was thinking," Harry said.

"Listen, tomorrow is Thursday. It's his day at the club. I'll go in and tell him you've got something to talk to him about. I'm sure he'll find a way out. He can figure a way out of any kind of trouble."

Judge Greenberg was a typical Tammany Hall boss. An East Side boy, the son of poor parents, he was a "self-made man," a lawyer, who had made Tammany politics an integral part of his career. He had risen high. Step by step, as regularly as the pages of a calendar, he had advanced from stage to stage until he attained the highest that Tammany had to give to one of its own—the judge's bench. He believed in Tammany with a religious faith. Tammany to him was like a mother who protected her young. His principal care was to keep his reputation clean and unblemished.

One of the characteristics which had helped his reputation was his respectability in religious matters. He was honorary president of the synagogue named after the town his parents had come from. From time to time he would make contributions to charitable organizations, and see that his gifts were properly publicized. When he spoke at meetings or at banquets for some religious institution, or at an orthodox gathering, he would wear the traditional Jewish skullcap. It was said that he even wore it when he sat at the bench, and that there was a *mezuzah,* an orthodox amulet, nailed to the door of the courtroom, for everyone to see. To Judge Greenberg religion was one of the steeds harnessed to the chariot which would carry him to the peak of a political career, and he guarded his religious reputation like the apple of his eye.

The Judge knew that Harry's wife had died; he had sent a wreath of flowers to the funeral with his card attached. He kept informed about all of the Tammany workers of the district, and knew the details of their personal lives. It was his business to know. He had only one standard for judging the behavior of his aides—was it good for Tammany or was it bad? That Harry was mixed up with a Gentile woman displeased him. Harry stood well with Tammany; he was a good mixer with the Jews and the Christians in the district, and the Judge was afraid that Harry's usefulness to Tammany would be hampered by his attachment to a Gentile; it would ruin his reputation among the Jews of the neighborhood. It had already occurred to him that it might be a good thing to have a talk with Harry and make him see the light.

Judge Greenberg spent every Thursday evening at the Tammany clubhouse. The "boys" would come in for a handshake and a few words. He had his own room there where the captains and lieutenants of the district could come to speak to him privately.

He was a small man physically, a handicap he tried to overcome by wearing shoes with specially built high heels; they helped a little, but not much. On this Thursday evening he sat in the huge leather chair at the writing desk in his room at the club and seemed to be completely lost in its capacious roominess. A thick cloud of smoke rose from the long cigar which he held between his teeth, while his large and unnaturally bright eyes took in the worried face of Harry who stood at the other side of the desk.

"It won't do, Harry," the Judge said severely. "I tell you it won't do." He pointed a finger of his little hand accusingly, his familiar gesture on the bench when some poor devil was brought before him. "You're fighting against religion; I don't know anybody who has won that kind of fight. A Jew has got to stay a Jew. You had a Jewish mother, and you've got to give your

179

children a Jewish mother. Everybody's got to stick to his own religion." He addressed the last remark to Maloney, who stood a little distance away from the desk. "Take Maloney over there. Would he marry out of his faith? No. Besides, it's bad for the party. If you lose your influence with the voters, you can't be of any use to us. No, Harry, you've got to put an end to it right away. Pay her off, and get rid of her. As soon as you can. Get married to a Jewish girl. Give your children a Jewish mother ... like your own mother."

"But Judge ... the children ... " Harry stammered.

"I don't want to hear any more," Judge Greenberg said. He stood up. "It's best for both of you. Anyway it's best for you," he added. "Mike, I'm relying on you to help him get it fixed up. Here"—he held out two long cigars—"and good luck."

As it turned out there was no necessity to talk to Mrs. Kranz. She had sensed the difficulties in the air. Her intuition told her that Harry was having trouble on her account, and she made preparations to meet it. She knew about the letter Harry's mother had sent from the old country. She even knew that Harry and Maloney had gone to get Judge Greenberg's advice.

When Harry got home he found her in street clothes. The two younger children were asleep. There was a locked valise standing near the door. At the other side of the room Rachel held her handkerchief to her eyes.

"What's going on?" Harry asked in dismay.

"Clara's leaving us. She's going back to her own house," Rachel sobbed.

"Why?"

"You know why," Mrs. Kranz said quietly. "I know what you've been going through. No, Harry, it's no use. It seems you can't fight religion."

"I won't allow a stranger in the house! I won't have any other stepmother!" Rachel wailed.

"Don't cry, Rachel." Harry went over to her and put his arms around her. "Don't cry. There'll be no stranger in the house. I'll take care of you. Don't cry."

CHAPTER SEVENTEEN

IRVING'S BUSINESS was doing well. He was able to give substantial help to his parents, and he had even been able to arrange for Nathan to stay for a year at a sanitorium in one of the southern states.

There was a vast change in Mary's life, too. She was Irving's right hand, something no one would have believed the modest, unpretentious girl the block knew could be capable of. But the block didn't know what a deep change had taken place in her.

The terrifying experience of the Triangle fire had had a profound effect on her. Her narrow escape from death, the sight of Sarah Lifschitz's flaming body plunging to the sidewalk below, all the horrors of the catastrophe, had left her stern and disillusioned, as though a new nature had been forged and fused in the flames. Her sensitiveness and naïveté were gone, and with them her compassionate sense of belonging to the world of the suffering and the poor. All she thought of now was how to escape permanently from the kind of life which might again confront her with the horror she had survived. That meant escape from a factory; she would never be safe from the consuming flames otherwise.

In the opportunity Irving had given her she saw her chance. She threw herself into her new work with all her energy, not noticing, not wanting to notice, that Irving's factory meant for others the same evils and dangers she was seeking to escape.

A new Mary had emerged from the Triangle fire, and Nat's attitude toward her while he was in the hospital had helped the process.

As the weeks went by, everyone in the neighborhood had visited Nathan—except Mary. He had made it clear that he didn't want to see her. Irving frightened her by telling her that her visit could only do harm as long as Nathan was so firmly opposed to it. Nathan's attitude gave her the feeling that she was being pushed aside, that she was somehow unclean, as though she had committed some sort of unspeakable crime. The "unspeakable crime," she felt sure, was her confession of love for him.

Nathan had already lost for her the glamour with which she had surrounded him. The religious aura in which his crippled limbs and his general helplessness had clothed him had vanished for her. With the loss of the aura of suffering—the mainspring of her love for him—Nathan had also lost for her the poetry and the beauty which had set him apart in her eyes as something so unique, extraordinary, and unattainable that she would be content to devote her life to adoring him.

The business opportunity Irving had given her presented her with a new interest in life. A vast world of new pleasures, experiences, sensations, and emotions opened up before her, such as she had never even imagined before. Her frequent visits to dressmaking establishments and exclusive stores made her more aware of her own appearance. Now she wore dresses which helped to bring out the lines of her small but well-developed body, her graceful arms and shapely, silk-stockinged legs. She now knew what it was to attract the admiring glances of men.

It soon became clear that Mary had an even greater talent for the business than Irving, with his shrewd instinct, had at first thought. She was quick to note the lines, the folds, the tulle knots and rosettes which were the fashion of the season, and she was able to make valuable suggestions to the designer. She attended fashion shows, went to matinees, strolled through the lobbies of fashionable hotels, observing the fashions worn by the elegant world, and at the same time adding to her maturity and experience. Often she designed her own clothes—her mother would sew them for her—and Irving would see in them new styles which had every promise of being sell-outs. In addition, to Irving's satisfaction, she turned out to be the best model in his showroom. It was enough for her to model a matinee dress, or a street ensemble, wearing on her pretty head a wide beflowered and befeathered hat, and to walk languidly across the showroom floor swinging her elegant parasol, her dainty feet twinkling in and out beneath the long dress, its semitransparent material clinging to her mobile body, for the buyers to place substantial orders without stopping to think whether the style was suitable for their trade or not. There were some buyers who refused to order a number until it had first been modeled by Mary.

So it was not surprising that she soon became an important factor in the business. More than one buyer asked Irving, with a sly wink: "Where did you find the *shikse?*"

At home Patrick McCarthy fumed and raged on the nights when Mary came home late. But he had lost his power. It wasn't he who was the provider of the family; it was Mary. It was no longer necessary to hoard odd coins for the monthly rent; the first of the month had no more terrors for Mrs. McCarthy. There was meat at the McCarthy table every day. The children had stout shoes for the winter and were provided with new and warm over-coats. Mrs. McCarthy could take it easy. There was no more need for her to work secretly at home on bundles of shirts and dresses. She could indulge herself in the extra milk and butter which the doctor had recommended to build up her strength. Grandma McCarthy could at last whip up new delicacies for the family, the pleasant dishes she remembered from the good days in Ireland.

No, Patrick McCarthy no longer had them terrified as in the old days. Grandma McCarthy told him plainly that he wasn't the cock of the walk any longer; that Mary was bringing more money into the house than he'd ever brought in; that Mary was no longer a child but grown up; that he had better stop yelling and cursing at her; and that if he didn't stop his goings-on, Mary would leave the house—and then they'd be back with the old poverty and misery. It worked. McCarthy was careful to keep his resent-ment to himself. Anyway, it gave him an excuse to visit Kelly's saloon more often—a pastime the family wouldn't have begrudged him, except that the drinking was so bad for his liver.

But within Mary's heart there was a vast emptiness. Her separation from Nathan had left in her a spiritual thirst which now became transformed into a physical yearning, and the new confidence she felt as a result of her success in business, and the many compliments she received, gave her the courage to translate her desires to reality.

Did not Irving's face remind her of Nat? Were they not chil-dren of the same father and mother? She could actually detect the same scent from Irving's body that she had been familiar with when she tended Nat. Irving's thick, black hair, with its tendency to curl into compact ringlets, was exactly the same as the hair she had so often combed. She came to see in Irving a Nathan who could move, who could caress and embrace her, whose hands were strong, and powerful, and tender. . . .

Then, besides, there was Rachel, who had clearly shown her jealousy from the first day that Mary had gone to work for Irving. She had wanted to quit school and work for him herself, without waiting to finish the commercial course she was taking. She had even thought of getting married to Irving right away. Since her mother's death she had felt insecure; she had awakened to reality from the lovely dream in which life had cradled her up to now.

Rachel was the spoiled child. Everybody had helped to spoil her—her father and mother, the neighborhood, her relatives, even the teachers at school. Her pretty face and figure had made up for all her faults. She would even escape punishment by her teachers when she neglected to do her schoolwork. All she had to do was to roll her eyes under the slumbrous, heavy eyelids for the teacher to forget any idea of punishment. Not only had her father pampered her as though she were an only child, but Mrs. Kranz had practically adopted her, treating her as though she were some sort of precious doll. Everyone flattered her; she was the acknowledged beauty of the block.

She had become accustomed to getting special attention from everyone, strangers as well as relatives, and she felt entitled to privileges beyond the portion of other girls of her age. If anyone neglected to pay her the homage she expected, she felt slighted. She lorded it over all her playmates, treating them as though they were her servants. Mary had been her special victim. If Mary appeared in school with a new ribbon in her hair, Rachel would be astonished and affronted. With the utmost assurance she would remove the ribbon from Mary's hair and put it on her own, as though it were her due. "Let's see how it looks on me," she would say with a winning smile.

Rachel had matured early. She looked much older than her years. Her breasts thrust forward against her dress, her hips were well rounded, her legs were long and shapely. She enjoyed her body. Ever since she was a child Rachel had found a secret delight in it, encouraged by the neighborhood's praise of her beauty. She grew up convinced that her looks could win all of life's battles and realize all her wishes. She would spend long hours

184

admiring herself. She was like an actress; life was unendurable without admiration. When it was denied her or withheld, she felt betrayed and unhappy.

Her uncle Silberberg's loan to Irving to set him up in business bolstered her self-confidence. Was not the loan in reality part of her dowry? She felt justified in thinking of Irving's business almost as her own. Several afternoons a week, instead of applying herself to her schoolwork, she would go to the factory and walk about officiously. She would peer over the shoulders of the girls at the machines, arrogantly criticizing their work. The girls would make fun of her and throw sarcastic and insulting remarks, frequently goading her into a hysterical outburst. Irving would have to come running from his office on the first floor to persuade her to leave the shop.

"Come on downstairs, Rachel. I want you to model a style for a customer," he said to her on one such occasion.

To regain her composure she pretended her visit had a purpose.

"Listen, darling, I have a suggestion. There's a model I saw at Saks. They're wearing the pompadour style again, with a lot of pleats...."

"Yes, I know. I saw it. Come on downstairs. I need you."

"You always take suggestions from Mary, why don't you take them from me?"

"Don't be childish, Rachel. You're good for one thing and Mary's good for another. Mary can suggest styles and you know how to model them," Irving answered placatingly. "Come downstairs, I want you to show my new number twelve to a customer. He's an important buyer. From Cleveland. Let him see how the number really looks."

Number twelve was a model which Rachel could show to advantage; she had the right figure for it. The dress seemed to be molded on her tall figure, holding her snug and smooth at the waist and falling in wide and stately folds. The buyer placed a large order.

There was an occasion when Rachel came into the showroom just as Mary was modeling a new spring style. The dress was a two-piece affair, the back of the jacket pleated, and the skirt longer at the back than at the front. The style was plainly designed for a young, slender figure, small in the hips; Mary's well-knit body showed the dress off to advantage. Rachel saw her

185

parading across the showroom floor, a wide hat on her head and a parasol in her hand. In a blaze of jealousy she insisted on modeling the dress. Irving whispered to her that the dress was not suited to her figure.

"Is that so? You'll see how it'll look on me. Give it to me, Mary. Let me try it on."

"Leave it the way it is," Irving begged. "It looks all right on Mary."

"I don't care. I want to see how it looks on me."

In the end, as Irving knew and feared, Rachel had her way. The style of the dress was altogether unsuitable for Rachel's well-developed, tall figure. Her breasts thrust forward exaggeratedly against the tight jacket; her wide hips strained against the skirt. The total effect was alarming, and the result was that the customer turned the number down.

When the buyer had left, Irving, tolerant and easygoing in business matters as he was, showed no anger. He tried to joke about what had happened and soothe the disconsolate girl.

"It makes no difference, Rachel. He'll come back—when he needs a pompadour style."

Rachel knew she'd made a mistake. But what irritated her most was that her good looks hadn't managed to serve her better and cover up her error. It seemed to her that she could see a sparkle of revenge and triumph in Mary's eyes, and she couldn't resist showing her resentment.

"I think you ought to remember, Mary," she said cuttingly, "that it was my uncle who put up the money for this place."

Irving flushed in anger and embarrassment. "Don't forget, Rachel," he said. "I'm paying your uncle back every cent I borrowed from him."

Rachel realized that she had made another mistake. "I didn't mean any harm," she stammered.

"I know you didn't mean it. Let's not talk about it any more."

Later in the day, when Mary had her hat and coat on, ready to go home, Irving came over to her and said: "Are you free tonight?"

"Yes. Why do you want to know?"

"How about having dinner with me?"

"I thought that Rachel ..."

"Never mind Rachel," Irving answered.

"You mean dinner with you and a customer?"

"No, with me alone."

"Sure. With pleasure!" Mary smiled gaily. "Just a minute until I powder my nose."

"Never mind. You're beautiful the way you are."

"Do you really think so?" She looked around to make sure that they were alone, and suddenly kissed him with her warm, moist lips.

"Hey, you're dangerous!" Irving said in mock alarm.

"Am I?" she asked. She tucked her arm in his.

The atmosphere in Neufeld's restaurant was warm and heady, thick with tobacco smoke, perfume, and the smell of overheated bodies. Couples danced to the strains of sensuous gypsy music. There were the pungent smell of wine and the savory odors of steaming delicacies. Pairs sat close together, the men glancing amorously into the low-cut dresses of the women. Women giggled and snuggled up close to the men.

Black-mustached waiters carried trays with sizzling steaks on wooden platters. Dancers in red-embroidered caftans, the men with their long-skirted coats, the women with their high heels, whirled around in an unending *karahod* to the rhythm of tireless cymbals. The diners, gaily colored paper hats on their heads, raised brimming glasses of wine. The cellar restaurant, in the dim reddish-brown light, was thick with tobacco smoke, hanging in dense clouds from the ceiling. Serpentine ribbons of colored paper hung from the overhead lamps and became entangled in women's hair. Confetti drifted onto the tables. Balloons floated about under the low ceiling; each moment one of them would burst with a sharp retort over the heads of the diners.

Irving had already reminded Mary a couple of times that it was getting late, and that she would find the door of the house locked. It had happened a few times before when she had come home late, and she had had to wait for a long time in the dark hall for her grandmother to hear her and let her in. But Mary was lost in excitement and exaltation. Her eyes sparkled, her cheeks flamed. She moved closer to Irving and held his hand tightly as though she would never let him go.

It was her first experience in this kind of Bohemian atmosphere. It seemed to her that she was far removed from reality.

living in a kind of dreamworld. She had never known that people could be so carefree, so gay, taking such pleasure in food and drink, finding such sensual joy in living. She closed her eyes to surrender the more to the atmosphere about her. She gave no thought to the lateness of the hour. The world had stopped still. She had only one desire—to yield to the languorous feeling that filled her, to have Irving, to have him for her own, to take him away from Rachel and the rest of the world, to have him for her own forever. She felt that she had always been in love with him. Her devotion toward Nathan had been no more than a reflection of the love she had always had for Irving. In the confusion of her thoughts Irving and Nathan became merged into one. It was as though they shared a common body; they were one and the same. When she had fallen in love with Nathan, embracing and caressing his crippled body, she was embracing and caressing Irving's sound and healthy body. Her face glowed in the ardor of desire; a flush of warmth spread over her. She moved closer to him, closed her eyes and murmured: "Irving! Darling! Take me with you!"

"Where? What do you mean?" he stammered.

"Anywhere, anywhere! I want to be with you."

Irving turned pale. He called the waiter, paid the bill, and led Mary out of the restaurant. A cab stood waiting outside, and they got in. The fresh air of the mild May evening intoxicated them more than the Tokay wine they had been drinking in the smoke-filled room. Trembling with desire, Mary pressed close to Irving. Her lips crushed against his cheeks, his eyes, and his lips, as though she were trying to communicate all her passion to him. She passed her hands over him. She was a warm pulsing breast from which poured the milk of desire. Irving was bathed in a sweat of uneasiness and fear. "Mary, what are you doing?" he barely stammered.

"I want you!"

He felt his resistance melting in the heat of the desire she had awakened in him ... and then, suddenly, he found himself struggling frantically against yielding.

Was it his instinct of hard common sense and calculation? That too. But more than that it was the innate inhibition inherited from his father and the generations before him. His father's face actually loomed up before his imagination for a moment. He saw

Moshe Wolf standing, desolated, dejected, his head bowed. "God, what will my father say?" And then there was Rachel. "After all, I'm practically engaged to her. Everyone knows it. And I took money from her uncle." No, he dare not yield. He must take himself in hand. But Mary ... the little Irish girl who had stirred his senses for as long as he could remember ... here she was, pressed close to him, breathing her hot breath on him, covering him with kisses, and murmuring to him: "I love you, Irving! I love you!"

She lifted her head from his breast, looked at him in the darkness with her big eyes.

"Irving, do you love me?"

"Ever since I can remember."

"Oh, Irving!" Tears began to fall from her eyes. Like a spring rain they washed away the lust of vengeance and desire which the unaccustomed wine had let loose in her. She sat quietly. When the cab stopped at her door she pressed her lips to his, got out, and ran upstairs.

The next morning Mary didn't put in an appearance at the shop where Irving impatiently waited for her all day. In the evening he walked up and down past the McCarthy house, but she was not to be seen. He met her brother Jimmy, who told him that Mary had stayed home in the morning and then had gone out, probably to church; anyway she was wearing a black veil. Irving went over to the church and waited on the opposite sidewalk.

He waited for a long time. Afraid to go inside to look for her, he went toward his father's store. When he reached 48th Street, he saw Mary coming along the street from the direction of Second Avenue. She wore no hat; her hair was unruly. She walked along thoughtfully, her head lowered. When Irving came up to her, she turned her swollen, red-rimmed eyes up to him.

"Where were you, Mary? I looked everywhere for you."

"I thought you'd never want to see me any more," she whispered.

"Why?"

"After what happened last night." She lowered her eyes.

"But nothing happened. You're a foolish girl."

"I'm worse than foolish. I'm ..."

"Don't you dare say it. You're the purest, the sweetest ... It was all my fault, not yours. It's my fault. I got you too excited. I shouldn't have taken you to that kind of place. It's my fault. When you didn't come to work today I really thought you didn't want to see me any more. It was all my fault, Mary. But honest, it won't happen again."

She stared straight into his eyes. "Why shouldn't it happen again? I wanted it ... and I still want it. I love you, Irving."

"But ... but ... if I could ... if it only depended on me, I'd take you, this very minute, just the way you are, to the first Justice of the Peace and get married. But you know I can't do it. You're a Catholic, and I'm a Jew. My father's orthodox; he'd never look at me again as long as he lived. I don't know what he'd do with himself.... It wouldn't be easy for you either, with your father and the whole family. And besides ... there's Rachel."

"Yes, I know. I'm mean and wicked. I know it's a sin for me to love you. I prayed to God all day. I prayed to Jesus to guard me from sin. I prayed to Holy Mary to protect me. But I can't help it. I'm sinful. I love you, Irving."

"You're not sinful, you're just honest about your feelings ... and you fell in love ... and you admit it."

"Irving, are you in love with Rachel?"

"No, I'm not in love with her, honest. But you know how it is. The folks have sort of matched us up ever since we were kids. And so we got used to the idea. And besides, everybody knows that it was her uncle's money that put me in business—even though I'm paying every cent back. What can I do? You know how it is. I haven't got the heart ..."

"I know, Irving, I know. .... It's too bad. ..." Mary seemed to be talking to herself, her eyes fixed on the ground.

She raised her head and looked straight at him. "Do you love me, Irving?" There was an expression of intensity on her face.

"You know very well I do. I'm crazy about you."

The yearning in his voice carried over to her like an electric current. She closed her eyes and came closer to him.

"Then I don't care. Nothing else matters. I want to be with you. I don't want anything from you, nothing, nothing! I only want to be with you, Irving. I want to be with you."

The next day she went back to the shop.

CHAPTER EIGHTEEN

WHATEVER HIS failings as a husband had been, no one could dispute Harry Greenstock's devotion to his children. He was always fussing about them. He was proud of them. Every Sunday and holiday the block would see father and daughters, dressed in their best, pleasantly promenading along. The very thought of entrusting them to the mercies of a strange stepmother made him shudder. When Mrs. Kranz left, Harry became father and mother to the children again. Increased devotion only increased his love for them. New springs of warmth and ardor opened up in his heart. The children satisfied all his wants. It wasn't long before he astonished his friends by dividing the pigeons among them. He gave them up, he said, to be free to give all his attention to the children.

Often he would walk with them over to the East River front. The neighbors would watch him, little Goldie in his arms and the others by his side, and they would exchange knowing glances at each other. Harry would smile and greet them as though there was nothing unusual about his circumstances, but they all knew that the proud eagle had had its wings clipped; he was no longer the same Harry. Gone was the proud, arrogant gait, the devil-may-care attitude. No longer did his shoes shine like mirrors, and his white shirt was no longer starched stiff as a board. His clothes didn't seem to fit so well; the knife-edge crease was gone from his trousers. Where was the derby hat that had sat so jauntily on his head in the old days when he and Maloney would stroll about the block, everyone looking admiringly at them from the tenement windows? Now the window watchers saw a Harry in a wrinkled suit, tieless, the shirt open at the collar, strolling with his children to the river to see the freight boats passing by.

There is a love intoxication which can so overwhelm a man as to make him capable of any crime in order to win the woman he yearns for. There is the drunkenness of the supersensitive worshiper of God—a love so intense that the worshiper convinces himself that it will please God if he torments his flesh as proof of his adoration. It is a consuming love in which all proportion, all reality, all balance is forgotten. Combined with Harry's normal feeling for his children was some of this ecstatic transport. It was a love which made him ready for the supremest sacrifice. His heart overflowed with adoration for little Bertha. She filled all his thoughts, leaving no room for the desire for women, for good times, for power and for money. He had changed entirely. His pride had disappeared. He never gave a thought to lording it over the block and playing the high and mighty. The child had him bound hand and foot. A new quality of humility filled him.

Little Bertha, sensitive as any fledgling bird abandoned by its mother in its nest, held her father fast. Her eyes gazed at him with infinite pathos. When she smiled it was as though the heavens were opened and a rain of joy were pouring down on the earth. She had heaven in her eyes; warm and brilliant sunlight shone out of them.

But all of this was Harry's enraptured fantasy. The child was like all other six-year-olds, just emerging from the semi-real world in which all children live—like a tortoise in its carapace—into the world of reality. It is an age when children frequently fall back for refuge into their childish dreamworld. When evening comes, and the child is driven away from the safety of the real world and left alone in its bed, it becomes afraid of the night and the darkness. It is as though the child is afraid it must return to the world from which it came. Going to sleep is the great crisis for the child. It is afraid to be alone; it must hear the voice of its mother, feel its mother's hand rocking it to sleep, hear the mother's voice singing.

Day after day little Bertha let herself be swallowed up by her childish world—the teachers at school, the children on the street, or playing with her dolls. But as soon as it was time for her father to come home from work, she watched for him like a faithful dog. She sat on the steps in front of the house and kept her gaze fixed down the street for his advancing form. The calls of the other children on the sidewalk could not attract her; she would stick to her post on the steps until Harry came along. The moment she saw him she would run toward him with little shrieks of happiness and clamber into his arms. She followed him like a shadow. She had to be near him while he shaved and washed. No one else could help her at the table. She would weep forlornly and simply refuse to go to bed unless Harry undressed her and held her hand until she was fast asleep.

Harry was so deep in the toils of his love for the child that he was afraid to leave her alone. He had dreams at night that someone was trying to take her away from him; he would wake up in a cold sweat. During the day, if he was working on a scaffold or some other dangerous perch, he would suddenly be terrified lest something happen to him, not out of fear for himself, but in a panicky realization that Bertha would be alone, without him to protect her. For no accountable reason, he would suddenly become convinced that she was ill. Such a fit of apprehension would overwhelm him that he would throw aside his work and rush home in the middle of the day, dashing into the house with his heart in his mouth—only to learn that the child was safely at school with the other children.

Apart from his worries about Bertha, what he wanted most of all was to see Rachel married to Irving. On that match he based his hopes for the children's security. With Rachel married, the younger ones would have someone to lean on. In his anxiety and worry he began to pay more attention to religious piety.

He paid a visit to Moshe Wolf, enrolled as a member of the congregation, and made a handsome contribution to Shmulevitch for the new synagogue which the congregation was preparing to open in time for the coming Holy Days. Before the holiday came around, Moshe Wolf was astonished to see Harry put in an appearance at the temporary quarters of the congregation on an ordinary Sabbath, when only a bare quorum of worshipers was in attendance.

"What's the matter? Is it a *yahrzeit* or something, Harry?" Moshe Wolf asked.

"Is a man supposed to go to *shul* only when it's the anniversary of someone's death?"

"That's the way to talk!" Moshe Wolf said with satisfaction. "It's about time, Harry."

"Well, after all, I thought as long as we're almost in-laws ..."

"Harry, we'll make you the sexton of the new synagogue yet," Schmulevitch said gleefully, pounding him on the shoulder.

193

"About a sexton I don't know . . . but I'll certainly paint the synagogue without charge," Harry answered in high spirits.

The change rejoiced Moshe Wolf's heart. Later in the evening, when the grocery was opened after the Sabbath, Harry came into the store.

"Moshe Wolf, I have something to talk to you about."

"What is it?"

"I'd like our children to get married as quickly as possible."

"What's the hurry? They're so young yet, and Irving's just getting on his feet."

"I'd like to see my daughter married. Who knows how long I've got to live? I'd feel more secure."

"What nonsense are you talking! You're crazy. A young man like you!"

"Moshe Wolf, I have no one in the world. Something can happen to me, who knows . . . and I have little children."

"You're talking nonsense. What can happen to you?"

"A man is only human."

"A man's in God's hands," Moshe Wolf answered.

"Let me see at least one of my girls settled. I want to see Rachel married."

"Well, is it up to me? Talk it over with Irving."

The day came when Harry talked it over with Irving. On a Sunday when Irving called for Rachel, Harry took him out into the yard.

"Irving," he said. "I've got no one but you."

"What do you mean?" Irving asked in bewilderment.

"Irving, you're like my own child . . . like Rachel. I'd like to see you both married. What do you say?"

Irving's thoughts flew around in confusion. He always supposed that some day, sooner or later, he would marry Rachel, but since his intimacy with Mary had begun, he had avoided the thought. Now that the question was put to him so directly, he was seized with panic. He stammered: "Sure . . . but we're too young yet. . . ."

"But you're engaged.

"Sure . . . sure. . . ." Irving said. His face was pale, and his heart was beating wildly.

"That's all I wanted to know," said Harry. He held out his hand.

CHAPTER NINETEEN

NATHAN WAS away from 48th Street for close to two years. After a year at the hospital he had, with the financial help of Irving, spent a year in the South in a sanitorium established for the treatment of infantile paralysis victims.

He came home on his own legs. Supported by crutches, he could walk for short distances. His right arm, except for the fingers of his hand, had complete freedom of movement; and he was able to perform some limited movements with his fingers. He could manage, though awkwardly, to hold a fork or spoon, and he could feed himself without help. Also, with the help of a mechanical device strapped to the palm of his hand, he could scrawl recognizable pencil notations on a pad. His left hand was permanently crippled; it dangled uselessly at his side.

What was most important was that he had recovered his self-confidence. At the sanitarium he had had the opportunity to go on with his studies. One of the professors from a neighboring college coached him, and from time to time he would be taken to attend a class. He had lost interest in studying law; instead he was applying himself enthusiastically to the study of mathematics.

To one such as Nathan, mathematics was as music to the blind. The most concrete of all, mathematics is at the same time the most imaginative of all the sciences. Though firmly rooted in exact knowledge, it is less bounded than other sciences by the limitations of reality. It moves about within the confines of its own cosmos like an unfettered meteor in the vastness of the universe; where it chooses to come to rest, there is the center of the world. Nathan could lean back on his wheel chair in the bright sunlight and let his mind wander about in contemplation of a mathematical problem. He would project a point in space and let his fancy rove about the position of his own infinitesimal body in the limitless distances of universal space. From mathematics he was drawn to metaphysics. He read a good deal in philosophy, especially the fashionable theories of Henri Bergson; but he was still deeply influenced by the belief in a personal god that absorbed him in the hospital.

When he got back to 48th Street, he hardly recognized his home. There was prosperity in the Davidowsky household. The apartment now took in all of the floor above the store. The rooms were freshly painted and newly furnished. His own room was fixed up like a studio, with a bookcase, a desk, a handsome standing lamp, and a comfortable couch. Vases and trifles here and there in the room gave signs of a woman's hand.

"Do you like it?" he heard a soft voice behind him say.

He turned and saw Irving and Rachel in the doorway.

"Rachel did all of it," his mother said. "She arranged the whole house."

Deborah seemed to have grown taller. She wore high-heeled shoes, a silk dress with a brooch pinned at her throat and a colored ribbon in her hair.

"Rachel did it all," she repeated. "She makes me wear new dresses from Irving's shop. Every day she brings another dress, and I have to try them on. She ties ribbons in my hair." Deborah seemed to be trying to apologize for her finery.

Nathan looked at his mother. She had become a different person. There was calm and peace in her face, a new light in her eyes. The shoulders which he remembered as always bent under a load of cares were now firm and straight. He began to feel some of the warmth and love of his youth for her well up in him.

She was not the only one who had changed. Moshe Wolf wore a neat, new suit. His beard was carefully trimmed. He wore a collar and a tie. The gold watch chain he had worn as a young man was draped over his vest.

"Everything is Irving's doing," Moshe Wolf said. "He even made us get someone to help in the store. There's practically nothing left for me to do. I can be a regular gentleman," he added jovially.

Nathan's heart swelled with joy. He turned to Irving. "How did you do it all?" he asked, his face radiant.

"It's nothing.... I have a small business, that's all...."

"A small business! He's doing better than some of the old

196

established firms. He's got the finest shop in the trade," Rachel said, taking Irving's arm proudly. "You just wait and see, we'll be ahead of them all."

"I'll see you this evening, Nathan," Irving interrupted. "I've got to go to the office. Remember, Ma, the best dinner you can make. I'll eat home tonight."

"You betcha," Deborah said in English. She'd been introducing more and more English phrases into her Yiddish speech ever since prosperity had hit the Davidowsky household.

"Wait for me; I'm coming with you, Irving," Rachel said. "Am I invited to supper, too?" she asked with a smile, as she and Irving left.

"She doesn't leave him for a minute. Since her father sent away the *shikse*"—Deborah heaved a sigh—"she's made this her second home. And the way she worked to get the house fixed up for you! She's just like one of the family."

"Well, isn't she one of the family, practically?" Moshe Wolfe remarked. "Everybody knows she and Irving are as good as engaged. It's just the same as though they were officially engaged."

These were happy days at the Davidowskys'. At Shmulevitch's temporary synagogue quarters a special service of thanksgiving for Nathan's homecoming had been held and Moshe Wolf had made a substantial gift for the new synagogue in gratitude to God that his son had been cured.

Nathan had returned after the High Holidays, on the second day of Succoth, the Feast of Tabernacles. Everyone on the block saw him walking across the street, assisted by Moshe Wolf, to Shmulevitch's prayer house. Jewish housewives wiped their eyes and murmured thanks to God piously; the devout Catholics crossed themselves reverently.

In the prayer house Nathan was called up to the Reading of the Law. Moshe Wolf's heart was full to overflowing as he heard Nathan's fine voice recite the ancient Hebrew phrases.

It was not only to please his father that Nathan attended the services. He felt the need to offer thanks to God. Nor did he mind when Dr. Chazanowitch, finding out about it, called him a "clerical" and accused him of joining the ranks of the "reactionaries"; the doctor was angry at him for several days.

After the service the entire congregation went over to the

Davidowsky apartment. Deborah had prepared honey cakes and cinnamon cookies. The carafe of wine passed from hand to hand. As was meet for this solemn Holy Day, with fervor and ecstasy they professed anew their faith in the just God in Heaven who watched over his people Israel. They rejoiced that Moses the Lawgiver had once trod the earth; that God had given the Jews their sacred Torah; that now they were safe in the blessed America which God had created as a haven and a refuge for the oppressed of the world. They wished each other joy in their children.

Shmulevitch, in his wide skullcap—for this occasion he had chosen the most imposing one of all—pounded Nathan jovially on the shoulders.

"Now that God has shown you his favor, it's time that you became a Jew."

"What else am I?" Nathan asked.

"No Jew's a real Jew until he has a wife. Without a wife you're only half a Jew. Look at Irving, he's getting ahead of you. Soon he'll be a husband."

"Rachel's already taken," Nathan laughed.

"Who said something about Rachel?" Harry called out. Since he had turned pious he let no important holiday pass without joining the worshipers at Shmulevitch's prayer house.

"We were saying," Shmulevitch said, "that you're dragging things out too long. How long are a boy and a girl supposed to keep company? Isn't it time to have a real engagement?"

"I talked to Irving about it. He says he has time," Harry replied.

"What kind of time? What does he know? A boy like him! Talk to Moshe Wolf! We'll talk to him right now. Moshe Wolf," Shmulevitch shouted. "Now that God has brought your first-born home to you—a man, and healthy, thank God—it's time to settle the other matter. It's time to have a real engagement. How long can a boy and girl hang around without getting married? And a girl without a mother . . ."

"For my part I'm ready now. . . ." said Moshe Wolf.

"Then what are we waiting for?"

"Irving says he has time. You talked with him yourself," Moshe Wolf said to Harry.

"What kind of time?" Shmulevitch repeated. "You're the father. It's up to you to take the thing into your own hands." He raised

198

his voice. "Friends, kinsmen! Joy to the bride and groom! I proclaim and make known to all of you that our kinsman, Moshe Wolf Davidowsky, has entered into a covenant with our kinsman Hirsch, Harry Greenstock. The boy Irving, in our holy speech Zebulon, the son of Moshe Wolf, pledges himself to Rachel, the daughter of Hirsch. Rejoice, kinsmen! Life and happiness to the bride and groom!"

There was a hubbub of congratulations and questions as to when the wedding would take place.

"Soon! Soon! You can start to get the wedding gifts ready."

"Good! Now we know that the match has been settled. Why should it be kept a secret?" said Shmulevitch to Harry. He had the satisfied air of a man who has done a good deed.

Irving hadn't been living at home for some time. He had his own apartment at a hotel; but he made it a practice to come home often to eat at the family table. On his next visit Moshe Wolf told him what had happened.

"We announced the match, Irving. Shmulevitch announced to everyone that you and Rachel will be married. When shall we have the engagement?"

Irving went pale. "What kind of engagement? What are we, children? We can wait for the wedding."

"But Irving, it's our custom—a Jewish custom—to have an official engagement."

"We'll be different."

"No, my son. We have to observe our ways."

"We've got plenty of time."

"Irving, you wouldn't bring shame on an orphan!"

"Who said anything like that? Who said I'd bring shame on an orphan? But what's the rush; we've got plenty of time!"

Everyone had come to visit Nathan. Everyone but Mary.

She hadn't put in an appearance, nor had he met her on the street. He knew that she was working for Irving and that she knew of his return. There could be no explanation other than that she was deliberately keeping away from him.

It was true. But the time came when she could no longer manage it.

199

"You haven't been to see Nat yet," Irving said to her. "He asks about you every day."

"He does?"

"From the minute he got home. You were the first one he asked for. It was funny . . . the moment he came in he said 'Where's Mary?'—just as though you were a member of the family."

"I thought . . ."

"What did you think?"

"Oh, nothing. . . ."

"After all, you used to be such good friends."

"I'll go up tonight," Mary said.

Nathan heard her voice outside in the corridor. It was like the old days, when she would bring him books from the library and call to him from the stairs.

"Nat, where are you!"

"I'm here! In my room. Come in."

She came in with her arms stretched wide to him as he sat at the desk with a book before him. He rested his arms on the desk and tried to raise himself—a movement he could customarily manage with ease. But this time he fell back to the chair.

He smiled wryly. Now, when he wanted most of all to stand up, his strength had failed him! He tried again, and this time he stood up.

"Nat! It's so wonderful. You can stand up!"

"I can walk, too," Nat answered with pride. He walked a few steps without his crutches, and then sat down on the couch.

"Jesus Mary!" Mary crossed herself and closed her eyes. Her lips moved devoutly. She went over to Nathan and put her arms around him.

"Nat, it's wonderful!"

"Let me look at you, Mary."

"I suppose you know you're looking at the head saleslady of the firm of Irving Davidowsky! A very important firm!"

Nathan looked at her. She was the same and yet not the same. She was stunningly dressed. The long skirt flowed down to her heels; the toes of her shoes peeped out like little mice from beneath the wide hem. The jacket fitted snugly around her delicately curving bust. Her waist was tightly corseted. The pointed collar of a white silk blouse showed above the opening of the jacket. On her hair perched a wide-brimmed hat with an ostrich feather.

200

In her elegant attire she seemed to Nathan like a little girl masquerading in grownup's clothing, but it was a disguise so natural that it seemed to him that it was the grownup who was real, not the Mary he had known.

"You've changed, Mary," he said at last.

"For the better or for the worse?"

"I can't say. I don't know."

His words, like a lightning flash of illumination, plunged her back into reality, away from the excitement of the reunion. She suddenly remembered how much she had changed, and the realization tore a cry from her lips.

"Mary, what is it?" Nathan asked in alarm.

"It's nothing," she stammered, her face white.

"It's so long since I've seen you," Nathan said. "I never thought of the changes that had to come with time. I thought you would stay the Mary I knew. And now I see you so different. Why should I have thought that you would wait as you always were... ?"

"Wait ... for what?"

"I don't know myself," Nathan said. His face flushed. "You didn't come to see me at the hospital. Even here—and I've been back for ten days—you've waited till now to come to see me."

"I didn't know whether you wanted to see me. When you were at the hospital you said you didn't want me to come to see you."

"There was a reason," Nathan said. "But now it's different. Now I want to see you. Now I want to see you very much. I want to see you often. I have so much to talk to you about." He lifted his right arm and put his hand out to her.

"Isn't it wonderful, Nat? You can move your hand—just the same as anybody else. Oh, dear Jesus! It's wonderful." She took Nathan's hand in her own and lifted it to her warm lips.

"What are you doing?" Nathan pulled his hand away. "Just as sentimental as before! I thought ..."

"Forgive me, Nat. I couldn't help it. It's like a miracle happening right before my eyes. I just can't get used to it ..."

"It isn't such a great miracle. I'm far from normal."

"Oh, no, Nat. You just don't realize it yourself yet. You can walk, you can move your arms ... almost the same as any other person."

"I'm thankful for what I have, Mary. Everyone has to live with the powers God gives him. I used to think that I was entitled to

201

everything, like everybody else. Now I've learned to be thankful for every separate blessing. I learned that at the hospital when I saw the way others suffered. Believe me, I saw all sorts of suffering—and I learned to be satisfied with what I had, and thankful for whatever God gave me, and ready to make the most of what I am and live as useful a life as I can." His voice trembled with earnestness. "Starting next week I'm going back to college. I've done all the preparatory work and I've sent in my papers. I've been accepted. I'll only need someone to take me up there in the subway and bring me home. Irving said it will be easy to arrange, and that it won't cost much. Besides, my friend Robert Hirsch has promised to help me. I don't have to be at class every day; I can do a good deal of the work at home."

Mary was silent. Her gaze went beyond the walls of the room into some far distance. Her eyes filled with tears, which ran unheeded down her cheeks.

"What is it, Mary?"

"Nothing," she said, and a smile, like a rainbow after a shower, shone out from her eyes. "I have to go now, Nat. You know the way my father is. He hasn't changed."

"When shall I see you again, Mary? I want to see you often. I have so much to talk to you about."

"I don't know, Nat darling. You see, I'm so busy all the time. I'm head saleslady; it's a responsible job. I'm always busy." Mary spoke half in jest. "Good-by, Nat. It was so good to talk to you."

Her eyes suddenly lost their warmth. She looked again at him—and she was gone.

CHAPTER TWENTY

IRVING, rebellious from his childhood against religious observances, was basically more strongly attached to his father's religious standards than his older brother. Nathan, like the educated and emancipated youth he was, had never for a moment given a thought to what his father might think of his feelings for Mary. To Irving, however, Moshe Wolf was the most important factor in making him dismiss any idea of marriage with Mary from his mind. He could oppose his father in small things— as, for example, in minor religious observances—but when it came to an important step like marrying someone of another faith, he accepted as impassable the barrier between Jew and Christian. It was not only consideration for his father, whom deep in his heart he respected, but also the religious fears which are more deep-rooted in the uneducated than in the educated that kept him from marrying Mary, however much he loved her.

Nevertheless, his affair with Mary made him content to let his "engagement" to Rachel remain nothing more than that. If he could have extricated himself, he would have—but he didn't know how. The same religious fears that prevented him from marrying Mary compelled him to maintain his relationship with Rachel. Then, besides, there was the fact that she was an orphan.

These two compulsions—to avoid marriage with Mary and to hold on to his "engagement" to Rachel—were the two facets of the single conspiracy which religion was opposing to his peace and happiness. Within himself he rebelled against it, but he knew very well that his only escape was in freeing himself from both family and religious ties. Lacking the courage to solve his dilemma by so drastic a step, he was able only to postpone the problem, to let things go on as they were. The result was that he found himself enmeshed deeper and deeper.

Now the hour of decision was coming inexorably closer.

After a week or two had passed without Moshe Wolf's calling in friends and clan to formalize the betrothal—as he had promised during the holiday gathering in his home—Harry Greenstock began to see himself as the victim of a piece of treachery. They were making a laughingstock of him; they were belittling his daughter! The suspicion tortured him. There was no thought in his mind outside the single obsession of leading his daughter—as quickly as might be—to the marriage canopy. It was the goal of his life; it would at least give him the comfort of knowing that his oldest child was provided for. And if she were married, the younger ones would be safe. It was the security of the family he was fighting for, and he put the whole strength of his purpose into attaining it.

He went to see Shmulevitch.

In Shmulevitch's efforts to speed the match there was something of a desire to please Uncle Silberberg, and something of a wish to earn the credit for performing a good deed in behalf of a motherless girl. Besides, as a near kinsman he was interested in Harry's family affairs. Thus he had become the guiding spirit in the matter of the match between Irving and Rachel. He was as vitally concerned as though he were arranging his own child's life. He went with Harry to Moshe Wolf and talked bluntly.

"Where is justice? How long must we wait? It's getting to be a disgrace! After all, you made a public promise."

"Does it depend on me? It depends on Irving. Go and talk to him. Maybe he'll listen to you," Moshe Wolf said apologetically.

"We'll go together. We've got to put an end to it, once for all," Shmulevitch said firmly.

"He can't play around with my daughter! He'll have to deal with me!" Harry shouted, pale with rage.

Shmulevitch grabbed him by the arm. "Let me do the talking. You keep quiet. You'll get nowhere by shouting." The three of them went down to Irving's shop.

The Harry of the old days wouldn't have been so timid. That he, Harry Greenstock, should go begging for his own child! But this was a new Harry, who leashed his rage and was as meek as a lamb. Anything for his daughter's sake! He would let them scorn him, anything, so long as it would help Rachel.

Irving froze in fright when the three marched into his office. He knew at once what the visit meant. His mind flew wildly about for an escape from the situation, for a way to fend off a final decision. He tried the light approach.

"What is it? A holdup?" he asked, with a forced laugh.

Harry's fingers tightened in a cramp. The best thing would be to grab this youngster by the throat and... ! He turned pale; his eyes became bloodshot.

"Listen to me, Irving," he said, ignoring Shmulevitch's attempts at calming him, "I only want to know one thing. Do you intend to keep your promise? And when?"

Irving put up a show of anger. "We're free people, me and Rachel. You can't use force in a thing like this. I'm going to take my own time."

Shmulevitch tugged at Harry's sleeve, and Harry, realizing that he'd made a mistake, trembled in anxiety.

"But after all, my son," Moshe Wolf said, "they have a right to know where they stand. Is it to be a wedding or isn't it?"

"I'll talk it over with Rachel," Irving replied sullenly.

"I'm asking only one thing—are you going to marry Rachel or not?" Harry persisted stubbornly.

"All I'll tell you is that if we do get married it'll be because we want to; not because I promised you," Irving said.

"Irving's right; he's right," said Shmulevitch. "He's a smart boy. What do you think? He's going to marry Rachel on your account? On account of the big dowry you're going to give her? Leave it to them. They know what they have to do.... What a business you've got here, Irving! My, my! Take a look! A whole floor! And all the mirrors! A fortune of money!"

"Whatever it costs, it's worth it," said Moshe Wolf. "Well, we better go."

Later in the day, when Rachel walked into the shop, Irving told her of the deputation that had visited him and about the "holdup" that they'd tried. "I told them that after all, we're in no hurry, and that trying to hold me up was an insult to you."

That evening Rachel came home with swollen, tear-stained eyes. "Who asked you to mix in my affairs?" she burst out to Harry. "You only belittled me in his eyes! I'll be ashamed to look at anybody. Why did you do it? If people find out that you tried to force him to marry me... ! You're making me out to be a cripple or something—"

Harry saw his mistake; no, his crime. A crime against his own daughter. He had shamed her in the eyes of her betrothed; he had made her unhappy. Now he was lost; whatever he did would be wrong. Rachel's tears terrified him.

"Don't cry," he begged. "I meant it for your own good."

"Why, why, why did you do it?"

Stunned and perplexed, Harry went to see Mike Maloney.

"You have to leave things like that to the kids themselves," Mike advised him. "Old folks aren't supposed to butt in. They only make things worse."

Yes, Harry could see he had made things worse. He blamed himself; dark thoughts crowded in on his mind.

Lately he had been getting spells of dizziness whenever he was working on a roof or a high scaffolding. Even though he wore his safety belt securely fastened, the dizziness persisted while all sorts of unnameable terrors would fill his mind. He would suddenly get the feeling that some awful accident had happened to Goldie or Bertha; he would see them run over by an automobile or pinned under the wheels of a truck. A cold perspiration would break out all over him and he would drop his work and rush home desperately—to find the children perfectly safe.

Ever since his encounter with Irving he was becoming more and more a victim to these dark thoughts. He convinced himself that Rachel was suffering all the time.

"What is the matter with you?" he would ask her out of a clear sky.

"I don't know what you mean."

"Why are your eyes so red? You've been crying."

"Leave me alone! Please leave me alone!" and she would rush out of the room.

"She hates me. She knows what I've done to her," Harry would think to himself.

His spells of dizziness became more frequent and his mind was filled with forebodings of disaster.

He got into the habit of dropping in frequently at Kelly's saloon, although he knew that alcohol was bad for his gall bladder. Every drink of whisky brought on an attack. And with the attacks came unbearable pain, as though an enormous weight were pressing on his chest. But when he didn't drink it was worse; for then the blackest forebodings filled him. What would happen to the children

206

if he should die? Ever since Sara's death nothing had gone right. "Oh, Sara, why did you leave me? I can't manage without you."

"Maybe if I die, Irving'll have more consideration," the thought suddenly came to him. "People will force him to keep his promise. My God, what am I thinking about! I'm going crazy."

But the dark thoughts persisted, lurked in a corner of his mind and gave him no rest. In bed, at work, all during the day, he felt the insistent demand to get the problem settled once for all.

One day as he perched on a scaffolding rigged up against one of the slaughterhouses in the neighborhood, his obsession of death, like a thief in hiding, emerged from the back of his mind and began to gnaw at him.

"Dear Father in Heaven," he thought frantically, "I have no one left but you."

From the deeps of his subconscious the words came to him. He saw himself alone and abandoned. There he was alone, naked, as he had come from his mother's womb. Even though the scaffolding was not high and he knew that beneath him, below on the sidewalk, people were walking, hurrying, calling to one another, still he could not see them. He was afraid that if he looked down he might get a spell of dizziness; he had experienced such spells before. There was a blackness before his eyes. He felt as though he had plunged into the midst of a deep night. He could neither see nor hear. A load oppressed his heart. Anxiety shook him. He was terrified at his sudden recollection of the attack he had only a few days before while he was working on a roof. It was fortunate that he had worn his safety belt then. Why wasn't he wearing it now? Dear God, he must get down from the scaffold right away. He mustn't think about death. Nothing would happen to him. He must be strong. He must think of little Bertha. . . . Tonight he would take her to a movie . . . just the two of them. . . . But between him and Bertha yawned the deep abyss beneath the scaffolding. Underneath, down there, was a street full of people— and he was here, alone. He was a prisoner on the scaffolding. He would never again be able to escape. . . . What sort of thoughts were these? . . .

"I must get down from the scaffolding before it gets too late," he thought. "It's time already. What time is it? It must be near twelve. I'll wait for the slaughterhouse whistle to blow. I won't work any more after lunch. . . . I'll take the children . . . I'll take

207

the pigeons ... I'll take the ferry to Staten Island. I'll take the pigeons.... Too bad the pigeons aren't here any more.... Where are the pigeons?..."

His ears were filled with the beating of wings. Everything became dark around him.... There was only the rush of bird's wings. White pigeons were cleaving the sky ... and he was flying after them. ...

From then on things happened quickly. Irving got the news on the telephone; an accident had happened; he was to come to Bellevue Hospital right away.

At the entrance to the hospital half of 48th Street wandered aimlessly up and down or stood in little groups talking in subdued voices. In the corridor of the hospital he saw his father, Shmulevitch, and Mike Maloney. Harry had been taken into the operating room. They hadn't been told yet how matters stood; they knew only that it was serious. There was a bad skull fracture; Harry was still unconscious.

"Where is Rachel?" Irving asked.

"Upstairs, near the operating room."

Outside the door of the operating room Rachel stood. She was alone. With the panic-stricken eyes of an animal she watched the doctors and nurses as they hurried through the corridor into the operating room. She didn't cry, she only looked dazedly about her. She had the same dazed look when Irving went up to her. She seemed not to recognize him. He took her arm and tried to lead her away from the door.

"Come on, Rachel. You can't do anything here."

Only then did she recognize him, as though his voice had recalled him to her memory. She stared at him with wide eyes.

"Where are Bertha and Goldie?"

"The children? I don't know. Mrs. Kranz must have taken them."

Her eyes suddenly filled with tears. She fell into Irving's arms and sobbed against him. He led her away from the door.

A little while later the doctors came out of the operating room. They were followed by a few nurses wheeling a stretcher from which only Harry's bandaged head showed. One of the doctors told Rachel and the others to go home; there was nothing now to do but wait. It was too soon to say anything definite. The crisis might last through the night—or even longer. In the meanwhile the patient had to have absolute quiet; nobody was to disturb him; they were taking him to a separate .room. He would be given the best possible care. Judge Greenberg had telephoned; so had some other important political officials. The family could be sure that everything that Bellevue could do would be done. In the meanwhile they must let the patient rest.

Irving did not go back to the office; he stayed with Rachel at the hospital. Toward evening—Harry was still unconscious, and there was no further medical report—Irving took her to his parents' house to spend the night.

In the morning there was no change. Harry was "fighting for his life." He had not yet recovered consciousness, but there was reason to hope that he might pull through.

In the afternoon Irving lifted the telephone in his office to call the hospital. As he was giving the number Moshe Wolf came in, flushed and breathless.

"Come quick, Irving! Hurry!"

"What's happened?"

"Harry's dying. He's just recovered consciousness. The first word he said was your name. He wants the marriage to take place before he dies ... right by his bed in the hospital room. Shmulevitch has gone to get a rabbi to perform the ceremony. Rachel is at the hospital. Hurry up. The doctors say they don't know how long he'll last. It's as though he's only staying alive to see his daughter married. ..."

Irving's first impulse was to go to the hospital with his father and get it over with. In the face of the demands of religion and simple human decency, what else could he do? He must marry Rachel now, whatever the consequences. But there was something he must do first; there was a responsibility he had to someone else. He must first talk with Mary.

"I'll be there right away," he said to his father. "You go ahead. I'll come right away."

"I'll go and get your mother, maybe a couple of the neighbors. But hurry, come quick." Moshe Wolf rushed out.

Mary was on the upper floor. She knew of the accident and she had sensed the truth when she saw Moshe Wolf burst in, and she knew exactly what was going on in Irving's mind. When he called her downstairs and closed the office door behind her, she steeled herself to act as though she were unaware of what was happening.

"What's the matter?" she asked.

"Harry Greenstock is dying. My father was just here. They want me to come to the hospital and marry Rachel at his bedside."

Mary was silent.

"There's nothing else I can do. I have to get married right away."

"No, there's nothing else you can do." Mary's face was set in a strange smile. Irving stared intently at her.

"Well, Mary, what do you say?"

"Why do you ask me?"

"Do you want me to go or not? You have to tell me."

"I think that you have to go."

"Is that what you honestly think? Do you really mean it?"

"Yes," Mary answered.

"Maybe we can find a way out."

"What way out could there be?"

"I mean later, when everything is over, and I can talk the whole thing over with Rachel."

"It'll be too late then," Mary said. She sounded as though the words were being forced out of her.

"What do you mean?"

"Nothing.... You didn't promise me anything, Irving. I took the responsibility. You told me at the very beginning that you couldn't marry me. It's my fault."

"It isn't a question about anybody's fault. But you've got to tell me everything you're thinking now—before I go to the hospital."

"I'm pregnant," Mary said quietly.

"Pregnant! Are you sure? Why didn't you tell me?"

"I wanted to be absolutely sure. I saw the doctor this morning."

"And you're still willing for me to marry Rachel?"

"What has my willingness to do with it? There's nothing else you can do. You promised her; you promised her father. You didn't promise me anything."

"What shall I do? What shall I do?"

"Go and marry Rachel," Mary said. She turned and left the office.

"Mary! Mary!"

210

"She's waiting for you, Irving," Mary called back from the door.

Irving went into Nathan's room in the Davidowsky apartment. In the hour of his bewilderment and desperation there was no one else he could turn to. From as far back as he could remember he had come to his brother with all his troubles. Now he came to him again.

He looked about the room wildly. "Is Pa home?" he asked in panic.

"No."

"And Ma?"

"She isn't home either. They went to the hospital. They're waiting there for you."

"I know. They want us to get married before he dies. What shall I do? What shall I do?" Irving wrung his hands, his face contorted in pain.

"What's happened? I thought you loved Rachel."

"Yes, I know. Everybody thinks so. I don't know myself. We grew up together. Of course I love her. She's a wonderful girl. I always took it for granted that if I should ever get married it would be to her. But now that we're both grown up...now I realize that Rachel's not for me. I'm in love with someone else."

"Why didn't you tell her?"

"There wasn't any reason to tell. We never talked about getting married. We just played together; we just had fun together—then we were engaged. No matter what happened between me and someone else, I always thought I would marry Rachel."

"You mean you would marry her even if you were in love with someone else?"

"Yes. There is someone else, but I can't marry her. She knows it and she understands."

"Why can't you marry her?"

"She's Christian."

Nathan was silent. He looked about the room. After a while he said: "And is that the reason you can't marry her?"

"It'll kill Pa.... It'll ruin the whole famliy. I'd made up my mind never to get married at all—it would be the only way—not to marry either Rachel or Mary...."

Nathan turned white. "Did you say Mary?"

211

"Yes, Mary.... But when Pa came and told me that Harry was dying and wanted us to get married right away, I was ready to go through with it. I talked to Mary about it. She was willing. But then I found out..." Irving stopped.

"What did you find out?"

"She's pregnant...."

Nathan kept a tight hold on himself. He leaned back on the couch.

"How did you find out?" he asked at last. His voice was quiet.

"She told me. Just now. She's been to the doctor."

"And are you...?"

Irving nodded his head.

Nathan got up from the couch. He got up without thinking about it. It was as though his limbs had regained their full powers. He began to walk in shuffling steps, without using his crutches. He went over to Irving who was seated at the desk. As he reached the desk he lost his balance and fell. Irving tried to stop him, but it was too late. He lay on the floor, making no effort to pick himself up. His right arm was stretched out toward Irving.

"Get out right away and get Mary and go down to City Hall."

Irving tried to help him up but Nathan motioned him away.

"Right away. Go right away," he kept on saying, his right arm still outstretched. His face had the stern expression of a judge in a courtroom pronouncing the verdict.

"Let me help you up," Irving stammered.

"Leave me alone. I'll get up myself." Nathan managed to raise himself onto his elbow. Irving helped him to get on his feet.

"I told you what to do. Why don't you go? It will be late. There's no time left. Hurry! Go!"

"How can I? They're waiting for me at the hospital!"

"Go. Right away." There was almost a hysterical note of command in Nathan's voice.

"How can I shame a dying man?"

"How can you shame a child who's just beginning life?"

"What about Rachel?"

"Write to her. Tell her everything. Tell her that you love Mary. Go! Go quickly, before someone comes in."

"And what about Pa? What'll he do?"

"What does that matter now? It's too late to worry about anything else now. Go quickly, before they come in."

Irving looked around helplessly. "All right, Nat, I'll go. You're right. I'm a fool for not seeing it myself. I'm going. Please make them understand that I couldn't do anything else. Please! Help me." The tears rolled down his cheeks.

"I'll tell them. I'll explain everything to them. Go, Irving. Go quickly." Nathan held out his hand.

"Thank you, Nat. Please don't hold it against me."

"All right, Irving. Don't worry. Everything will be all right."

"And you don't blame me for what happened with Mary?"

"I don't blame anybody."

Irving left the room and went down into the street. He hurried furtively out of the block, like a thief.

Mary was in the shop when he got there. She was attending to her duties as though nothing unusual had happened.

"Come quickly, Mary. Get your things on and come with me," Irving ordered her, taking her hand.

"Where to?"

"I'll tell you later. Come quickly. There's no time to lose."

They rode downtown in silence. As they went into City Hall, Irving halted on the stairs. "We better get everything settled, Mary," he said. "About the difference in our religion, you know how my family looks at those things. And the same with your family. There's going to be plenty of bitterness. I'm not going to become a Christian and I don't expect you to become a Jew. Let's agree—now—that the child... Naturally I'd want the child to be Jewish and you'd want it to be a Catholic. Let's agree that we won't bring the child up one way or the other. Later it can decide for itself. Is that all right with you? Do you agree?"

"Yes," Mary nodded.

"It's a promise?"

"It's a promise," Mary answered. She held out her hand. Irving put his hand in hers.

The wedding canopy leaned against the wall of the hospital room. Rachel sat by her father's bed holding his hand in hers. The tears streamed from her eyes.

Near the foot of the bed sat Mike Maloney. He was wearing a dark suit, the coat buttoned closely about him. He held his stiff derby hat on his knee. His face was pale, his lips were pressed

213

together tightly. There was an expressionless look in his cold blue eyes.

A doctor held Harry's wrist. Harry's face was almost entirely hidden beneath the white bandages. The sound of his labored breathing filled the room.

Outside the door the rabbi whom Shmulevitch had brought to perform the marriage ceremony paced up and down impatiently. He waved his hands violently as Shmulevitch pleaded with him to wait. Mrs. Davidowsky walked up and down the corridor, grim-lipped, wringing her hands and muttering to herself. Standing alone against a wall of the corridor, Clara Kranz held a handkerchief to her eyes.

Moshe Wolf was downstairs in a telephone booth. He had called Irving's office a dozen times and each time they had told him that Irving had gone away with Mary and that he wouldn't be back. Moshe Wolf couldn't believe it. How could he believe that his son would betray a solemn promise to a dying man?

"I don't know what's happened! He told me he would come right away," he said to Shmulevitch in helpless bewilderment.

They looked at each other. Both of them looked at Deborah. She shrugged her shoulders and pressed her lips tightly together.

"He'll come. He must come. He promised me. I know he'll come."

Inside the room it was quiet, as though death, entering the room, was sending silence as his advance messenger. The doctor looked at Maloney. Maloney avoided his glance.

The dying man was aware only that he was floating in a strange, nebulous cloud. He seemed to be falling, falling, into a black nothingness. The only thing that saved him from plummeting into the abyss was a thin, tenuous thread of awareness that vibrated within him, now stretched to the breaking point. There was something he must wait for, something he must first do. What this compulsion was became dimmer and dimmer to him, he only knew he must wait for it to be done. "Quicker ... quicker." His lips formed the words, but no sound emerged. The doctor, watching him closely, threw another disquieted glance at Maloney.

Suddenly Rachel got up from her chair and looked down at her father. She was no longer crying. Her eyes were wide and there was an unearthly glow in them. There was a strange serenity in her face. She bent over Harry and said in a distinct, emotionless voice: "Don't worry, Papa. I'll take care of the children. Good-by, Papa. Good-by."

Moshe Wolf opened the door and went inside. He stood quietly by the bed while the doctor felt Harry's pulse. "The end is near," the doctor said. "It will be over in a minute."

Moshe Wolf bent over the bed and softly recited the orthodox ritual. Harry's lips moved faintly as though he were repeating the words. *"Shema Yisroel*—Hear O Israel, the Lord our God is one."

"Forgive me," Moshe Wolf whispered to the dying man. "I did not want it so. Forgive me."

CHAPTER TWENTY-ONE

IN A copper stand which Deborah had brought with her from the old country, a candle burned, a *yahrzeit* candle for the memory of the dead. As though mourning for one dead in in his own household Moshe Wolf sat on a low bench. He had made the symbolical rent of mourning in the dress Deborah wore; he had made a rent in his own coat. He sat on the mourning bench and he recited the moving and prescribed verses from Lamentations in the traditional chant.

"How doth the city sit solitary. . . ."

"You mourn as though our son were dead in reality—God forbid it. . . ." Deborah complained bitterly.

Moshe Wolf made no answer. He sat on the bench, swaying over the open prayer book. "She weepeth sore in the night, and her tears are on her cheeks. . . ."

"It's her fault. I knew she'd bring misfortune to us from the first day she stepped in the door."

Nathan looked up from the table at which he sat. "It isn't her fault; it isn't his fault. They had to get married," he said.

"Had to?" Deborah repeated; Moshe Wolf raised his head from the prayer book and looked at Nathan.

"In reality she was his wife already. She's pregnant."

"Pregnant?" Deborah repeated. There was complete unbelief in her voice.

"Yes. They were in love. It's natural and it happened. She'll soon have a baby. Irving's baby."

Moshe Wolf's eyes were horror-stricken in his ash-gray face. He looked wildly about him as though a yawning abyss had opened up before him to engulf him. Deborah tore at her hair and clawed her face and shrieked in agony. Moshe Wolf did not move from the stool. He bowed his head toward the floor. His shoulders swayed in prayer. His voice rose and fell in the same cadence with which he had chanted the Lamentations: "My grand-child will be a Gentile.... The grandchild of Davidowsky will be a Gentile...." He got up from the bench and walked uncertainly up and down the room. Suddenly he stopped. "We once had a son," he said to Deborah. "Now we have no son. Our son is dead. His name must be blotted from our memory. His money is unclean to us. He is dead to us." He returned to the mourner's bench and resumed his ritual chanting.

Later he went into the kitchen, washed his hands at the sink and stood near the window to recite the evening prayers. He went into the kitchen—not into the parlor, nor any of the new rooms. He prayed at the kitchen window, as he was used to pray in the days before Irving's money had bought new rooms and new furniture for the flat.

It was not only Moshe Wolf and Deborah to whom Irving's marriage to Mary had brought bitterness and grief. Everyone on 48th Street felt that an unforgivable crime had been committed against poor Harry. The feeling was so strong that it even overcame the suspicions and prejudices between Christian and Jew on the block. Jew and Christian equally predicted that the marriage would come to a bad end. "No good can come of it," they said. The story went around that Harry had died with a curse on his lips; they all knew that the dead man would never rest in his grave until justice was done. And since the guilty pair were not on hand to receive the block's wrath, its anger was poured out on the heads of their unlucky parents. "McCarthy's in-law," they called Moshe Wolf scornfully. Nor was McCarthy spared.

For several days the McCarthys didn't show their faces on the street, and there was talk of breaking into the house to see what was going on. One morning the neighborhood woke up to discover that the McCarthys had moved away from the house quietly during the night.

Of the people involved, the only one to walk through the block with head high, and firm, unashamed glance, was Rachel. She accepted the expressions of condolence on her father's death from the neighbors, Jew and Christian alike, with calm dignity. No one could sense in her attitude any resentment against Irving's desertion of her. She sorrowed only for her father. She wept bitterly when she was indoors at Mrs. Kranz's; she had moved into her

217

house after the funeral. The other children were there, too, with the approval of Judge Greenberg and Mike Maloney, whom Harry had named in his will as guardians of the children and executors of his estate.

Moshe Wolf applied himself doggedly and determinedly to resume his old life. He moved back into the old, crowded quarters. Again he slept on the cot near Nathan. The kitchen became again the family's living quarters, parlor, dining room, and the room for prayer.

He let the helper in the store go, and got up himself at dawn to take in the cans of milk and the fresh bread and rolls which were delivered early, and prepared the store for the day's business. He swept the floor, cleaned the entrance, hardly finding time before the first customers appeared to run upstairs and recite his morning prayers. There was no time to linger over them; those days were gone with Irving. Such luxuries were now left for the Sabbath, when the store was closed. Nor could he permit himself any time to pore over the holy writings, to study the week's portion in the Bible, or to chant the psalms.

The duties waiting for him in the store would force him to rush downstairs, and as he took off his prayer shawl and phylacteries and put the prayer book away, he would think to himself: "The dear God knows that I have no time. . . ." He would hastily swallow some food and run into Nathan's room. "Nathan, are you all right?" He knew that Nathan needed his help in the morning to dress.

Nathan had to adjust himself, too, to the altered circumstances which Irving's marriage had brought about in the Davidowsky household. He wanted more than anything else to make himself useful and helpful in the day's work. He yearned for an end to his role of parasite. He wanted by his own efforts to justify his existence and the new-found physical and spiritual blessings that had fallen to him.

He satisfactorily passed the examinations which would readmit him to college, and he accepted the financial help which Irving sent him through Dr. Chazanowitch. He held no grievance against his brother, and he managed to avoid the faintest feeling of envy. Nevertheless he couldn't help feeling a strong sense of guilt, especially when he saw how valiantly his father struggled against the poverty that had resumed its sway over the household.

It wasn't long before Moshe Wolf learned that Irving was contributing money for Nathan's studies through Dr. Chazanowitch and that Deborah was getting money from Irving every week. The news stunned him. He stopped talking and fell into a lonely, solitary existence.

He showed the same warm affection toward Nathan as before, but the boy could sense the change in his father, although Moshe Wolf never let a word pass his lips.

Quite otherwise was the way Deborah took the family troubles. Not for a moment did she accept the situation. She refused to give up hope that eventually Irving would rid himself of his Gentile wife and come back to the family hearth. Not only would he come back to the family but he would marry his destined bride, the right bride for him—Rachel. His promise to Harry must be kept; how otherwise could it be? The dead man would never rest; he would demand justice for his child. Therefore Deborah made no effort to avoid Rachel, she tried in every way possible to keep the girl close to her. It was as though she thought that by watching over Rachel and Harry's other children, she could placate the dead man and prevent him from summoning the curse of heaven on Irving. She had sought out Rachel shortly after the funeral.

"Rachel," she said to the girl. "You're like my own daughter to me. Help me win back my son. The *shikse* worked some sort of magic over him. He was dazzled by her. She caught him in a trap. But he'll escape from her. Just wait and see. . . ."

"I have nothing against them," Rachel answered. "I wish them luck—all the luck they're entitled to," she could not help adding, unable to control her bitterness.

Deborah moodily shook her head.

After an awkward silence Rachel said: "Do you think that Mr. Davidowsky"—it was the first time she had failed to refer to him as Moshe Wolf—"would arrange for someone to recite the *kaddish* for my father?"

"He's been saying the *kaddish* himself right along," Deborah answered. "Right after the funeral he started. Every Friday and

Saturday, in the *shul*. He would do it on the weekdays, too, but they don't have enough people for the services."

Rachel was so touched by the news that she went over to the store to thank Moshe Wolf.

It wasn't long before the old relationship was re-established between Rachel and the Davidowskys, just as though nothing had happened. Moshe Wolf lavished warm affection on the Greenstock children. It made no difference to him now that they had gone to live with Mrs. Kranz. Besides, Mrs. Kranz went out of her way to see that the children should remain in their faith. Every Friday she saw to it that they were neatly washed and combed and dressed in their best. Then she would send them over to Moshe Wolf's for the Sabbath evening meal. On Jewish holidays, too, the children would be at the Davidowskys. Deborah took them with her to the synagogue for memorial services.

In spite of all that had happened, Harry's orphaned children were at home in Moshe Wolf's home. Deborah treated them with more affection than she had ever shown her own children. It was as though she were seeking to buy absolution for her son's sin. There was warmth and love and comfort for little Goldie and Bertha; more, it was as though in the Davidowsky household they found satisfaction for some unconscious urge to be with their own, to stay close to the roots of their origin and their faith.

CHAPTER TWENTY-TWO

RACHEL HAD decided against looking for work in an office; what she wanted was a job as model or salesgirl in a dress shop. An unconscious impulse drove her to find the same kind of job as Mary's.

In one of the smaller dress shops to which she applied, the owner seemed interested. After eying her appraisingly and having her walk up and down a few times, he asked if she had had any modeling experience.

"Oh, yes," Rachel answered eagerly. "I've had a lot of experience. I've modeled dresses for buyers in a wholesale place."

When the owner asked for the name of the firm, Rachel refused. She could not give the name, she said; she had private reasons. The owner seemed suspicious, but he appeared to be willing to engage her. Did she know that the job didn't pay much? Yes, she knew that; she didn't expect to stay a model; she wanted to learn selling.

The shop owner, a dapper figure of a man, with sparkling dark eyes, took her on, and Rachel went home elated and happy. At last she would be earning her own living. It wouldn't be much— eight dollars a week—but now she could pay Mrs. Kranz something toward the care of the children. She would make good—she must make good! She would learn selling and become a successful saleslady. Then she could support her sisters; she could keep the promise she had made to her father on his deathbed.

But it took only a few days in the new job to wake Rachel from her dreams. The store owner hardly let her alone; he never took his eyes off her. He watched her while she changed to model a dress for a customer, walking brazenly into the dressing rooms while the girls were half naked. The others didn't seem to mind his ogling and suggestive remarks, but Rachel flushed with embarrassment. At first she was too timid to protest, but when the owner began to take liberties with her, she protested. "Were you so modest where you worked before?" he asked sarcastically. "It won't get you very far. You better come into my office before you go home."

Later, seated at his desk in his office, he said to her: "I'm afraid you won't do. You haven't got a bad figure, but you don't know how to handle a model's job. If you want to stay on, you can work in the basement, sorting merchandise. The salary's the same, but, naturally, the work's not so pleasant. Think it over and let me know."

Rachel had lost her pride. She was on her own now; there was no one to lean on for protection.

"I'll take it. I have to earn my living," she answered.

"All right," the owner said. "Report tomorrow morning at eight. You'll go to the basement with this card." He gave her a slip. "But it's a shame, with a figure like yours"—he eyed her again—"and such a pretty face." As Rachel started to leave, he stopped her. "Wait a minute," he said. "Why don't you have dinner with me tonight? There's a nice Italian restaurant I'll take you to. Maybe I can help you."

"I'm sorry, but I don't make any dates."

"Not with anybody?"

"No. I'm in mourning." Again she turned to go.

"All right, whatever you say."

But things were no better in the basement stockroom where Rachel worked with a few older women. Not only was the work unpleasant and the room crowded, but even there she wasn't safe from annoyance. The overseer, a coarse, pimply adolescent, bothered her from the moment she reported for work, and the store owner, hoping that by now she would be more amenable, called her into his office each few days to ask whether she thought she was ready to try the modeling job again.

Rachel had to quit. She dismissed the possibility of using her stenography. She would learn the dress trade, whether or no, and prove herself in the business that had brought Irving his success. The next job she found was in Brooklyn, a long trip from home. It was a temporary job for the Christmas season, selling lingerie. It didn't take her long to learn that her good looks were far from being an asset; salesmen, floor managers, overseers, and foremen hung around her; the other girls were jealous and showed it. She quit that job, too.

Her comfortable world seemed to be at an end; she would never be able to keep the promise she had made to her dying father to take care of the children. She knew that the little money left of her father's estate wouldn't last long. Mrs. Kranz begged her not to worry; Mike Maloney and Judge Greenberg would take care of everything; nevertheless the weight of her responsibilities pressed heavily on her shoulders. Everything was going wrong. She had thought that it would be easy for her, that her pretty face would see her through. Now it turned out that her pretty face and figure meant only trouble. She began to neglect her appearance. Gone were the days when she would stand in front of the mirror, admiring the graceful figure and the "classic features" that everybody was always praising. She wanted to be like other girls, like the run-of-the-mill girls she would meet in the streets and the stores; girls who had no other gifts but skillful hands with which to earn their livelihoods.

One evening she came home from her latest job tired out. In front of the door stood a sleek and elegant automobile. She gave no special thought to it; it was probably calling to pick up one of Mrs. Kranz's boarders who had had a stroke of good luck. Inside the house she was surprised to see several people in Mrs. Kranz's parlor. In the heavily draped, dimly lighted room she barely made out the massive and clumsy figure of her uncle Silberberg. He was sitting between Mike Maloney and Judge Greenberg. From Uncle Silberberg's chair came the sound of strangled coughing and grumbling. Then came an annoyed growl. "Don't you pay any attention to me?"

"Oh, Uncle, I'm so happy to see you."

"Happy! Ha!"

"Oh, yes I am, Uncle! I'm so glad to see you!"

"But you never bothered to let me know what you are doing! I have to find it out from strangers!"

"I didn't know that you'd be interested."

For Uncle Silberberg the remark was like a stab, digging through the barriers of fat that had accumulated about his family feelings. Now he recognized the situation for what it really was. Here were helpless, homeless orphans, the children of his own niece. Yet they had not turned to him because they did not know whether he'd be interested in their lot. What was the use of the fortune he had accumulated? Here were his own kinsfolk and the forlorn orphans of his own flesh and blood too terrified of him to come to him for help. He had had to learn of their troubles from strangers. Judge Greenberg had had to write to him.

"So you didn't know if I'd be interested?" He began to shout, more out of anger at himself, although he looked wrathfully at Rachel. "My own family! And you didn't know whether I'd be interested!" As though he were trying to convince them that the fault was not his he yelled at the top of his voice. "Where were you? What are you doing?"

"I'm working," Rachel replied.

"Where? What kind of work?"

"What's the difference? I have to make a living for myself and the children."

"No. You don't have to. That's what I'm here for. It was your duty to let me know. You knew you could come to me."

Judge Greenberg interrupted in his quiet, authoritative voice.

"Your uncle is right. I'm afraid we're all somewhat to blame. Your uncle called up the moment he learned what had happened. He phoned me right away. He is undertaking to provide for the children, and for you, too. Everything is already arranged with Mrs. Kranz. That's why we're here now. You're going back to school. You don't have to go to work. Your uncle will take care of everything."

"I want to keep on working," Rachel said. "I don't want to go back to school."

"Why not?"

"Because I want to earn my own living."

"Yes, but in order to earn your own living you have to learn some skill. Isn't that right?" Judge Greenberg said persuasively. "Don't you agree?"

"I don't want to go back to school. I'm old enough to begin earning my own living."

"I don't see anything wrong in that," Judge Greenberg said. "What kind of work do you want to do, Rachel?"

"I don't want her to work." Silberberg shouted. "I want her to go to school. I want her to go to college. I want her to wear fine clothes, and live in comfort, and meet nice people, and boys from good homes. I want her to be a lady. I'll take care of everything. I don't want her to go to work."

Rachel looked at her uncle with warm eyes in which grateful tears were beginning to gather.

"But I want to work, Uncle," she said to him pleadingly. "I'll be unhappy if I don't work. I want to have a career."

"I don't see any harm in it," Judge Greenberg broke in. "What kind of work do you want to do?"

"I want to work at women's wear."

"Women's wear?" Uncle Silberberg asked in surprise.

"Yes. I want to sell in one of the large stores. I want to learn all I can about the trade. I want to design new styles. I want to be a designer...."

"Why didn't you tell me that? I'll send you to the best designing school. I'll give you a letter of recommendation to Berman on Fifth Avenue. There you can learn everything. But I want you to go to school. I want you to be a lady," Uncle Silberberg declared vehemently. His big moon face glowed with eagerness and affection.

PART II

CHAPTER ONE

FROM THE depths of the dark African jungles, heavy with the narcotic aroma of the tropical forests, a melody came creeping—a melody whose primeval rhythm stirred and intoxicated the white man in far-off Manhattan.

Who had brought the strange rhythm to Manhattan? Had it come from the night haunts of New Orleans, borne on the swell of the Negro wave to Harlem? Had it come from the dives and brothels of Harlem to capture the streets of New York? In any case, the jungle motif with its licentious beat swept New York into a primitive dancing madness.

The Middle Ages had known such a dance mania; it had come and gone. But the madness that swept over New York at the beginning of the jazz age shook the foundations of respectable family life and brought in its wake a revolutionary shift in the morals and behavior of the American woman.

In the dark primeval forest the manlike ape had sought to shut out threatening terrors in the tearing convulsions of mating lust.. Now the rhythmic beat of the jazz madness had brought the terrors of the African night eastward from the jungles—and now, too, there was refuge from them only in self-forgetfulness and self-abandonment through the narcotic of naked desire. The rhythm penetrated into the white man's blood and stirred the primitive instincts within him, the dark heritage of his jungle past. In Manhattan, in America, in Europe, the pulse of the white man answered the jungle, surrendering to the call of the primitive past. Broken were the bonds of the discipline which had chained him for generations. Deep buried lusts, long held prisoner by religious interdiction and sacrosanct social custom, broke out of their centuries-old prisons. New York broke out in a veritable rash of dance halls and night clubs. Elderly dowagers took lessons in dancing from slick young teachers, and venerable heads of families—pillars of society—from the Wall Street banker to the schoolteacher who earned hardly enough to provide for his family sported black silk socks and patent leather shoes and went for lessons to the studios of dancing teachers. Doctors prescribed dancing lessons as a cure for the ailments of tired patients. Bank directors and board members exchanged addresses of dance studios at directors' meetings. In the lobbies of the big hotels, in cushioned chairs in dimly lighted alcoves, sat elegantly dressed, pallid-faced young men waiting for the "hotel mice"—the rich wives, widows, spinsters—the permanent residents of the large hotels. "Gigolos," these pale young men were called in Europe; America christened them "lounge lizards."

Every hotel had to have a dance hall; almost as though it had been decreed by legislative act. The floors were small and crowded, the better for dancing couples to press bodies closely together under the dim lights, dancing cheek to cheek, young and old mixed together in a dancing mass. The perspiration soaked through the thick layers of powder on the wrinkled faces of old dowagers, bouncing up and down to the tune of the "Turkey Trot" or the "Grizzly Bear" or the "Bunny Hug." They swayed about, body pressed to body, a solid moving group, all signs of individuality lost in it. Captive worshipers, held in thrall by the dance mania, swayed back and forth to the wail of the woodwinds and the wild, rutty call of the blaring saxophones.

The dance mania had its influence on American family life. The social independence of women can properly be reckoned as beginning with the rise of the jazz age. Not only did it break down the barriers which had hemmed women in, and into which the social mores and traditional education of the times had held her, but it made her man's equal. Woman felt free, an individual in her own right. She arrogated the right to go wherever she pleased —and whenever she pleased. She was seen alone in places where earlier her presence would have been unimaginable. She smoked and drank—not only in the intimacy of her own home but in public places.

With the rise of the dance craze the woman claimed for herself rights which had been the exclusive privileges of men. Now the husband and master would come home at the end of the day to find the house deserted; let him cool his heels and wait for his dinner until his wife came home from her "five o'clock" *thé*

230

dansant; the precious privilege of coming home late—the exclusive prerogative of the male! The husband had to watch his wife dancing with men who were strangers to him; he had to watch her responding—like a woman of easy virtue—to the intimate embrace of a gigolo. And if he dared to protest, he was laughed at as an old fossil who was way behind the times.

The dance mania went further. It undermined the sanctity of the marriage bond and degraded it to an inconsequential arrangement which could be entered into or abandoned at will, on the slightest whim. The pendulum swung to the far extreme; now it was the wife who suggested a divorce to her husband. Wives changed husbands and husbands changed wives—like the casual changing of a garment.

The dance madness had its unavoidable effect on the appearance of the American woman; it had its particular effect on her attire. Up to 1912, before the dance mania gripped New York, the American woman of fashion wore dresses of heavy black satin or silk which covered her from chin to toes. Apart from the ribbons and bows and folds which the fashion decreed, her dress was not very far from the crinoline, impossible to wear without the stiff fishbone corset which enclosed the curves of her body in an unyielding harness. The corset dominated her body and determined her figure. An expensively embellished gown was intended only to bear witness to her husband's wealth and to be worn only for show; most often it hung in the closet. And when the woman did wear it she felt as though she were dressed up for a parade. The folds and billows and pleats were all designed to give the wearer a tall and stately appearance. And there was the wide hat with its arching ostrich feather, and the fox collar and the dainty parasol! It was impossible to imagine wearing an elegant dress without carrying a parasol! Altogether the ensemble was more like a military uniform for female cadets. The dresses trailed behind them the faint odor of lavender from their long stay in scented closets—a far cry from the heady perfumes of the modern woman.

In 1914, under the influence of the dance craze, a revolution began in woman's clothes—more properly an evolution, since female dress was to pass through gradual transformations until it reached the radical styles of the later years. The corset was still the power behind the throne, determining the female figure. But instead of raising the bosom, tightening the waist and emphasizing the hips, as the old fishbone corset had done, the modern corset narrowed the hips and flattened the bosom. With the fishbone stays abandoned for a simple elastic material there was no longer a wall of iron between the woman and her dance partner. In spite of the war raging in Europe, Paris was still the center of fashion. And Paris decreed that woman should resemble a bird, with bird of paradise feathers on her head, and a dress with a long train. Brought over to America, the dress was designed with a Moorish note—a harem dress, narrow at the ankles, resembling Persian pantalettes, and forcing the wearer to move along in mincing steps. The rhythm of the dance could no longer express itself in the free movements of the old-fashioned waltz, which seemed to have in it something of the eternal battle between the sexes—the man constantly pursuing and the woman constantly retreating. The modern dance was a willing, harmonious coming together, the dancing couple continuing their co-ordinated easy swaying until the rising tempo of the music and pressure of body against body ended with the convulsive climax of the music. The narrow hem of the dress, compelling the wearer to take small steps, was deliberately designed to suit the dance movements of the jazz age.

But in the close intimacy and warm sensuality of the dance the corset, simplified though it was, was for the woman an unwelcome barrier between herself and her partner. In 1915 the corset began to disappear from the feminine wardrobe. Dress materials changed; heavy velvets and rustling satins gave way to clinging, transparent flesh-colored chiffons. It was the "lingerie dress" that now adorned the American woman.

It was not yet the frank and revealing garment it was ultimately to become, although it was short enough to reveal the delicate stockinged ankles. Eventually the woman was to find a new freedom of easy, natural movement. The beauty and grace so long concealed, the resiliency of the limbs, the harmonious play of delicate muscles—rid of the restrictions of corsets and fishbone stays—had never known such freedom since the ancient days of the Greek tunic.

Irving Davidowsky was quick to recognize that the "lingerie dress" had come to stay. He saw that a new era was beginning in the garment industry, and he sensed the vast possibilities which the new one-piece dress presented to the smart businessman for mass production. There was no need for careful and laborious cutting and modeling; the dress required no fitting to individual figures. It did away with the endless complicated ornamentation of pleats, folds, and ribbons which the earlier fashions had demanded and which required the painstaking labor of skilled dressmakers. The simple lines of the dress, free of complicated trimmings, made it easy to produce anywhere. It could even be manufactured outside the factory; by home workers whom contractors could hire cheap.

The new style had another advantage, well suited to the extravagant nature of the American woman who longed for change; she changed her attire with each change in fashion. Rich or poor—there had to be a new hat each season. Why not new dresses too? Why not several changes within a single season? A woman was not a bird whose foliage must do for the whole summer. She must be always new, always different. She must attract men.

And her man liked to see her in something new. Up to now it had been only the rich who could afford such luxuries; the proud and haughty ones who took whole caravans of dresses with them wherever they went. No woman of society would dare be seen twice in the same dress. Why not give the same privilege to the woman of lesser means, the white-collar worker's wife? Why shouldn't every salesgirl, every shopgirl, have the chance to buy pretty clothes and to show herself to her boy friend in colors and style that would enhance her charm?

Up to the appearance of the negligee dress that possibility was barred to the average woman; materials were too high, manufacture too costly. The new style for the first time promised the possibility for mass production of attractive clothes, with a consequent radical reduction in price, so as to bring the cost of dress down to the purse of the masses. And the only way to do that was to introduce rigid economies in the cost of materials and production techniques.

Irving Davidowsky, by now a recognized manufacturer in the ladies' wear industry, went to his bank and had a talk with Mr. Grossman, the vice-president and treasurer. The bank was growing rapidly with the needle industry it served. Its vice-president had been a clothing manufacturer himself—even a worker, as he was fond of saying. He still held a few silent partnerships with

233

some of the important firms in the trade. He was sympathetic to Irving's ideas and plans.

"I like ambitious young men," he said, putting his hand patronizingly on Irving's shoulder.

"Especially when they're successful," Irving commented. He could afford the free tone. He had a name in the credit markets. His position in the industry, his well-established business with its large staff of salespeople and extensive trade all over the country, made him feel he was entitled to take an independent attitude with the powerful vice-president. Without revealing the details of his plan—that might have been too dangerous in view of Grossman's connections with his competitors—he only told him that he had something in mind that might revolutionize the garment industry.

"I don't like revolutions," the vice-president said.

"Not even if they show a profit?" Irving asked drily.

Fifteen minutes later Irving had in his pocket a letter to the head of a huge Paterson silk mill guaranteeing his competency to take over the entire output of a particular crèpe-de-chine which the mill turned out. The mill was able to sell the piece goods at a low price; it paid substandard wages to the unorganized workers in the mill—and even less to the large numbers of child laborers the mill employed.

With the source of supply established, Irving proceeded to organize the production end of the business. His factory was unionized, and under the prevailing wage rate he, like other manufacturers, would be unable to put the negligee dress on the market at a price low enough to make its mass sale possible. But a way was found out of the dilemma; the cut material was "smuggled" out of the factory and, through the agency of contractors, was sewn together by home labor. Though the unions had won recognition after the successful strike of 1910, exploitation and sweating of the home worker were still widespread; the union carried on a ceaseless and unavailing struggle against such practices. Although the progressive elements of the city and the majority of public opinion demanded action against homework and child labor, it seemed to be impossible to force through the necessary legislation either in individual states or in the Congress. Years and years were to go by—with the legislation continuing to be buried in committee pigeonholes, although the politicians of all the parties

234

coquetted with the question when election time came around. Powerful forces combined in opposition to the adoption of the legislation; let the children of America keep on sweating out profits for the corporations!

What was most bewildering was that the very people who, it might have been expected, would range themselves on the side of the children—high dignitaries of the churches—"Suffer the little children to come unto me"—emerged as the defenders of the manufacturers and industrialists. They fought side by side with the lobbies in Congress and the state legislatures to defeat the laws which the "radicals" were introducing and which would "ruin the economic life of the country." They utilized the moral content of the religion of which they were the custodians—not to save young children from the yawning maw of Moloch, but to feed the fire in Moloch's belly. From church pulpits came the thunder of fiery pronunciamentos declaring that to forbid the labor of children under sixteen would be to jeopardize the very existence of the American home; that if the state or the federal government were granted the right to send inspectors into people's homes to see whether children were engaged in child labor, the authority of the father, the natural head of the family, would be destroyed; and with it would go the respect which children owed to their parents. A new, alien tyranny would wreck the peace of the home and corrupt family morale.

In the meantime the brisk traffic in child labor went on. The prevailing low wages and high rents forced all the members of the family to lend a hand in earning the common livelihood. Fathers, mothers, older brothers and sisters—the ones on whom the burden of providing fell most heavily—could hardly wait for the younger ones to grow up so that they could be harnessed to the yoke of American industry. In the states which had no legislation of any kind against child labor, children worked in glass factories, warping their young lives in front of fiery furnaces. In the Pennsylvania coal mines children scooped the water out of flooded levels. In the New Jersey textile mills children worked at the looms, their tiny hands barely able to tend the spindles, their heads sinking to their breasts in fatigue, until, like the slave children at the looms in ancient Tyre, they were jarred into wakefulness by the overseers.

And in that progressive sector of America, in the great metropolis on Manhattan Island, conditions were not much better. Public opinion was sufficiently on the alert to compel the politicians in Albany to adopt some sort of controlling legislation, while the bills against child labor itself were being constantly amended and debated. Even in the union shops, and with union approval, children under sixteen were employed. In the tenement flats it was the parents themselves who harnessed the children to the treadmill after school hours and late into the night, working on the bundles which contractors supplied.

"I don't want to know anything about hours. You're your own boss. You'll get paid for whatever you turn in, by the piece. Whether you do it in the daytime or at night—that's your business, not mine," the contractors would say to the home workers. "Nobody can tell you how many hours you can work in your own home, or who you get to help you. This is America; it's a free country."

The tenement flats of the poor became transformed into factories in the long winter evenings and the hot summer days. There were bundles of all sorts. Besides dresses and shirts and waists there were artificial flowers, and there were flats where children helped to make cigars, breathing tobacco dust into their young lungs. Tubercular sputum and clots of blood colored the tobacco leaves, or were spat out onto the fabric of a dress to dampen it for the pressing iron.

When unfamiliar steps would be heard outside on the dark stairs, alarm would seize whole families. Maybe it was the official of a society come to snoop around to see if under-age children were working. Neighbors would communicate with each other, warning of the impending danger by means of prearranged signals, and in a moment the work would be hidden away under mattresses. There were only curses for the investigators. "I'd like to know if the society will pay my rent on the first, instead of giving me advice about the children!" would be the greeting. There was no law preventing parents from putting their children to work in the house; it was to be a long time before such a law would be passed. What! Destroy the authority of the head of the family and undermine Christian morality! There were only pious speeches and promises from state officials and the governor. Home labor went on freely and openly in the richest city in the world.

Without the sweat of little children America could not exist; its economy would collapse!

And now to the shackles on the wrists of the children of the richest city in the world, a new weight was added: "Davidow-sky's bundles."

CHAPTER TWO

IRVING'S FACTORY was laid out without any sort of
plan. It was haphazard, like other plants; purely provisional,
driven into expansion by the increasing tempo of the demand
and the desperate efforts of production to catch up with it.

Located in an old, down-at-the-heels merchandise warehouse in
the east twenties, the factory was not much better than a warehouse for human beings. Gradually one floor after another had to
yield to the living merchandise at the expense of the dead merchandise formerly stored there. No improvement in the building accompanied the change. There was the same lone elevator which
had carried cases of leather, straw-packed bales of tea, bundles of
wool, motors and electric machines to the upper floors. Now it
carried elderly Jews, men and women, young girls, children—
human freight—to the same dusty, dark, and bare lofts. The lower
floors were still packed with merchandise—cases of oranges and
other fruit, sacks of foodstuffs; the lease held by a produce dealer
on the lower floors still had a long time to run. At night freight
trucks and produce vans would park at the building to load and
unload merchandise. In the early morning and late evening streams
of factory workers passed in and out of the doors.

The building had had no stair wells; they had been hastily installed only lately as a concession to the fire laws. But in actuality
the stairs were completed only up to the floor where the factory
office and showrooms were located. It was the upper floors which
housed the workers. On one of them rough partitions had been
hastily put together, dividing the floor into sections and separating
the cutters from the sample makers and the sample makers from
the drapers.

These classes of workers were the aristocrats of the needle industry, with higher wages and better working conditions. There
were two toilets on the floor on which they worked, one for the

men, the other for the women. On the other floors all the workers, men and women, had to share a single toilet.

In the section nearest the elevator were several long tables, piled high with bolts of chiffon, heavy moire, transparent voile, pongee, heavy shiny satin, stiff rustling taffetas. There were bolts of cheap dress linen and soft crepes in a wide variety of colors.

The materials were laid out for cutting in a manner which would allow the minimum waste. The success or failure of a style depended largely on the cutter; months of experience were needed for perfection in the craft. The cutters stood at long tables and with heavy shears or razor-edged knives cut parts of garments from the piles of merchandise, following the paper pattern supplied by the head cutter. It was only the expensive materials that were cut by hand; the cheaper materials were handled by electrically driven cutting machines. Busy gangs of youths—boys and girls—under the supervision of an experienced overseer—removed and assorted the cut pieces.

Part of the cut material went to the floor where drapers and bushelmen worked on garments to be manufactured on the premises; most, together with the appropriate trimmings and accessories, were packed into bundles and carried off into a separate stockroom, ready to be delivered to the contractors for completion into finished garments, at rates far cheaper than could be managed under the union scale. These were the renowned "Davidowsky bundles."

Elsewhere on the floor were the drapers, who worked at long rows of muslin-draped dressmaker's dummies. Here the workers were mostly middle-aged women and adult girls. They draped the cut material on the dummies, tacking the pieces on to the muslin with large, loose stitches, preparing the garment for the operators at the sewing machines. Most of the drapers were women who had been seamstresses in the old country, working under the warm Italian sun in a Neapolitan back street or on a Sicilian square, or who had come from a distant, snow-covered town in Russia, or from a gloomy Galician village. Under the beam of a kerosene lamp in a Jewish home as young girls they had accumulated their dowries working for local dressmakers. They had woven their young dreams into the dresses and blouses and petticoats they sewed. Now they were in the New World, in the "golden land"— Italian mothers, their children left unattended in tenement flats,

239

mature Jewish girls with the factory for husband and the sewing needle for child—most of them had long abandoned the young dreams they had cherished in the villages and towns of their youth. Now they stood or knelt in front of the dressmaker's dummies, draping them in satin and silk, crepe and batiste, day in and day out, hour after weary hour. They adjusted the folds of material, modeled the waists, tacked the soft stuffs on the arching bosoms. The work paid well; up among the higher wage levels of the industry. The union had managed to establish a scale of fifteen dollars for a fifty-hour week.

The sample workers worked in the room next to the drapers. They, too, were among the better-paid workers of the industry, since the work required much experience and training. They were mostly middle-aged men—there were few women—who had brought their skills with them from the old country. It was their job to put the garment together according to the sample provided by the designers.

These were the favored classes of workers in the trade. The rooms they worked in were cleaner, and they worked in greater comfort. Since the operation they performed required individual attention, there was plenty of room to stretch and move about; they didn't have to poke their elbows in their neighbor's side.

The upper floors of the Davidowsky plant were a hive of mass production. The freight elevator opened directly into the mouth of a Gehenna! The loft was filled with a rumbling and a buzzing, the vibrating and hammering of electric motors driving the belts over the wheels of the sewing machines, revolving at a dizzying speed. It was here that the operators worked, in a solidly packed mass. The area from wall to wall was crowded with rows of machines, jammed close to one another. The windows, smaller than on the floor below, were locked tight, grimy and dust-covered. Naked electric bulbs hung straight down from the ceiling over the sewing machines. The air was like a Turkish bath. A thick and humid heat, mixed with the escaping steam from the leaky radiators, hung in the air, which was heavy with the electricity which drove the motors and with human sweat; heaviest of all with the feverish activity which boiled, bubbled, and seethed under the flying fingers of the workers.

At the machines, row on row, sat middle-aged and elderly men, bearded and clean-shaved Jews, old women, faded girls. They sat closely pressed together, elbows close to their sides, unable to move their arms without bumping against their neighbors. There were intense Italian faces and mournful Jewish faces. The men sat in their rolled-up shirtsleeves. Some were bareheaded, others wore hats. Sweat poured down from foreheads under the brilliant glare of the lights. The eyes of all of them—the black-bearded as well as the venerable graybeards, or the clean-shaven young men with the bold forward-thrust noses—were like secret beacons, revealing their secret thoughts; their eyes told of their lives, of their joys and sorrows, of their hopes.

Eyes are like sponges; they soak into themselves a man's experiences, they reflect back his ancestry and his heritage. They are like breasts filled with the milk of awareness. Look into a man's eyes, and—without words, without any concrete exchange but only through an intuitive understanding—you sense the partnership of all mankind. You are his brother. You understand him. You bind yourself to him in a realization of common brotherhood and common destiny.

Most of the workers in the factory had lived half of their lives under foreign skies, in other lands. They had brought with them the dreams of their young years, and from these dreams they drew the milk of comfort for their hard life. They sat at the machines, pressed close to one another like galley slaves at the oars of a slave ship, and they thought of the homes that had spewed them out. Many of them, especially the older Jewish workers, still had wives and families in the old country. The war which was raging on the European continent had taken away the possibility of any contact with them. They drew the long lengths of material under the darting needle of the sewing machine. Their hearts raced with the swift tempo of the machines, and in the secret depths of their thoughts they bathed in the quiet waters of their intimate dreams. Some of them thought of their wives and children on the other side of the ocean; others thought of the homes they had already established in the New World, of the small children whom they saw so rarely in their waking hours. They dreamed of the future, of homes and green fields and flowing streams—the scenes they had known in their youth on their native soil.

The aging, unmarried girls, from whose cheeks the dank air of the factory had exhausted all the freshness of youth, and from whose bodies the machine had drawn the marrow of their bones, each dreamed of a new life which she would sometime know . . . sometime, sometime, sometime . . . when God . . . or fortune . . . would smile on her and send her the one she was destined for. A shining prince would come in the guise of a black-haired young revolutionist—he would have to be a revolutionist—and would invite her to a moving picture theater . . . no, they would meet at a masquerade ball which the union would be giving for some important cause, and there he would ask her to be his wife. . . . Or maybe it would be a man past his youth, a young widower with children—not too many children; she would make a concession, a compromise in her dream. . . . Others thought of green gardens, heavy with roses, maybe of an arbor overhung with ripe grapes in the autumn—in the middle of Manhattan, on Delancey Street— the same as it was in good, sunny Napoli.

Most of the operators were new to the trade. It was the easiest way for a greenhorn to earn a living, to be able to send a few dollars back home to a wife waiting for the good tidings that her husband had already saved enough money for a passage for herself and the children. . . . Sewing at the machines was the greenhorn's first introduction into the garment industry, and therefore it paid less than any other branch of the work. The operator was always worried about his job. Whereas the sample maker had to be an experienced hand, the operator could be easily replaced. He was always liable to be fired for the slightest cause; there were hundreds of others waiting to take his place. When business was slow, the manufacturer would try to keep the cutters and sample makers on as long as possible; they were the backbone of the shop. The first to be sent home were the operators, finishers, and cleaners, and so the operators sweated to stay in the good graces of the foremen, making frantic efforts to beat the production of their neighbors.

They would sit at their machines, shivering in their skins as, with a sixth sense, they felt the approaching presence of the foreman, whom Davidowsky had hired to keep an eye on them. "Quiet, the angel of death is here," the operators would whisper to each other. They would bend over the work that flew past the darting needles, their thoughts flying along with the beat of the electric motors. When the foreman was around, it was wise to think of nothing but sewing the garments piled beside the machines.

Where the pressers worked, on the floor above, the light of the electric bulbs was half hidden in the thick clouds of steam that rose to the ceiling from the damp cloths over the garments on the ironing boards. Gradually through the cloud of steam one could distinguish heads, then hands, then bodies. The one-piece dress being manufactured had little padding, and it took an experienced presser to emphasize the line which had to be given to the garment. Handling the heavy iron, too, demanded physical strength; the presser had to be hardy enough to stand on his feet all day. Most of the men were big, with wide chests, red faces, and powerful forearms. Because not enough men were available, women, too, worked at the ironing boards, but they were reserved for the less important job of ironing the lower half of the garment. The upper part, with its folds, pleats, sleeves, throat line, and waist, and all the other details which the designer had included on the sample garment, were left to the experienced men pressers.

For all their appearance of strength and robustness, most of the pressers were likely candidates for "the proletarian sickness." Their lungs would inhale the clouds of hot steam rising in the room all day, and it didn't take long for the healthiest of them to leave the industry permanently maimed.

When the garment came out from under the pressing iron, stiffened in all its folds and pleats, it traveled up another floor to the finishers and cleaners. Here the final touches were put on the garment—hooks and eyes sewn on, buttonholes finished, and the various trimmings applied. Among the workers were old, gray-bearded men, the energy drained out of them by long years at the machines, old women, grandmothers, driven by stark need to help earn the family livelihood, and youngsters, sixteen and under, getting their first taste of the trade. Now, in the winter twilight, as the evening gloom crept in through the dust-covered windows, girls and boys—almost children—sat under the glare of electric bulbs and pulled the loose threads from the sewn garment. Their fingers moved quickly, cutting off the ends which the machine had left. Their eyes were heavy with fatigue; they were drowsy from the monotony of the task and the steam which oozed out of the radiators. Some of them looked toward the small windows where the winter night sent in its last beams of light. Their young eyes could see the clean snow falling softly to the sidewalks. They thought of snowballs, of the crunching sound of the soft snow. But their fingers moved swiftly and assiduously.

Thus it was in Irving Davidowsky's garment factory, not much different from the thousands of factories of the country where tens and hundreds of thousands of workers sweated away at making the dresses which clothed America's women.

CHAPTER THREE

FOR ALL their growing wealth, the Davidowskys had many problems to worry them. Their chief comfort was little Nat, now a boy of three. He was healthy and energetic like his father, and he resembled his father with his keen brown eyes and strong, determined jaw. He chattered away, curious about everything, asking hundreds of questions which Mary was hard put to it to answer. He wanted to know about heaven, about God, how things got to be created—the questions which all children ask and which parents can never answer to the child's satisfaction.

The family lived in a comfortable—one might say a luxurious—apartment, an eight-room flat near Riverside Drive, the fashionable residential section. They kept two servants, one of them a nurse for the boy; Mary still spent most of the day at the business. She and Irving went out a good deal to restaurants, night clubs, and the popular five o'clock *thés dansants*. Irving kept a watchful eye on all the fashions as they appeared, but it was Mary who had the eye for style. Her glance took in every line of a new fashion and she was able to determine, as though with a sixth sense, which particular innovation of handling or design would capture the buyers' fancy.

As with Irving, the business was her major interest. Styles, fashions, materials, and design were always on her mind. She spent a good deal of time on her appearance. After the birth of the baby she had begun to show a tendency toward plumpness, and she tried valiantly to keep her figure slim and stylish. Massage and exercise became a regular morning chore.

She had made up her mind to travel far with Irving along the road to material success. They wanted to forget the past and all of the memories bound up with it, and to throw the memories of their poverty overboard like useless ballast. Wealth—that was the goal of their new life.

Completely sundered from her past, Mary was new-born, Eve-naked, facing only the new world of her choice. This world was made up of the important employees of the firm—Goldenberg, the head designer, and Mrs. Rosenkranz, the head saleslady, their constant visitors and steady companions. Knowing the difficulties they would meet, both Irving and Mary had cut themselves off from all their old religious connections, though retaining their profound beliefs. They belonged to no clubs or societies; they made no acquaintances or friends among their neighbors.

Irving did have some friends in the industry. Some among them were comrades from the old neighborhood, schoolmates and playmates who had found their way into the garment industry much as Irving had done. Some of them lived near him and he would be invited to their homes.

Mr. Grossman, the vice-president of Irving's bank, invited him to his home and suggested that he join the local synagogue.

"You never mentioned what congregation you belong to, Irving," he said on one occasion.

"Oh," Irving stammered. "I belong to my father's synagogue on the East Side. That's where I used to go when I was a kid."

"On the East Side? That's all right for the old-timers, like your father, with their old-time rabbis. We've a fine rabbi . . . speaks a first-class English. A young fellow like you ought to be connected with a modern temple, not with one of those old East Side *shuls*."

"Well, I'm really an old-timer myself," Irving commented.

"Anyway, I'll send Dr. Silberman, our rabbi, to see you."

Not long after, Irving got a telephone call from Dr. Silberman. The rabbi didn't wait for an invitation; he named the time himself—"At eight o'clock tonight. I hope I won't be disturbing you," and he hung up.

When Irving answered the doorbell that evening he saw an imposing, elegantly clothed young man, looking more like a successful lawyer or actor than a rabbi. He asked him in. The rabbi seemed to be eager to meet Mrs. Davidowsky, and expressed his disappointment when he learned she was not at home.

"You know, Mr. Davidowsky," he said, "we have a splendid Ladies' Auxiliary at the Temple. I am sure that Mrs. Davidowsky would be very interested in making the acquaintance of our fine women. We are starting a kindergarten, too, in our Sunday school. I understand that you have been blessed with a fine son."

Irving was not given to evasion. He preferred to meet and settle all issues head on. He made no exception in the present case.

"I'm afraid you won't take me into your congregation," he said evenly. "I'll be delighted, of course, to make a contribution to the Temple, as much as I can afford. But I'm afraid that joining the congregation is out of the question. Nor will my wife be able to join the Ladies' Auxiliary. She is a Christian—a Catholic. My son hasn't been circumcised."

The rabbi stared in surprise.

"And what about yourself?" he asked at last.

"Why, I stay a Jew, just as my wife stays a Catholic. We have agreed that the child will choose his own religion when he grows old enough to decide."

"Very modern, very modern, indeed," the rabbi commented. He got up to go. "Thank you very much for being so frank with me, Mr. Davidowsky."

"And what about a contribution to the Temple? If you like, I'll send you a check."

"I'll have to talk it over with our Board of Trustees. We'll let you know. Good-by, Mr. Davidowsky."

Irving saw no more of Rabbi Silberman, nor did Mr. Grossman, of the bank, renew the invitation to join the congregation. Their conversation was confined to business affairs. With the rest of Irving's acquaintances it was the same. No one asked him about his private affairs, and there were no more invitations to their homes.

It was no secret in the trade that Irving's wife was an Irish Catholic, and that his child had not been received into the Jewish faith; the latter was the most serious of all—worse than conversion. . . . So it was wiser if conversation with Irving limited itself to business affairs. He was someone to be reckoned with in the industry. The Davidowsky firm was already so firmly entrenched and so solidly placed that Irving didn't need to plead with the bank for credit; the bank sought him as a client. It happened more than once that some envious competitor tried to hurt him by producing a competing line and selling at a lower price, or tried to damage his reputation among the out-of-town buyers by spreading rumors about religious conversion. But the efforts to

247

start a boycott against him among the Jewish retailers were not successful. Irving was resourceful; he had new and fresh ideas. The retailers and buyers had to come to him. Besides, he made it his concern to emphasize the fact that he was still a Jew. He made lavish contributions to Jewish charity organizations, hospitals, and other Jewish causes. He let himself be seen in places favored by the Jewish businessmen of his acquaintance; he took visiting buyers to kosher restaurants.

His wife didn't mix into his religious life and he didn't mix into hers, he told his friends. He told it to himself, too, to comfort his feelings. But inside he was perplexed and dissatisfied. When the High Holidays came around, the Days of Awe, he hardly knew what to do with himself. He kept the factory closed—like the other Jewish firms—but he was too restless to stay at home. He would wander about the streets; once he had gone into a small synagogue in a side street where he knew nobody would recognize him. A deep longing for his father came over him, an aching yearning to see him.

But Moshe Wolf had not only refused to see him since his marriage; he had even forbidden the mention of his name in the household. His mother visited him at his office from time to time, and he would press generous sums of money on her. She would try to refuse.

"What's the good of it? Will your father enjoy it? He would sooner work like a horse and get up in the middle of the night to drag in the cans of milk. And do you think he's got the strength for it? Don't I hear him groaning all night? And when I give him his meals he pushes the plate away and asks where the money came from. Where did I get this dress, he wants to know ... or where did I get the rent money from? He cross-examines me like the police in the old country. Now he's stopped talking altogether. He doesn't say a word; just shakes back and forth over his prayer books. He goes down to that Hasidic prayer house of his on the East Side. Whenever he can get the chance he goes down there. And not a word. ... Believe me, my son, my life is bitter. One son a cripple, the other ..."

Irving would try to make light of his mother's remarks. On one of her visits he said: "Do you know, Ma, I'm buying an automobile. I'll come to take you out for a ride."

"Where will you take me riding? To the cemetery? You haven't got a home you can take me to."

"What do you mean?" Irving got angry. "I have a wife... and a child...."

"But your parents have no daughter-in-law and no grandchild just the same. To us, my son, they're Christians."

Irving bit his lips.

"How's Nat?" he asked after a pause.

"How should he be? All of a sudden he's got to be a regular loudmouth with the socialists. He thinks that this is Russia; he wants to throw over the tsar."

Conversation with his mother left Irving bitter. "It's only because I'm not rich enough, or strong enough. That's why they have no respect for me," he thought. "Just wait till I make enough money, then they'll take me the way I am. They'll forget my wife's a Catholic and my son's not circumcised. It's only the rich Jews who can afford the luxury of a Christian wife. The rich can have everything—not the poor. Just wait till I've got enough fat on my bones; just wait until the firm grows. Then they'll talk differently. They'll all come sucking around then."

He didn't believe it himself, but the thought was enough to induce him to throw himself body and soul into business, with the single purpose of raising the Davidowsky firm to new heights. It was as though the business had usurped all the intimate and sacred feelings in him—his reverence for his father, his love for Nat, even his devotion to his faith.

The situation was not greatly different with Mary.

After the birth of the child she had begun to feel a longing to see her mother and her grandmother so that they, too, might love her child. She was proud of the baby; she had brought him into the world; she loved him with all her heart. It took a long time for her to summon the courage to go looking for them, but there was no difficulty in finding out where they were. She knew that if her parents still lived in the general neighborhood of 48th Street, they would be attending Sunday mass at the church on Second Avenue. She went there herself and took up a post in a dark corner. Irving was under the impression that she was going to mass at St. Patrick's on Fifth Avenue. He did not interfere in her religious life. He knew that she had remained a devout Catholic, and he interposed no objections. Near her bed she even had a small crucifix, but Irving raised no question about it. It was Mary's; it had nothing to do with him.

The day she went there, she saw them all in the church. Only her grandmother was missing. Her father seemed to have grown taller and thinner; her mother seemed old and shrunken. They were poorly dressed—so it seemed to Mary when she thought of the comfort of her own life. Her heart was full. She felt sinful and degraded. She fell to her knees before the wooden crucifix, closed her eyes, and prayed silently. It was not for herself that she prayed—with her sins so heavy on her, how could she pray for herself?... Nor did she pray for her child. He was "outside," shut out from grace; not baptized ... she could not pray for him to Jesus. She prayed for her parents... more for her father than for her mother. When she got up from her knees, she saw the family leaving the church. They passed close to her. She looked straight into her father's face. For a moment he stared back in astonishment, then a yellow pallor spread over his face. His thin lips trembled as though he were murmuring something—a prayer or a curse?—and he shifted his eyes from her. When the others saw her, Mrs. McCarthy stood still with fright. Sylvie shouted out in joy. Mary came a step closer; her mother came toward her. Then Patrick McCarthy seized his wife's arm in a strong grip— Mary could tell from the grimace of pain on her mother's face that it hurt—and pulled her away after him. "Jimmy! Sylvia!" he growled in a threatening whisper, and the young ones went out after them. She was alone; they had thrust her out of their lives.

Instead of going home Mary followed them from a distance, furtively, so that she should not be seen. They lived on 40th Street, close to the East River, in a poor neighborhood full of stables and half-wrecked houses with closed shutters. Mary wandered aimlessly near the foot of the block and halted at a candy store. She couldn't go home until she found out how things stood with her parents and how she could help her mother. She saw her brother Jimmy come down out of the house. How big he had grown! He was growing out of his clothes. He needed a new suit, Mary thought. Sylvie came down after him. He was walking along energetically, with his father's long stride. Sylvie ran after him on her thin legs.

Mary shrank into the doorway. They seemed to be headed for

the store. That meant that her mother could still manage to give them a couple of pennies each Sunday after church. . . . Maybe things were all right for them. . . .

Sylvie saw her and ran toward her, shouting "Mary! Mary!" in her excited young voice.

"Sylvie, stay where you are!" Jimmy yelled. His voice was like his father's; he had his father's angry face.

Mary threw her arms about Sylvie. The tears choked her.

"Don't touch her!" Jimmy shouted angrily. "Don't let her touch you, Sylvie; I'll tell Papa."

"Jimmy, Jimmy!" Mary looked at the boy with pleading eyes.

"Judas! Christ killer!" he shouted at her. Mary stared at him in fright.

"Judas! Christ killer!" the boy shouted again. He looked at her contemptuously. "What were you doing around the church? Why don't you go to the synagogue with the other sheenies?"

Mary lifted her hand and slapped him hard on the cheek. Then she turned and walked away.

"Judas! Christ killer!" Jimmy repeated. He picked up a stone from the gutter and threw it after her.

The stone hit her on the leg, but she felt no pain. She walked on faster. She only felt a flood of bitter hatred toward all her past, toward her father who kept his tyrannical rule over the household, who was instilling a blind hatred into his children, who cast the shadow of his black hatred on everyone about him. "What have I got to do with them?" she muttered to herself.

A deep pity welled up in her heart—pity for her mother, for herself, her child, for Irving, pity for the whole world divided into warring camps. Her tears melted the hard knot of bitterness that constricted her heart. She walked along the streets, the tears pouring down her cheeks, then she took a taxi and rode home.

When she reached the apartment she burst into the baby's room, lifted him up out of his crib, and held him close. She remained exalted all day. She felt the need to cling more firmly to her new life. She lavished affection on Irving and the child. She embraced and kissed Irving, telling him how wonderful he was, and thanked him again and again for taking her away from the squalor of 48th Street. She never wanted to go back there. She never wanted to hear of it again. She didn't care what happened there.

251

She wanted to separate herself altogether—completely—from the past.

"What's happened to you, Mary?" Irving said. "Did something happen today? Where were you all morning?"

She told him about her meeting with her parents and brother and sister.

"Don't take it so hard," Irving comforted her. "I get plenty of that from my own mother. My father refuses to have anything to do with me; even Nat has turned his back on me. Exploiter, he calls me. And all because I wanted to make something of my life. That I give hundreds of people a chance to make a living doesn't seem to mean anything to them. They don't stop to think that I'm helping to develop an industry for the benefit of the masses, not for the privileged few. Doesn't that count for anything? Everybody's got his own philosophy. We wanted to help them—your parents as well as my parents. We wanted to lift them out of the muck they've been living in ever since they came here from Europe—with all the nonsensical ideas they brought here—Christian, Jew, proletariat, bloodsuckers. . . . That's the old stuff; it was all right for people on the other side of the ocean. Here, in America, there's no place for it. If they want to stay in the dirt and stew in their own juice—all right, let them. But they can't drag us back with them to that kind of a life. I'm an American. They can't hold me back."

"Oh, Irving, you're so clever! I never thought that . . . I used to think . . . Well, never mind. . . ."

"What did you think? Come on, tell me. What did you think?"

"Oh, it was only something foolish."

"Go on, tell me!"

"Well, the truth is that when Jimmy called me those names, Judas and Christ killer, I was ready to go to the nearest rabbi and ask him to convert me to your religion. Not only me, but little Nat, too."

"Why? Just because that ignorant kid brother of yours called you names? In that case I ought to go to a priest right away and get converted, the way my father and mother call me 'goy.' We'll have to change our religions every time someone decides to call us names!"

"Sometimes I think, Irving, that if you can't change to my religion, I ought to change to yours."

Irving looked at her in surprise.

She went on. "Because it would be easier for you. Then your family would take you back. And you could belong to the same temple as your business friends. I know how you feel when your holidays come around. I can tell how you miss going to the synagogue."

"What sort of ideas are you getting into your head? Come on, tell me what's on your mind."

"I'm thinking about the baby. It's bad for the child to be without a religion. When he goes to school ... with other children ... he'll not know where he belongs. . . ."

"Yes, that's true. It won't be easy."

"That's why I'm always thinking of it. Even if we can't bring ourselves to get converted, we ought to at least see that the child belongs somewhere. If not in my faith, then in yours. It terrifies me that he might die unbaptized, uncircumcised."

Irving was silent.

"Let's think it over for a while," he said at last. "I don't like to do things in a hurry. Anyway, Mary, I want you to know that I appreciate what you're offering. I know what your religion means to you." He took her in his arms.

Irving had a strong feeling for individual rights. In business he was a paragon of correctness. He considered a promise sacred, regardless of the losses it might sometimes mean. He was almost fanatically careful of other people's money, as careful as he was about his own. Whatever else they might say about him in the trade, they had to concede that he was a rock of reliability. "A good loser as well as a good winner," they said. It was this principle of punctilious honesty that had helped to build his reputation in the business world.

He carried the same principle over to his domestic life. Mary was an equal partner with him in relation to their personal life and their child. Only in that way, he felt, could they build a life together, securely fortified against the bitterness their families felt toward them. Had Mary taken any step toward baptizing the child, he would have seen it as a violation of their agreement, a threat to destroy their family life. In the same way he was afraid to accept a suggestion from her—obviously the result of a momentary weakness—which might make her unhappy and permanently disrupt their life together. He wouldn't do it in business and he certainly wouldn't do it in his own family affairs—regardless of the "profit" he might make out of the transaction.

The following day, as they sat at the dinner table, he delivered his decision. "I've thought a good deal about what you said last night. It was sweet and generous of you to make the offer. But it wouldn't work out. I know how you feel about your religion, and you'd be taking a step you'd regret all your life. It's best to let things stand the way they are."

CHAPTER FOUR

THE HIRSCH family lived on West 60th Street, on the third floor of an old and dignified brownstone house. Mildred, the daughter and first-born of the family, was a professional masseuse whose clients, mostly elderly men and women, lived in the neighborhood.

The family consisted of Dorothy Hirsch, the mother, who was a widow, and the two children, Mildred and Robert. Mildred, a spinster who looked older than her years, supported the family. Not long after they had come from Germany, the father had died after losing all he had in the Wall Street crash of 1907. There were rumors that he had taken his own life, afraid to face the debts he was unable to pay. But that was something the family never talked about. The Hirsches had wealthy relatives, but the widow had refused all offers of help. She had paid her husband's debts by selling most of the family possessions and had kept the family together by giving music lessons—she was an accomplished musician— until Mildred had finished a course as masseuse.

The pride and joy of the family was Robert. Both women lived only for him. They begrudged spending any money on themselves that might interfere with keeping him at college. They asked nothing and expected nothing from him in the way of helping toward the family budget, and they would have thought it an act of treachery to the family tradition if Robert were to interrupt his studies and go to work. Mildred was the one who worked. She rose early every morning, carefully combed and brushed her thick black hair—the only mark of youth about her—and put on her professional-looking white nurse's uniform. With her gaunt body, her long face and protruding teeth, and with the long gray coat whose scraggly fur collar had long ago lost any resemblance to the skin of the animal from which it came, she looked like a hard-working German *hausfrau* as she went on her calls. She performed

255

her duties neatly, emotionlessly and efficiently, never overstepping the rigid boundaries of her position. She trailed after her a scent of disinfectants and a cold, impersonal atmosphere. Her strict and unbending demeanor had lost for her, one after the other, her few rich patients; now she had to be content with clients in more modest circumstances who asked for no more than they paid for. Her earnings were small, but Mrs. Hirsch knew how to manage.

The mother dominated the household. She had only to give voice to the slightest wish and both children would hurry to obey without a word of protest. She took care of the house; scrubbed the floors, polished the furniture, aired the bedclothes, and kept the apartment clean and spotless.

By dint of considerable sacrifice Mrs. Hirsch had managed to save from the opulent days a few pieces of the elegant furniture they had brought with them from Germany. There was a Biedermeier china closet which held some pieces of Meissen porcelain, a Dresden coffee credenza, a bookcase filled with German classics and fine editions, a Biedermeier table in pale mahogany, some chairs upholstered in blue, a delicate Empire period chaise longue—on which only guests were permitted to sit—and the large grand piano.

Mrs. Hirsch practiced at this piano every day. A few invited guests came over every second Monday of the month to hear some chamber music, mostly Mozart and Bach. Mrs. Hirsch played the piano, her daughter the cello, and two old friends—Mr. Bachrach, an old friend of Mr. Hirsch, who had also lost his money in the Wall Street crash, and Mrs. Lehman, a music teacher, Mrs. Hirsch's friend—played the violin. Robert sat at the piano turning the music for his mother.

The regular guests at the concerts were a couple of old family intimates and the few friends Robert would invite. After the music, chocolate and little cakes were served.

In addition to Mildred's earnings there was the small income from a trust fund which Mr. Hirsch had left. Next to nothing was spent on clothes. The family goal was to keep Robert at college.

Mrs. Hirsch watched over him like the apple of her eye; she had watched over him from the time he was a child. He was now in his early twenties and was studying philosophy at Columbia, where he also helped the renowned Professor Korngold in preparing a new history of German philosophy. But his mother still treated him as though he were a child. She took care of his laundry, told him what to wear, supervised his manners and behavior. He had to give her an accounting for every hour of the day, how he spent his time when he wasn't at school, where he went, whom he had visited. She advised him about whom he should associate with and whom he should avoid; she never dictated to him; she simply advised him.

"I'm thinking particularly, Robert, of the Davidowsky boy. It's a great pity. He was so gifted and promising. And it's quite right of you not to neglect him after his terrible misfortune. But after all, to visit him at his home, to spend so much time in that awful neighborhood! They are East European Jews, I understand, from Poland. I'm sure they have very little culture. You can bring the young man to one of our music evenings if you feel you must, but as for visiting him at his home—I'm afraid that wouldn't do. There is nothing you can learn there...."

To "learn" something was the sole duty of Robert's life, according to Mrs. Hirsch. Everything he did, everyone he visited, every book he read, was considered from the viewpoint of whether it would help him to "learn" anything. It was pure "culture" Mrs. Hirsch was thinking of. Anything practical or useful was far from her thoughts.

At first Robert had started to study law, and his mother had dreamed of the time when he would be a famous lawyer—Robert could be nothing less than renowned. But when he had shifted to philosophy, Mrs. Hirsch, instead of complaining, was pleased that her Robert would be able to devote himself to higher things. The only complaint she had was that he hadn't asked her advice in the matter.

In the son—Mildred thought of him more as a son than a brother—the two women placed all their hopes. They saw in him the realization of the proud family aspirations they had cherished so long. Robert would restore the dignity of the Hirsch name; he would cover the Hirsch name with glory. He would not only become famous in the academic world, he would be a respectable and moral individual who would set an example to the entire community. Mildred clothed the boy in all the trappings of the dream she had long nursed of the destined one she would some day find. He would not be a rich man, but he would be noble, learned, and profound. She wanted Robert to be like her ideal.

257

Mother and sister, therefore, watched tremulously over every step Robert took. Would he be able to "learn anything useful" to enrich his knowledge, to ennoble his character, to enhance his personality? No Jewish matriarch of any era bore so cheerfully and so courageously the burden of the family livelihood as did the women of the Hirsch family for the sake of the family name.

Strangely enough, the overindulgences and extravagant attention the women paid to him did not spoil the boy. He was a serious youth with a strong sense of self-discipline. Life was a very serious affair to him. He believed in the pantheistic God of Spinoza, the sum total of all creation, of the universal good of which he himself was a part. It was by living a moral and ethical life that one could best render homage to God. For Robert, Spinoza was not only the prophet and seer who had uncovered the true Divinity; he was also the highest example of the God-serving man, the man of moral purity, the high priest of God in the modern world. To follow in Spinoza's footsteps was his highest ideal. He was content to live modestly and humbly. But for the tearful opposition of his mother and sister, he would have found work to help the family finances. Since they refused to hear of that, he was careful not to spend an unnecessary penny on himself.

Since Nathan's return home and his resumption of his studies Robert had been visiting him frequently. The two spent many evenings together. Once or twice he had brought him to his own house for one of the Hirsches' musical evenings, his sister helping him to carry the invalid chair up the stairs. Often he would take Nathan to college. Every moment he could spare he would spend with his crippled friend.

It wasn't out of a feeling of virtue that he was so loyal. He actually enjoyed the East Side atmosphere—in spite of his mother's disapproval—and he was impressed by Nathan's strong character and the stoic resolution with which he faced his lot. He wondered most of all at Moshe Wolf's complete devotion to his son. Moshe Wolf he venerated, standing in awe of the saintlike purity of the old man's nature.

On a winter evening the two sat in Nathan's room. Through the closed windows came the faint rumble of wagon wheels clattering over the cobblestones of the street, the cries of children and the scoldings of impatient mothers. Against this background the two discussed the subjects that interested them—death, God, the meaning of life.

Nathan sat on the couch, a few books scattered about him. His pale face, with its large and eloquent eyes, was fringed with a thin beard which gave him a deeply pious look—as though he were a figure from a distant time, such a figure as might have been seen walking on the Jerusalem streets. The other, dark and intense, might have been one of the crowd gathered about an ancient prophet outside the Temple gates. His dark brown eyes looked downward behind half closed eyelids as he talked in a careful and deliberate manner, seeming to be seeking for the exact words to express his thoughts. His black hair grew long in front of his ears, softening his characteristically long family features.

Nat, aglow with his enthusiastic faith in a personal God and a special providence, was fervently challenging the pantheism which Robert, like many of the young intellectuals, passionately championed.

"I simply can't understand it," Nat said. "Why should the rabbis of the Amsterdam ghetto have put the ban of excommunication on Spinoza? Instead, they should have found a place for him in the Rabbinical Sanhedrin. He was faithful to their tradition. He lifted monotheism to unapproachable heights, far beyond human reach. He followed in the path of the rabbi-philosophers, a loyal follower of Maimonides and his school. And yet, what good is it to know that there is a creative force if it has no will? Jewish philosophy has taken Yahweh—with all the dominating role he played in the life of our forefathers—and expunged from him all those qualities with which man might have direct contact. It's like a mathematical formula which solves mankind's greatest riddle, but which the mind of man all the same cannot understand, because it rests on concepts far beyond his reach."

"How can we, who have barely reached the outer fringes of knowledge and science, expect to conceive that which is the entirety of knowledge?" Robert asked. "By painful experience we win to new worlds, we broaden our horizon—yet we cannot have a conception of what will be known only tomorrow, or in later generations. How can we conceive something to which our senses have no approach and our intellect no road? We can conceive of the frame, but how shall we conceive its substance and content?"

"The concept of divinity," Nat answered, "is not a luxury; it is a necessity for man's existence, a must for his life. That is why it was molded into the very embryo of the first man. It is what we thirst for, what we search for, our driving force, our hunger for God. He exists in us, not outside of us. The further the horizon of our knowledge extends, the richer the sum of our experiences—and thus the reach of our concept—all the more will man be limited to the tiny island of his own ego, the elemental bond which binds him to his creator."

Sometimes Moshe Wolf would come up from the store when Robert was there. He would sit quietly in the corner of the room and listen to what these young thinkers discussed, and strain his mind to grasp some of their philosophy. Nat's stout defense of God against Robert's Spinozism gave Moshe Wolf keen satisfaction. Although he didn't altogether understand what his son was saying, he nevertheless felt that it was his side that was being upheld.

"Just like it says in the Holy Writings," Moshe Wolf could not help interjecting. "The spirit of holiness rules in the heart of man."

"You see, Robert, my father belongs to a sect of devotedly worshipful Hasidim. For all their lack of science they've reached a higher truth than the Jewish philosophers. *They* are the followers of historic Judaism, not the philosophers."

"Maybe you'll both drink something?" Moshe Wolf said. "You're talking so long your throats must be dry. I'll make some tea. It'll be ready in a minute."

Moshe Wolf enjoyed playing host to these "modern sages"—although they were cut from a different cloth than the ones he had known in the old country.

One evening as the two friends sat together there was a new visitor—a "princess of Judah," as Robert thought of her the moment he saw her.

And Rachel actually seemed like a princess to the carefully sheltered youth, a princess from some strange and faraway world. The room in which they sat was suddenly filled with a scent of delicate perfume. Two luminous dark eyes smiled at him, framed like some strange sapphires between long-lashed lids below thick, half-moon shaped eyebrows. Her forehead was wide and smooth, the nose straight and symmetrical. The fresh smiling lips revealed her white teeth, resembling the two strands of pearls which she wore at her throat beneath the open fox collar.

"Oh, I'm sorry. I thought you were alone, Nat," she said in her warm and vibrant voice.

"Come in, Rachel. Do you know my friend Robert? This is Robert Hirsch. I thought you'd already met him here."

"I've seen him before, but we've never met."

Robert blushed like a young girl and got up from his chair.

"This is Rachel, our neighbor and friend."

"Rachel! What a lovely name!"

Rachel came toward him and held out her hand. The black gloves she wore seemed to emphasize the whiteness of her skin. She opened her jacket and sat down; Robert could hardly conceal his delight.

"I came to invite Nathan to a concert on Monday," he said impulsively. For the first time in his life he forgot the reserve and modesty his mother had been drumming into him all these years. "We have little concerts at our house, chamber music. We're going to play Mozart, that is, my mother and sister. . . . If you'd like . . . I mean . . . Miss Rachel . . ." Robert stammered. "If you'd do us the honor . . . I'm sure that my mother and sister will be happy to . . . they'll be honored to . . ."

"It's a splendid idea," said Nat. "Rachel could take me and you wouldn't have to come for me, Robert."

"And my mother will be delighted, I'm sure. She'll be very happy to have Miss . . ."

"Miss Greenstock," Nat said.

"Rachel Greenstock." Robert pronounced the name slowly.

"Well, then, it's agreed," Rachel said. "Now I must really go."

Robert opened the door for her. She thanked him with a flashing smile.

"Tell me about her. Who is she?" Robert asked when she had gone.

"She's our neighbor. And a very good friend." There was an enigmatic smile on Nathan's lips.

"Doesn't she look exactly like a princess of Judah?"

"Yes," Nat said. "Exactly."

"Rachel! What a beautiful name! I always worshiped the biblical Rachel. . . ." Robert seemed to be speaking to himself. He didn't notice Nathan's amusement at his own enthusiasm.

CHAPTER FIVE

BLENDED DELICATELY as in a minuet were the soft harmonies of the piano and strings in the scherzo of the Mozart trio. But at the concert at the Hirsches' home, the piano and the cello, usually so harmonious, seemed to be engaged in some sort of venomous duel. The elderly Mr. Bachrach tried hard to co-ordinate his fiddle strokes with the rhythm of Mildred Hirsch's cello, but even when he did succeed, the piano motif galloped ahead under Mrs. Hirsch's nervous fingers. Mr. Bachrach's race flushed a beet red. He tried to let Mrs. Hirsch know, by hoarse whispers and exaggerated gestures, that she was losing the tempo; he was surprised that she wasn't aware of it herself. But Mrs. Hirsch seemed to be playing a wild solo. She galloped along, at a mad pace, in a sort of unheeding trance.

Whatever it was that was happening, it had apparently affected Mildred, too. Bent over the cello, she seemed to be wailing over her own fate, wandering off into an elegiac solo, ignoring the accompaniment of the fiddle, paying no attention to the piano chords.

And all because Robert had brought that young woman to the concert, without having asked his mother's permission to invite her. He had made such a to-do about the importance of the new visitor that his mother, contrary to the usual custom, had served chocolate in the special service; Robert himself had taken the cups and saucers out of the cabinet and had gotten them ready for the occasion. He had also persuaded his mother to buy a chocolate cake at the bakery. And all this for an *Ostjüdin* from the East Side; for the companion of his crippled friend! Robert's behavior had unnerved his mother even more. He was nervous before the girl came, and when she did arrive he blushed like a schoolboy. And now, as he sat by his mother and turned the pages at the piano, she could clearly see that his thoughts were not on the music but with that young woman who had the temerity to sit so grandly on the divan in her flowing silk evening dress.

"Yes, we know that you're a model in a dress house," Mrs. Hirsch thought angrily. "And you can't impress us with your evening dress, which you probably borrowed from the place you work at in order to make an impression on my son. And it's bad taste to come to an unpretentious concert in a fancy ball dress, with that crippled friend of yours, as though you were going to a ball. And that son of mine! Look how he stares at her with those eyes of his, as though he'd never seen an evening dress before! No sense of shame before his mother and sister! Just stares at those imitation jewels that she's got all over her!"

But well disciplined as she was, Mrs. Hirsch did not betray her feelings. She was so natural and friendly that Rachel could discern nothing in Mrs. Hirsch's attitude toward her other than the most courteous hospitality. Mrs. Hirsch's fingers were steady and her manner calm as she poured chocolate into the delicate cups and passed them around. She praised Rachel's gown and made admiring remarks about the ornaments she wore.

Mildred was less able to control her feelings. The smile that uncovered her large teeth was more like a grimace of distaste when she offered the chocolate cake to Rachel. Rachel sensed the hostile atmosphere into which she had stumbled. She was entirely innocent. She had no designs on Robert, but the attitude of mother and sister, which she felt so plainly behind their appearance of cordiality and friendliness, tempted her, in the contrariness of her feminine nature, to establish a closer relationship with the boy. It was as though a hidden impulse, stronger than herself, was forcing her to throw little glances at him, to flirt a little and to respond to his enamored gaze. And all the time he acted the lovesick calf, hovering about her, to everyone's astonishment and his mother's chagrin.

When it was time for the guests to leave, Robert put on his coat. With a new self-assurance and confidence, as though it were a perfectly natural thing and one to which he had been accustomed all his life, he said: "Don't wait up for me, Mother. I'll probably come home late. I'll help Miss Greenstock to take Nat home."

Mrs. Hirsch could hardly believe her ears. It was not so much what Robert said as it was the ease and assurance with which he said it. She wanted to say: "Miss Greenstock brought your friend here, and I'm sure she can manage to take him home alone." What she said instead was: "All right, Robert, but don't forget to put your rubbers on. It's snowing outside."

An hour or so later Rachel sat opposite Robert in the ice cream parlor on First Avenue, near the moving picture theater. It was she who had suggested that they go in. He gazed at her with his hungry, lovesick eyes, his hand in his pocket fingering the solitary twenty-five cent piece he had to his name. He trembled in fear that she would order something that would take all of it; he still would have to take the trolley home. But the warm smile in her eyes made him forget all his fears.

Did she like music? he asked her. Why, of course, she answered. The following Thursday the famous German conductor, Nikisch, was directing the Philharmonic. Did she enjoy Wagner? ... Thank goodness, she had changed her mind.... She wasn't ordering a chocolate sundae, she was having a cherry soda ... that was only five cents. He would leave five cents for the waiter and then he would have fifteen cents left, Robert thought joyfully.... Would she do him the honor of going with him to hear the Wagner concert on the following Thursday? Robert was frightened at his own boldness.... She would be delighted, but she must first remember if she was free on Thursday.... Yes, it was all right, she would keep the evening free. But the tickets must cost so much! But then they could sit in the gallery, couldn't they? She wouldn't mind it at all; she'd love to sit in the gallery with the students. Couldn't they sit in the gallery? ... Oh, no, he would get good tickets; you could appreciate Wagner only in the best surroundings.... Would she allow him to take her to dinner before the concert? ... By now Robert was so carried away that he could hardly believe it was real; he must be living in a dreamworld.... Dinner? My goodness, I'll bankrupt you! ... But it will give me such pleasure ... please don't refuse....

She was moved by his earnestness and lapsed into silence. Then she said: "If you insist; but really, it isn't necessary...."

"Oh, please, I beg of you." His fervor amused and at the same time impressed her.

"Then of course I'll go with you," she said. She smiled at him, her eyes glowing in excitement.

On the short walk to Mrs. Kranz's boardinghouse she held

tightly to Robert's arm; a moist snow was falling and the street was slippery and wet. Robert breathed in the girl's delicate scent. The warmth of her hand on his arm went all through his body.

"We'll meet on Thursday, at six?" he said at the door of her house.

"Yes." A smooth hand, cool as alabaster yet burningly warm, touched his. Robert went home with a melody in his heart.

The tuxedo which hung in Robert's closet he wore only once or twice a year on special occasions, when the family was invited to dinner at the home of a wealthy relative. Before he left the house on the following morning, he took it down on its hanger and looked it over carefully.

"Do you think, Mother," he asked, "that this will need cleaning? Will it be all right if it's just pressed?"

It was so unusual for Robert to show any interest in such things that Mrs. Hirsch stared in astonishment.

"Why are you worrying about it now?" she asked. "It's still a long time to dinner at Cousin Hirsch's; not until Easter."

"This is for a special occasion," said Robert with a broad smile.

"I won't ask you what the special occasion is; I'll only ask you when it is," Mrs. Hirsch said in her calm voice.

"This Thursday."

"Then there won't be time enough to have it cleaned. I'll press it myself." Mrs. Hirsch took the jacket from his hand.

"*Mutter*," said Robert; the German style of address was still used in the Hirsch family. "I'll need a few extra dollars. Do you think you..."

"Well, if you must have it..."

"Yes, Mother...."

"How much do you need?"

"I think five dollars will be enough."

Mrs. Hirsch winced. Five dollars meant a large drain on the family budget. He had never before asked for more than a dollar or two, for a concert or a book. Five dollars was an enormous sum. But she hid her feelings.

"Of course you can have it, Robert."

"I'm taking someone to dinner and a concert. Nikisch is directing a whole evening of Wagner with the Philharmonic. The overture to *Meistersinger; Lohengrin*..."

265

"Five dollars will hardly be enough for dinner and the concert, Robert. You'll need at least ten...."

Robert's face fell. "As much as that?"

"*Kindlein,*" his mother said. "The tickets alone will cost five dollars; you'll have to have desirable seats. And then dinner—I suppose you'll eat in a nice restaurant; that would be proper—will cost three or four dollars. And a taxi to take your guest home; how else? You'll need at least ten dollars."

Ten dollars! Almost half of his sister's weekly earnings! Robert thought of Rachel, and remembered the scent of the perfume she wore; it was enough to banish all his fears—she was worth any sacrifice!

"I must have it, Mother," he pleaded. "I promised."

"Of course you must have it. Here is five dollars; you'd better go at once and get the tickets. Hurry before they're sold out. We'll manage the rest somehow. Now hurry along."

Later in the day Mildred cleaned Robert's dinner jacket while Mrs. Hirsch pressed the trousers at the ironing board. They worked in silence, hardly exchanging a word.

As Mildred rubbed away with a soft cloth at a stain on the coat, she suddenly broke out bitterly: "Of course it's that awful girl he brought to the house."

Mrs. Hirsch kept on sliding the iron back and forth. There was no change in her manner. She was turning over in her mind the problem of getting the extra money for the boy.

"Suppose it is? As long as it makes him happy," she said.

She decided she would pawn her gold brooch.

In the softly lighted French restaurant Robert sat opposite Rachel on the comfortable black-leather-covered chair in one of the booths. He felt his face flaming. He was sure that everyone was looking at him, and that everyone envied him. He didn't care. He had money in his pocket—he kept fingering the bills. He nodded acquiescently to everything the waiter said to him. He allowed Rachel to do the ordering; he was content just to gaze at her. He hardly noticed the food on the table; he forgot to drink the wine. He was drinking in her large eyes, her black hair, her long, smooth cheeks, her delicate ears and the long coral earrings dangling from them. He was drinking in her perfume.

Words bubbled out of him—about the music they were going

to hear, about his studies at college. He told her of his plans. He, was helping his professor with a history of German philosophy, a very important work.... He was preparing for an academic career; his mother and sister were very eager about it....

Rachel listened to him intently.

He kept up the flood of talk. "I never knew," he said, "that perfumes could have such magic about them. Now I understand why the Eastern peoples set such store by them.... Even the Gods loved perfumes and incense.

"Do they interest you so much?"

"Oh, yes, they've always interested me. But it's only now that I'm beginning to understand their magic. I guess my forefathers are beginning to come to life in me. You know that our fore-fathers loved pleasant perfumes. Take the Song of Songs—'how much better is thy love than wine! and the smell of thine ointments than all spices.'..."

"I've always loved perfumes, too," Rachel said. "I used to buy little bottles of perfume with the few pennies I'd get from my father. My friends used to laugh at me. They bought ice cream while I bought samples of perfume...."

"Oh, I can understand that; there's something of the East about you. You're like Sulamith, right out of the Song of Songs...."

"Oh, Robert..." Rachel blushed.

"I mean it, honestly. When I saw you for the first time I thought that that must be the way the princesses of Judah must have looked."

"You musn't say things like that." Rachel flashed a brilliant smile at him.

"It's true.... The moment I saw you I felt as though a wind from the Bible was sweeping over me.... And your name... Rachel..."

"You mustn't talk like that," she repeated. "You're liable to turn a girl's head and break her heart.... I didn't know..."

"But Rachel, I'm in earnest...."

"You'd better eat... your food is getting cold. You're danger-ous with that talk of yours.... But I like what you say about perfumes. I love them. I'm more envious of a woman's collection of perfumes than of her jewels. I read about a new perfume from Paris just the other day—Amber, they call it. It's like frozen honey. I tried some at Altman's. The salesgirl put a drop on my blouse—it lasted for days and days. It's almost intoxicating."

Robert no longer tasted the food or the wine. He was eating and drinking frozen honey. It intoxicated him, too.

Later he sat beside her in the dimly lighted concert hall. He didn't hear the music. He held Rachel's warm fingers in his own, and he could feel the scent of amber, like frozen honey, penetrating into his skin, filling his veins like wine. He was aware of no one else in the concert hall, there were only Rachel and himself. The hall became transformed into a scented rose garden. The scents and perfumes were wafted from thousands of hidden flowers. Every blossom bloomed and sent out its odors. The roses, the carnations, the violets, the arbutus—all of them gave out the sweet scent of honey. He was floating with Rachel in a cloud of perfume.

At the door of her house, before she left him to the darkness of the night, she let him taste the honey fragrance of her lips.

He lay in bed, eyes wide open, and dreamed of the perfume of honey. He could still feel its taste on his lips. He let himself be bathed in it. He swam in its sweet scents—like a river—and he dreamt of love. . . .

In the morning he rode downtown to Altman's and went to the perfume counter. Yes, they had the new Amber perfume, imported from Paris. A tiny vial cost seven dollars and fifty cents. The larger vial was fourteen fifty. The bigger size was of course more economical. . . .

In the Biedermeier cabinet, where the Dresden coffee service was kept, there was a rococo porcelain figurine. It showed a romantic scene—a maiden in a wide, colored crinoline sitting on the river bank by the stump of a tree, thoughtful, her finger at her cheek. Behind her stood a cavalier in short colored trousers and richly colored jacket. He was looking at the maiden pleadingly. Near them stood a naked Cupid with a bow and arrow aimed at the heart of the maiden. The skin of Cupid was pink and cream. He wore a red sash over his middle.

Robert had known the figure ever since he was a child. It had never had any special significance for him; simply a piece of porcelain, a memento of old Germany. But now it began to speak eloquently to him. He took it out of the case and went with it over to an antique shop on Madison Avenue.

"What do you want for it?" the dealer asked.

"Fourteen dollars and fifty cents."

The dealer gave him the money.

A few evenings later, as the Hirsches sat at the table over the evening meal, Mildred got up from her chair and pointed to the Biedermeier cabinet.

"*Mutter!* The Cupid figure is missing!"

"I forgot to tell you, Mildred," Mrs. Hirsch said quietly. "There was an accident. While I was cleaning the shelf the figure fell and broke. I was so upset about it I didn't want to tell you."

Robert's face flushed red.

CHAPTER SIX

IRVING'S DECISION about the child's religion, sensible though it seemed, had brought Mary no peace of mind. She became obsessed with a kind of terror for his welfare.

When little Nat saw his mother, he would stretch out his hands to her, staring solemnly at her with his big eyes. It was impossible to resist him. All his movements, the look of his eyes, the curve of his lips, expressed a pathetic helplessness which bound Mary to him hand and foot. However urgent her other duties, she simply could not leave him.

One evening she dressed to go with Irving to a show of the new spring fashions of a leading designer. Before she left the house she went for a final peep into the baby's room. When he saw her, he stretched out his little hands toward her, and she threw off her coat and bent over his crib.

"Mary, we'll be late," Irving reminded her.

Mary didn't answer. She kissed and caressed the child, oblivious of everything else.

"Mary, what are you doing? You're waking him out of his sleep. He'll be restless all night."

Mary paid no attention.

"Mary, what are you doing?" Irving repeated.

"Please, Irving. Let me stay home. I want to stay with the baby."

"What are you talking about? You know how important this style show is for us."

"I can't go, Irving. Please! Call Miss Dobkin. She'll be glad to go with you."

"Are you out of your mind? Miss Dobkin's no designer. All she can do is follow orders. You know we can't just copy, we have to combine, and you're the only one who can do that."

"But, Irving, darling, I can't go. Honestly, I have a terrible headache. I'll be absolutely of no use to you at the show."

"Then take an aspirin or something. Come on, Mary," and Irving took her arm.

Most of the time she would let herself be persuaded to go. This night, however, she firmly refused to leave the house.

"I just can't go any more, Irving. Please, I beg you, let me stay at home."

"All right," Irving answered. "Whatever you say. You'd better lie down. And leave the baby to the nurse, you know how nervous you make him. She's always complaining that he doesn't sleep all night."

"I'll leave him soon. I'll go to my room."

Later, however, when Irving came home from the style show, Mary's room was empty; she was fast asleep in a chair beside the crib.

The situation got worse. Mary was becoming high-strung and nervous and constantly worrying about the boy. If the nurse was a bit late in bringing him back from his daily walk, she would imagine every kind of disaster. If the boy had the slightest illness she almost went out of her mind. She had all sorts of mad fancies and obsessions. In the midst of a visit, or at the office, or at the theater, she would suddenly start in alarm, convinced that something dreadful had happened to her child. She would get home in a panic—to find everything calm and little Nat peacefully asleep. Often she would jump up out of bed at night, trembling all over, and rush into his room to make sure that he was all right.

One day Irving got a frantic call at the office to rush home at once; something terrible had happened.

When Irving arrived, half out of breath, Dr. Glicksman, their family doctor, met him at the door.

"I'm afraid it's the mother who's the patient, not the child," the doctor told him gravely.

"What happened?"

"The youngster suddenly developed a high temperature—nothing unusual; he probably ate something that didn't agree with him. But Mrs. Davidowsky got so frightened that I'm afraid the shock might have some sort of lasting effect on her. She's on the brink of a nervous breakdown. You'll have to be very careful with her. I think she'd better stay in bed for a few days."

271

In the bedroom Irving found Mary kneeling before the crucifix hanging near the bed. She was praying with such ardor that she did not hear him come in. Her eyes were closed and her face was flushed. She was murmuring: "Oh, dear Jesus, have mercy; have mercy!"

When she saw him, she threw herself into his arms and sobbed. "Oh, Irving. He's dying," she moaned, the tears flowing down her cheeks.

"That's nonsense. The doctor says he'll be all right in a couple of days. You must get hold of yourself, darling."

"Oh, I'm so afraid."

"What are you talking about? He has a little fever, that's all. Dr. Glicksman says it'll soon pass. You've got to calm yourself, darling."

"Irving, God's punishing us. Oh, dear Jesus, take my life, not his! He mustn't die, not now, not now! Dear Jesus!"

"Mary, you must get hold of yourself. Come, you'd better lie down. You need rest. You've had a shock. The doctor says you have to rest. Nothing is going to happen to the baby. Please, darling, come, I'll put you to bed."

"Irving, he mustn't die! He mustn't die!"

"He'll not die. Don't be silly. You don't know what you're saying." Irving was at the point of tears himself.

"Irving, I'm afraid. God is punishing us. I'm so afraid...."

She held him close as though she wanted to draw some of his strength into herself.

"Mary, darling, please be calm. For my sake! For the baby's sake!"

He put her into bed, and covered her with a blanket. The doctor gave her a strong sedative and she fell asleep. By the time she woke up, the boy's temperature was normal.

But although Mary seemed to get over her panic, Irving could see that he would have to be firm. "It's no use, Mary," he said. "You can't take care of him by yourself. You'll simply make yourself sick, as well as the child. Get another nurse, the best children's nurse you can find, and let her devote herself entirely to him. Please, Mary, you'll only break down again and you won't do the baby any good."

"You're right, Irving. Oh, yes, you're right," she said with resignation.

272

But the shock had settled deep in her. She was unable to rid herself of her worries because the child was neither Jew nor Christian. Her fears gave her no rest.

Since her marriage she hadn't attended any church regularly, although she would sometimes drop in during a week day when she felt the need. She would kneel near the door, bow her head, and murmur a prayer. Sometimes she would do no more than gaze at the crucifix and let herself be immersed in the love and grace that flowed from the tortured figure on the cross into her aching heart. Since her marriage she had not attended mass; she felt that she could not partake of the Host until she had received absolution for her sins—and she had not gone to confession out of fear of revealing that her son had not been baptized; she knew what a cardinal sin that was.

The believers in ancient religions cannot free themselves from the desire to join in the mystic ritual of their faith. No matter how alienated from his religion, the Jew, when Yom Kippur, the Day of Atonement, comes round, will feel an unease and a thirst—as though the martyred blood of countless forebears is pulsing in his own veins, demanding that he come closer to his God. The Catholic, too, however far he is severed from the church, feels almost a physical need to unite himself with his God through the sacrament of the mass. Mary was envious of the worshipers who could participate in the sacred ritual. She yearned to be part of the Mystery—but it was forbidden; she had not made her confession to the priest; her sins had not been forgiven; she was not pure before God.

After little Nat's recovery she began to go to church more often. Once she found herself in the enormous vault of St. Patrick's. Near the door she saw several lines of people waiting patiently at the rows of confessional booths to receive from the unseen priest the penance which would wash them clean of their sins.

Before one of the booths the line of people was small, and moved along quickly. Mary joined it.

As the line drew closer to the confessional, her heart began to beat faster. She thought for a moment of leaving the line, and joining the longer line near by. No, the line at which she stood would be best after all; it was moving along more quickly; the priest was probably a kind and patient man ... he would under-

273

stand her . . . he would be tolerant with her. At the other booth the priest must be much stricter; he was keeping the penitents in the booth for a long time. In the midst of her indecision it was her turn to enter the confessional.

At first the priest in the booth was a voice reciting a prayer. Then he was simply an ear.

"I haven't taken part in the Holy Sacrament for over four years," Mary began, hesitantly.

"Why?" The voice was young and full of energy, but sympathetic.

"Because I haven't been to confession."

"And the reason?"

Mary was silent.

"Open up your heart to God, my daughter. There is no sin for which God's mercy cannot grant atonement if you come before Him with a believing heart."

"I married a man outside the Church."

"With the consent of the Holy Church?"

"No."

"Then your marriage is not sacred. In the eyes of the Church you are an unmarried woman, living in sin. Has this sinful union borne fruit?"

"I have a son of three."

"To what faith does the child belong?"

"He has not been baptized."

The dark booth became silent. All Mary could hear was the deep breathing of the priest. It was a full minute—it seemed like an eternity to Mary—before she heard the priest's voice. This time it was harsh and stern. It had a brazen tone—as though it were emerging from some metallic throat. It was now the voice of judgment.

"Why did you not baptize the child?"

"My husband is a Jew. He comes from orthodox Jewish parents. We decided that the child would belong to neither church; we would let him decide for himself when he is grown up."

"When he is grown up . . ." The priest's voice rang with sarcasm. "What makes you so sure that he will attain an age at which he can make his own decision? What sort of guarantee have you that he will grow up? What will happen to his soul if he dies?"

A paralyzing numbness swept over Mary's nerves. It seemed to her that the metallic voice thundering out from the little window held the power of life and death over her child's future. She was terrified, and her fear threw her under the spell of that mighty voice. She was bound hand and foot to the confessional window, too terrified to move.

"Why don't you answer?" the voice demanded

"I don't know. That's why I've come...." Mary stammered.

"You came to save your own soul. But what about your child?"

Mary was silent again. Then she said: "But the child isn't only mine; he belongs to his father, too."

"And has his father a faith?"

"He is a Jew."

"An observant Jew?"

"He is loyal to his religion."

"And you?"

"What do you mean?" Mary asked in fear.

"Are you true to your religion?"

"Of course, Father, how else would I be here now! That is why I came here."

"So you are true to your religion." Again there was sarcasm in the priest's voice. "You come to the Mother Church to save yourself in the hour of your need. You raise your hands to your Redeemer; you believe in Him and you bring your heavy heart to Him in terror and in fear...."

"Yes, yes ..." Mary sobbed.

"But your son you have cast into the dark jungle of unbelief. You have left him on the other side of the wall, outside the Church, in the dark night where the Devil rules. In the night, in the dark forest, you have left your son to the beasts that prowl while you yourself seek salvation and protection under the warm wings of the Church?"

"Father, what can I do? I made an agreement with my husband not to have our child baptized. He didn't even want to let the child be Jewish—though I asked him to—because he didn't want to do anything that might break my heart. How can I break his heart? He will never forgive me all his life."

"How can you talk of agreement?" the priest's voice thundered. "Was it an agreement that concerned your own soul? No, you made an agreement concerning the soul of your child, your child's

275

life, his salvation in Jesus. Who gave you that right? You can do what you like with your own life, but you cannot dispose of the soul of your child for your own peace, for the peace of your house, for your own comfort. See how selfish you have become! You do not risk your own faith for the sake of your comfort—no, you hold on to your faith. You come to the Church for absolution so that you might partake of divine bliss and be enfolded in the arms of your creator. But what of the salvation of your child? What of his future in Heaven? You have balanced his future on the scales of your own welfare. What will you do if your child dies without grace? Do you think you will still be able to find peace in your heart? That you will be able to live your life in contentment? The knowledge that your son is doomed will torture your days and rob you of your sleep at night."

"Yes, Father...I tremble at the thought of it. That is why I have come to you."

"Welcome words, my daughter! Then it is not for your own soul that you have come; it is to save the soul of your child, to bring him under the healing wings of the Church."

"Yes," Mary answered. Now she was completely under the power of that unseen voice. She was hypnotized by eyes which she could not see. She was under the spell of the voice which rang in her ears. Her will was powerless. Every thought was enslaved under the blows of that metallic voice hammering in her soul.

"What shall I do, Father?" she asked. She was obedient now. She was a suppliant, submissive to the demands of the church.

"Our lives are not in our own hands, my child," the voice went on. Now it was filled with tenderness and sympathy. "None of us can know what the coming moment will bring. We are in God's hand. Act now, my child. Do not wait. Not even for a single day. Go home and bring your child to me. I shall be waiting. You will know me, and I shall know you."

"Not today, not today, Father," Mary pleaded in a weak and helpless voice.

"Why not?"

"I can't bring him today. My husband will soon come home."

"When then?"

"Tomorrow."

"At what time?"

276

"Tomorrow, at eleven in the morning. When I take him out."
"I shall be waiting for you. Eleven in the morning."

She struggled no more. She knew it was an act of betrayal against Irving; she was doing something that would create an eternal abyss between them. But there was no help for it. She had to do it. She was completely under the power of the voice that had given the order, that had told her what she must do.

In the morning she dressed the boy herself. She dressed him in white, and told the nurse that she was taking him downtown to buy him a new coat.

When they arrived at the church, little Nat asked: "Is this the store, Mama?"

"Yes, darling. This is where we will buy you a new coat. You will see. But you mustn't tell anyone. You mustn't tell anyone where you have been. Do you hear? Not Papa, and not the nurse ...no one."

"Why, Mama?"

"Just because I want it that way. Promise me you won't tell."

"All right, Mama.

When she mounted the steps, a short, thin young priest came toward her. He had a long nose and big, restless, staring eyes. He smiled at her and greeted her quietly. Mary looked at him in surprise. Such a small and thin body ... and that mighty, thundering voice. ...

"I am happy that you have come. Come with me." He took the boy by the hand, as though the child already belonged to him, and led the way with firm steps.

Mary, her head bowed, followed them.

277

CHAPTER SEVEN

THE FIELDS of France were drenched with the blood of France's best sons, but from Paris there still came the style creations for the elegant ladies of the world. New York shipped guns and bullets to France—and France paid for them with cosmetics, perfumes, liqueurs, and styles. In the white and gold salon of the Waldorf-Astoria Hotel, Chambrun of Paris was giving a show of the creations just received for New York's world of fashion.

The salon was crowded with buyers, models, and designers. The heads of all the important New York firms were there. Chicago, Cleveland, Philadelphia—all the large centers—had sent representatives. Besides, of course, there were the ladies of the fashionable world. In the spirit of the times the show was combined with a five-o'clock cocktail party. A famous orchestra played the latest dances, while several couples, pressed close together on the small dance floor, moved about to the rhythms of the tangos and fox trots that were sweeping New York. In the middle of a dance there was the blare of a trumpet—the signal that the show was on.

The current Parisian styles were strongly influenced by Rostand's *Chanticler,* the dramatic success of the season. From the wide steps that led down from the platform at the end of the salon, one model after another began to descend. They seemed to be completely covered with feathers. All that could be seen was long, fluttering feathers and the faces of gorgeous models rising out of nests of feathered costumes, and delicate feet darting in and out from below long feathered dresses. The audience broke into applause. This was something new—an unmistakable success!

There was a second signal. Between the rows of feather-bedecked models a girl walked gracefully down toward the audience. Her tall figure was draped in delicate black lace. From both sides of her thick black hair spread bird of paradise wings, throwing a soft shadow on the girl's brunette skin. A feathered scarf around her throat lifted and fell. There was a flaming red rose at the point of her deep cut *décolletage*. The folds of lace, like a black avalanche, descended down the graceful form over the shimmering silk gown underneath. From beneath the narrow hem the points of her little shoes appeared and reappeared. She walked majestically, as though aware of her importance, like some proud, fantastic bird from a strange world.

Irving and Mary were among the guests. Since she had had her son baptized, Mary had become much calmer. She knew it would not be long before Irving must learn about it; the child was constantly chattering away about the baptismal ceremony and the church, though his words were too confused to be understood. Sooner or later she would have to tell Irving, and she expected that the outcome would be serious. But the feeling of relief that had come to her with Nat's baptism was worth any consequences. Let happen what must; she was ready for it.

Her newly found peace of mind had given her a renewed interest in the world about her. She had become more carefree, had stopped worrying about the boy's health, and was not spending so much time at home. She had begun to take more interest in business affairs, and in the new modes. She had begun again to attend fashion shows, theaters, and night clubs.

Mary was the first to recognize the model coming toward the audience between the rows of feathered girls.

"It's Rachel!" she whispered.

"Where?"

"The girl in black, coming toward us."

Rachel came closer to their table. She was carrying a card with the figure five inscribed on it. As she approached the table at which Irving and Mary sat, she stopped in surprise. But only for a moment. She allowed an exaggeratedly friendly smile to appear on her face and nodded to Irving, who had his eyes fixed on her. He answered with a stiff bow. Mary kept her head turned away.

Rachel turned as though to go on, then, seeming to change her mind, she turned toward the table again and, with a coquettish gesture, held up the numbered card in her hand as though to identify the dress she was modeling.

It was only when she had left the table that Irving was able to shake off the embarrassment that had gripped him. He turned to Mary.

"I understand she's head buyer at Berman's. What's she doing modeling Chambrun's styles?"

"To show her figure. She's been doing it often, at most of the big fashion shows."

"Why does she need to do that?" Irving asked in surprise.

"I suppose she wants to. She knows what she's doing."

They were silent for a little while.

"I wonder what happened to her sisters," Mary remarked.

"They're all right. They're being well taken care of. Their uncle is taking care of them. . . . Do you think that Chanticler style will be good for us?"

"No, it's too vaudevilley. It's good for actresses. It'll never be a mass production number."

"I believe you're right."

"I don't know if it'll be popular even among the smart set. That kind of style needs the European background, huge salons, big receptions. That kind of thing is past. Today a girl wants to show her figure, not her dress. Paris can't teach us anything any more; we can teach Paris," Mary commented.

"I think you're right," Irving repeated.

They sat on only for a little while longer. The shock of Rachel's sudden appearance—they hadn't seen her since they had left 48th Street—was too much, and before the newer models were shown, Irving said: "I don't think there'll be anything here to interest us. Let's go, Mary."

"I shouldn't like Rachel to imagine we're leaving on her account," Mary said.

"Let her think what she wishes," Irving replied. They walked toward the elevator.

They were silent as they rode home in a taxi, lost in their own thoughts.

It was too early for bed. They went into the living room. Mary picked up a deck of cards and started to shuffle them at the card table.

"I've done something terrible, Irving," she suddenly said.

"What is it?" Irving asked. He turned the leaves of the newspaper he was reading.

"I took Nat to church. . . ."

"Yes, I know. He's always chattering about it. I don't think it's the right thing to do. You'll get him all mixed up. I'm opposed to it, you know that."

"I may as well tell you the whole thing. You'll have to know it sooner or later. I took him to church to have him baptized." Her head was bent low. Her voice was calm and her hands kept on shuffling the cards, but her fingers were trembling.

"What!" Irving shouted, leaping up from the chair.

"I've brought my child into the Church," Mary answered quietly.

Irving's face turned white. Every vestige of blood seemed drained out of it. His eyes stared blankly in front of him. He swayed, as though he were about to fall; and then he fell back into the chair. He covered his eyes with his hands and whispered: "How could you do it? How could you do it?"

"I couldn't help it, Irving." She dropped the cards on the table and went into the bedroom.

She waited for him to come in to her. Before dawn she went back into the living room and found him lying fast asleep on the couch, still dressed. He was breathing heavily. She threw a light blanket over him. He opened his eyes and saw her. "It's you," he said. "Why aren't you sleeping?"

"Come in to bed, Irving. It's cold here."

"I'm all right." He closed his eyes.

In the morning when Mary got up, Irving had already left the house.

"Mr. Davidowsky left early," the maid said. "He said he had a breakfast appointment."

"Did he leave any word about dinner?"

"No, he didn't say anything."

All day Mary wandered about the house. She made up her mind that if he did come for dinner it would mean that everything was all right. She had known how he would take the news of Nat's baptism, and she had been prepared for his anger. But she had hoped that after the first shock had passed he would accept the situation and make the best of it. Now, she told herself, everything depended on whether he came home to dinner or not. She rehearsed the arguments with which she would try to make him see that what she had done was right. She must make him understand the terrifying ordeal she had lived through while little Nat was ill, and the constant torment she had experienced, the physical and spiritual torture she had suffered. He would understand; he would have to understand!

"What else could I do? He had the choice. He could have let the child be Jewish. If he didn't choose to follow his own religion, then he has to allow me to follow mine. There was nothing else to do! There was nothing else to do!"

He came home at the usual time. When he entered the living room, Mary had a drink ready for him. Little Nat was playing on the floor.

"Did you have a hard day?" Mary asked. It was her usual question.

"Not specially."

"Will you have a drink?"

"I think so."

"Nat waited up to say good night to you."

"How are you, young man?" Irving picked the child up in his arms. "Were you a good boy?"

Mary watched them. She saw no change in his attitude toward Nat. But maybe there was a change—had Irving returned the child's kiss...?

Dinner went along much as usual, Mary asking about the business, and Irving answering at first tersely, then more expansively. There were growing difficulties with the union, problems with the contractors... there were a lot of protests about the bundles for homework... he was thinking of quitting the manufacturers' association... there wasn't enough protection for the manufacturer in the new agreement with the union as long as competing manufacturers stayed outside the association and could give out their work where they pleased....

Mary looked at him intently. Had those dark rings suddenly appeared around his eyes? Was the stern curve of his mouth the result of business difficulties or was it because of what had happened with his son? How he has changed, she thought to herself.

After dinner they sat in the living room. She again lifted the deck of cards to lay them out in a game of patience. Irving picked up the evening newspaper. She broke the silence.

"Irving, you'll have to listen to me. I know that what I've done is a great shock to you. But if you only knew how I've suffered..."

282

"What are you talking about?"

"I want to explain how the whole thing happened."

"I don't want to discuss it."

"You must. You must know the way I feel. ..."

"I don't want to know about it."

"But..."

"We made an agreement, didn't we?"

"There are things that can't be handled by agreements. This isn't a business matter."

"I know that. You don't have to tell me that. Do you think it was easy for me to stick to the agreement? I have a religion, too. I have my own people, too. You know that."

"I didn't know you cared so much about your religion. I never saw you practicing it."

"Maybe we Jews don't practice religion the way you Catholics do—but we don't change our religion as quickly as others. A Jew would rather die a thousand times, he would let himself be burned at the stake, rather than deny his religion!"

She looked curiously at him. He had never seemed to her so Jewish as he was now. His eyes in their dark rings, his bold nose, the curve of his mouth, seemed to reveal his bitterness. She had seen that expression on the faces of so many Jews. Suddenly it seemed to her that Irving's face was like his father's.

"I gave you the choice of having your own way about it," she said. "You didn't want to do it, so I had to take the road that seemed best."

"Who says I didn't want to do it? Maybe I did want to do it."

"Then why didn't you?"

"You know why I didn't. Because I had consideration for you."

She looked at him helplessly.

"Irving, darling. I don't deny that you're right, but I don't regret what I've done. No, Irving. You can do whatever you think you ought to do—but I couldn't do anything else. You'll never know what I've been through." She lifted her handkerchief to her eyes.

"What's the good of any more talk? The thing's done. You say you couldn't help yourself. I can understand that, but I can't help feeling the way I feel. There's no use talking any more. We'll both have to take the consequences. I have to go out now. I have to see my lawyer—about some labor troubles."

283

"The lawyer?" Mary asked, frightened.

"I forgot to tell you about it. I have to see Shulman and some others."

"Why didn't you ask him up here, the way you usually do?"

"There's going to be a whole group of independent manufacturers. We're meeting at a hotel. You better just throw a blanket and a pillow for me on the couch. I'll come home late; I don't want to disturb you."

It was an uncomfortable week that followed. Neither of them could find the old footing; a wall had been erected between them. Irving himself hadn't realized the depth of his concern. It was as though forces were at work within him independent of his own will and as though his ancient heritage was protesting within him. His wife and his son seemed to be strangers to him. He reproached himself for it a thousand times. What grievance could he have against the child? Was it the child's fault? But he couldn't help himself; she had killed all the loyalty and trust and deep intimacy between them. The bond that had held them to each other was gone. The love that kept them together—the physical as well as the spiritual—was violated. And what was as bad, he saw in what she had done the low esteem in which she held his own background and descent. The Jew was no better than a Judas to her—that was the name her brother had called her—and she wanted to save her child . . . their child . . . from the curse that lay on his father. If that was the way things stood, what sort of relationship could he have with her? If that was the way things were, then his father and mother had been right about his marriage. . . .

Yes, she saw the Jew through the eyes of all the other Gentiles, as something inferior. His faith was no faith at all in her eyes. He had no God. He was cursed in the hereafter as well as here. They were making a hell for him in this world . . . in the future world God would do the same. . . . "She had contempt for me all the time she was with me. While we ate together or worked together . . . while she lay in my arms and conceived my child," he thought to himself.

Well, then, what was the sense of any life between them? What sort of life could there be for them when that was the way she felt about him? He was a Judas, a Christ killer! No, it was his parents who were right; not he. They hadn't let common sense,

284

practical considerations, make them betray their faith. They, with all the long chain of martyrdom behind them, were the ones who were right. . . .

He tried to fight against his broodings. Mary was young, she was inexperienced, he told himself. What she had done was in a moment of unreasonableness, out of her love for the child, out of her fears for the child's future. Of course she didn't think Jews were Judases and Christ killers. He remembered her attitude toward his brother Nathan. And the respect and love—almost the veneration—she had had for his father. Maybe the thing to do was to find out how they could correct the error. That's all it was—an error. He would talk it over with Shulman, his lawyer. After all, he was the child's father. . . . The thing had happened without his knowledge and consent. . . . He should have something to say about it, too.

His mind cast about desperately in doubt and disquiet. Should he save the sinking ship of his home—or should he let it go down, a wreck? He decided not to take his lawyer into his confidence. First he would have another talk with Mary. Maybe she would be willing to repair the damage she had done, and let the child choose for himself, when the proper time came, what his religious faith was to be. But he kept postponing the talk with her; subconsciously he was afraid of being compelled to take a decisive step. Events brought the decision sooner than he expected.

On Sunday afternoon Irving was at home. There was a ring at the doorbell. Irving opened the door. He found himself face to face with a black-coated young priest.

"You are Mr. Davidowsky, I presume," said the priest, with a friendly smile.

"Yes," Irving answered. The priest stepped inside the door.

"I am Father McKee. I am happy to know you." The priest put out his hand. "I am responsible for bringing your son into the Catholic fold. I trust you are content, Mr. Davidowsky, that your child has at last entered into the true faith." The priest looked at Irving benignly.

Irving was astounded, and froze with resentment. Loud, abusive words rose to his lips. But he restrained himself, and answered in the same bland and confident tones as the priest had used.

"I suppose you know that you baptized my son without my consent?"

"We do not require the father's consent, Mr. Davidowsky," the priest replied. There was no change in his tone. "You see, the Church does not recognize a marriage entered into without the Church's sanction."

"The laws of the state recognize a marriage without the sanction of the Church."

"Indeed," the priest said, as though he were hearing the fact for the first time and was surprised and impressed.

"Yes, sir. And it is my intention to annul the baptism on the ground that it was without my knowledge and consent." Irving continued in the same bland, smiling tone.

"Will the child's mother consent to the annulment?" the priest asked.

"I am hoping so," Irving replied. "The whole thing, you see, was a mistake.

They had both been standing in the entry hall of the apartment. A door to one of the inner rooms opened and Mary came into the corridor.

"I have come to visit my child in Christ, and I learn that it is Mr. Davidowsky's intention to annul the baptism," the priest said, looking straight at Mary.

"Who said that?"

"Mr. Davidowsky just told me so. And he tells me that he expects that you will give your consent."

Mary looked from Irving to the priest. Her voice was firm and steady.

"I will never consent to having the baptism annulled."

"You see, Mr. Davidowsky? Believe me, the day will come when you yourself will be thankful."

When Mary and Father McKee came out of the child's bedroom, Irving was gone.

He did not come home that evening. Instead there was a telephone call from his office to let Mary know that he had gone on a business trip and would be away for several weeks. A few days later Irving's lawyer called her on the phone. There was something very important he had to talk over with her, he told her. He would like to call on her at her home.

CHAPTER EIGHT

MARY'S FIRST impulse—when the lawyer told her that Irving had left her for good and was asking for a legal separation—was to make him pay dearly. A blind rage swept over her. All of the old prejudices she had kept in control burst the bonds in a flood of abuse.

"And why? Just because I dared to bring my own child into my own faith? They're all that way, every one of them! Young and old—every one of them—they all hate Catholics! He had the chance to bring up the baby as a Jew, and he refused! Now he wants to break up everything just because I wanted to give my child a religion! That's the way they all are." Her eyes were flaming. "All of them . . . Irving, his mother and father . . . even Nathan. . . ."

She paused. Even her blind rage had to hesitate before the doubt that entered her mind. Contradictory and confused thoughts raced through her brain.

"No. Not his father. He's different. . . . But even he refused to have anything to do with us after we got married. . . . Every one of them . . . they all hate us!" Again her prejudices broke their chains. She hardly recognized herself. . . . "Those Jews! They'll pay for the trouble they're causing. I should never have expected anything different. I should never have had anything to do with them. My father was right. . . ."

Again she stopped. Somewhere in her fury she had stumbled against a barrier which even her unbridled anger could not cross.

There are experiences and happenings in the lives of everyone so profound in their effect that they always remain the compass needle pointing the course we must follow. Whatever roads we tread, these events rear up like signposts beckoning us onward. Their pull is so powerful that there is no turning back.

Such a decisive event had been Mary's experience in Moshe

Wolf's grocery store on 48th Street so many years before. She could feel again that first surprise, as though her eyes had been suddenly opened and she had seen the store for the first time; as though Jesus himself had pointed the store out to her. And then everything that had happened...Mr. Davidowsky's friendly smile and the good things he had pressed on her. From then on the Davidowsky's were no longer the "cursed Jews" whom her father was always abusing. They were different Jews. All the Jews on the block were different. Jesus had led her to them. Mr. Davidowsky and Nat—dear Nat—and even Mrs. Davidowsky, who had wanted to give her money; and Irving...yes, Irving...her baby's father.

The two emotions struggled inside her. Sometimes one would prevail, then the other. But most of the time they contested furiously, like fighters in a ring. "They'll pay dearly for it," she thought darkly. "I hate him and his family, all of them." Then would come the warm, intimate feeling. She could not throw it off her, like an old garment. "After all, they're my own people, my child's people. I found a home with them...no, it wasn't a home...they're Jews and I'm a Christian. There's nothing to hold us together. It was never real. It was a lie. It had to burst, like a soap bubble....And now does he imagine he can throw me out? And that that smart lawyer of his will get rid of me.... No, Irving wouldn't do that....His lawyer said he wants to make a settlement with me.... It isn't a question of money. He'll assume all responsibility, the lawyer said. I can name my own terms. The best thing would be for me to get my own lawyer. But what's the good of it? He never loved me...or the baby, either. We were always strangers to him. He's a Jew and we're Christians. God, what shall I do? I've got to be careful.... I need a lawyer, someone, to advise me. I need someone to protect me. I'm all alone. There's no one to help me. I know what I'll do; I'll go to Father McKee. He's my confessor. He'll know; he'll tell me.... She can have him. Rachel can have him. And they can have their Jewish wedding, with a rabbi and with Shmulevitch and with that Mrs. Kranz, for all I care."

Father McKee had had a hard childhood and a miserable youth. He was the son of a poverty-stricken farmer who scratched a bare living from the stony soil of an upstate New York farm.

The family made a living during the summer from the scant crops and the milk from the two cows they kept. In the winter the father of the family earned some money cutting wood. They were all hungry more often than not. Joseph, the boy, had shown a marked aptitude for study, and the timely intervention of a Catholic society saved him from the fate of a hired hand. His undeniable gifts, his correct behavior, and his unusual piety attracted the attention of the local bishop. Supported by a small church stipend, he was sent away to study.

Everything that he had, Father McKee knew he owed to the Church. It was the Church which had rescued him from the mean farmhouse, not much more than a shack, where the cold crept in all the winter and hunger prowled all the year. The Church had transplanted him into light, warm, sun-drenched halls where there was ample food for his body and spiritual nourishment for his soul. First the seminary and then the church had become the home he had never known. He paid back the debt he owed with all the love and gratitude of a humble nature. He studied diligently. He did everything that was required of him, never even thinking of questioning those who were in authority over him. He advanced quickly, and when he was ordained, his unquestioning nature saw himself as a part of the authority which Jesus had placed on the earth to represent and guard His divinity. There was no doubt in his mind that every creed other than the Catholic was sinful and pagan. Everybody, Christian as well as Jew, who did not surrender unquestioningly to the authority of the Catholic church was doomed to eternal darkness. He practiced the duties of his calling with fervid, almost fanatic, devotion. He was the shepherd of his flock; they had been entrusted to him for their keeping. He was responsible for their souls, for their spiritual integrity, for their destiny in this world and in the life hereafter. For all of the blandness and suaveness of his manner, he was as strict toward those entrusted to his care as he was toward himself. Back of all the kind charity of the manner with which the seminary had taught him to deal with people was the bitterness of the memories of his cruel childhood. To the pity and love for people he had learned at the seminary he added a hard core of the stern judgment which life had meted out to him.

Father McKee was on duty in one of the confessional booths when Mary walked into the church. The matter on which she had come to consult him, she thought, was a secular one, so she waited for him to be finished. He came out of the booth and started to walk off in his sedate and unhurried steps.

"Father McKee," Mary called after him softly. She went toward him.

He looked around. His face was stern and tired. There were large dark patches around his eyes. His skin was an ashen yellow; his lips were wan and dry. He seemed to be annoyed at the interruption, but his face quickly softened in a warm smile.

"I am glad to see you, my daughter. How is my son in Christ?"

"He is well, thank you, Father."

"Do you want to see me?"

"If you're not tired and have a moment's time, Father."

"I am never too tired to do God's work. Come with me, my daughter."

He was only a few years older than she was; how strange that he called her "daughter," she thought.

"I would like to see you privately."

"Of course. How else. It is too late for confession; come up to my study."

Upstairs, she burst out abruptly: "I am separating from my husband."

"Oh!" the priest exclaimed in a tone of regret.

"Do you approve?" Mary asked.

"It is only that I hoped you would help to bring him into the Church; to save his soul through the only true faith."

"My husband a Catholic? No, Father. He's leaving me because I had the child baptized. . . ."

"Stubborn blindness . . . again the sin . . . Jesus Christ, extend Your grace over them." The priest closed his eyes for a moment in prayer. "What is it you want of me, my daughter?"

"I need a lawyer, someone to protect my rights . . . and my child's. I need a lawyer I can rely on. I thought that maybe you . . ."

"Oh, I see, I see . . ."

"Why, Father, the business is really half mine. I helped him to build it. I was with him from the very first day he started. You might even say we started it together."

"How is that? Did you both invest equal sums of money?" the priest asked, not entirely out of curiosity; he was seeking to learn

290

something of the background of this soul that had entrusted itself to his care.

"Money?" Mary laughed bitterly. "Where would I get money? We were both of us poor kids on 48th Street. He got the money from the uncle of the Jewish girl he used to go around with. She thought he was going to marry her."

The priest leaned forward. "You say he used to go around with a Jewish girl? That he was promised to another girl before he married you?"

"He wasn't altogether promised. But everybody thought they would get married. In a way he gave his word to marry her, but later he changed his mind."

"Gave his word? To whom?"

"I don't know exactly," Mary said, flushing. Why had she brought up the subject of Irving's promise to Rachel's dying father?

"I suppose he promised the girl's uncle, the one who gave him the money to go into business," the priest said.

"Yes, he promised her uncle," Mary said, grasping at the suggestion. "Yes, it was her uncle. But he paid him back. He considered it a loan, not a wedding gift. He paid back every cent."

"I see, I see. And what did she say when he broke his promise and married you?"

"Who?"

"I mean the Jewish girl."

"Oh, she didn't say anything. It didn't make any difference to her. You see she still had her rich uncle, and he was taking care of her and the other orphans."

"Orphans?"

"Yes. Her father died."

"When did he die? Before Mr. Davidowsky broke his promise or after?" the priest persisted.

Mary flushed. "I really don't remember."

The priest lapsed into a thoughtful silence.

"It was like this," Mary went on. "They all thought that Irving was still free, but we had already been married before her father died. Secretly married. And they all still thought he was engaged to Rachel."

"That was while you were working for Mr. Davidowsky, I suppose."

291

"Yes."

The room was cool, but Mary felt as though she were burning up. With her handkerchief she mopped at the perspiration that bedewed her face.

"I understand. You worked in his business and you were married to him secretly. No one knew that you were man and wife and they all thought that he was engaged to his Jewish friend. Rachel, her name was, you say. A biblical name."

"Yes."

"And you were a partner in the business, you say. You didn't just work there; you were a partner."

"First I just worked for him as a saleslady. Then, after we got married, naturally we just worked together. I designed and adapted the styles, and I modeled. I have a very good eye for fashion. I gave him the idea for the model that was our first enormous success. I designed it, and then we began to make it in large quantities. That's what made the firm rich, and really established the business. We enlarged the factory and employed hundreds of people, and gave out lots of bundles for homework. He can't deny it. I helped him from the very beginning." Mary was talking rapidly. She was glad the conversation was getting away from the uncomfortable circumstances of her marriage.

"You must be very competent."

"I used to work in a waist factory. Do you remember that terrible fire in the waist factory on Washington Place a few years ago? The Triangle fire? I was caught in it...."

"Indeed," the priest said. "Tell me about it. I've heard so much about it."

"It's hard for me to talk about it. Every time I think about it I seem to see Sarah's..." she paused, and then stumbled on: "Sometimes I have nightmares about it... even now.... I wish I could forget...."

"I can understand. But please tell me, who is this Sarah that you mentioned? Forgive my curiosity, but a priest must know so many things. He must know everything about his flock. And I am eager to hear about that terrible fire from the lips of one who lived through it."

"She was a girl named Sarah Lifschitz. She saved my life."

"She really saved your life? How did it happen?"

"Yes, she saved my life... and she was killed. She blazed up like a torch . . . she fell from the window like a flaming torch . . . and before that the glass from the broken window kept digging into her. . . . Please, Father, don't make me talk about it. I can't bear to remember it."

"I understand. I understand."

There was a moment's silence. Then Father McKee came back to the subject.

"And what did you do for her?" he asked.

"For whom?"

"For Sarah Lifschitz, the one who saved your life."

"What could I do for her?"

"I mean in your own shop, the one you ran with Mr. Davidowsky, did you think about Sarah Lifschitz and others like her who died in the fire?"

Mary felt the priest probing deep into her conscience.

"I will tell you the whole truth, Father. I never thought of it. . . . You see, Father, it was this way. . . . Nobody's in business for pleasure. We had to have everything figured out to the last penny. Before we produced any garment, we had to figure out whether it would pay us to work on it. And we had to think of the competition, too. We couldn't afford to be different from others. We had to do the same things the others did. Irving always said that business is one thing and charity's another, and that they couldn't be mixed together. And he's right. There are a lot of things you have to take into account when you're in business. You wouldn't know, Father, but the competition is pretty bad. . . ."

"Yes, yes, I understand. It certainly would seem that you've been quite a help in the business. . . . You're certainly entitled to a substantial share . . . maybe an equal share . . . in everything your husband has." There was a smile on the priest's lips. Mary noticed it, just as she noticed the irony in his words "Yes, my daughter, I guess you'd better go to a lawyer. You have undoubted experience in business matters; you are well acquainted with worldly things; you'll be able to make your way. Unfortunately, there is no way I can help you in these things." The priest got up from his chair.

With a heavy heart Mary left the priest's study and went out on the street. What was the phrase she had used when he questioned her about Sarah Lifschitz? "I never thought of it. . . ."

293

What was it she hadn't thought of? Was it Sarah Lifschitz, half out of the shattered window, her flesh pierced by the jagged edges of the broken glass and holding her by the arms until she could find a foothold on the balcony beneath the flaming floor? She had not thought of her—because she had wanted to forget her. That was the truth of it. She had wanted to forget everything about her past—her youth, her childhood, her mother, Nathan, her grandmother, all the things that were closest and dearest in her life.... She had thought only of one thing—how to build the business, how to earn more and more money, how to get more clothes, how to make more and more money out of others ... out of others, each of whom was a Sarah Lifschitz or a Mary Mc-Carthy....

Yes, she had revealed the truth ... to herself as well as to Father McKee. And it was the naked truth that was burning like an open wound in her heart....

A light snow was falling. It was still early afternoon, but it seemed like dusk. Snow-laden clouds hung in the sky. The street lights were turned on. People hurried along the sidewalks. The middle of the streets were packed with thick lines of barely moving automobiles and wagons drawn by big-bellied horses.

Mary walked fast. Where should she go? She felt that she had no home. She knew that she should go to the apartment on Riverside Drive, to her child, but without volition her steps were taking her in the opposite direction. Something was happening to her; there was something she needed. What it was, she did not know; all she knew was that there was something she needed, some place to find a foothold. She was not hanging suspended in the air, clinging with bleeding hands to the iron rail of a small balcony far above the street. Her feet were not groping for a safe niche on the smooth, unbroken wall.... Yet she felt as she felt then ... as she felt when she was a small child and was turned away from the Italian grocery with empty hands ... and at the same time it was as though she was clinging to the rail of the balcony while the Triangle floor blazed in flame inside....

There would have to be another miracle or she would fall....
"Sweet Jesus, help me! Sweet Jesus, help me!" her lips murmured, just as they had murmured before she found the blessed firmness of the grating beneath her feet....

She did not know what help it was she sought, what it was she

294

prayed for. Her voice came thin, as though someone were strangling her throat, her heart was heavy, and her spirit low. She wasn't aware how she was pushing her way through the compact crowds on the sidewalk. Now she had crossed Madison Avenue ... Park Avenue. She hurried along. Third Avenue. ...

Her body was drenched with perspiration; her face was hot and flushed; her heart beat wildly. The thought raced through her mind—"I'll let myself be run over. I'll let myself be crushed under the feet of the horses." No, she didn't want to die; she wanted to live. She must live. She must start a new life. She had a child. She had to live. She had to live for her child.

She halted at the El station on Third Avenue. She was tired. She must go home to see little Nat. She must put things in order. Everything was so confused. The El trains rumbled and thundered overhead.

She called a taxi. "Riverside Drive and 75th Street." The taxi lurched forward. She leaned forward in her seat. "No," she said to the driver. "Take me to Second Avenue, near 47th Street."

That was where she would go, to the small wooden church, to the carved wooden crucifix. ...

Every once in a while the sky showed gray through the thick clouds overhead. A few trees pathetically held out their naked branches against the gray sky. For a moment Mary stood motionless near the church and looked toward the river. She could see the faint shimmering of the water of the East River under the darkening sky. She went inside. The church was in almost complete darkness; a few candles flickered in the iron holders and threw their dim, trembling light within the vaulted room. Mary looked at the picture of the Mother with the Christ Child on her lap. She crossed herself. Completely hidden in the shadowy darkness, the massive carved wooden crucifix, its outlines merged completely into the surrounding darkness, still made its presence felt. It dominated the vaulted interior of the church; the outstretched arms on the crucifix conquered the darkness. She threw herself on her knees before the crucifix. She kept her eyes closed and thought of Christ's suffering face. Somewhere in the darkness above her head the face gazed down at her. She tried to shut it out from her mind's eye ... but Jesus' living face and His eyes were looking at her ... only at her. He could see her, He could hear her. ... She could pour everything out to Him, everything.

295

...Everything she had concealed from Father McKee, everything she had concealed even from herself, everything she had tried so hard to banish from her memory ... she could tell everything to Him. ... She did not need to find words, or to picture concrete images in her thoughts. All she needed to do was to open the pages of the book of her life and place them at the feet of Jesus. ...

"I took Irving away from her ... I forced him to marry me. Not because I loved him but because I wanted to triumph over her; to show her that I could take him away from her. It was his brother, it was Nathan I loved. He needed me ... and I wanted to serve him, to help him. Instead I made Irving marry me. I made him break his promise to a dying man. They were waiting there for him; the wedding canopy stood by the bed ... and I stole him away. Not because I loved him. No! Because I knew he was a good businessman. I wanted to be rich. I wanted to live in luxury, not the way my mother and the others lived, in dirty holes all their lives. I wanted to have beautiful clothes, and an easy life. And I wanted to have a lot of money in the bank, so that I would never again be poor and have to come to others and beg them to give me work. That's why I worked so hard and made Irving work so hard for the business to grow. I confess it all, dear Jesus! We rented an old building, without thinking about the safety of the people who would have to work there, and we changed it into a factory, and every time I visited one of the upper floors where the operators worked, I would think of that Saturday afternoon in the Triangle firm ... and the flames licking near the door. I saw Sarah's face with the crown of flames around her hair ... but I closed my eyes. I drove every memory of that day away from my mind. I didn't want to see Sarah's face; I didn't want to remember her young body and the way the broken glass was cutting into her breast. ... I even tried to forget You, dear Jesus, forget how You enfolded me in Your arms when I hung on to that iron balcony and how You carried me down to the balcony You provided for me on the floor below, so that my life might be saved. I didn't want to remember it; I didn't want to think of it. I didn't want anything to prevent me from forcing my husband to make more and more money. I wanted money, and all I thought about was how to make it so that we would never, never be poor again. That is the truth, dear Jesus, the whole truth . . . the whole truth. . . ."

And the miracle came to her. The knot of bitterness in her heart melted. Scalding tears streamed from her eyes. She was empty of all thought and feeling.

How long she stayed there she did not know. It might have been an hour or an eternity. But when she rose, the road was clear to her.

Irving was Rachel's. She had stolen him from her; now she must give him back so that he could make good his promise to her dead father. She would give him back, freely, with an open heart, and she would do all she could to make the divorce easy. He could make arrangements about the child through his lawyer. For herself she wanted nothing. She would find work. She would live like every other working girl. She would leave the house as soon as she could find a suitable place for herself and little Nat in some humble neighborhood. She would go back where she belonged. She would go back to the East River, back to 48th Street.

She dried her eyes and went outside.

CHAPTER NINE

NOT MUCH was changed on 48th Street. Moshe Wolf still made his scant living in the grocery store, rising out of bed at dawn, snatching a moment of prayer in the kitchen, and then downstairs to get the store ready for the day.

He knew that his wife was visiting Irving, that she was getting money from him, and that Nathan was keeping up his studies with Irving's help. There was nothing he could do about it. All he could do was to remove himself from all of them, even from Nathan, and burrow deeper and deeper into his own hiding place, like a tortoise in its shell. He became even more rigidly pious. What else had he to expect of the world; he would live righteously to prepare for a world of eternal justice.

So far as Nathan was concerned, it had not taken him long to find out that in allowing Dr. Chazanowitch to persuade him to resume his studies, he had undertaken something beyond his physical possibilities. More, beyond his spiritual possibilities. At the beginning he had approached his studies enthusiastically. Robert Hirsch came for him a couple of times a week and wheeled him away in his invalid chair, down the subway steps, and uptown to Columbia. When Robert could not come, there was a man whom Irving had hired to help him. But now he knew that the task was more than he could accomplish. His pessimism led him to neglect his studies. He resented having to be helped by strangers. It was one thing when his father—or Mary—did things for him. But when he had to turn to strangers, to someone hired for pay, all the hopelessness and helplessness of his condition again overwhelmed him.

"Pride and arrogance, that's all it is! The cheap vanity of showing the world that a cripple can go to college!"

Even Dr. Chazanowitch, unaware of it though he was, wanted to show off with him—a trained monkey that had learned to ride a bicycle. "Here you are, everybody! See what I've done! Here's a totally crippled boy and I'm making a lawyer out of him!"

But he did not abandon his studies, nor did he see any reason why he should refuse Irving's financial help. He needed it so badly. "God gives everyone his work to do," he thought to himself. "He has saved me from uselessness and has given me enough to survive in my own little world. Let me be content to be a little drop in the sea of life. The heights are not for me. What I have now is enough. Let me make it useful."

And there was someone who had encouraged this resolve: Heimowitz, the tailor across the street.

Heimowitz had shown him nothing but contempt from the moment Nat made preparations to return to college instead of continuing his activities in the radical circle to which Heimowitz belonged.

"So you've gone over to them." To Heimowitz "them" meant the bourgeoisie, the exploiters, the manufacturers. "Naturally, your brother is a manufacturer, and so you become a lawyer. Your brother cuts the throat of the workers and you'll make it all right and legal with your smooth tongue. I didn't expect it from you."

To Nathan, Heimowitz was still the conscience of 48th Street, the embodiment of protest and struggle against the forces of oppression and exploitation.

"Who says that a lawyer only has to defend manufacturers? Doesn't the worker need a voice in court, too? Maybe I'll devote my career to the workers."

"Oh, yes, we know how you'll take the side of the workers. We've heard that tune before. All you intellectuals say that's what you'll do, while you're still raw, but as soon as your feathers begin to sprout you fly over to where the pickings are better. If you really want to be useful to the workers you don't need to wait until you finish college. Anyway, it's your brother's money that's paying for it. Money that he squeezes out of the workers' sweat and blood, and which you'll have to be grateful to him for all the rest of your life! Come with me. I'll show you where you can really learn something. You'll learn more from real life than from all the colleges put together."

Nathan had gone with him. Heimowitz became his instructor in sociology and the neighborhood was the university. The block's official socialist was getting older, but the advancing years meant only that he was growing bitterer toward the capitalist system and more hardened in the labor struggle. Even his tongue was freer. He talked against everyone—God, Tammany, the manufacturer, the government—mostly against the Jews. No, he didn't spare the Jews.

"Oh, we're fine revolutionists, we are," he said to Nathan. "For the Gentiles we're revolutionists; not for the Jews. We want to overthrow all tyrants—except our own. We yell that all religion is reactionary, dark, medieval, a curse on mankind. But just dare to touch Shmulevitch's skullcap and you'll see what'll happen. We sneer at the other fellow's pot, but whatever's cooking in ours is kosher, and nobody dares say a word. Take Shmulevitch. You saw how he built the *shul*. Jews gave money for it. Your father pawned his shirt to give him money. They tore money from the living and the dead. And what did he build the *shul* for? Do you think it was for Jews to pray in? For his kosher chicken business, that's what it was for! The whole thing was for the sake of his business so that he could get a rabbi to give his slaughterhouse a clean bill of health. And how do we feel about our own millionaires? It's all right to shout against Rockefeller and Vanderbilt, but just say a word against Schiff and they'll call you a traitor to the Jews! Take yourself. Here you are, a radical, and you're always babbling about all the exploiters of the world. But do you ever say a word against your own brother? Naturally; he's the one you get money from to study."

"What have you got against Irving? What's he done?"

"What's he done? Come with me and I'll show you."

The block, like the rest of the East River neighborhood, was infested with the plague of homework—the bundles of cut material which the contractors sent to the tenement flats to be sewn together into finished garments. Every flat had become a factory. Even the sick presser, Chaim Melamed, whom 48th Street watched out for—even Melamed was busy working. His whole family, wife and children, was working with him.

Heimowitz dragged Nathan up to the second floor of the tenement house where Melamed lived.

To Nat's astonishment, the sick man whom he had seen for years propped up on a chair in front of the tenement door was now busy in the small, unkempt kitchen, its windows facing a small yard where the wash hung out on lines. With one hand he

300

held on to the table while with the other he dragged the hot pressing iron along the damp cloth which was spread over a finished dress. A cloud of steam rose up from the damp rag, and Melamed brought a heavy stick of wood down on the board to insure that the crease would hold.

In another room, crowded with two beds, Melamed's daughters were stitching buttonholes or sewing buttons on finished dresses. Two smaller children played around on the dirty floor. Melamed's wife, a thin and sallow woman, sat at the sewing machine, her feet pumping back and forth on the treadles. An old woman with disordered gray hair stood at the stove in the kitchen and poked around among the pots. Bundles and pieces of material lay scattered around. The window was shut tight. It was cold outside, the snow piled heavy in the yard, on the window sills and the roof. The kitchen itself seethed with heat from the gas stove on which Melamed kept his iron hot. The room was full of the sour smell of cooking food and the sickly sweet odor of gas.

"Guests!" Melamed exclaimed in surprise. A smile appeared on his pale, moist face. Unnatural red patches stood out on his cheeks. He wiped his face with the damp rag he was using at the pressing board, his smile uncovering the solitary tooth left in his mouth. "Tell me something; tell me some good news, Heimowitz! And you crawled all the way up those two flights, Nat! You see, Nat, if I got rid of my sickness, you can get rid of yours too!" Melamed coughed and spat into the sputum cup which stood on the pressing board. He continued his chatter. "What can I tell you? Nothing. I suppose as long as you came up, you have something to tell me."

"Nothing. Just so. We just came up to see if you were working," said Heimowitz.

"Why shouldn't I work? I always told them at the union that the only reason I was sick was on account of the slack season. Give me work and I'll get better, I told them. But they didn't want to believe me. They said I've got consumption and I need to go to an institution. To Denver, they said. Who's got the money to go to Denver? My benefit money they took away because I didn't pay dues! Give me work, I always begged them, and I'll get better. But they didn't believe me. And now you see for yourself . . . the minute it gets busy in the trade, I get healthy, my wife

301

gets healthy...." Melamed began to cough again and clutched at his chest.

"I see you're still coughing," Heimowitz said.

"That's the gas; it gets in my throat. The oven leaks. And suppose I have a little consumption, so what! So I'm supposed to lay down and die? I'm supposed to get thrown out of the union? I'm supposed to stop working in a shop? All right! So along comes the contractor. He doesn't ask questions—whether I've got consumption or I haven't got consumption! What business is it of his? He gives me a bundle of material. Whatever I finish I get paid for. I'm my own boss. I work when I want and how much I want. Nobody can tell me when I can work and when I can't work. I work, my wife works, my children work. Thank God, we can buy a piece of meat once in a while, at least to make some soup. Do you smell it? That's what's cooking on the stove.... This is my mother-in-law. We can even manage to take her in to live with us. Since her son died, she hasn't had a place to live. So she does the cooking. Because, after all, it's not me who's the real worker; it's my wife. I only help a bit. I'm still on charity.... There's got to be somebody in the house to cook a meal."

"You're still on charity?" Heimowitz asked.

"Of course. I'm supposed to be a sick man. It's my wife who takes the bundles of work. My wife and the children."

"But you just said that you're working. And I can see you at the ironing board."

"Who's working? I'm working? Can I work? I'm a sick man." Melamed shrugged his shoulders. "As long as I'm in the house, and I have nothing to do, so I press a bit. After all, I've been a presser all my life. I'm just helping her out a bit. But you don't have to tell anybody about it, just the same. Why should the charities find out? After all, what harm am I doing if I help out a little bit and help to earn a few pennies? And after all, the contractor begs me...."

"But it's bad for you."

"What harm is it? Work doesn't do me any harm. It's good for me. When I'm at the pressing board I forget that I'm sick." Melamed smiled again and bent over the sputum cup.

When they got down into the street, Heimowitz continued his tirade.

"I tell you, Nat, the Jewish bosses have enslaved their own

brothers in America worse than Pharaoh in Egypt. After all, in Egypt they had some pride left. Here in America—you see yourself what they've made out of a worker, one of their own brothers. They throw him a crust of bread, like a bone to a dog, and he pays with his pride. He works—and he takes charity! That's the condition they've brought him to."

"Whose fault is it?" said Nathan.

"It's my fault, it's your fault, it's everybody's fault—because we allow it."

"Do those bundles come from Irving?" Nat broke in.

"What's the difference? If it isn't Irving, it's for some other black-hearted dog, some other capitalist like Irving. Whatever their names are—Markowsky, Nathanson, Cohen and Levy—all of them yesterday's immigrants, practically just off the ship, or at the most, children of immigrants—like your brother. Born in poverty like the rest of us, and worked in shops themselves! Or they've seen poverty in the home, seen their own fathers coming home from work knocked out and exhausted, seen them fall on their food like animals and sleep like animals, seen them living like cattle, leaving their house before the sun rises and coming home in the dark of night. Never getting a chance to see their own children...."

It was already evening when Nathan got home. A light snow was falling. His father was in front of the store sweeping the sidewalk and steps. Deborah stood in the doorway.

"What do you have to work yourself like a dog for?" she called to her husband.

Moshe Wolf made no answer. Nathan could hear his heavy breathing. Bitterness and shame over his own helplessness swept over him.

All that evening he watched his father. He watched him as he stood back of the counter and served the customers. He watched him dragging the cans of milk, the crates of groceries and the sacks of sugar up from the cellar storeroom. He watched while his father swept out the store, put the merchandise in order, stowed away the packages and sacks and boxes before he closed the store for the night.

Moshe Wolf had become an old man. Nathan could see that his father's beard had become altogether gray. His eyes were sunk deeply in his head. His hands had become old. Nathan noticed for the first time how old his father's hands were, old and wrinkled and trembling. He looked at them upstairs, in the flat, when Moshe Wolf stood at the kitchen table and began to chant the evening prayers before sitting down to his evening meal. As they held the prayer book, the hands seemed to tremble. They seemed to join in the old man's prayers—the wrinkles and folds of the loose skin were eloquent with prayer.

Nathan looked at his father as he stood bowed in prayer. He thought of his father's attitude toward Irving. It had seemed to him nothing but the blind fanaticism of the old country. He had not agreed with his father's attitude, but he respected his dignity and pride. "His money is unclean," his father had said, and he had refused to touch it. . . . And here he was in his old age, working like a beast of burden—and he had only to stretch out his hand and he would be able to live in peace and comfort, even in luxury.

"I wouldn't have been able to do it," Nathan thought. "How small I am compared to him! What is the intelligence and logic of the individual against the logic and intelligence of an entire history and civilization and tradition!"

"What are you staring at me for?" Moshe Wolf asked kindly. He sat down at the table and began to eat.

"He's looking at the way you're spoiling your life with your own ignorant obstinacy. At your age you still have to drag the sacks of groceries! We could be catching a breath of fresh air—living in some peace—and God sends a *shikse* into the house—" Deborah sighed as she handed Moshe Wolf a cup of coffee.

"You were right, Pa," Nathan suddenly said.

"What do you mean?"

"I mean about Irving. You were right. I understand now. Now I know that I can't take his money any more. . . ."

"What's the matter?" Deborah demanded, alarmed. "What happened!"

"Nothing happened," Moshe Wolf said. "A man who has no reverence for God can't have respect for his fellow man."

Later, as Moshe Wolf helped Nat to bed, his trembling fingers rested with benediction on his son's dark head.

CHAPTER TEN

I N THE between-decks, in the bellies of the ships which carried the great stream of Jewish immigration from the old world to the new, a glowing Jewish idealism came with the Jewish masses to the New World. It was an idealism which had its roots in the age-old martyrdom of the Jew, forged and tempered in the fires of the Russian revolution in which Jews had played so ardent a part.

With their idealism they brought, too, the entire baggage of social ideas and ideologies of the various radical groupings in Europe. They fought each other bitterly over their competing attitudes toward the end aim of the social struggle. Not for a moment were they able to agree as to the shape of the world to come—whether socialist, according to the Marx-Engels theories, or anarchist, according to the Bakhunin-Kropotkin ideas. But this was all the music of the future. So far as the immediate task was concerned they all held the same view—to fight shoulder to shoulder against the slave labor of the sweatshop. Many of them neglected their personal careers and all their personal interests to devote themselves to raising the Jewish masses out of their economic chaos, organizing them in trade unions and lifting them up from the degradation in which the employers kept them to the dignity and greater security of collective action.

The Jewish worker was like a plant trying to thrive in a new environment. He had reached his maturity in an atmosphere of persecution and oppression. Through it all he had kept in his heart the dream and the longing for the Messiah who would some day appear to create that just world which the prophets of old had foretold. That had been the only ray of hope on his dark horizon, the consummation he had prayed for by day and by night in the pious life he had lived in the old country. Now, in the new world, he kept the dream of a Messianic redemption alive in the sweatshops where he labored. But, under the new conditions, the Messiah who would bring about the better world would not be a divine Redeemer—it would be the social revolution.

This ideal, or rather dream, of social revolution sustained the Jewish worker during the long hours of his back-breaking toil in the sweatshop, just as the dream of a Messianic redemption had sustained him and his parents in the pious prayer houses in the old country.

Yet the dream of a better and juster world, instead of being bound up with America, the country which was now their home, had as its arena Russia, the very country that had driven them out.

The leaders of the unions, preoccupied with actual and immediate problems, managed to reorient their thinking within the framework of the realities of American life and American attitudes. But the intellectuals, busily engaged in spinning the web of Utopian socialist ideals for the workers, simply floated around in space. They felt rootless in the new world; they could not integrate their ideals with its soil. To them America was no more than a temporary halting place; they still had to weave their dream of social revolution out of the old-world threads. Everything that was good in their dreams of the social revolution was bound up with Russia, the country in which they had fought and bled. They left America entirely out of their reckoning. The lectures they gave to the Jewish working masses did not deal with American social conditions, nor did they explore the ways of improving them by methods suited to the standards of American life.

It was as though they were simply biding their time in an inn or hostelry for travelers. Their life was bound up with what was happening in Russia. They made plans for Russia; they talked Russian among themselves and read Russian books. It was only when they had to speak to the masses that they would condescend to use Yiddish, the language of the masses, coarsening and vulgarizing it, using it as a means to spread their interpretation of the events which were taking place in a country the masses had left forever behind them.

It was on the occasion of a lecture given by such a group, in a school for social science, that Nathan Davidowsky, son of immigrants, sat before an audience in his invalid chair. He had been

306

invited to expound his ideas to a class of workers and union functionaries.

"America is our home," he said in his earnest voice. "Not a place where we have found a temporary haven, until the sun of the revolution rises in Russia. America is our spiritual home. It is the country which should be nearest and dearest to us, because it is most closely related to our ideals of a better world order—if not yet in accomplishment, then certainly in ideals and potentialities. The founding fathers designed it so that it might become the leading force in the creation of a new world order.

"Not only through its legislative institutions does America point to the highest moral order yet achieved in the world. Through its institutions it aims at achieving the highest ideals of the ancient prophets. America has brought into harmony the two philosophies which have been at the opposite poles of human thought. It has made peace between them. America is the first country in history to establish a synthesis of the religious-moral ideal of the Hebrew prophets and the rational-ethical ideals of the Greeks. Thomas Jefferson is a unification of the two civilizations, the link which joins Isaiah and Plato. And in the same way the American Bill of Rights, the Declaration of Independence, and the Constitution are a synthesis of the two cultures which have their source in the Judaeo-Christian teachings of both Testaments. It is, if you like, the new Christianity which has been so long in coming.

"Our fathers came here to a strange and alien world. They were unable to adjust themselves. They stumbled into the shops and were exploited by their own kinsfolk, their own people. They thought that the sweatshop was America. But we, their children, who know of America's traditions of freedom; we who have gone to public school and learned American history, we know the true America. We know that there is another America—different from the one our fathers know. We do not need to direct our ideals of social justice to a country strange to us, to a land to which we will never return. Our gaze must be fixed on the land where we have found a home, on the country which has received us as equal partners. It is here, in America, that our life must be lived. Our future is here, in America. We must build our life in the New World—our world.

"We must free our parents not only from their physical slavery

307

to the shop; we must free them from the psychological and moral slavery which the sweatshop has bred in them. We must fight not only for a better physical life, but for a better moral life, too. The sweat system under which our parents work has robbed them of all human dignity. Their human pride has fallen victim to the struggle for existence, the fear of unemployment, the terror of the landlord, the never-ending fear of hunger. They must be given back the high moral pride which they brought with them from the old country. They must be rid of the shackles of demoralization and degradation. They must learn the pride and dignity of free American citizens.

"It is impossible to exaggerate what the vicious sweatshop system has made of the worker. I have seen how the degrading contractor system has transformed a consumptive worker's home into a sweatshop in which his own wife and children become ready candidates for the same disease which the sweatshop gave to him. And not only that. This man, sick for years, has had to take up the pressing iron again—even though he continues to take the money the charitable institutions give him. Crippled them physically and spiritually—that's what the contract sytem in the garment industry has done to the worker!"

"What about your own brother? What about Davidowsky's bundles?" The shouts came from a few in the audience who resented Nathan's argument in favor of an American orientation; that argument struck at the roots of their radical ideas.

"Yes, I know about Davidowsky's bundles. That is why I'm here; to fight against them!"

"But you take his money to study at Columbia," someone shouted sarcastically.

Nathan paled, but there was no hesitation in his voice as he answered.

"Yes, it's true. I admit that I thought that I was right to take help from my brother. But since I found out about Davidowsky's bundles I have refused his help. I've given up college. I admit I was late in finding the honest thing to do. I should have followed my father who refused any help from him long before I did, on religious grounds."

Nathan's frank confession seemed to change the audience's attitude toward him. He could feel a new wave of sympathy coming to him; but the angry comments continued. What? Disassociate the social revolution from Russia, the birthplace of revolution? Think in terms of America? Unheard of! Insane! Dangerous!

"Sure, Tammany will teach Marxism to the Bowery bums!" someone shouted scornfully. "The Republican corporation lawyers will teach socialism to their capitalist clients!"

"Tammany isn't America, nor the corporation lawyers either! America is the Constitution, the Declaration of Independence, the Bill of Rights! These aren't only empty words; they are living principles and laws! They contain the promise of freedom for all. Today they are closed up in a sealed book, but the leader will arise who will break open the seal. We already have seen the signs of the coming of such a man. It was in the Constitution that Lincoln found his greatest weapon in the fight against the South. Even Theodore Roosevelt made the attempt, and Woodrow Wilson, too, though they didn't have the courage to carry the job through. But tomorrow will bring the man who will have the courage. He will lift our Constitution as Moses did the Commandments, and say: 'This is what is written and this I will do.'"

When Heimowitz helped Nathan down from the platform, a middle-aged man approached them. He had a young face, although his hair was gray. He had a friendly and intelligent smile. He took Nathan's crippled hand in his and shook it warmly.

"Don't feel too bad at the way they laugh at you. They don't treat me any better. What you had to say was more than interesting, it was necessary. You aren't alone in your views. There are others, and the number is growing all the time."

"This is Comrade Zelikowitz, our Assemblyman," Heimowitz said. "He's the manager of the waist makers union."

Nat had heard of him. He was one of the union leaders who had risen from the ranks. He had come to America as a young man with the stream of Jewish immigration and had gone through the poverty and hardship which were the lot of his fellow Jews in their first years on American soil. At first he had been a cigar maker. Then he had become an operator, dragging his Singer sewing machine—the "hand organ" as it was known—from shop to shop. Earning a bare livelihood in the daytime, he spent his nights in study. The East Side had elected him Assemblyman and one of his fellows to Congress. The two had been the first to propagandize Americanism to the Jewish masses. He had no thoughts of returning to Russia; he dreamed instead of the time when America would become the paradise which the radicals insisted could be built only in Russia.

"You can help us. We need intelligent young men like you," he now said to Nathan.

"How can I help? I've got nothing but this mouth of mine," Nat said with an apologetic smile.

"You've got a head and a heart too. That's all we need. We don't need you to do acrobatic tricks," Zelikowitz said. "We need you to talk to workers' groups just the way you talked tonight. We haven't got time to make speeches; we're up to our neck with the strike. The halls are packed with workers and we need someone to give them words of encouragement, to give them heart through these difficult days. We have plenty of Yiddish speakers; we need English speakers, too. Young man, you can be of great help to us."

"Do you really think so?"

"I'm certain of it. It's my business to know. Where will I be able to get in touch with you?"

"You can always get him through me," said Heimowitz, who was standing behind the wheel chair.

"And who are you?"

"Don't you recognize me?"

"Oh, it's Heimowitz. How do you come to be here?"

"Who else do you think brought him here? And listen to me. I've got something to tell you." He drew the Assemblyman to one side. "After all the boy needs to make a living."

"How does he get along now?"

"From his father, a poor man, with a poor grocery store on 48th Street; he barely manages to make a living."

"Davidowsky, did you say? Not the same family as 'Davidowsky's bundles'?"

"Yes, that's his brother. I knew the bastard when he was a baby, but they both refuse to have anything to do with him; this young man gave up college because he won't take any help from his brother."

"Don't you worry. We'll employ him in the union. We need him. Bring him to the office tomorrow. I'll arrange everything."

Nathan would have been hard put to it to explain the miracle of his new-found fund of energy. It was as though vast reservoirs

310

of strength had accumulated within him during the long years of his inactivity; now the reservoir was spilling over in work for the labor movement. He plunged into an intensive study of working conditions in the garment industry. Forty per cent of the workers' earnings, he found, went for the rent of their flats in the vermin-infested tenements. Tenement rents had climbed sky high as a result of the cessation of building during the war. Prices of farm products, as a result of the enormous exports to the Allies, had climbed twenty per cent. General living costs, because of the huge influx of Allied gold into the country to pay for war materials, had become abnormally high. The entire country was catapulting into a period of "prosperity." But the wages of the workers, especially in the needle trades, had not increased; on the contrary, they had declined. And now the manufacturers were taking advantage of the weakness of the unions to smuggle work out of their shops so that contractors could farm out bundles for homework, thus cutting the earnings of the union workers. The specter of unemployment constantly haunted the workers in the industry.

The manufacturers, Nat learned, instead of investing their own capital, were borrowing money from fly-by-night, insecure banks, and paying exorbitant rates of interest. Most of the manufacturers—in most cases former workers themselves—were caught in the prevailing American get-rich-quick fever. They were seeking feverishly to escape from the class of the exploited and join the ranks of the exploiters. The fear of poverty had aroused in them an unbridled appetite. Brothers, kinsfolk, meant nothing to them. They were thinking only of one thing: how to get a foothold on the ladder which led to wealth, no matter who had to be trampled on and crushed in the process.

By day Nathan dictated articles for the English-language publications which the union issued; in the evenings he lectured at union meeting halls.

A new social awareness had arisen in America with the inauguration of President Wilson. Wilson did not wage war on the monopolies and the huge corporations with the bluster and fury of the temperamental Teddy Roosevelt—for all of his bluster, the corporations had known that Teddy would expend all his revolutionary zeal in sound and fury. Wilson awakened the country to a new conception of social justice with a logical, irrefutable, academic calm. In the same way he led the fight against the accumulation of enormous fortunes at the expense of the people. The time for such legalized looting at the expense of the people was past. Wilson's great virtue was that he knew how to awaken a social consciousness in the academic circles from which he came himself. Professors left their lecture halls and took their students on tours of factories, mines, and mills.

Academic circles in New York began to interest themselves in labor conditions in the garment industry and began to arouse public opinion. Nathan played his part in the public enlightenment. The sight of a crippled youth on the lecture platform made a tremendous impression.

Evenings Heimowitz would take him in his wheel chair to the union meeting rooms. There was an urgent need to strengthen the solidarity of the workers within the union ranks. The manufacturers were preparing to launch a violent attack on the union —it was no secret—and it was necessary to strengthen the organization, recruit new members, give courage to the older members, collect workers' dues and accumulate a strike fund to carry them through the expected lockout by which the manufacturers hoped to break the union's back. There were all nationalities among the workers. The meetings were a babel of Yiddish, Italian, and Slavic tongues. There were many Irish and native-born Americans, too, in the ranks; these, of course, spoke English, as did those of the foreign-born who had been in the country long enough to acquire the language. The Jewish workers were comparatively easy to organize. It was more difficult to organize the Italians and Slavs; the same was true of the Irish, who were under the direct influence of the church.

Heimowitz took Nathan from one meeting to another. The crippled speaker who spoke from an invalid chair became a prize attraction, popular among the workers. The fact that the brother of the well-known and well-hated Irving Davidowsky was appearing at union meetings and talking against his own brother aroused a special interest.

The small, narrow room on the first floor of Beethoven Hall was packed with workers. They spilled out of the hall, on to the stairs outside, and down to the street.

On the small stage in front of the hall sat a group of people with tired faces, unshaven, their eyes heavy with fatigue. These were shop chairmen, union workers and organizers. In front of them, on his wheel chair, Nathan sat. Behind him, like a guardian angel, stood Heimowitz.

For a while Nathan looked at the faces before him. The smoke of stale cigarettes and cigars dimmed the yellow light that spilled from the dust-covered electric lights. Out of the clouds of smoke, faces emerged clearly now and then. Eyes of old and young— sad Jewish eyes, sad Italian eyes, eyes of fathers, mothers, sisters, brothers—united and merged into one another. It was as though one single enormous eye stared and bored into Nathan's face. Speaker and audience fused into one body. The cares, the burdens, the sorrows and the lust for battle poured from the audience to the speaker; love and loyalty to the workers poured from the speaker to the audience. Nat became one with them. He forgot that he was crippled; he was leading them in battle. He was standing with them on the picket line; he was guarding the doors of a shop, blocking with his body the attack of the strikebreakers. He was fighting back with powerful vindictive blows. He was healthy, he was normal. He was a giant.

That is how the audience saw him, too. They forgot that it was a cripple who was sitting before them. His pale face shone earnestly from the sparse frame of his thin dark beard. His eyes glowed with loyalty and trust. Every movement, every expression of his face bore witness to the love which beat in his heart for the cause of the workers. A deep wisdom seemed to shine forth from his high forehead.

"What are we all? We're lost souls, helpless and unprotected. Anyone can buy and use our strength and our life—even our human dignity, for his own purposes and profits. They don't care that the places in which we work are fire traps; they take more care of the warehouses where they store their goods. They are careful to protect dead merchandise; they do nothing to protect living beings. Your only salvation is in your collective strength. Without it you are nothing but a labor commodity to be bought and sold on the open market at whatever price the boss decides to pay. With it you are the inheritors of the earth, for you are the ones who make it bloom with your toil."

Nathan would come home from the meetings exhausted and drenched with perspiration. Heimowitz tended him with selfless devotion and watched over him with fatherly concern. There was in Heimowitz's attitude something of the spiritual veneration which his parents, the pious Hasidim in the small Polish village, had paid to their rabbi. Nathan was Heimowitz's rabbi; he was preaching the word for the revolutionist and freethinker of 48th Street.

Heimowitz's God was the social revolution. That was his Messiah. That was what would wipe away all tears and loose all the bonds of slavery. His belief in the social revolution satisfied all his needs. He had no other personal life. He had lost his wife during his one-man struggle—here on 48th Street—while he fought Tammany and the other social evils. She had simply died from the poverty, heartbreak, and trouble that had come from her husband's crusading zeal. His children—two daughters—had left him long before. One of them had really sunk to the depths; she had married a union leader who had later become a jobber selling piece goods to the manufacturers; Heimowitz even suspected him of being a contractor. He cared nothing for them, nor they for him. He lived alone, behind the cleaning and pressing store, in a dark, windowless room. His bed and a few odds and ends made up the furniture. He cooked for himself on a small gas stove.

He lived for no other goal than the revolution. Just as a pious Jew, before he goes to bed at night, gives an accounting to God of his actions during the day, so did Heimowitz give an accounting to himself before he went sleep each night as to what he had done for "the cause."

The fact that he was taking Nathan to meeting halls each night gave Heimowitz a new life. He felt elevated through Nathan's activities, as though through Nathan he had found his own true mission. He thought of himself as an indispensable part of Nathan's labors. He would say: "Tonight we're going to Clinton Hall. There we have to deliver the goods!" And when Nathan was through with his speech, Heimowitz would say: "We gave it to the bloodsuckers, the bosses! We let them have it!"

"All right, let us go now. We have no strength left. Don't you see the way we're sweating; worse than working at the pressing table," he would shout, driving away the people who crowded around after the speech.

He would never take Nathan directly home. He would take him into his own store and set about brewing some tea.

"It'll soon be ready. Just a little while. You rest. You're tired."

He had tried on occasion to "kidnap" Nat. When they were kept out late at night he would actually refuse to help Nathan up the steps to his father's house.

"It's all right. You can sleep here. I'll put you in my bed and you'll sleep. Tomorrow morning early, anyway, I've got to take you to the union office, so it'll save the job of climbing those stairs."

"What are you talking about, Heimowitz? You know my father waits up every night until I get home. He'll be worried."

"All right, so I'll run and tell him that you're sleeping here. Now I'll make you something to eat."

Moshe Wolf saw plainly how the little tailor was trying to steal his son, and he couldn't prevent a growing feeling of jealousy.

"Why should he have to take you to the meetings? Why can't I take you?" he demanded.

"Because you have to know everything that's going on. Heimowitz was practically brought up in the unions. He's an old war horse. He knows where it's most necessary for me to go."

A contest developed between Moshe Wolf and Heimowitz as to who should be the boy's bodyguard. Moshe Wolf began to accompany them to the meeting halls and listen to his son's lectures. He would listen to Nat's eloquent attacks on working conditions and add his sighs to the sighs of the audiences.

"Like the Jews in Egypt," he would say mournfully. "They gave them no straw and still demanded their bricks."

CHAPTER ELEVEN

IT IS ONE of those unquestioned axioms in New York that a hot summer will always be followed by a severe winter. True to the general belief, the winter of that year came early and lasted until late in the spring. February and March brought unusually severe snow storms which blanketed the east coast states. New York was helpless; the city was hardly finished with cleaning one snowfall off the streets when they were covered again.

The enormous piles of snow heaped in the gutters and over-flowing on the sidewalks disrupted traffic. People were late for work and late getting home. The subways were packed to suffocation; the streetcars were jammed. On the sidewalks pools of melting snow added to the treachery of the icy surface beneath. Pedestrians trod gingerly, carefully placing one foot in front of the other.

From early in the morning Moshe Wolf had been hacking away with his shovel on the sidewalk in front of the store, trying to clear away the caked ice. He had already swept away the drifts of snow that had fallen during the night. He was hot from the exertion. The sweat ran out under his hat down his gray-bearded face, but his hands and feet were freezing with cold. He had lost one of his rubbers in the slush. He groaned. His back ached. He was putting his last ounce of strength into the work.

Deborah stood on the steps leading down to the store. Her head was wrapped in a shawl and she was wearing a heavy coat. She looked dolefully at her husband, shaking her head and grumbling in a resigned voice.

"Woe is me . . . a street cleaner . . . in his declining years."

Moshe Wolf made no answer.

"What are you killing yourself for?" she kept on. "Nobody's

going to stick his nose in the store anyway. Have you got customers? Have you got anything to sell?"

What she said was true. The grocery store was sinking from day to day. Moshe Wolf kept on trying; anything rather than be dependent on his son. At least he would hold on to the illusion that he wasn't dependent on Irving. He knew very well that Deborah was getting money from Irving, but at least, as long as he held on to the store, he could have the feeling that it was he, Moshe Wolf, who was keeping up the household. But it was getting harder and harder. Deborah was refusing to help him. Oh, no, she said, she wouldn't give up her few remaining years to slaving in the grocery when she had a son who was willing to support her in comfort.

"If you're crazy," she said to Moshe Wolf, "and you're willing to drive your own flesh and blood away from you, and refuse to take money from him, that's no reason why I should suffer."

Moshe Wolf had to neglect the store more and more. He was constantly being torn between attending to the store and taking care of Nathan. The store wasn't prepared in time; the groceries were unorganized or misplaced, the milk froze in the cold, the bread and the crackers and the cakes got moldy—and the customers began to disappear from day to day. To add to his troubles, over on First Avenue, near the new synagogue where Shmulevitch now had his kosher poultry store, a new Jewish grocery store had been opened, and Moshe Wolf's store was almost completely deserted. He sat all day in the cold, half empty store, warming himself at the gas oven, beating his palms together and reciting the Psalms, sometimes from memory and sometimes peering into the open prayer book on his lap. Only a loyal few of the old customers poked their noses into the store once in a while, asking for articles which in most cases Moshe Wolf didn't have on his shelves.

"You stubborn old mule!" Deborah said. "Close the store and come upstairs to get the cold out of your bones. I'm making a pot of coffee."

Moshe Wolf knew that Deborah was right and that the only thing to do was to close the store altogether. But closing the store meant to admit that he was through, that he was content to live on Irving's blood-money, which he had sworn not to touch.

He thought of looking for work in one of the factories where many of the orthodox Jews he knew worked at sewing shirts, in a factory where a man could gather with his fellow Jews to recite the afternoon prayers—and work the extra time to make up for their devotions. But who would take care of Nat? Although the boy was not entirely helpless—thank God!—still he needed someone around to help him. After all, there were some things he could not manage for himself.

Moshe Wolf felt abandoned and alone. Each morning he poured his heart out in prayer . . . and then the day had come when the miracle happened; his prayers were answered. Nathan had a job; he was working for the union. The crippled Nathan, who had to be wheeled around in an invalid chair! Heimowitz would take him in the evenings to meeting rooms where strikers were assembled, and Nathan would address them. And in the daytime someone came—sometimes a young man or a young girl— and he would dictate to them and they would take it down by stenography, and later what he dictated would be printed in the papers! Could anyone believe that these words which came from his son's lips would be written down and printed? And they paid him money for it! Nathan, his crippled son, who he thought would have to be cared for all his life, had saved him from the sin of coming to Irving for help! Who would believe that Nathan could now contribute twenty dollars a week toward the family livelihood?

Twenty dollars a week! It was enough to pay the rent; enough to keep body and soul together. It was more than Moshe Wolf had ever made out of his store. The miracle put new spirit into Moshe Wolf.

Deborah put her own construction on what was going on— her older son had undertaken to ruin his younger brother, and her husband was helping in the work. Nat was going around to union meeting halls and agitating the workers against Irving! Her heart bled. Moshe Wolf's household became transformed into a hell.

"A murderer's heart you've got to have! To carry on against your own brother! To blacken his name in people's eyes! And you, you old fool, you have to help him!" she complained bitterly when both Nat and Moshe Wolf were home.

"And what if he's a thief, a bandit? Are you supposed to keep quiet about it?" Moshe Wolf answered angrily. "In America such things happen. One brother is a district attorney and the other is a gangster. So do you think that the district attorney will keep him out of jail just because he's his brother?"

"Who did he ever do any harm to? He gives people a chance to make a living. He gives jobs to hundreds of poor people who could starve without him. I know why he's put himself against Irving—" she glared at Nathan—"he's jealous because he can't do what Irving can do. He's jealous because he's a helpless cripple, God help us! And because his brother's a success, a man who's making a name for himself. . . ."

"Deborah," Moshe Wolf shouted. "I'll not allow it! Our holy Torah declares . . ."

"Don't throw your Torah at me. You see what he's doing. He's stirring everybody up against his own brother. And you, you fool, you help him against his own flesh and blood!"

"I'm not jealous of Irving," Nathan said quietly. "I never had any ambition to be rich."

"Then why are you against him?"

"Because he's draining the life blood from the poor," Moshe Wolf answered hotly. He had heard Nathan use the phrase at a meeting.

"Is he the one that makes them work? Poverty makes them work. Do they work for Irving? They work to put food in their stomachs. He gives them a chance to bring a crust of bread into the house. They're satisfied. They bless him for giving them work. Instead of thanking God that your own child has climbed out of poverty . . . How many times we prayed to God—take us out of this prison, do something to let us get rid of 48th Street, from the store, from chopping the ice in the winter and burning from the heat in the summer. No day, no night! And when at last God gives an ear to your prayer and listens to your cries and lets your own child make something of himself . . . you want to destroy him! Your own flesh and blood! I won't let you do it. I won't let you destroy my child. I won't let you do it!" Deborah broke into tears.

"It's his own fault," Moshe Wolf replied. "What does he have to try to be so rich for?"

"You're a stubborn fool, Moshe Wolf. About him"—she pointed to Nathan—"we know. He wants what Heimowitz wants, to throw over the Tsar. But what's bothering you is something else. I know it. It's because he married that one. You're right; I don't say you're not right. But I tell you it won't take long. God will listen to my prayers. He knows the tears I shed every night. He'll leave her, you'll see. And then everything will be all right."

Strange as it might seem, Deborah Davidowsky had an intimate friend and confidante on 48th Street. It was Harry Greenstock's one-time mistress, Mrs. Kranz.

A common ambition bound them together—the longing to see Mary's and Irving's marriage destroyed. Then, too, Deborah had learned to have a certain amount of reverence for Mrs. Kranz. She was really moved by the latter's devoted treatment of the Greenstock orphans. A real mother could not be more devoted than Mrs. Kranz, Christian though she was. The block rang with Deborah's praise of her.

"She even makes sure that they keep to Jewish ways," she said to Mrs. Shmulevitch. "I've seen it myself. And the way she gets them ready for the Jewish holidays! As though she were a Jew herself."

She enjoyed her evening visits to Mrs. Kranz, when she could unburden her heart over the misfortune that had destroyed her household. Mrs. Kranz was understanding.

"Irving is still my son. No matter what he did, he's not the one to blame."

"The man always falls into the trap, and it's the woman who sets it for him," Mrs. Kranz commented.

"I could even say—may God not punish me for saying it— that he's my only son. I shouldn't say it, because after all Nat is also my son, but what can I expect from him—for all of his learning and education. A married man he'll never be. . . .God knows, from Nat I'll have no grandchildren; only from Irving can I expect to see grandchildren to rejoice my old age."

"You'll have grandchildren. Jewish grandchildren. You've earned that blessing." Mrs. Kranz was a great comfort.

"Irving was always my favorite. He worried about me from the time he was a child. The first penny he earned he brought home to me. I always knew he'd amount to something. And then that *shikse* comes along, and sets a trap for him and takes him away from a helpless orphan."

320

"Nothing good will come of it," said Mrs. Kranz. "Irving is a Jew, and he should marry a Jewish girl, just like he promised Harry, and give his parents a Jewish grandchild. Everything will be all right; you'll live to see everything all right."

"May it soon come to pass, dear Father in Heaven! I'll go to Harry's grave myself to tell him the news," said Deborah piously. "If only Rachel doesn't do anything foolish. I hear she's going out with some young man, some educated friend of Nat's. Some no-good..."

"Oh, she isn't serious about him. She's only passing the time. She only thinks about Irving. I know."

"Keep your eye on her, dear Mrs. Kranz. Watch out for her. She must wait for Irving. She must help her poor dead father to find some peace in his grave. Watch out for her, dear Mrs. Kranz. Such a treasure! She mustn't—God forbid—fall into the wrong hands.... He's getting to be a rich man, that son of mine. Everything he turns his hands to is gold. What a life she'd have with him! We could all be happy... dear Father in Heaven!"

"Don't worry, Mrs. Davidowsky. Rachel knows what she's doing."

"God will reward you for the care you're taking of the poor orphans, for what you're doing for Rachel."

Everything Deborah told her of Irving's business progress Mrs. Kranz passed on to the girl. She kept her hopes high with renewed promise, and blew on the flame of envy in Rachel's heart.

"She knew what she was doing, that Mary," Mrs. Kranz said. "She knew what a prize she was getting. Did you hear, Rachel? Irving has taken another two floors of the building for his business. He's giving out thousands of bundles. The whole neighborhood is working on Davidowsky's bundles. He has a tremendous business."

"Yes, I know. I hear about it in the trade."

"His mother told me that Mary doesn't come to the business any more. They haven't seen her around the shop for a couple of months. And he doesn't go out anywhere with her."

"I'm really not interested," Rachel remarked.

"I know you're not interested, but what's the harm in knowing what's happening with them?"

"I told you I'm not interested. I don't care to know anything about them."

"I know, I know! Are you going out this evening?"

"Yes, Robert is coming for me. We're going to a concert."

"Why are you putting on your evening dress? You know the boy is too poor to get orchestra seats."

"Who said anything about orchestra seats? He got tickets on the top gallery. He got them from a friend of his."

"And you're wearing an evening dress to sit in the gallery? And all your jewelry? Rachel, I've told you before, the boy's spending his last cent on you. He's a poor boy. Does he know you're not serious with him?" Mrs. Kranz looked at the girl with motherly concern.

"He knows it," Rachel said impatiently.

No, she had no serious intentions toward him. In her heart of hearts—although she never admitted to herself how deeply envious she was of Mary—all her yearning was toward Irving. She was unable to escape from the grip of her envy. Not because of Irving's success in business. She had had her chance to marry more than one wealthy and successful manufacturer, or professional man, or budding lawyer well on the way to a successful political career, all of them attracted by her beauty and some of them by the rumor of her uncle Silberberg's wealth. She had scorned them all.

Irving had left her suspended in mid-air. She belonged to him. He had been stolen away for a while, that was all. Now it was simply a contest between her and that other.

It wasn't long before Deborah learned that her prayers were being answered.

When Irving came back from the trip which had kept him away for a few weeks, Deborah put on the new coat which he had given her—and which she kept hidden from her husband—and went down to his office.

"I wanted to see you, Ma," Irving said. "I have something to talk over with you."

"I suppose it's about your brother. I suppose you've heard about the speeches he makes against you."

"No, it's not that. He's doing what he thinks he's got to do, and I don't hold it against him. I suppose he thinks he's accomplishing wonders. He's saving the world at the other fellow's expense. If he was in my place, here at this office, he'd do just

322

what I have to do. He thinks that it's all under my control—that I can make a revolution in the industry and give the workers all the blessings he's promising them—and that I just refuse to do it. But I'm willing to see conditions improved. I'm willing. It's the customers who aren't willing, the banks, the manufacturers, the whole industry. I've got to stand up against my competitors if I want to stay in business. Do you understand, Ma? I wanted to see Nathan finish college. I wanted to see him become a lawyer. But he wanted to become a labor agitator; all right, his job is to attack me, and my job is to protect the business."

"Why is it you look so bad, my son? Look how thin you're getting! What's happened to you?"

"That's something else, Ma. That's what I want to talk to you about."

"What happened?" asked Deborah in fright.

"I'm afraid that Pa was right."

"Right about what?" She came closer to him, her heart pounding.

"You used to say, Ma, that fire and water don't mix. It's Mary. Things are bad, Ma. We'll have to separate."

"What happened?"

"She had the child baptized."

"Didn't I know she would do it? Everyone sticks to his own! Oh, you fool, you fool, you fool! What makes you say it's bad? It's good, my son! God has listened to my prayer, he has seen the tears that I poured out each night." Tears began to stream down Deborah's cheeks.

"What's good about it, Ma?"

"You'll get rid of her."

"I'm rid of her already."

"What do you mean?"

"She's gone away from the house. I was away from the city for two weeks on business, and when I came back she was gone."

"And the baby?"

"She took him with her."

"Do you know where she is?"

"Yes, she's living in a hotel. She sees my lawyer, but she won't see me."

"So what do you care!"

323

"They're my wife and child, aren't they? She doesn't want to take any money from me."

"You're lucky, my son, that it happened this way. That's what Rachel's father, who died before his time, wanted—that you should make good the sin you committed against his orphan."

"Ma, don't talk about it."

"Why not? My heart's been talking about it all the time. It's only my lips that were quiet. Do you think it's nothing that you brought shame to an orphan; that you fooled a dying man on his deathbed? Do you realize what you did, my son? It's only justice that you should get rid of the *shikse* and marry the girl who was destined for you. The poor girl waited for you all the time."

"Who waited for me?"

"Rachel! Who else? She could have been married ten times already, if she wanted. Doctors, lawyers, all of them were after her. Her uncle wants to give her a big dowry. And she refused them all. She knew what she was waiting for. Her heart told her that you would come back."

"Ma, please don't talk such foolishness. I'm a married man."

"You'll soon be free. You'll not be married for long. Let's go and tell your father."

"You mean that Pa will make up with me?"

"Make up with you? He'll throw his arms around you! Now that God has helped us and that you're rid of her at last, you'll be like a newborn son to him. I'll tell you something, my son; the way I think, all their anger against you is because you disgraced a poor orphan and married a *shikse*."

"Maybe Pa feels that way. But not Nat. Nat will never make up with me."

"That should be your worst trouble. Where are you living? How are you managing?"

"Sometimes I stay at the apartment, sometimes at a hotel; I can't stand the apartment since she left. It's so empty and lonesome. I wish I could be with you and Pa and Nat. I want to talk to them. They've got the wrong idea about me. They think all I'm after is money; but we were so poor...."

"I know, my son."

"Why couldn't we all live together now? I have a fine place. I have enough money to go into any business I want. Why do they have to stay in that prison over there? What's the good of all

324

the money I make if my own parents don't have some pleasure out of it? I'm so lonesome. Please, Ma, come and live with me."

"I'll come, my son. And your father'll come, too. And let me tell you something—even your brother will come. What else could he do? Without us he can't manage. When he sees that there's no one to take care of him, he'll come and beg to be taken in with you. Just let me go and tell your father the good news."

When Deborah got home, Moshe Wolf was seated at the kitchen table reading from the Book of Psalms. Nat sat at the other side of the table bent over a book. Deborah threw open the door. Before she had time to take off her coat she announced: "It's over! It's finished! The trouble is over. You'll have no more reason to be against Irving."

"What happened?" Moshe Wolf asked, without lifting his eyes from the prayer book.

"Thank God! Irving has left the *shikse.*"

"Why?" Moshe Wolf asked. He pushed his glasses up to his forehead. Nathan raised his eyes from the book. He turned pale and his right hand, as was always the case when he was excited, began to tremble.

"Because he wanted to get rid of her, that's why," Deborah answered. She had taken off her coat and was now shaking the snow off the shawl she had worn over her head. "They're already living apart. He'll soon be rid of her altogether. He's going to get a divorce."

"But why?"

"Just so. What's the matter? Aren't you glad about it?"

"Why should I be glad? It doesn't hurt me and it doesn't harm me. But before a man divorces his wife there must be a reason. After all, he married her."

"She baptized the child. If you have to know the whole thing, then there you have it. Well, now are you satisfied?"

"What is there for me to be satisfied about? Why shouldn't she baptize her own child? Did he bother to have the boy circumcised? What did he think? Just because he paid no attention to his religion, she shouldn't pay any attention to hers? To tell the truth, she was right to do it. What do our sages say—the calf belongs to the cow and the child belongs to the mother."

"Moshe Wolf! What are you saying?" Deborah stared at him open-mouthed. "Have you gone crazy? I'm telling you that your

325

son has repented of his mistake. He's going to divorce the *shikse* and he's going to make good his promise to Harry and marry Harry's orphan. And you tell me about your sages! Did your sages say that a Jew should marry a *shikse*?"

"The sages say that a Jew must be a good and decent human being, that he should do harm to no one, Jew or Christian. Yesterday he took the girl, married her and gave her a child; today he changes his mind and sends her out of his house. Oh, no! Just because she's a Christian? He knew that before, when he married her."

"Moshe Wolf! What's come over you? Your son wants to be a Jew again. Don't you understand that? He wants to make good the sin he committed against a poor orphan."

"At whose expense? At the expense of his own wife and child?"

"Moshe Wolf! You're taking her part—against your own son!"

"Who knows if he's even supporting her? Of such a man, of a man who has thrown God out of his heart, it's possible to believe anything."

"Moshe Wolf! Do you know what you're saying? It all comes from being with those socialists. This is what they've done to you, my husband!" She looked scornfully at Nathan. "Maybe you'll take the *shikse* in here with you. Who knows what to expect . . . if that's the way you stand up for her!"

"I think you're right. I think that's what we ought to do. We have to find out where she is with the child. She's alone in the world. She has no one. We have to find out how things are with her. Maybe she needs help," Nat broke in eagerly. Until now he had been silent.

"Moshe Wolf! Do you hear what your son is saying?"

"There's nothing wrong in what he's saying. Our sages teach us to have pity on all God's creatures. Whatever she is, she's a creature of God—she and the child."

"I won't listen to any more. Either we'll all go to live with Irving or you'll stay here yourself. He wants us to come and live with him. He told me so himself, with his own lips. He'll support us in comfort. He wants to help Nat. He wants to make us happy. It's time we had a little pleasure in our old age." Deborah burst into a storm of loud sobbing. "If you don't want to go, then you can stay here!"

"Pa," Nat said quietly, "I think the best thing would be for

326

you and Ma to go and live with Irving. I can manage for myself all right. You don't have to worry about me. I have friends, and they'll help me. I can earn my own living now." He tried to get up from the chair.

"No, my son. Where your place is, there is my place too." Moshe Wolf went over to him. "If your mother wants to go, she can go. I'll stay here with you."

"I'll go," answered Deborah, taking up her shawl. "My son needs me." She left the room quickly.

CHAPTER TWELVE

THERE ARE NO words in the language which throw so much terror into the hearts of the workers as "slack season" and "fired." Other words might conjure up the fear of death, but they do not plunge a man into the same dank prison of worry and care; at least, they can be fought against. But the fear of hunger, of finding one's self without a roof over one's head, thrown out on the sidewalk, is greater than the fear of death. For in America no one has the right to go hungry. In the small towns and villages of Poland or Galicia the worker might be hungry, but he would still feel that he was a respectable and respected man. He might not have a roof over his head in the sunny towns of Italy, but he would still have the feeling that he was where he belonged and that the skies over Italy were his skies.

It was not so, here in America. In America you had to have a roof over your head. You had to have something in the bank, or some credit at the grocery. Otherwise you were no longer a respectable human being; you were a bum.

In their old homes in the Slavic or Italian towns and villages a man's neighbors had no more security than he did. All of them depended on God's pleasure from one day to the next. If there was no home of their own, then they could move in with a brother or a sister, or else friends made a place for them in their own crowded homes. If they were hungry they could sit at the humble table of a neighbor. The common need they all shared created a bond.

It was otherwise in New York. Hardly had the slack period set in, between manufacturing seasons, when the black cloud of care descended on entire families, neighborhoods, and streets. The first to sense the oncoming of the slack season were the small neighborhood grocery storekeepers. There would be a different expression on their faces. They were slow in handing the loaf of bread to the child who had come to get it on credit.

"Tell me, my dear," the grocer would say. "Is your father working?"

The same change came over the butchers. But they didn't employ the diplomatic language of the grocers. They talked plain and to the point.

"Go home and tell your mother if she wants some meat she can cut a piece off her own rump."

The real ogre was the landlord, or the collector who came around regularly for the rent. As long as one could manage to keep a couple of beds and a few sticks of furniture under a roof, it was home. Fed or hungry, at least the family was together. But as soon as the pitifully few pieces of furniture were thrown on the sidewalk—then the home ceased to exist. The couple of chairs, the table, the pots and dishes, the few clothes, the mattresses, the bedding, the treasured piece of cut glass and the other odds and ends that spell home—put these out on the street, and the family was no longer a family; it was scattered and broken. And this specter of want and unemployment played into the hands of the manufacturers in the garment industry.

Every year, in the between-season slack period, the manufacturers renewed their efforts to break the union and take the reins into their own hands. One of their chief weapons was the subcontractor.

These were small fry, ex-operators and the like, who managed to gather around them a few friends, kinsfolk, and factory acquaintances, and wheedle a loan out of some wealthy relative. The next step would be to rent some cheap basement floor—or convert their own homes into a workshop. Then they would go to the big manufacturer or jobber and undertake to turn out particular lots of garments for a flat price. Not all of them ran open shops; some of them were even one hundred per cent union. Yet they could turn out the work at rates cheaper than other union shops, principally because the hands preferred to work with someone they knew, someone with whom they could feel at home, rather than in a large factory under the supervision of a strict foreman or boss, and in an atmosphere in which they felt alien and oppressed.

329

During the slack season it would be the small subcontractor who was the first to suffer.

At the Davidowsky plant Irving was talking to Herschel Spiegelwasser, one of his subcontractors. "I'm sorry, Herschel. There's nothing I've got for you. I have to keep my own hands occupied. Otherwise they'll eat me up alive. After all, my own factory comes first."

Herschel, with his small, close-cropped beard and bloodshot, squinting eyes, scratched his head in bewilderment.

"But Mr. Davidowsky," he pleaded, "ten families depend on my small shop for a living—Jewish families."

"Hundreds depend on mine, Jewish and Italian as well," Irving answered.

"And there's no work at all?"

"Nothing."

Herschel Spiegelwasser walked out with bowed head. The heads of the ten families who depended on him for a living were waiting for him in his shop, idle for the first time in a long time. The idleness worried them. They knew that Herschel had gone to Davidowsky's shop for work, and they were hoping that he'd come back with good news; but by his hesitant entrance, his bent head and bowed shoulders, by his worried scratching of his beard, they could tell that the news was bad. Herschel looked at them silently and the workers looked at him; they knew what his silence meant.

"Go back and tell him we'll do the work cheaper," old Moshe Yossel called out. He was a kinsman of Herschel's and, in a way, the spokesman for the shop. He had grown children and was a little less afraid of speaking his mind.

"How much cheaper?" Herschel asked.

The workers looked at one another. Every one of them had a family to support. Every one of them had thought that by working for a kinsman, instead of one of the large manufacturers, they'd be in less danger of being fired.

"Whatever he can pay. Somehow we'll manage," Moshe Yossel said finally.

"How'll we be able to do it?"

"We'll manage somehow; we'll manage somehow. We'll work a few hours more and we'll speed up more. So we won't have ten

330

dollars a week. We'll manage with eight. Anyway, its better than going hungry."

"If only the union doesn't find out," remarked one of the more timid hands.

"If you don't tell them, they won't know."

"Moshe Yossel is right. We'll manage it, Herschel, we'll manage it," said Leib Ber. He was an enormous, hairy man with a deep voice. "Will the union pay the rent when the landlord knocks at the door? Will the union pay the bills in the grocery? In the butcher shop? Sure they'll pay! Like hell they'll pay! The union knows how to take—not how to give."

"All right, all right, don't growl. The union isn't so bad. It's a good thing. Without the union you'd be worse off. But now we can't help it. When there's no work, you have to take what you can get."

Herschel went back to Davidowsky. "Mr. Davidowsky, we'll do the work for less," he said. "I talked to my help. Somehow we'll manage."

The same sort of thing had happened every year. But this year the manufacturers had adopted the tactic of smuggling the work out of the shops and dividing it among the subcontractors and contractors at prices below the union levels even before the slack season came on. In the peak of the season, when the shops were usually crowded with workers and the sewing machines whirled at full speed, the bosses began to send the workers home day after day, with the explanation that there was no work on hand. The slack season seemed to have come like a premature and unexpected plague.

The small shops in basements and tenement flats were busier than ever, whereas the large, regular union factories were deserted. Only a skeleton staff was kept in the plants, so as to keep the organization intact—a few cutters, sample makers, experienced pressers. Chief among the victims were the machine operators and the finishers.

The streets of the East Side were packed with throngs of careworn and harried workers, running for help to their lodges, to charity organizations or to more fortunate friends. They pleaded with relatives to lend them enough money to placate the rent collector, so that they would at least not be thrown out bag and baggage into the street.

Harried housewives took boarders into their tenement flats. Children were shoved into any available corner, parents slept in windowless, airless rooms. The only bedroom with a window, together with the only comfortable bed, was given over to the boarder. The mother of the family bent over the washtub doing a stranger's laundry instead of her own children's clothes.

That these things were taking place in the middle of the season, at a time when the workers would usually be earning enough to put by a few pennies for the slack season, meant that something strange was in the air. Something must be happening.

The union knew what it was. The bosses, after they had distributed the work among the cheap subcontractors, were preparing to stage a lockout. They were going to let their own factories stand idle. They were going to make an attempt to break the union, rescind the concessions they had been forced to make, and restore the clothing industry to the sweat system that had existed before the strike of 1910.

The workers were not entirely alone. There were some New Yorkers—and these from the comfortable and even wealthy Jewish circles—who were not unaware of the injustices to which tens of thousands of families were being subjected. They saw with concern how greedy manufacturers were seeking to get rich quick on the sweat of workers, the need of wives and mothers, and the hunger of children. And they knew how the Jewish manufacturers' attitude toward the Jewish workers was imperiling Jewish prestige all over the country. In an attempt to prevent the impending calamity they tried to bring about some sort of compromise between the warring factions. One of the most active figures in the attempt to forestall open conflict and bring peace to the industry was Mrs. Weiss, a progressive and civic-minded woman who held an important post in the manufacturers' association. She was representative of the new class of women who were beginning to play a part in American political life. She wasted little time on the Utopian dream of a single, ready-made panacea which would solve the conflict between capital and labor all over the world with one grandiose gesture. The struggle, she knew, was a long one and would have to be solved gradually; the immediate injustices must

332

first be put in order. The welfare of tens of thousands of families depended on the course of action adopted by the employers. She was familiar with the lives of the men, women, and children in the garment factories. She knew that the first and most necessary steps would have to be the improvement of working conditions, higher wages, shorter working hours, better sanitary conditions in the shops, and a more decent attitude on both sides. These advances could not be achieved, she was convinced, without first getting rid of the enmity and distrust which contaminated the relations between the employers and the workers. Both sides must recognize that they were dependent on each other; both sides must understand each other's rights. It was only by good will and understanding on both sides that the curse could be lifted from the industry.

With the decision of the manufacturers' association to precipitate a general lockout, she had come to the conclusion that she must undertake the task of influencing public opinion over to the side of the workers. The pressure of important sections of the city would compel the manufacturers to abandon their belligerent policy. The progressive forces in the Democratic party were with her. She had already won over one of the promising Tammany members, the city sheriff, a man who was on the threshold of an important career. One of her close friends, a social worker in an important settlement house on the East Side, had enlisted the interest of the enormously powerful Jewish multimillionaire banker, Mr. Koenig. He had promised to be present at an informal gathering at her home where the issue of the impending lockout would be discussed.

The few guests whom Mrs. Weiss had invited were beginning to arrive. The sheriff brought a newcomer with him, a tall, handsome man, expensively and impeccably groomed. Mrs. Weiss greeted them and saw that they were comfortably seated. The sheriff, his thin hands clutching his brown derby, as though he was afraid to let it go, had a deferential air about him. He would not contribute much to the discussion, his attitude seemed to say, but he would listen and learn. Mrs. Weiss, plump and hearty, patiently schooled him in some of the highlights of the issue while he listened intently. But there was little time for it; other guests were arriving. There were a tall, rawboned Senator, a couple of professors of political economy, a few topnotch journalists, a couple of influential women, and two members of the manufacturers' association known for their liberal and progressive attitude on labor matters.

Now most of the guests had arrived. The representative of the union, gaunt and middle-aged, seemed to be lost somewhere in his clothes. His skin was a pale, jaundiced yellow. His movements were quick and restless, as though he had quicksilver instead of blood in his veins. Nathan Davidowsky was there in his wheel chair, together with two other union workers. Only the multimillionaire was missing. They all waited impatiently for his arrival; his lateness seemed to spread an air of nervous unrest.

At last he came, accompanied by his social adviser and secretary of his philanthropic activities—the "director," as the small, bearded Dr. Yudelman was known. The secretary's darting and restless glances behind the thick glasses caught the eyes of Mrs. Weiss; he flashed her a smile of triumph—he had brought the millionaire.

Mr. Koenig, his white starched shirt ballooning out of his dinner jacket and a carnation in his buttonhole, bestowed patronizing smiles around the room, carefully measured according to the social station of the recipient. For some the smile seemed to emphasize the vast abyss that separated their respective places in the community. For others the smile was more friendly, though not without condescension. He sat down near an influential rabbi whom he knew and with whom he exchanged a soft handshake. It was Yudelman who supplied the finishing touch to his employer's greetings. The social adviser completed them, smiling warmly at all those who had been overlooked. His employer must make no enemies—especially among the journalists, for whom the millionaire showed only scant respect and whom he dismissed with a cold bow.

Mrs. Weiss opened the discussion.

She talked briefly. She explained that she had taken the initiative in calling this small meeting together. She had asked members of both sides—she knew how concerned they were about the situation in the needle industry—to put their views before a representative group of influential citizens, in order to explore the possibilities of avoiding hunger and need for tens of thousands of families. It was entirely on her own responsibility that she had

334

asked them to come. The union had sent its representatives, the manufacturers' association had refused. However, she had succeeded in having a couple of influential members of the association, not officially, but on their own initiative, to come and present the manufacturers' side in the matters under dispute. The union representative would first present the workers' side of the dispute.

The union representative went into a long discourse in which he reviewed the entire history of the relations between the union and the manufacturers since the 1910 agreement had been signed. His speech was academic, full of facts and figures. But it held the attention of the listeners; it was clear they were eager to learn the facts.

After the union representative had finished, one of the manufacturers presented the association's side. His speech, too, was full of facts and figures. The union, he said, through its unrealistic demands, was driving the industry out of New York's metropolitan area into the suburban towns. He charged that the union was trying to deprive the employer of the right to run his own shop. They wanted to take away the employer's right to hire and fire; that meant to destroy all managerial initiative, a "must" in any business. The manufacturers, he said, could not go as fast as the union would like in raising the wage standards of the needle trades; the condition of the industry wouldn't permit it. They all had sympathy with the honest grievances of the workers, but there was no choice but to follow the general economic pattern of the country.

The manufacturer's remarks seemed to make a marked impression on his listeners. There was an increased tenseness of interest when Mrs. Weiss introduced Nathan Davidowsky as someone who had an intimate knowledge of the life of the garment workers. "He can tell us," she said, "about the needs of the working people better than anyone else. He lives and works among them."

There were murmurs of surprise when Nathan was wheeled to the center of the room; he had been sitting quietly and unobtrusively in a dim corner. He smiled, as though apologizing for the fact that he was a cripple, and then he began to talk.

"The real heart of the differences between the manufacturers and the workers is, I think, more a moral than an economic matter. It is more than the details of working conditions which decide

335

the relationship between employer and worker; it is the basic fact of labor versus capital that determines the relationship between them. What is the worker? He is the owner of a labor power which he offers to the employer, but at the same time he is a human being who shares a common destiny with the employer—often of the same religion, always of the same human family. When one human being oppresses another, he is betraying God and his commandments. When one citizen betrays another, he is committing an act of betrayal against the state.

"It is true that the Jewish manufacturers in the garment industry are tiny gnats compared to the vast industries in Gentile hands. When Gentile owners treat their coal miners, or weavers, or steel workers, like cattle or machines, their eyes only on profits in dollars and cents—that is a betrayal of the state, a betrayal against the Constitution which our lawmakers will have to correct and repair. But when a Jew, a man who has escaped from the same tyrannical regime as his brother, who has found with him a common home and a common refuge in the free world, who is bound to him by a common martyrology and a common faith—when such a man has only a dollars-and-cents attitude toward his fellow Jew it is a sin against God! It is more than a sin against the country which has given him refuge—it is an unnatural crime which undermines the prestige and the very existence of all the Jews in America. Let others speak of the way the American coal magnates treat the Slavic coal miners. I will tell you about the attitude of Rubenstein, Perlman, Kalmanovitch—or of my own brother, Davidowsky—toward workers who are their own kinsfolk, members of their own families, worshipers in the same faith.

"Nothing stops them. They smuggle work out of their own shops to be done in subcontractors' cellars or in poverty-stricken tenement flats. Instead of making the garment industry an asset to America's economy, they degrade it into the kind of slave system that is the curse of the backward Slavic and Asiatic countries, where children toil in weaving mills and factories."

Nathan went on to describe the plague of the "bundles" which had blanketed the East Side. He talked of the Davidowsky bundles, and what they meant in countless households. He described what he had seen in the poverty-stricken tenement flats of his own neighborhood. He told of the consumptive presser, Chaim Melamed. He told of the degradation and degeneration which the

336

contractor system had brought into the ranks of the workers. He told of the cellar shops of subcontractors, where union workers were compelled to work at starvation rates out of fear of losing the roof over their family's head. The manufacturers were not only seeking to destroy the union but, more important, they were seeking to destroy the dignity of labor. They were seeking to bring the laboring masses down to the level of a degraded pauper class that they could kick about at their pleasure. What was it but the lust for money, the greed to get rich quick—the curse of the country—that had made the Jewish manufacturer forget every human obligation to his own brother! The common hunger and persecution he had shared with those who now worked for him should have intensified the sense of kinship. Instead the taste of money had only given him an unbridled appetite. He was fleeing hysterically from the fear which poverty had implanted in him. He was desperately striving to get rich quick, so as to exorcise the beast of hunger which still was in his bones. He was his own victim—blind to every human value.

"Before there can be any harmony between employer and worker in the garment industry," Nathan ended, "the manufacturer and the worker, too, must free themselves from the fear of hunger; one of the hunger for riches, the other of the hunger for bread. The manufacturer must feel a sense of dignity in the part he plays in American industry. He must be content with an honest reward for his abilities, his experience, and his business competence. He must believe in the industry, in its importance to the country, in its possibilities for the future. His goal must be the creation of a sound industry—not in making a fortune overnight. Then the industry might become a pattern for all business to follow. That is the contribution which the Jewish garment manufacturers can make to the economic life of the country—a contribution which will be in the spirit of the teachings of the Jewish prophets. That is the debt which they owe to the country which gave them refuge from oppression and bestowed on them the blessings of equality."

Nathan's words met with a mixed reception. One of the garment manufacturers stalked out of the room, declaring that he had expected to take part in a realistic discussion of the crisis in the needle industry; instead he had to listen to "anarchistic, revolutionary speeches."

337

The rabbi came to the rescue, in diplomatic, soft-spoken and careful phrases praising the manufacturers for their generous philanthropies. Even one of the union representatives jumped up to emphasize that the opinions expressed did not reflect the union's stand and went beyond the boundaries of union policy. He ascribed Nathan's observations to his youth and inexperience.

Everybody waited to hear what the millionaire would say. For all his apparent interest in what Nathan had said, there was the fear that the idealistic and fervent appeal might have scared him off. It came as a surprise, therefore, when Mr. Koenig got up from his chair and said in his heavy German accent: "I am in complete sympathy with everything the young man has said. I warn these employers that if they insist on carrying out their ill-advised plans for a lockout, I will put all my influence on the side of the union. And if there's a strike . . ." He paused, as though he were estimating the size of his contribution to the empty union treasury—while the union representatives held their breath. Instead, shaking a threatening finger at the manufacturer who had remained in the room, the millionaire declaimed: ". . . If there's a strike, I will join the striking workers on the picket line myself."

The tall man who had come with the sheriff had been following the discussion with close attention. He kept his eyes fixed on Nathan. A helpless cripple, he was thinking, yet somewhere he had found the energy to devote himself to the cause of the workers. What was the source of the moral strength which fortified the boy's will? When the excitement of Nathan's talk had somewhat subsided, he went over to Nathan. There was a warm smile on his face. Then he bent over the crippled figure and said in a sympathetic voice: "Allow me to ask you a personal question. I'm interested in your circumstances. . . ." He hesitated.

"Please ask anything you like," Nathan said. He smiled with his frank, confiding smile.

"Have you always been this way?"

"Oh, no," Nat replied. "It happened when I was eighteen years old. Infantile paralysis."

"At eighteen?" the other repeated. "I thought it was only children who . . ."

"No," Nat interrupted. "Adults get it, too."

"I didn't know. I must ask your pardon. All the time you were speaking . . . when they told me of your activities in labor matters ... I've been wondering where you find the energy to concern yourself with others' needs when your own are so great."

"I guess it's just because my own needs are so great," Nat said quietly, "that I can understand the needs of others."

The other was silent for a moment.

"I understand. Thank you. What is your name?"

Nat told him.

"Mine is Franklin Roosevelt."

CHAPTER THIRTEEN

THERE WAS A good deal of grumbling around the
unions over the kind of speeches Nat was making; he was
departing from the Marxist line and going off on tangents
that were anathema to the socialist-minded leaders. There was too
much talk about God and ethics in his exposition of labor versus
capital. What was worse, he was ignoring the very existence of
the class struggle; this, in the eyes of some of the union leaders,
was nothing but arch heresy. "He talks too much about God to
suit me," one of the leaders remarked after a particularly offending speech. "Where's the class struggle!" They tolerated him
because he attracted audiences, and because the period was critical.
As long as he kept up the spirit of the workers, he would do.

But his speech at Mrs. Weiss's home sealed his fate. He had
made a bad mistake. His talk had made a stronger impression than
the address of the union representative—a fact that was to be
neither forgotten nor forgiven in certain of the labor groups. It
was clear that they would have to get rid of him. All sorts of accu-
sations began to be made against him—he was betraying working-
class interests and introducing anarchist ideas under the cover of
his talks about God and ethics and human dignity. Didn't he have
a brother who was a manufacturer? Probably his attacks against
him were merely a blind. In actuality he was working against
labor. Who knew? Maybe he was in the manufacturers' pay.

A few days after the incident, when Heimowitz wheeled Nathan
into the union office, nobody paid any attention to him. When
Heimowitz went to ask what hall he was to take Nathan to that
evening he was shifted from one official to another, until finally
he was told that he could take "the cripple" back home; they would
let him know later. So far as Nathan was concerned, no one said
a word to him.

Heimowitz was bewildered, but it was not for him to ask any

questions—after all they probably knew what they were doing. He took Nat home.

The following day an item appeared in the East Side Jewish daily which was regarded as the official mouthpiece of the union. "A new type of faker has appeared in the ranks of the movement, whose idea seems to be to throw sand into the workers' eyes, babbling about God and poisoning the minds of the workers with dangerous anarchist ideas. In one breath he damns the bosses with revolutionary phrases borrowed from the anarchists, and in the next he weeps tears and promises them that if they will only treat the workers kindly all differences will be overcome and the Messiah will walk the earth—in other words the union won't be necessary at all. Unfortunately, the fact that this dangerous sentimentalist has been left crippled by infantile paralysis makes audiences give him sympathetic attention, thus adding to the danger. There are grounds for suspicion that he has been hired by the bosses to confuse the workers; he has a brother who is one of the worst sweatshop exploiters in the garment industry. Fortunately, the union has become aware of the danger and is seeing to it that the trouble-maker no longer harms the movement."

The article was the final blow. There wasn't a union anywhere in the Jewish trades who would have anything to do with Nathan after that blast, nor was there a meeting hall at which he would have dared to show his face.

Most painful of all was the confusion of poor Heimowitz. "I don't believe what the newspapers say, Nat," he said, when he came to talk it over with him. "I don't believe that you're working for the bosses. After all, I know you. But something's rotten somewhere. Instead of talking about socialism you're always talking about God. God and socialism don't mix."

"Why not?" asked Nat.

"How many rabbis or priests have you seen that are on the side of the workers? From all I can see and from all I know, the rabbis and the priests and God himself are on the side of the capitalists; on the side of the exploiters against the exploited."

"Then you haven't seen enough, Heimowitz. Not all priests and rabbis are enemies of the working class. There are many of them on the side of the workers—even in the dispute that's going on now between the union and the manufacturers' association. The ones who aren't on the side of the workers are betraying God's

341

teachings. Wherever God's word has come to us—through Moses, or the Prophets, or through Jesus and the Apostles—God has championed the oppressed against the oppressors. God is always on the side of the workers and against those who exploit them."

Heimowitz fidgeted restlessly in his chair. "I'm not so educated as you," he said, "and I'm not going to debate with you about what the Prophets said—or Jesus. All I know is what kind of harvest grows from all this religious superstition. Wherever there's darkness and exploitation and reaction, there's where you'll find the priests or the rabbis. In Russia the priests marched ahead with their crucifixes and the Cossacks came after with their knouts, and in Poland I saw for myself plenty of times how the priests helped the landowners to keep the peasants in slavery. And what about here in America? All the ministers on the pulpits, with their solemn faces, helping the rich to exploit the poor! Have you ever heard any of them say a word against Vanderbilt or Carnegie or Gould or Jacob Schiff? Have they ever said a word about child labor? And what about our own rabbis? All they're worried about is to see that, God forbid, we shouldn't eat ham—it isn't kosher! And now that the masses are beginning to throw off the chains of religious superstition, along come intellectuals like you and help to shackle them on again. Oh, no, Nat. Religion and progress don't go together. It's as plain as the nose on your face. Karl Marx said it; if you're for religion you're against the workingman."

Heimowitz stalked out of the room, leaving Nat bewildered and perplexed. It was as though Heimowitz's impassioned outburst had opened up a window through which Nat saw the abyss that yawned between the worker and God. "Whose is the fault?" he asked himself. He thought of that day of destiny in ancient Jerusalem, that day when Jesus stood before Caiaphas the High Priest. Caiaphas still lived; he still pronounced his judgment on the Galilean. Through the generations, up to today, the judgment went on.

Moshe Wolf had to become the breadwinner again.

Although he had been neglecting the grocery, he hadn't given it up entirely. Giving up the store would have meant giving up the flat, and where was there for them to go? Most of the houses on the block were to be torn down. Besides, Moshe Wolf had been afraid to give up the store for another reason; he didn't have too much confidence in Nat's ability to make a living. As long as the boy brought home a few dollars every week from the union, that was fine, it was a contribution toward the house. But Moshe Wolf still relied on the grocery, keeping the store open for the few customers who were left. There were not many; most of the neighbors had moved away. Tony the bricklayer was still there, and Zelig the junk dealer with the aging Long Anthony. There was no hair left on the horse's mane; it had been rubbed away by the harness, and his tail was no longer thick enough to whisk away the flies. But he still made a brave attempt to carry on. Every morning the bells on Zelig's junk cart let the neighborhood know that he was still pulling along the old tins and pots and pans and dented ironware.

Kelly still had his saloon at the end of the block and Mike Maloney was still a frequent visitor. And, of course, Mrs. Kranz still kept her furnished rooms for her down-at-the-heel "artists."

Even some of those who had moved a few blocks away remained loyal. There were newer and more modern grocery stores on their own blocks, but just the same they came over to Moshe Wolf out of friendship.

Now that he had once more to depend on the store for his livelihood, he applied himself to putting the place in order. Again he awoke before dawn, while the night still covered the city, and went downstairs to take in the fresh bread and rolls, the bundle of newspapers, the butter and milk and cheese. He begged additional credit from the suppliers; he had always been punctual in paying his debts and his reputation was good.

He stayed in the store from early morning until late at night. Without Deborah to help, the entire burden was on his shoulders. Yes, he thought, it was different without a wife in the house.

He hardly found time for his daily prayer ritual. There would be time only to throw his prayer shawl over his shoulders, put on his phylacteries, and hurriedly mumble the morning prayers. Well, God would see and understand. It was only that the time was lacking. "You know already, dear God, what is in my heart," Moshe Wolf thought. It was the fact that he could devote so little time to Nat that worried him most.

He had to leave Nat alone for half the day at a time. There were times when Moshe Wolf was so occupied with the store that

343

he completely forgot that Nat was upstairs waiting for his father to come and help him dress. Moshe Wolf's conscience tormented him, but he could not help himself; there was no one to whom he could leave the store; there was nothing to do but wait for a moment of quiet to come when he could close the door and go upstairs.

All morning Nat lay patiently on his bed. Though he was able to take a few steps, handle a book, and even manage to write after a fashion, he was unable to dress himself. His fingers were not flexible enough for that. If people only realized, he thought, what art it required for such a simple thing as fastening a button, how thankful they would be to God!

He thirsted for God more out of longing and love than out of faith. His love did not grow out of his faith; on the contrary his faith grew out of his love. When he was alone and waiting for his father, Nat felt the need to come under the shelter of divine grace and to unite with it. His idea of divinity was not that of an abstract, unseen power from which man must be eternally separated by his very nature and of which he could have only a dim understanding. It was a special providence, a real force which was directly related to him—not as a member of the human family, or as a Jew—but directly, actually, individually. Through this contact with divinity he could be all of creation, yet a separate entity within it. He could be an individual, yet boundless; not lost like a drop of water in a vast ocean, but a drop which was at the same time the whole ocean; part of the Godhead, yet containing it.

He was too unpracticed in religion to be aware of the ways in which man might unite with divinity, or to be able to have a clear conception of a divine power. The abstract concept of the intellectuals he had long ago discarded as something which had no meaning for him.

It was not through intellect or faith, but through love and service that Nat came close to God. Service to God meant service to man. The secret of God was limitless love; love toward everything created, toward the world, toward man and toward eternity. Love was the purpose of creation; it was the goal, the uniting of creator and creation in a perfect harmony. And the road lay in service to man, in a yearning to come closer to the ultimate purpose. In this mission he saw the purpose of his life, and he prayed in his heart that he might fulfill it.

344

"You who have raised me up from physical and spiritual death! You who lighted in me a spark of your own radiance! Hold me bound to you; do not let me fall again into the deep night. Let me do your will, crippled as I am. Let me serve you through service to all created things. Let me strive toward the eternal purpose where your love and your peace dwell!"

Man becomes ennobled through his own thoughts. New vistas and horizons are opened to him, as though he is drinking in from the breasts of mercy and grace new perceptions and intuitions. Man soars on buoyant wings. Boundaries are erased between the reality of the present and the magic dreams where eternal childhood reigns. Man, alone with his need for divinity, becomes a child again.

As he lay on his bed it seemed to Nat that he was a child again. He could not summon up a recollection of his early childhood, but he remembered an experience of his youth. He remembered lying helpless in the first days of his illness, unable to move. He lay on his back, his eyes fixed on the ceiling, as though he were seeking for the reason, the purpose, of the plague that was devouring him. He remembered the light, cool fingers of a girl's hand on his crippled body and he could feel a stream flowing from them which penetrated into his pores and stirred his blood. And he remembered how his flesh, which he had thought dead, had come to life. The recollection was so indescribably sweet that he closed his eyes. It was a dream; it could not be real—he had wanted only to dream, to dream. . . .

Now, too, he closed his eyes. He wanted to dream again of the cool caress of sensitive fingers. He could feel it again. . . . A shudder passed along his spine as though an electric current were going through him. He kept his eyes closed, unwilling to abandon his dream.

But the sensation of the touch of cool, soft fingers on his skin was so real, so actual, that he opened his eyes in fear, to convince himself that it was a dream, after all, and not reality. He looked about the room. No, it was a dream. The room was still. Through the windows came the soft shadows of the misty spring day, so light and soft that they covered the walls of the untidy room with a pearly radiance and hid the outlines of the objects strewn about and wove them all together into a single ethereal softness. The

345

early spring day filled Nat with warmth and light. He felt the beneficence which the spring was bringing on its wings.

He closed his eyes again. He felt that something, someone, was approaching him, coming nearer to him. It seemed to him that he could hear footsteps on the stairs, hear the door opening. Now he could feel a soft breeze blowing, the faint breeze that beating wings send out before them. He felt the wind across his face. He did not want to open his eyes, lest he disturb the dream. There were footsteps approaching his bed. Light footsteps, surely they could not be made by human feet. They came closer. Someone was standing by his bed; he could feel the light of the day being blocked from his closed eyes. Then he heard—clearly heard —a voice.

"Nat! Darling Nat!"

"Mary, it is you." He spoke with his eyes still closed. What else could it be but a dream!

"Yes, Nat. It is me. I had to see you. I had to."

Only then did he open his eyes. It was real. Mary was before him, bent over him.

"What are you doing here?" He spoke as though he were still living in his dream.

"I live near here—with my child—on Second Avenue. I couldn't help it . . . I had to come to you."

"I knew it, I knew it," Nat murmured. He seemed to be trying to come back to the real world.

"You knew it?" she asked. "What did you know?"

"I knew that you would come," he wanted to answer—he would have answered in his dream. But now he was awake. Instead he said: "I knew that you had left Irving; that you'd gone away."

"I live in a furnished room on Second Avenue, with a family. It isn't very comfortable; only until I find work."

"What do you mean? Work? And what about Irving?"

"Irving owes me nothing. I should never have married him. He belonged to someone else. I stole him away from her. It was all my fault. My place was somewhere else."

"What are you saying? You loved him."

"I don't know any more. Maybe I did; maybe I didn't. Maybe I loved someone else and thought that it was Irving I loved. Anyway, it is all my fault."

Nat's face, in the dark shadows of his thin beard, became pale

346

as chalk. Mary fell silent, as though she were afraid of what she might say.

"Of course I loved Irving," she said. "I bore his son."

"Then in that case you haven't stolen him from anyone and you owe a debt to no one," Nat said. Now he was calm. "And so far as taking Irving away from someone else—maybe I'm more responsible than you."

"I know about that," Mary said. "Still I took him away from another ... when her father was on his deathbed ... I shamed her. That's where everything had started—the chasing after money, the factory, the bundles. No, Irving is not as bad as you and your father think; it is all my fault. I made him do it all. I wanted to forget who I was, forget my poverty, forget 48th Street. I wanted to run away from everything in my past and to escape into a different world. I wanted to drown my conscience with riches ... forget my father and mother and all their poverty ... I wanted to forget Sarah Lifschitz. ... Forget you too, Nat. I wanted to feel secure. I wanted to be part of that other world ... and I pulled Irving along; I made him follow after me until he became estranged from his own flesh and blood. It isn't Irving's fault. It's all my fault."

Nat was silent.

"But now everything will be different," she said. "Rachel can have him now. She can have him now, with all his money and his factory and his bundles. She can have them all. I have nothing against them and I want nothing from them. Nothing! Nothing!"

"And what will you do?"

"I don't know yet. I'll look for work. In a factory. I want to be a worker, not an employer. But I don't know yet what I'll do about little Nat. Did you know that he had your name? I don't know yet where I will keep him. For the time being, I'm with strangers. I've left him with them now."

"Why shouldn't you move in with us? Stay here with us."

"Here ... with you ... all of us together?" She looked at him, trembling.

"I don't think my father'll be against it. I think he would want it that way."

"You think your father would be satisfied to have me and my child here after what I did to him?"

347

"That's what I think. You don't know him; he has nothing against you for having the baby baptized."

"What?"

"I heard him say so myself. If you love your child, it's natural that you should want to give it your own religion, he said."

"He said that?"

"Yes. I heard it myself. We were thunderstruck to hear him say it. I think that's why my mother left the house and went to live with Irving."

"I might have known, Nat."

"Why shouldn't you come here to live with us?"

"It's the dearest wish I could have, Nat. It's something I never even dared to dream about...." She broke into tears.

"Please, Mary, don't cry..." Nat put his crippled hand on her shoulder.

She dried her eyes and looked about the room. "Yes," she said, with a sudden smile, "you can use a woman around the house. That's easy to be seen. But Nat, I just realized! Why are you in bed? Are you sick?"

"No. My father is busy in the store. But he'll soon come up."

"Oh, I see! Let me help you. Please, Nat, let me help you to get dressed."

"No." Nat flushed with shame. "My father'll soon come up."

"But, Nat, I used to help you... when I was a stranger to you. Now I'm your sister-in-law, and goodness, I'm the mother of a child. Please, Nat. You don't need to be ashamed before me."

And he listened to her as a child listens to its mother, and he felt no shame that he was not ashamed before her.

"Tell me, Nat, have you had anything to eat yet? Who prepares meals for you?"

"My father'll soon come up. He'll make me something."

"I'll do it now. I've known my way around your mother's kitchen—ever since I was a little girl."

Moshe Wolf came up from the store in a great hurry, as usual. Going up the stairs he mumbled to himself: "Just my luck. Today of all days."

"I didn't have a minute to come up to you, my son," he said as he came into the room. "It was so busy—just before Passover. You must be starving...." He suddenly stopped and stared.

348

"You're dressed! Who helped you?" He looked around the room. "The place is cleaned.... Who was here?"

"The neighbor's girl. The Gentile neighbor's daughter," Nat said with a smile.

"What neighbor? Who?" Moshe Wolf stammered.

"Mary."

"Mary? Which Mary?"

"Your daughter-in-law. Irving's wife."

Moshe Wolf turned white.

"What is she doing here?"

"She has nowhere else to go, she and the child," Nat answered.

"I don't understand. And where is Irving?"

"She has left him."

"That I already know. But doesn't he support her? Doesn't he give her enough to live on?" Moshe Wolf began to stammer in rage.

"She won't take anything from him."

"Why? For what reason?"

"For the same reason that you won't take money from him. She doesn't want to live on Davidowsky's bundles."

"So." Moshe Wolf said. "And where is she? And the child?"

"They are with strangers."

Moshe Wolf tugged at his beard, wrinkled his brow, and screwed up his eyes. His gestures showed the struggle that was going on inside him. The skeleton hands of past generations were reaching up to pull him down into the darkness. He tried to ward them off, drive them back to their silence and exorcise them. "What does that mean? How can it be that she has no place to go?" he said. There was pain in his voice. He strengthened himself against the dark forces. He fought against them, overcame them with the strength of the mercy that rose up within him. He became strong as a lion, the dark forces destroyed. Then he said quietly: "Where is she now?"

"She has come here to us."

"So, she has come." Moshe Wolf bowed back and forth, uttering the words in the Psalmist's chant. "Then she must stay. I drive no one from my door."

"And the child?"

"What sort of a foolish question is that?" Moshe Wolf seemed

349

to be reproving him. "Where else should the child be but with the mother?"

"Then go and tell her, Pa. She is waiting."

"Where?"

"In the kitchen. She is getting some food ready."

"Woe is me! She doesn't know how to keep the dishes kosher!" Moshe Wolf moaned and went into the kitchen.

Mary looked at him timidly, but Moshe Wolf kept his gaze turned away. He pointed toward the shelf where the dishes stood.

"On the left shelf is where the dishes are that we use for dairy foods," he said. "And on the right shelf the dishes for meat. Be careful. Don't get them mixed."

"I'll be careful, Mr. Davidowsky," Mary answered humbly. There were tears in her eyes.

CHAPTER FOURTEEN

THE EAST RIVER neighborhood was home to Mary. Here she had grown up, and it was here, on Second Avenue, near 47th Street, that the small wooden church stood where she had prayed. Where the church was, there was her home. The doors of the church were open all day for the devout. Catholic churches, like the ancient prayer houses among the Jews, are not simply shrines, to be visited only on the Sabbath day when congregants, dressed in their starched best, come to pay God his due. The church is the house of God, open all day for the devout.

Although she had left Irving, she thought of the Davidowskys as her family. She had no other family. Her father's attitude, and her brother's, had completely estranged her; nevertheless she had tried to find his whereabouts, but without any luck. She had learned from the old priest at St. Boniface's that her mother had died and that her father had not been seen at the church since. With her mother and grandmother gone, there was left only her sister Sylvia for whom there was love in her heart.

The Davidowskys were the only family left to her, and she felt the bond that united them becoming stronger. No matter what happened between her and Irving, he was the father of her child. She belonged to him and his, even now that she was ready to surrender him to the woman she felt he belonged to. Irving's mother, she knew, had never felt any affection for her. She knew of all the conspiring and maneuvering and the plans that had been discussed at Mrs. Kranz's house; of the deep plots to rid Irving of her and bring him back to Rachel. But Deborah's attitude toward her did not change her feeling toward Moshe Wolf. She instinctively felt that for all his refusal to condone his son's marriage to a Catholic, for all the bitter opposition that stemmed from his deepest religious convictions, she had a protector in the old man. She knew that the devout Jew—had not Jesus sent her to him in

351

her hour of need?—would not permit any harm to come to her. No matter how bitter he was against his son, and certainly against her for baptizing the child, he would still feel a warmth toward his own flesh and blood, the characteristic Jewish family feeling which no offense could stifle. She remembered all his devotion to Nathan, and she knew that in the depths of his heart Moshe Wolf thought of her and her child as his own, as part of his own family.

Then there was her old feeling for Nathan. She could frankly face the truth now; her marriage to Irving was simply the sequel to her longing and love for his crippled brother. She had married Irving because he was Nat's brother—and because she couldn't be Nat's wife. But her marriage to Irving had not changed her feeling for Nat; on the contrary, it had become deeper and more intimate. It was the physical side of it that had disappeared. But her feeling of nearness to him was stronger, more whole, and noble.

She could not imagine her life outside the aura of Nat's personality. The sweetness which he had brought into her life had made up for the bitterness of her youth. The physical thirst she had felt for him and which had become transmuted to a feeling of deep sisterly love had ennobled her. She had given his name to her child. And even though she had been barred from seeing him during all the years of her marriage, she longed to serve him. She had only been waiting for the day when the Davidowsky family would be united so that she would again have the chance to help the helpless boy.

There was someone else who was close to her heart of hearts. Someone dead, not living. It was Sarah Lifschitz, whom Father McKee had summoned back for her from the shadows of forgetfulness. Father McKee's question—"What have you done for Sarah Lifschitz?"—was like a lash that had ripped away the veil behind which she had hidden herself. Sarah Lifschitz had entered into her heart like a living presence. She had never had any other real friend. Even her early relations with Rachel had been mostly filled with envy; there had always been a rivalry between them—Irving had only been its latest object. Now that she had dropped all her worldly ambitions and had reverted in her thoughts to the younger Mary who had slaved in a factory, Sarah Lifschitz had become alive for her. Everything that Sarah had done for her—letting her flesh be pierced by the jagged glass, sacrificing her life to save Mary from certain death—everything was resurrected into a living memory. However brief had been the friendship between the two girls, Sarah Lifschitz now became the most intimate companion of Mary's life. It was almost as though she had become resurrected in Mary. Mary had become in her own imagination the little Jewish operator, the victim of the Triangle fire, and was demanding justice for all of the other victims of the catastrophe.

It was all so clear to her. That was where she belonged. That was her world. The world where the Sarah Lifschitzes labored and died. The world of the East River, where her real family was; Moshe Wolf's family. When she had found Nat neglected and alone, it seemed to her that she was the one he was waiting for; that Moshe Wolf was waiting for her, too. She was returning where she belonged, to the home she should never have left. And when Moshe Wolf pointed out to her the shelves where the meat dishes and the dairy dishes were kept, she knew then that it was Jesus who had sent her back to this Jewish home, just as he had sent her—so many years before—to Moshe Wolf's store.

In the meantime she still stayed on in the furnished room on Second Avenue. She had enough money for her immediate needs; she needn't worry about finding work. She took care of Nathan, cleaned the flat, and cooked the meals. She sometimes felt that she had never been away—everything that had happened was no more than a dream.

It was true that Moshe Wolf preferred not to eat the food she prepared. He couldn't bring himself to rely on her attention to the prescribed ritual cleanliness, although he knew that she was being careful. Moshe Wolf kept his own dishes and pots and pans in a separate cupboard. But he raised no objection to her cooking for Nat and herself and the child. Yes, he knew that she was bringing the child with her into the house. He could hear the boy's voice. He had even stolen a quick glance at his grandchild. After all, a child! The child was not responsible. But still Moshe Wolf could not help it; the sight or sound of the child would give him a sharp pang of pain—and at the same time of joy. His grandchild!

But his grandchild was a Christian! The Cross had been brought into his pious Jewish home! He made it his business not to come

353

upstairs to the flat in the daytime while Mary and the child were there.

Late in the evening, when she was gone, he came upstairs. He stood in his accustomed place in the kitchen and poured out his heart in prayer. It was not easy for him to bridge the abyss between Jew and Christian which now confronted him in his own house. A Christian mother and child were under his roof all day! And what if she had brought a crucifix with her! But why should she not keep it by her? Moshe Wolf suddenly thought. It was her religion, hers and the child's. Again he felt himself torn by the ancient struggle. The thought tortured him—that his own grandchild, the issue of his son's loins, the child who should have been destined to carry on the generations-long chain of Jewishness— was a Christian, a Catholic!

"My grandchild is a Christian! I have lost my place in Israel. The ancient chain has been broken. My grandchild will begin a new line of Christian generations, who will not know my God. They will be the enemies of my people. They will be pogromists against the Jews!"

He began to feel unclean, as though he were one of the unbelievers who had danced and capered around the golden calf.

"And I have allowed her under my roof. I have allowed her in with her crucifix; under my own roof!"

Was that his sin? That his son's Christian wife and his baptized grandchild had come under his roof? Or that he had allowed them to bring the crucifix into his home? But the crucifix was a part of their Christianity, inseparable from it. No. It was not a sin. What he had done was not only in accord with his feelings as a man and a father, it even carried out the dictates of his religion. God had commanded it—"As I am merciful so must you be merciful." "The compassion of a father toward his children," said the Torah. Were they not his children?

He had never felt that Mary was a stranger, or alien to him. Though she was a child of Christians, she had almost a Jewish heart. Surely she had earned great blessings for herself; surely she would reap a great reward; surely she would have a portion in the world to come. He had held nothing against her even on that awful day when Harry was on his deathbed. Irving's had been the sin. Irving had seduced her; she had only asked that he make good her shame. What she had done was right. Even having

354

the baby baptized—what else could she do? She simply wanted the child to follow in her own faith.

And then her appearance here, when his wife had left him alone with his crippled son. He downstairs in the store, and his son upstairs, helpless and alone. She had come, and in her coming he saw the hand of God. God had sent her so that she might help him take care of his son. How, then, could he turn her away? No, his conscience could be at rest. What he had done was just. And as for the child—was it the boy's fault that he was born of a Christian mother? No, no one was to blame for what had happened—except maybe Irving—Irving, and his own fate!

He saw himself as banned from Israel. Not because of Mary or the child, but because of his bitter fate. God did not want him. It was not a threat; it was a judgment. God wanted to destroy him. He wanted to blot his name out of the scroll of the chosen.

He would not let his name be blotted out! He would fight for his honor against God and destiny. He would hold on fast, he would cling with the last ounce of his strength to his faith and his people. "Could I have barred them from my door?" he asked himself. "No, dear Father in Heaven. There was nothing else I could do. You yourself have said in your holy Torah—'The compassion of a father...'"

And while Moshe Wolf struggled with his soul Mary kept guard over the ritual cleanliness of Moshe Wolf's home. It was a sacred obligation to her, almost as though it were a part of her own faith. It even seemed to her that there was something mystic in the rite of keeping separate the meat and dairy dishes in the Davidowsky household. They must never be permitted to come together; if they ever did come together something terrible might happen. She was more careful than Deborah had been. Every time she took a plate or a cooking utensil from the shelf she looked eagerly at Nat. Was this right? Was it kosher? Nat howled in laughter when he saw her standing in indecision, worried about some plate she had in her hand.

"Nat, please tell me if I'm allowed to put butter on this plate?"

"Why not? The butter isn't poison."

"Please, Nat, you know what I mean."

"Do you know, Mary, since you came into the house it has become a really kosher Jewish home."

355

"And what was it before?"

"Oh, it was nothing to the way you take care of things."

"Nat, do you think it will be all right if I cook a chicken in the kosher style? Do you think your father will eat it? I know how to do it. I saw your mother do it often."

"You can try."

She went to a kosher butcher shop on Second Avenue and asked for a chicken—"a strictly kosher one."

The butcher looked at her sarcastically. "What do you mean strictly kosher? All my chickens are kosher. This is a kosher butcher store. I can give you one of Shmulevitch's special kosher-slaughtered chickens if you want, but it'll cost you two cents more on a pound."

"I'd like to ask you something," Mary said, hesitating. "I want to cook the chicken kosher style. Will you please tell me how to do it?"

"What do you need to know for? You're not Jewish, are you?"

"No. But my father-in-law is a very religious man and he'll only eat kosher. Please tell me how to cook the chicken kosher."

"Oh, I see." The butcher grinned. "All right, I'll tell you, but listen with attention. First you take the chicken and put it in a bowl with cold water and let it soak there for half an hour. You hear? Half an hour, not a minute more or less. Then you sprinkle it with salt; sprinkle it very well with salt, so that all the blood is drained out. Let it stay that way for an hour. Then you wash off the salt and put the chicken to boil. And then, when it gets to taste like straw—then it's a chicken kosher style. If that's the way you want it, you're welcome to it." The butcher slapped his apron-covered belly with glee as he finished the instructions.

Mary, with little Nat, left the store. On the way home she passed the small wooden church near 47th Street. She decided to go inside and ask Jesus to help her. She would pray for everything to go along well. She would pray that Moshe Wolf might eat the meal she would prepare.

The carved wooden figure was almost entirely hidden in the deep shadows that hung in the small church. Mary could see the pierced sides, the feet nailed to the wood, but not the face. In a niche beside the great altar there was a statue of the Mother carved in pale marble. A few candles burned before it.

Mary came closer and looked reverently at the Madonna's face.

356

A trembling seized her. It seemed to her that she knew that face, that she had seen it somewhere, in dream or in reality. The face seemed somehow familiar and close. The regular, long lines of the oval face, the full eyes, set in the half-moon sockets; the bold eyelids beneath the high and serene forehead, the long, thin nose. The pale marble seemed almost alive, the half open mouth seemed to tremble. The face radiated love and pity.

Mary stood in transport before the figure. Then she knelt down, closed her eyes and poured out her heart in prayer.

"You see, Holy Mother, he was very good to me when I was a child. He helped me in the time of my greatest need. And I was so bad to him! I brought so much trouble to him. I took his son from him and later I brought his grandchild into the Church. And he is such a pious Jew, and he suffers so for what I have done. But still he allowed me to come into his house, and he even is willing for me to live with them. He is all alone and his son is a cripple. And today is Friday, and I want to prepare the Sabbath meal for him, according to their religion. I bought a kosher chicken and I want to cook it for him so that he can observe his Sabbath as he is used to. Dear Mother, please let me succeed in preparing his Sabbath meal and let him eat it. And please intercede with your Son so that He might turn the heart of my father-in-law to my child—I so want him to love my child. Please, I beg you from the depths of my heart, grant my prayer."

When Moshe Wolf came up from the store just before dusk, he was astonished to see Mary fussing over the chicken at the kitchen table.

"What is this?" he asked.

"Mrs. Davidowsky always used to cook a chicken on Friday, so I bought a chicken at a kosher butcher's—and I'm cooking it in the kosher way. Today is Friday...."

"Chicken? What kind of chicken is it?"

"Oh, Mr. Davidowsky, it's a kosher chicken. It's one of Shmulevitch's chickens. It had the stamp on it. I bought it at a kosher butcher's on Second Avenue."

"And do you know how to get it ready?"

"Yes, Mr. Davidowsky. The butcher told me. A half hour's soaking in cold water ... just a half hour, then an hour for salting.

It's been salted for twenty minutes already . . . just another forty minutes." She looked at the clock.

"An idea for a Christian to get in her head!" Moshe Wolf said to himself. He shrugged his shoulders, in doubt as to how he should take the whole business.

But his heart softened. All the things Mary was doing! Running around to get a kosher chicken, learning how to cook it according to the kosher laws. . . . But at the same time something in him fought against the idea that a Christian should be preparing a Jewish Sabbath for him. He said no word and went downstairs.

At night, when he closed the store for the Sabbath and came into the flat, he found the table set in all its Sabbath whiteness, just as Deborah used to prepare it. On the table stood the two tall brass candlesticks which they had brought from the old country. The candles were lit, and at the end of the table, before his chair, were the two Sabbath loaves, covered with a white linen cloth.

"Who did all this?" Moshe Wolf asked, his mouth agape with surprise.

"I always used to see Mrs. Davidowsky do it, and I did everything just the same way. I used to love to see the candles burning on the table on Friday night. It's such a beautiful custom," Mary said with a smile. As she sat at the table, little Nat beside her, she seemed the typical demure and modest Jewish housewife, dressed in her best for the Sabbath eve.

Nat sat quietly in his chair, waiting to see what his father would do. But Moshe Wolf hardly knew what to do. His heart wouldn't permit him to hurt the girl, when she had tried so hard. He went into the kitchen, washed at the sink, and then changed into his Sabbath suit, the one he always wore when he went to the synagogue. Well, let things be. He would not go to Shmulevitch's *shul* to pray as he did every Friday night. He stood near the wall and chanted the prayers. His lips murmured the Sabbath prayers, but in his heart he prayed to God to show him the way as he blundered along the road and knew not where he was going. Was it a sin that the Christian girl who had come into his house was leading him into? Was it a sin that his heart was becoming softened toward her and to the child—the Christian child—who was his grandchild? Was it right that he, the pious Jew, should sit at the Sabbath table which she, a Christian, had prepared?

His heart trembled at the thought that—who knew?—maybe he was abandoning the Jewish path. But again, how could he shame a human being who was doing so much for his crippled son? And for himself, too? His lips chanted the Sabbath prayers in the traditional mournful melody. "Have pity on me, dear Father in Heaven," he prayed in his mind. "Teach me what to do."

When he finished his prayer, he knew what he must do. Whatever the circumstances, this was the Sabbath, when the pious man must forget all cares and anxieties of the soul, when there must be only rejoicing. What else than that God had ordered it so?

He turned to Mary with a kind smile on his face. "You've done everything just as though you were reared in a Jewish home," he said.

"I guess I really was. I spent more time in your house than in my own."

Moshe Wolf looked at her benignly. Then he said: "And where is the wine for the grace?"

Mary flushed. Had she done something wrong after all?

"I didn't know what to do about the wine. I was afraid to buy it," she said apologetically.

"You were right, my ..." He almost said "my daughter." The words almost escaped from his lips. "The question of wine for the grace is a very delicate matter. I have it always ready." He went to a cupboard and took out a flask of wine and the silver beaker which had been a gift from Deborah's father in the old country, filled it, stood at the table and began to recite the benediction.

Mary put her fingers to her lips to keep little Nat quiet while Moshe Wolf was chanting the prayer. She watched him reverently, as though he were reciting the High Mass. He did not offer the wine to Mary or the child; nor to Nat, as had been his custom, so as not to embarrass the strangers at his table. But when he had recited the blessing over the fresh loaf, he handed a piece of it to Mary and the child.

"Let him have some of the Sabbath bread," he said to Mary.

"Take it, take it," Mary said to the boy. "Grandpa is giving it to you." There was a tear in her eye, her heart was singing. "Oh, thank you, Holy Mary. Thank you."

When Mary brought the food to the table, Moshe Wolf was

overcome again with doubts. As though to get a final assurance he asked: "Are you sure that the chicken was kosher?"

"Oh, yes, Mr. Davidowsky. It was one of Shmulevitch's chickens. The butcher charged two cents a pound more for it, on account of the kosher stamp."

It was the two cents a pound extra that convinced Moshe Wolf. Shmulevitch, he knew, appraised the spotless cleanliness of his kosher poultry shop as worth the premium in price.

CHAPTER FIFTEEN

FOR ALL the stoicism of her manner, there was a raging fire in her heart as Dorothy Hirsch fought against the "intruder" who was stealing her son Robert from his family, his sphere, and his academic studies. She hadn't denied him anything; she kept him supplied with the money he needed in order to satisfy Rachel's empty extravagances. She sold one family possession after another—and all for the sake of the girl for whom Robert had conceived such a wild passion.

The Dresden coffee service had already disappeared from the house; the guests at the chamber music concerts at the Hirsches' had to take their hot chocolate from ordinary cups and saucers. Even the Biedermeier cabinet had gone, and the embroidered tablecloth with the matching napkins.

Robert constantly needed money to take Rachel to restaurants and concerts, and his mother was terrified lest, in his obsession, he might resort to getting into debt with strangers, or—worst thought of all—to doing something against the law. Better for her to give him the money he needed.

Mildred grew paler each time she saw her mother sell some household treasure to the Madison Avenue antique dealer who by now was a frequent visitor to the Hirsch household. She didn't dare protest, but the careworn expression that had become part of her since Robert had brought Rachel into the house showed how she was suffering. Thick patches of gray began to show in her hair. Her long cheeks seemed to droop. On one occasion, when she saw a family treasure disappear, one which she had been used to from her early childhood, she was unable to control her sighs.

Mrs. Hirsch put a warning finger to her lips. No one must know of the situation, or why the things were being sold. But when the dealer left the room, Mrs. Hirsch said unemotionally, as

361

though she were talking to herself: "The boy must be saved from harm. Better these things should go than that he should do something foolish."

Mildred did not know how her mother hoped to "save" the boy by giving him everything he wanted at the expense of stripping the household, but she could not question her. The Hirsch children did not ask questions of their elders.

As for Robert, all the while he was draining the family dry to pour on Rachel unasked and unwanted attentions, he had the naïve conviction that his mother and sister, too, were sharing his joy.

His was one of the unsuspecting natures which have no notion of the sins they commit against others. He honestly believed that he was making his mother and sister glowingly happy—how else, since he was so happy himself? It was impossible for him to conceive that his mother and sister could have any life apart from his own; it followed, therefore, that they must be in agreement with his own ideas of what was good or bad for him. And since they had no other desires but to see him happy, then what made him happy must of necessity make them happy, too. The things which were beautiful and desirable to him must have the same appeal to them. He was convinced that they must love Rachel just as ardently as he loved her.

"Wasn't she beautiful tonight, Mother? Did you see how the red scarf she wore suited her white dress? She looked like a Rembrandt painting."

Sometimes she was a painting from Rembrandt, or a Raphael Madonna, or even the Mona Lisa. But to all of his transports his mother had the same answer.

"Yes, Robert. Rachel looked beautiful tonight. Didn't you think so, Mildred?"

In spite of her rage against this "upstart" who was destroying her house, Mrs. Hirsch gave no sign of her feelings when Rachel was present. Her attitude and self-control influenced Mildred, too, so that it was impossible for Rachel to read anything but warm hospitality and friendship in their bearing toward her. But her instinct told her that things weren't as they seemed on the surface —especially since her conscience wasn't easy. She began to feel a sense of guilt. She had long lost the desire to use Robert for the purpose of showing herself at elegant restaurants, theaters and concert halls, or to escort her to fashion shows. She had already stopped regarding him merely as a substitute, good only until she should at last get Irving.

Robert's devotion and adoration was beginning to move her, and she felt herself responding to him with a feeling that was more than friendship and less than love. But she did not want the feeling to overcome her. She fought against it because she still thought of herself as pledged to Irving. Like Deborah, she refused to accept the reality of Irving's marriage to Mary. It was no marriage at all. All she had to do was to wait and bide her time until she was able to triumph over her. That triumph seemed to her to be her life's goal.

Not for a minute had she given Irving up. All the more was he hers since his business had been started with "her" money, with her help and influence. Her envy of Mary was thus more than the competition for the love of a man; it had another side—Irving's wealth and his business success.

Rachel had given a willing ear to everything Irving's mother was always telling her—that she must fulfill the will of her dead father. Her father, Deborah told her, had pledged her to Irving; it was her duty to do everything she could to take him away from the *shikse* who had cast a spell on him and stolen him away. She must take him away from Mary and marry him, just as her father had wanted her to do with his dying breath.

All of these motives struggled against allowing her growing feeling for Robert to prevail, but his devotion and the new vistas he had opened up for her began to have their effect. His family's sacrifices for him impressed her, and she began to be ashamed of all the heartaches and trouble she must be causing them. What sort of opinion must they have of her?—the way Robert was spending money on her, forcing Mrs. Hirsch to sell her household treasures; she had noticed with each successive visit how one article or another would be missing from the room. And never with a single word or sign did they show any resentment, but continued to receive her with such warm hospitality. She was ashamed—and her first impulse was to break up the relationship.

"You know, Robert, that I'm not in love with you and I'll never be in love with you," she said to him one evening.

"I know. I expect nothing from you," Robert answered. "How could I ever hope to earn your love?"

363

"Then why do you spend so much money on me?"

"Because it gives me such pleasure. Isn't it enough reward for me to be with you at a concert or at the theater? That's all I expect...."

"But it's too much for your pocket. It's terrible, Robert. It would be much better for both of us if we didn't see each other again."

"Oh, Rachel, please don't drive me away."

"No, Robert, we must face the truth. There's no sense to continuing. You know there's someone else."

"I know, Rachel. I know. But just let me be near you, please."

"There's no sense to it! There's no sense to it!" She began to cry.

For a while she refused to see him. One evening when he came, she sent Mrs. Kranz down to tell him she was out, although all the time she longed for him and the life he had made her a part of. She was so used to having him by her side, to feel his love and devotion; he was as necessary to her as the very air she breathed. She longed for the concerts at the Hirsch home, and for the books he brought her to read; to go walking again with him in Central Park, to hear his enthusiastic comments as they stood before a painting in the Metropolitan Museum. She had grown so accustomed to his sphere of life that she could no longer live outside of it. Everything—her home, Mrs. Kranz, Irving's mother, her job—all of these seemed strange and alien to her.

"Mr. Hirsch, there's no use waiting." She heard Mrs. Kranz say. "Rachel is out for the evening. She told me she'll be home very late."

"I only came to invite her to a chamber music concert at my house next Monday. I know how much she enjoys them."

"I'll tell her, Mr. Hirsch. I'll give her the message."

In the morning there was a letter from his mother. "We have all become so used to you, so used to your pretty presence enhancing the concert. And I know that the pleasure of the evening will not be complete if you are not there. I beg you not to refuse my son's invitation, in which I and my daughter join, to be with us. Robert will call for you on Monday."

364

Rachel knew how much anguish it must have cost Mrs. Hirsch to write the letter. Yet she had written it.

The following week when Robert wanted to take her to a concert at Carnegie Hall, she flatly refused to go. Finally she let herself be persuaded, but only on condition that she pay for her own ticket and that they sit in the gallery. Robert was appalled. How could he take her to the gallery, to stand against the railing, or sit on the steps? She, Rachel, in all her elegance? But what was he to do? He had to be with her, to sit by her side, to feel the waves of warmth and perfume which came from her.

They sat close together on the gallery steps at Carnegie Hall. They were huddled among other young couples sitting close together like themselves, their coats and hats piled near them, holding each other's hands and listening to the Chopin nocturne the pianist was playing on the stage. The notes fell like drops of rain falling on a shingle roof on a day of early spring, bringing the joyful tidings that the winter would soon be gone and that spring was here at the door. They listened to the falling raindrops. A new sensation overwhelmed Rachel; it was a feeling she had never felt before. She tried to imagine that she, too, was a student; they were students together. She worked; she was a waitress in a restaurant, so that she could pay for her college course. They were engaged. They had common interests and they were working together, doing the same research. They were studying medicine—it made no difference to her what it was they were studying —and music was their passion. They were poor, but they saved their pennies, denying themselves food, so that they could come to hear the famous pianist....

How good it felt! Maybe she would translate it to reality. Maybe she should wipe her past out of her heart, put an end to her dreams of Irving, and be with Robert, help him study, do what his mother and sister were doing. She would continue working and help him to complete his studies, help him work on the book that he talked so much about. The book would make him famous; he would be given a teaching post. And they would all live together, themselves and his mother and sister, in the small, modest home, and they would have their concerts of chamber music on Mondays, and she would be the hostess and she would serve hot chocolate and sweet cakes to their guests.

And put an end to all her dreams? To the dreams she had

nursed through all the years, waiting for Irving to come back into her life? The dream was now so close to becoming reality; it only depended on her. She could be Irving's wife, the true, the only Mrs. Irving Davidowsky—not like that interloper. . . . She would be the head of the Davidowsky firm. She would travel to foreign countries with Irving. She would take trips to Europe— to Paris, Berlin, Vienna—to look at the fashions. She would go with Irving to style shows and everyone would admire her ele- gance and beauty. She would have dresses from the best coutu- rières. She would dictate the mode. Women would dress according to the style that Madame Davidowsky decreed. "Madame David- owsky wears this style," salesladies in exclusive shops would tell their customers. Madame Davidowsky. Her name would be on everyone's tongue. Fashion magazines would write about her. She would be able to wear expensive jewelry, visit the fashionable resorts. There would be a rich apartment on Riverside Drive, and in the winter, Florida; and trips across the ocean, when the war was over.

No, she had no right to sacrifice herself; if not for her own sake, then for her sisters. She must see that they were cared for. She owed it to her dead father. She had promised him on his deathbed that she would take care of the children.

It was high time to put an end to the affair. She looked at Robert with pitying eyes as her thoughts raced along. Mrs. Kranz insists that I meet Irving. She's right. Now is the time. It's what I've waited for all these years. Yes, I must see him. His mother begs me to meet him. Why do I put it off? Look what they're doing to him—she thought of him now with deep pity. They're driving him crazy. They're all against him—his father and his brother. Whoever heard of one brother trying to ruin another! And now they've taken *her* into the house. Mr. Davidowsky threw out his son and wouldn't have anything to do with him because he married a Christian, and now, even though she bap- tized the child, he's taken her into his house just out of spite. He's not as pious as he makes out to be, the old man. Whoever heard of an orthodox Jew doing anything like that! The whole thing is to hurt Irving. Oh, I must see him! I'll see him tomorrow. I'll let him know what's going on. Oh, Irving, you'll realize what a mistake you made. . . .

The pianist's racing fingers were pouring out a tragic melody.

The raindrops had turned to blood; they were no longer dropping from a soft spring cloud onto a shingled roof. The cloud was Robert's heart, and it was from his wounded heart that the blood drops were falling, falling onto soft, white hands, her hands, Rachel's hands. . . .

Rachel looked at him. He was absorbed in the music. He seemed to be in a world apart. She had never known that he had such beautiful eyes. How big they were, how dark and glowing, and how penetrating their gaze! It seemed to her that he was looking into a strange and distant world. His hair was tumbled over his forehead. She had never before noticed that he had such soft, curly hair. And that lock of hair that fell on his forehead! And his face was so young, as though he were still a child . . . and so beautiful! The soft glow that shone in his eyes and the dear smile on his young, fresh lips! And that lock of hair tumbling over his forehead. . . .

What a shame that the highest goal he could ever aspire to was to be a teacher! A feeling of deep pity welled up in her, and she put her hand on his head and ran her fingers through his hair. She passed her fingers softly over his forehead and put her palm over his eyes. She felt a cool fire which seemed to pour from his eyes onto her skin. She kept her hand over his eyes for a while, then she took it away.

She saw his eyes fixed on her. Oh, God, she had never seen such sadness and joy as were now in his gaze. He took her hand and buried his face in her palm. She could feel his soul trembling and fluttering in her hand, like the newborn, naked fledgling in her father's dovecote. Just like her father, she wanted to take the little fledgling and put its mouth to hers.

On the way home, Robert said: "I've decided to give up college."

"Why?" She stopped and stared at him in astonishment.

"What's the good of it? What's the good of studying philosophy? The most I can ever be is a teacher."

"Well, what's the matter with that?"

"I want to earn money."

"But how?"

"I have a chance to get in with a banking firm. A friend of my father's, a financier in Wall Street, is willing to put me in his

367

office. You know my father used to be in Wall Street. It's a chance for a career for me."

"And what does your mother say?"

"She's unhappy about it, of course. In our family we've always had academic careers. It's been that way for the past four generations. My father was a Doctor of Law before he went into Wall Street. Of course my mother's heartbroken at the idea."

"Then why are you doing it?"

"I have no time to wait. Don't you see, my parents and grandparents grew up in Germany. But I'm in America. And in America it isn't everybody who can allow themselves the luxury of studying for the sake of study. There's no time for that. Studying's got to pay dividends right away. Otherwise it's got to be put aside in favor of something practical."

"And you really want to give it all up?"

"Oh, no, I don't *want* to give it up!"

"Then why are you doing it?"

"I want to earn money, a lot of money. And I think this'll give me the opportunity."

Rachel was quiet for a while.

"Robert, there's something I want to tell you. I'm meeting Irving Davidowsky tomorrow. You know that I used to be engaged to him. My poor father chose him for me. We were practically engaged ever since we were children. You know what happened. Irving has separated from his wife and is going to be divorced. We'll probably be getting married soon."

"I know," Robert said quietly.

"And you still want to give up your studies?"

"Yes."

"Why?"

"Because I think that if I go into the business world and earn money, then you'll think more of me. And that's all I want from you. Your affection and your friendship."

Rachel laughed.

"Why are you laughing?"

"Oh, how innocent you are, Robert! Don't you know why I like so much to be with you and why I want to go to concerts with you? It's because you're different from others. You know music, and literature, and painting, and philosophy, and so many things. I feel uplifted when I'm with you. If you're just another

368

businessman, what'll I want you for? There are plenty of business-men who are after me. And how about Irving? He's a business-man, a very successful businessman. If I want you at all, Robert, then it's just the way you are."

Robert stared at her.

"Robert, do you really want to do something for me, so that I can always remember you? Always, always?" She looked at him with glowing eyes.

"Yes, Rachel."

"Then please don't give up college. Let me dream about you and always think that if I wanted to I could have been a teacher's wife. That thought will help me all my life." She turned toward him and kissed him full on the mouth.

"Rachel!"

"Please, promise me."

"Yes, Rachel, I promise."

When Robert returned home, he called out to his mother—"Mother, I'm not going to take that job in Wall Street. I'm go-ing to go on with college."

Mother and sister, for whom Robert's decision to quit school had been a fearful blow, stared at him.

"When did you decide that?"

"Tonight. Just now."

"Oh, I see," Mrs. Hirsch said.

"Rachel doesn't want me to quit studying."

Mrs. Hirsch sighed. "And I couldn't persuade him," she thought.

A rush of jealousy struggled with the feeling of gratitude that the girl had persuaded her son not to break the long traditions of the Hirsch family.

CHAPTER SIXTEEN

IT WAS harder than Deborah had thought to induce Irving to agree to a meeting with Rachel.

"Is Rachel a stranger?" she demanded. "She's the one you should really be married to. You never had a wife; you had a ..."

"Stop it, Ma. I won't listen to anything against Mary, do you hear, no matter what she's done!"

"But at least it's no more than right that you should talk to her. Who says you've got to discuss getting married right away? After all, I don't even know if she wants you. Maybe she isn't dying for you. Do you think there aren't plenty of men who are waiting to grab her? Anyway, just now she's going with someone else, a college boy."

"She can go out with anybody she likes. I'm not interested."

"You're still sticking up for that ..."

"Ma!"

His attitude changed when they both found out what everybody knew and what all 48th Street was gossiping about—that Mary had moved near the Davidowskys and was at the flat every day, taking care of Nathan and keeping house for Moshe Wolf. At first Irving did not believe it, but when he was convinced that it was true, he was furious.

"It was wrong for me to live with a Christian, but it's all right for them... !" he said bitterly.

"Do you think it's your father's doing?" Deborah argued. "Your father's a fool; he was always a fool. This is all the cripple's doing. He's the one who convinced your father. She wormed her way into the house in the first place by taking care of the cripple; that's how she bought your father off. And now it's the same thing. She heard I wasn't in the house any more, so she came and fooled your father. You know he'd do anything for Nathan—he'd even get converted himself!"

Yes, his mother was right. Everything was clear now. His father had never cared for him. He remembered as a child his father's coldness to him; it was only toward Nathan that his father had shown any love and devotion. A wave of jealousy and resentment swept through him. He no longer thought of Nathan as an unfortunate paralytic. He saw him as stronger than himself; Nathan, the cripple, with all his helplessness, had stolen from him first his father's love and now his own wife! Ancient grievances came back to him. Nathan had fought with him from the very beginning for Mary—and he had won her, won her with his weakness. With all his success, for all of his huge business, for all his wealth, Irving meant nothing to his father or to his wife. He was the black sheep; they had thrown him out; they would have nothing to do with him; they wouldn't even take his money. And they were blackening his name. And now they had taken her in and made peace with her even though she had broken her sacred promise and had baptized the child. All because the cripple wanted her to wait on him. . . .

He remembered how, when he was younger, his father always looked down on him because he didn't want to waste his days and nights in studying things he'd never have any use for. Instead he had searched for ways to earn a living, so that he could get ahead and lift himself and the family out of their poverty. How contemptuous his father had been each time he brought a few dollars home to his mother to help pay some of the bills which his father had contracted—always giving away groceries on credit and never getting paid for them. And how proud his father had been of Nat's progress at school.

"I was never anything to him. Everything I've made of myself I've got only myself to thank for. The only one who ever encouraged me was Ma. Ma's right. I've got to make up to Rachel. And I will make up. I'm through with any responsibility toward Mary. She's done me enough harm—had me thrown out of my own family—and now she's in league with Nat to finish me off altogether."

"My son," Deborah prodded him, "you'll find no peace till you make good the sin you committed against the dead. It's the dead man who's fighting against you."

371

"What shall I do?" Irving asked.

"Bring the thing to a finish, the sooner the better. See Rachel and make good for what you've done."

"But how can I do anything as long as Mary's still my wife?"

"She never was your wife. She fooled you from the beginning."

"We have a son."

"The child's a stranger. It'll grow up to be your enemy."

"But I won't go to visit her at her home," he finally said. "I'd be ashamed to face her sisters until I've had a talk with her."

For years and years, ever since Irving had abandoned her at her father's deathbed, Rachel had waited for the moment when he would come and beg her to take him back. She had gloated in imagination over the circumstances in which the reconciliation would take place. She had rehearsed a thousand times what she would say, how she would act, the clothes she would wear. Especially the clothes. Somehow she had the feeling that it was with the clothes she wore that she would get her revenge for the injustice committed against her.

When the day came Mrs. Kranz, naturally enough, helped her, murmuring words of advice.

"No, not the blue dress with the red scarf. That's too loud for an occasion like this. If I were in your place I'd wear the long velvet dress with the low-cut neck. I think dark colors would be best for an occasion like this," Mrs. Kranz advised.

Rachel followed the advice. The dark velvet brought out the brunette tone of her skin, and the lines of the dress emphasized her classic figure. She wore long golden earrings. Around her throat she wore a single strand of pearls. In order to avoid the gossip of the neighbors and to keep the matter secret from her sisters, who. now that they were growing up, began to suspect that something was in the air, it had been arranged that she and Irving were to meet in the lobby of the Waldorf-Astoria over on Fifth Avenue. They were to meet for dinner at six o'clock; at that hour the dining room of the hotel would not be too crowded. They would be able to find enough privacy to talk things over at length.

Mrs. Kranz accompanied her to the hotel.

In the softly lighted lobby they saw Irving a little distance away. He was seated in a deep chair, his eyes buried in a newspaper.

No, her returning knight errant was not sending any couriers ahead of him to announce his coming with fanfares of trumpets. He was not even dressed in a formal dinner jacket, but in an ordinary business suit—and he was apparently so immersed in the financial pages of the paper that he had not been watching for her to enter the lobby. Rachel began to suspect that her pretentious attire was an exaggeration, was somehow out of place. All the drama had gone out of her entrance. She felt as though she had been set down naked in the middle of the street and someone had drenched her with cold water into the bargain.

"Shall I go up to him and tell him you're here?" Mrs. Kranz asked.

"No. You better go away now. Leave it to me," Rachel said.

She went toward him with firm and quick steps.

"Hello, Irving," she said, trying to control her embarrassment.

"Rachel!" He jumped up from his chair. Seeing her elaborate dress he flushed. "Forgive me! I came straight from the office. I had a hard day. It looks as though we're going to have a strike. I had no time to go home and change. I was afraid it might make me late."

"Well, it's a good thing that you decided not to be late—this time."

"Oh, Rachel!" He sat down beside her. "I'm so grateful to you for coming. I thought you'd never forgive me for what I . . ." He stammered and did not finish.

"You owed me nothing and there's nothing I have to forgive you for," Rachel answered.

"I'm the one who suffered. It was myself I committed a crime against."

"I don't see where the suffering comes in. You were married, you had a child, and Mary was a great help to you in business."

"Yes, all that's true," Irving agreed. "But it's what happened later. It's this way. . . ."

He began to pour out all the details that had led to his separation from Mary. And as he talked on—with not a word about Rachel and his betrayal of her—she saw more and more clearly that this was not the returning knight errant of her dreams, who had come to throw himself at her feet and deliver his life into

373

her hands. This was not the reunion she had imagined. It was very far from it. What she was listening to was no more than a bare recital of facts that seemed to have more to do with a business transaction.

"You see, it was like this ... I can't deny that Mary was a great help to me in the business. She had experience, taste, a feeling for popular style, for what would sell and what wouldn't sell ... you know what I mean, Rachel. Yes, so far as the business is concerned, everything was all right, but when she baptized the child, you see ... that meant quite plainly that she was breaking the agreement we made. It was a definite agreement we made when we went to get the marriage license...."

Rachel felt as though she had been caught in a trap. There he sat, her knight errant, returned to repent for the deep wounds he had inflicted on her pride, for violating her young dreams, for disgracing her father on his deathbed—and he showed no sign of it by a single word or gesture. He was thinking only of himself; he did not see her, he saw only the outrage that was committed against him, not the crime he had committed against her. It was Mary's broken promise about the child that rankled in him, not his own broken promise to Rachel. Was it for this he had met her? So that she should be a listening ear for him while he spilled his complaints? What did he think she was to him? And why had she come? Whom was she seeking? Whom had she expected to find in him?

There came to her the memory of a bygone incident. He had come to take her to the Lenchiz ball, the first ball she had ever gone to. She remembered how her mother, on her sickbed, had sewn a little wad of bread and salt into her dress to ward off the evil eye. She remembered the new shoes her father had bought her for the ball. She rode in a carriage with her knight to her first ball—and he talked only of her rich uncle, trying to persuade her to intercede for him so that he would lend him money to go into business.

"Nothing but business," the phrase ran through her mind. This man sitting beside me, she thought, is not a man at all. He has no life of his own. "Nothing but business." He didn't look at her the way Robert looked at her. Robert would forget everything else. She was all he craved. She could feel him drinking in her beauty, intoxicating himself with the joy of her presence.

And was it for Irving she wanted to exchange him? For this machine beside her who thought of nothing but money and business, of nothing but what was in his own interests; of nothing else but getting richer and richer? "And it's for this I've waited all these years. It's this I've been jealous about."

She suddenly broke into his monologue. "I'm not interested. I don't want to hear any more." Her voice was cold.

Irving looked at her in astonishment.

"But I thought that you came to meet me to hear about the way everything happened!"

"You know why I came. But now I've changed my mind. Now I've got another reason. I came to tell you that I have nothing against you, and I'm thankful that you broke your promise to me and married Mary instead. I've learned lots of things. I've learned that there are other things in life besides business. No, you owe me nothing, and Mary owes me nothing either. I'm thankful to both of you. And I'll tell her that myself."

"You'll tell Mary!"

"Yes, I want her to know that I'm not standing between you. It's something your mother has talked into you... and into me, too. I know that my father would forgive you if he knew how I feel. I wish both of you a happier life than you've had up to now. Good night, Irving."

She got up from her chair and walked away, leaving him staring after her, his newspaper in his hand.

It was only when she got home that she gave way to her feelings. She locked herself in her room and let the tears come. But they were not tears of disappointment and resentment; they were tears of release and regret, tears of shame and terror... shame that she had not understood her true worth, and terror over the gamble she had taken with her own happiness.

She looked at her tear-stained face in the mirror. She saw how the tears had left a track down her heavily powdered cheeks. "I hate myself! I hate myself! I hate myself!" She threw herself on the bed and sobbed aloud.

Mrs. Kranz, who had been waiting impatiently to hear the outcome of the meeting, didn't know what to think when she saw Rachel come home so unexpectedly early. And she was bewildered when Rachel locked herself in her room and refused for a long time to let her in. At last Rachel opened the door.

"Rachel, darling, what happened?" Mrs. Kranz asked in fright.
"Nothing bad happened! What happened was good!"
"Then why are you crying?"
"Because I'm ashamed of myself. Because I was a fool, a fool, all these years!"
"But what happened? Tell me!"
"I found out what a fool I've been. I've been jealous over a ... a ... businessman all the time. I've been wasting all my hopes on someone who means nothing to me. And all the time I've been ignoring the happiness that was here and waiting for me, and that I came close to losing for good. Oh, I've come to my senses. I've awakened from an empty dream. Money and business and the factory and styles and troubles with workers—that's all he knows. Nothing but business. And what I really wanted was around me every day—poetry and music and beauty. And real, self-sacrificing love. ... Do you understand, Clara? It was just the same as smearing my face with paint and powder. I hid my real self under everything that was artificial, just the same way as I disguised my real self with all these fashionable clothes. Others told me it. My aunt in Brooklyn wiped the paint off my face with a handkerchief when I was sixteen and went to visit her for the first time, and I was angry at her and I didn't want to have anything more to do with them. But now I know she was right. Now I understand."

Mrs. Kranz hid her face in her hands. "It was my fault, Rachel," she wept.

"No, Clara. It was not your fault. You meant it for my own good. You wanted to see me happy." She caressed the older woman's graying head. "It was the fault of all of us. We thought that happiness and comfort could be found only in money, in a successful business, and that's what you tried to get for me, because you love me and you love the children and you loved my poor father. And you thought that if I married Irving, the children would be happy and secure. And that's what I thought, too. I believed that if I waited for Irving I would be keeping my promise to my father. No, Clara, it was a mistake. He can't give anything, neither happiness nor security, because he has nothing to give. Do you hear, Clara; Irving has nothing to give besides business. But business isn't life. Life is a home, a good home, and a decent family where everyone is ready to help the other.

376

And it's love, Clara, love! It's that that my poor father really wanted for us on his deathbed. It was that he was striving for; not money. We didn't understand him, but that's what I really promised him. Do you remember what I said to him just before he died? Papa, I said, don't worry, I'll take care of the children. And I thank God that he has opened my eyes and made me see the truth." She burst into hysterical weeping.

"Then why do you cry again? Why aren't you happy? Why aren't you laughing?"

"It's the way I treated them! What must they think of me?"

"Who?"

"Robert's mother and sister. How will I be able to face them? How will they be able to have any feeling but hate for me?"

"Then go to his mother and tell her everything."

"How can I tell her?"

"Tell her the truth. Tell her everything. She'll understand you and forgive you, and she'll take you to her heart."

"But I won't have the courage to face her."

"You don't have to be afraid of anything. Those eyes of yours would melt a stone wall," said Mrs. Kranz with a smile.

"And I almost ruined them with all this stuff! Here, you can have them all for yourself." With a push of her hand Rachel sent the vials and jars of cosmetics from the little table beside the bed scattering to the floor.

"Oh, a little paint does no harm. It adds interest; it attracts the men," said Mrs. Kranz, picking up the scattered things. "My mother taught me that when I was small, in Vienna, and she knew what she was talking about. She was a dressmaker for the stars in the Vienna opera," Mrs. Kranz continued, slightly crestfallen.

"Oh, Clara darling, I didn't mean to hurt you!"

"I know, my child. Anyway when you go to see Robert's mother it won't do any harm to use a little dark stain below your eyes."

"Oh, no, Clara, never again. Starting today I'm going to get along with the color nature gave me."

"That's all right for you," Mrs. Kranz laughed. "But what about the others that nature hasn't been so liberal to?" She carefully rearranged the little cosmetic vials on the table.

"Well, a teacher's wife won't need make-up. I told you that Robert is going to go in for teaching, didn't I?"

377

"Then you'll be a professor's wife! How wonderful! In Vienna we used to think highly of a Frau Professor. It's almost as important as a Frau Geheimrat."

"Or as Frau Davidowsky of the firm of Davidowsky!" Rachel laughed gaily. She suddenly sobered. "Yes, and I want to see Mary, too. They say that she visits the Davidowskys and takes care of Nat, the way she used to do. I'm going there to see her."

"To see Mary? Why?" Mrs. Kranz asked in surprise.

"To make up with her."

"Do you really mean it? Are you joking?"

"No, Clara, I mean it."

"But what have you to make up for? What harm have you done her?"

"Plenty, Clara. All the time they were together I was only waiting for something to break up their marriage. I was like a dark shadow between her and Irving. Don't you see, Clara, how I have sinned against her?"

"I don't see it. How on earth have you sinned against her?"

"Because I was waiting for Irving. He knew about it; everybody knew about it. His mother was always convincing him that my poor dead father would never forgive him for what he had done. Naturally that had an effect on his attitude to Mary. It wasn't because she had the baby baptized that they separated. That was only the excuse. The real cause was me."

"No, Rachel, I can't agree. I can understand that you owe an explanation to Robert's mother and sister. That's only right. But you don't owe anything to Mary. Oh, no, she owes plenty to you."

"I owe her my gratitude. Gratitude for freeing me from a burden that others wanted to put on me."

Mrs. Kranz shook her head. She couldn't bring herself to agree.

Dorothy Hirsch made things as easy for Rachel as she could. The girl's unexpected visit did not frighten her, and she was quick to grasp the situation. Rachel's modest dress and demeanor told her everything. She was not powdered; her face had the natural color of her ripe young girlhood, with honest lips and clear, frank eyes. Mrs. Hirsch could hardly conceal her surprise; the girl's beauty shone out all the more glowingly without the covering make-up. Rachel started to say something, but Mrs. Hirsch took her by the hand and sat her down beside her.

"I know everything. Robert told me that you insisted he must go on with his studies. I'm grateful."

"What must you think of me?" Rachel began. "The things I've done! The way I've behaved!"

"What have you done that's so terrible, my dear? You tried to frighten Robert away, and he wouldn't be frightened." Mrs. Hirsch looked at her admiringly. "And he was right. I wouldn't be scared off, either, if I were in Robert's place."

"There was a reason why I wanted to frighten him away."

"I know that, too. Robert told me."

"But now everything's changed. I have..."

"Yes, I know. Robert told me everything, and about the talk you had yesterday. You should have seen his happiness when he came home last night. I've never seen him so happy."

Rachel flushed in embarrassment.

"Mrs. Hirsch, didn't Robert tell you that I'd like to help out for his studies? I have the means for it."

"Robert doesn't need it." Mrs. Hirsch took hold of Rachel's hand. "He has the money for college. His father left money for that. And you need every penny for yourself."

"But I don't want to be someone special and apart. I want to be one of you."

"You are one of us, my child."

"But I want to take some part; I want to help...."

"You are helping. By being so sweet and modest. There's nothing dearer you could give us."

"But all of the beautiful things that have been taken away from here." She looked around the room and pointed to the case that had held the porcelains.

"That was a sacrifice for love. Such sacrifices are sweet." Mrs. Hirsch pressed Rachel's hand in her own.

A few days later Rachel said to Robert: "Let's go up to Nat's and tell him about us."

"Fine! I almost forgot about him. I haven't seen him for a long time. I'll bet you he won't want to believe it. You'll see how surprised he'll be!"

When they brought him the news Nat struggled up from his chair and held out his right hand to Robert. Rachel took his left hand in both of hers.

"I chased him and chased him," she laughed, "but he wouldn't let himself be chased away."

"There's nothing surprising about that. I wouldn't have let myself be chased away either."

"When are you coming back to college?" Robert asked. "Everybody on the campus asks about you. You remember Professor Samuel, the old professor of law? 'Where is your friend?' he always asks me, each time I run into him."

"The college will have to buy me a horse and carriage if they want to have me there," Nat said, laughing, "I can't get there myself. There's no way for me..." he broke off and looked at Rachel. "You've changed somehow, Rachel. I can't put my finger on it, but you've changed. Your whole appearance is different. What have you done to yourself? I'll bet you that Mary won't recognize you."

"Where is she? I thought that I'd find her here."

"She must be in the kitchen. It's the youngster's mealtime."

"Mary! Mary!" Rachel called; "Mary, where are you?" She ran inside to the kitchen.

Her "rival" was sitting at the table giving little Nat some food. The boy, now four years old, with curly hair and the characteristic bold Davidowsky nose, looked at Rachel curiously with his large, lively, searching eyes.

"Mary, darling," Rachel cried out.

"Rachel, is it you?" Mary got up from the chair, letting the spoon fall from her fingers, and her face paled, as though all the blood had fled from its surface.

They fell into each other's arms and burst into tears. The child, left alone and seeing his mother crying, added his lusty howls.

"What's going on in there?" came Nat's voice from the other room. With his shuffling steps he came into the kitchen, Robert after him.

"Please, Nat, take the baby inside with you. Go to Uncle Nat, darling. I'll come right in."

"Wait a minute," Rachel cried. "Is this your baby? Your little Nat? Let me look at him." She tried to take the child into her arms but he resisted, crying all the louder.

"He's frightened because he heard me cry. Stop crying, Nat; nothing's wrong." Mary tried to quiet him.

380

"She made you cry," the child whimpered, pointing at Rachel. "Oh, darling, I'm so sorry," Rachel said soothingly, bending toward him.

"No, darling, no! She didn't make me cry. She made Mama happy, so happy! Don't you see? Mama's smiling." Mary tried to force a smile to her face, but instead she broke into tears again.

"Come, Nat, come with me," said Nathan. "That's the way women are. You come with me. We're men. Give me the plate, Mary; I'll feed him."

Mary dried her eyes and the two girls looked at each other.

"I saw Irving," Rachel said, without any preliminary. "And do you know what he talked to me about—just imagine! He invited *me* to dinner, and he spent the whole time talking about *you*. How he misses you, and how he longs for the baby. He simply doesn't know what to do with himself. Not a single word about me; only about you, as though I was his mother and he was pouring his heart out to me. I could have slapped him!"

"Why didn't you? He's earned it honestly enough."

"I was afraid you might scratch my eyes out for it afterward," Rachel laughed. "But seriously, Mary, I wasn't sure of it before, but now I know that Irving is really in love with you and has always been in love with you. They simply talked us into believing that we were engaged to each other, but it was you he loved all the time. Irving always knew what he wanted, and no amount of talk could make him change. He married the one he loved."

"And still it didn't work out."

"The trouble is that everyone helped to spread a story that had no foundation—that Irving disgraced me and broke his promise to me. He never promised to marry me, and he hasn't committed any crime against me. He did what he should have done, and you did what you should have done."

"But, just as you see, it was all no good."

"No, Mary. We've simply got to forget everything that these old-fashioned people have talked into us, making you an interloper between Irving and me. The truth is that I was the interloper; I came between you and Irving. From now on things have to be different. You owe me nothing, and so far as I am concerned I have only a feeling of deep gratitude to both of you. I am the happiest girl in the world. I love Robert."

"You have changed, Rachel. What has happened to you?"
"I'm in love, Mary. And you're in love, too. I know it."

When Rachel had gone Mary couldn't stop thinking about her. Rachel had changed; she was the same, yet not the same. It was as though she had emerged from a shell which had concealed her true essence. Her face, free from cosmetics, shone as though a veil had fallen from it; she was only now revealing her true and real self. Mary was seeing the real Rachel for the first time.

CHAPTER SEVENTEEN

T WO MAJOR anxieties harassed Nathan's mind and gave him no rest. What was to happen now? He could not sit idly by while his father slaved for a meager livelihood. Besides, he knew what sort of shopkeeper his father was. Without Deborah around he was probably handing out groceries on credit with a free hand—it wouldn't take long until the store would have to close for good. His father didn't know that Mary was contributing some of her own money to the needs of the household. Which meant that it was again Irving who was helping to support the family. No, he could not sit idly by. God had saved him from total helplessness; it was time he did something for himself. What would be the end?

He had come to the conviction that his expulsion from the union was something that had been inevitable. It was neither his fault nor the union's. He was not the kind to yield unquestioningly to the union "line" and to carry out orders blindly—though he knew that an organization, if it were to exist at all, had to function like a machine. But he was too much the individual for that. The best way for him to propagate his ideas would be to put them in a book. But for that he would need a lot of help. Most of all he needed to know more. He had long ago learned that law was not for him. He would never make a good lawyer. He lacked the necessary talent for partisanship; nor would he ever be able to make a compromise with his own conscience or his own feeling of justice. No, the law wouldn't do. What he must find was some way to give voice to his particular ideas on social and religious questions. First he would have to do some intensive studying in political economy, the history of religion and philosophy. He would have to spend a lot of time in libraries. How could he manage that when he wasn't able to earn a penny for himself and had to depend on others for the most basic needs?

There was something else.

He was still held in the throes of an emotion he thought he had long succeeded in banishing—a consuming envy of his brother Irving. There was nothing physical in it. The emotions which Mary had once aroused in him he had completely suppressed in himself the moment Mary had become his brother's wife. The strict moral boundaries with which Jewish tradition had fenced in the married woman were actual and concrete for him. His brother's wife was holy. Not even in his uncontrolled unconscious thought did he entertain any physical feelings for her. His envy had to do with the fact that Mary and little Nat belonged to Irving, not to him. Deeply ingrained in his nature was the intense feeling of the Jew—carried over from the ancient Hebrew law—toward the continuity of the generations, the urge to be father to a son. To some extent Nat considered that Irving had been no more than his, Nathan's, proxy, his vicar, in marrying Mary. Mary was his widow; Irving had married her. He was dead; his seed could not sow a new generation. The younger brother had married the widow of the older, as the law had commanded, and the first child was called by the name of the dead man so that "his house shall not disappear out of Israel."

He was not envious of Irving's relationship to Mary. On the contrary, he had found a deep satisfaction, even a sort of sexual release, in bringing the two together. He had rejoiced in their marriage and in the knowledge that they were building a common life. He had died a hundred deaths when he had heard of the cleavage between them, in agony lest it might lead to a permanent break. He felt bound by numberless ties to his brother's personal life, as though that personal life were a fulfillment of his own. However bitterly he had fought against Irving's labor policies, a close family bond tied him to his brother. He prayed to see Mary and Irving reconciled, and because of this deep desire his heart went out in gratitude to Rachel for making everything right between her and Mary. With Rachel's betrothal to Robert the gravest obstacle to the success of Irving's marriage was overcome.

From the day Mary had brought her son into the house a deep attachment had grown between Nathan and little Nat. It was as though the child could sense all the confusion of the complicated relationships between Nathan and Irving. Nathan became a second father, indistinguishable from his real father. "Uncle Nat" meant the final authority for the child; his word was law. It was even enough for Nathan to show himself at the door for the child to stop rebelling about going to sleep, or to perform willingly some other unwelcome duty.

Nat's devotion to the child had its effect on Moshe Wolf. Deborah had not been wrong when she told Irving that Moshe Wolf was ready to do anything in the world for "the cripple." It was true. Moshe Wolf venerated him; he could refuse him nothing. Whether it was the deep feeling of pity which consumed him day and night, or some unsuspected magic which Nat exercised over his father—Moshe Wolf's only goal in life was to help his crippled son, to lighten the heavy burden which the paralysis had thrust on the boy's shoulders. Thus Nathan's slightest wish became Moshe Wolf's most sacred obligation, regardless of how it conflicted with his own feelings. What he would have considered arch infamy in Irving, he accepted or condoned in Nathan. Not alone had Nathan persuaded Moshe Wolf to allow his Catholic daughter-in-law to become the mistress of the household—now Moshe Wolf's heart was becoming softened toward his baptized grandchild, as well.

Gradually Moshe Wolf became accustomed to both of them. He would keep his gaze fixed on the child, no longer pretending to ignore him, as he had done at first. He often—too often— forgot that the child was a "goy," who would "hate the Jews." Now all he saw was a child—his grandchild.

One evening before Moshe Wolf had come up from the store, Mary and Nathan sat talking about Irving. "He's more sinned against than sinning," Nathan said. "It's the fear of hunger that he still has in his bones, the curse of everyone who has known poverty. He means well, but he just doesn't realize how his fear of poverty leads him to sin against others. If he could only free himself of the obsession that accumulating wealth and squeezing profits out of others will rid him of his fear! If he could only realize what greater riches he could store up for his conscience! He's got a conscience, no different from the rest of us. You'll see, he'll come back to us. He'll begin to see things the way we see them. You're the only one who can help him, Mary. He'll listen to you. You've been in the same position and you've emancipated

385

yourself. Why can't you get Irving to see things the same way?"

"Not Irving. You don't know him. All he thinks of is business."

"I know. His mad chase for money isn't normal. He's just running away from poverty, frantically searching for security. Someone's got to stop him short. Someone's got to tell him straight. Someone's got to say to him: 'Irving, you're running away from poverty and flying straight into unhappiness!' Nobody but you can tell it to him, Mary. He won't listen to anybody else. He has no confidence in us. You're closest to him."

"You know the reason that led to our separation," said Mary. "It was something entirely different."

"You mean, the difference in religion?"

"I broke the promise I made him."

"You acted according to your conscience. And that wasn't the real reason anyway. The real reason was the whole atmosphere of suspicion created by ignorant, superstitious, or simply evil-minded people. But now Rachel has cleared it all up. There's no reason now for you to believe that you've taken anything from anybody. Even my father—and he was the one who was the chief opponent to your marriage—has made peace with the situation."

"Are you sure that your father has made peace with the situation?"

"Well, maybe the Jew in him hasn't, but the father—and the grandfather—in him has."

"But he hardly ever has anything to do with Nat."

"That's your fault. You're always acting as though you're guilty. You act as though you'd committed some sort of crime in giving your son your own religion. Why don't you act natural? Why do you have to make a secret of the child saying his prayers? Let my father see what's perfectly plain—that he has his religion and you and the child have yours. He doesn't hide his religious practices from you; don't hide yours from him. There's nothing to be ashamed of. I'm sure that my father—just because he's a religious man—will think more of you for it. Besides, why don't you move in here altogether? When Pa sees the child around all the time, he'll get accustomed to him more quickly. You can have my room."

"And where will you sleep?"

"I'll sleep near my father, in the small room. In the daytime

I'll probably be out of the house anyway. I'm only waiting for the spring to come, and then I'll spend most of the time in the library on 42nd Street. I'd be going there now if there was anyone to take me. There's a lot of research and reading I've got to do."

"Nathan, why didn't you tell me! I can take you there every day."

"And what about little Nat?"

"I'll take him along. It's only a short walk. It'll be good for him, now that the weather is milder."

"Just the same, you ought to move in with us. The way it is now it's too hard for you—coming over here every day to take care of me."

"But what will your father say if he sees me bringing up a Catholic child in his own home?"

"I think he'll be happier that way than if the child is given no religious training at all."

"Do you really mean that?"

"I know it. I know my father."

Later that evening Mary saw for herself that Nat was right. Instead of taking little Nat to the furnished room to put him to sleep before returning to prepare the evening meal for the family, Mary kept him with her, and sat him next to her at the table. After Moshe Wolf had washed his hands he recited the blessing over the fresh loaf of bread. Then he cut a slice off the loaf and handed it to the child—as had been his custom with his own children. The child lifted the bread to his mouth. Moshe Wolf glared at him, just as he used to glare at Nathan and Irving when, as children, they had started to eat before pronouncing the prescribed blessing.

"Why don't you recite the blessing?" he started to scold, and stopped, realizing suddenly who the child was. Seeking to soften his harshness—or to hide the pain he felt—he added: "I suppose they have a blessing over the bread, too. Let her recite the blessing with him. Bringing up a child like a *goy* . . ."

Nathan turned to Mary. "Father wants you and Nat to recite the grace."

"Come, darling, say the prayer that I taught you," Mary said to the boy.

Little Nat folded his hands and repeated after his mother: "Our father who art in heaven, hallowed be Thy name. Thy kingdom come, Thy will be done, on earth as it is in heaven. Give us this day our daily bread, and forgive us our trespasses, as we forgive those who trespass against us, and lead us not into temptation, but deliver us from evil. Amen."

Moshe Wolf sat quietly and waited for the prayer to end. He closed his eyes so as not to see; he tried not to hear. The childish voice went on. Moshe Wolf struggled against the impulse to get up from his chair and leave the table. But how could he commit the sin of shaming them? Were they at fault for believing in their God and addressing their prayers to Him? If only his own children believed as fervently in the God of their fathers! As he brooded thus, fragments of phrases came to him. He wanted to shut them out, but he could not help hearing. Some of the meanings were not quite clear, but what he could understand seemed close and familiar. "Our father, who art in heaven." Was it not like—may God forgive him the comparison—the sacred words— *Avinu shebashemayim*—our Father in Heaven ... ? But still there was that ache in his heart; a Christian prayer at his table! His own grandchild!

During the meal he held back the sighs which struggled to escape his lips. He must not shame the "strangers" at his table. But afterward, when Mary had cleared the table, Moshe Wolf took out the Book of Psalms and began to chant the sacred words, bowing to and fro: "The Lord is my shepherd, I shall not want. He maketh me to lie down in green pastures ..."

Mary did not know that the prayer her father-in-law was chanting was in its essence the same as the prayer she so often intoned in church. She did not understand a word of it, yet she felt the common bonds that unite all those who make their devotions to God. She understood the sorrow which the words he was chanting evoked. They seemed to go directly into her heart. The tears streamed from her eyes as she washed the dishes at the sink; tears of sorrow, but tears of comfort, too. The comfort which enclosed her and her child in a bond of worship with her father-in-law, the pious Jew, Moshe Wolf.

CHAPTER EIGHTEEN

WHAT WAS happening at Moshe Wolf's house was no secret to 48th Street. The block wasn't quiet about it. And not 48th Street alone. The repercussions traveled all over the neighborhood, as far over as First Avenue, where Shmulevitch's new synagogue, the Rodeph Sholem, stood, and where he had opened his new kosher poultry place.

Moshe Wolf was not entirely pleased with the new synagogue. It wasn't the new synagogue itself that bothered him—what could he have against a synagogue?—what bothered him was the synagogue's president, his old friend Shmulevitch. There had been differences between himself and Shmulevitch over the question of hiring a rabbi. The hiring of a rabbi for the synagogue involved the problem of where his salary was to come from. Most of the members of the congregation were poor folk, small storekeepers, pressers, operators, carpenters, cigar makers—hardly the kind who could support a rabbi in some degree of dignity, the way the more moneyed Jews in the blocks farther north maintained a rabbi in their own well-established synagogue. But Shmulevitch had a ready answer.

"The rabbi'll make a living out of me," he said, banging his enormous fist on his hairy chest. "I'll make him the kosher inspector of my slaughterhouse, and he'll be able to make a living out of it. The congregation won't need to spend one cent on him for salary—except whatever you want to give him for circumcisions, *bar-mitzvahs*, weddings and funerals, God forbid. Everything else he'll have from me."

The "trustees" whom Shmulevitch appointed to the synagogue's board of directors were well satisfied. As long as they could have a rabbi, let the money come from anywhere! And a rabbi who wouldn't cost them anything was a bargain not to be refused. But Moshe Wolf was uneasy about it.

"It isn't right," he said. "A rabbi should make his living out of the synagogue. He shouldn't depend on a kosher slaughterhouse to make his living."

"Why not?"

"Because things aren't done that way among decent Jews. Among decent Jews the rabbi is the boss over the synagogue. Here a kosher slaughterhouse will be the boss."

Moshe Wolf's arguments convinced the trustees. They saw that Moshe Wolf was right; there was no sense in having a rabbi who would have to make his living out of inspecting Shmulevitch's poultry. It was too dangerous; Shmulevitch might just as well be the rabbi himself. They decided to get along without a hired rabbi until the congregation could manage to support one properly. In the meanwhile one of the congregation would have to lead the prayers. Shmulevitch promptly reserved the honor for himself. Had he not been the leading spirit in establishing the synagogue? Then what more right than that he should be the temporary rabbi? But he nursed his grievance against Moshe Wolf.

When the Sabbath just before the Passover holiday came round, Moshe Wolf felt the need to observe the day with his fellow Jews, to listen with them to the Reading of the Torah. He knew there would be trouble with Shmulevitch; the things Shmulevitch had been saying about him had reached his ears. But he couldn't help it; on this Sabbath he would have to go to the synagogue.

The synagogue was not altogether completed. The balcony—the women's section—was only half finished; Shmulevitch was holding up its completion until he could manage to raise an additional mortgage. Moshe Wolf came in after the service had started. Shmulevitch, in his most imposing skullcap and with his prayer shawl over his shoulders, stood swaying before the Ark. Moshe Wolf put on his prayer shawl and began to pray. Shmulevitch, before the Ark, was in the midst of a series of fancy cantillations, aping one of the currently popular cantors and showing off. He did not notice Moshe Wolf come in.

There were not many worshipers; not more than ten—a bare quorum—were scattered among the benches. Devout though they were, they had torn themselves away reluctantly from their stores and shops where the clamoring customers waited, to observe the

390

pre-Passover holy day. Shmulevitch, as a matter of fact, had complained about the few worshipers on such an important day. Nevertheless the few who were there urged Shmulevitch with grumblings and gestures to hurry the services along. "What's he getting so fancy for all of a sudden? What's he dragging it out for? Who's got time for it? A storeful of customers is waiting!" Shmulevitch continued on with his arpeggios and improvisations; their impatience made no impression on him. Suddenly, in the midst of a passage he particularly fancied, he caught sight of Moshe Wolf. As though this was what he had been waiting for he forgot all about his performance and raced through the rest of the service. With the concluding words he advanced to the edge of the pulpit, banged on the rail three times with his fist, and called out in his stentorian voice: "Brothers! Jews! Our holy synagogue is defiled! A sinner in Israel is among us!"

The congregants froze in astonishment. They were friends, neighbors; not a sign of a stranger in their midst. What was Shmulevitch talking about?

"I will not take out the Holy Scroll from the Ark in the presence of an apostate," Shmulevitch yelled at the top of his lungs.

Two or three old women, standing timidly near the door, began to wail and wring their hands. "Dear Father in Heaven, have mercy!" Were the bitter misfortunes that they remembered so well in the old country happening here in the New World! "Dear Father in Heaven!" Their sobs grew louder.

The panic began to spread to the men. Frightened voices began to call: "Who is it? Who? Who? Say the name!"

"There!" Shmulevitch pointed his enormous hand toward Moshe Wolf. "He threw his wife out of the house and took in a *shikse* and her child!"

"Have you gone crazy?" a voice called out resentfully. "What are you talking about, Shmulevitch?"

"As God is my judge," Moshe Wolf began to stammer. "God forgive his evil tongue! My wife left me, to go to live with my younger son. She left me alone, with my crippled son on my hands, and my daughter-in-law and my grandchild came into the house to help me!"

"Do you hear it, Jews! He confesses! The *shikse*, he says, is his daughter-in-law, and the child is his grandchild! His son left her! He's going to divorce her, thank God, and marry a good Jewish

391

girl. And this man who poses as a pious Jew, takes her into his house with the baptized grandchild. That's why his wife left him. Would she stay in the same house with a *shikse* and with a baptized grandchild?"

"But it was God's own pity! She had nowhere to go," Moshe Wolf stammered.

"Do you hear?" Shmulevitch shouted. "When the son took her in he threw him out of the house—he said the *Kaddish* over him! And now he takes her in himself!"

A jumble of voices filled the synagogue.

"What has he got against the old man?" "What's it got to do with us whether he takes a daughter-in-law into the house or not? Does that make him unclean?"

"You can pray with an apostate if you want!" Shmulevitch's voice drowned out the others. "But I'll not let him defile the Lord's house! A baptized grandchild! Take a look in the bag where he keeps his prayer shawl! You'll probably find a crucifix there!"

"It is forbidden to shame a man in the eyes of the world! It is forbidden to spill human blood! It is forbidden! It is forbidden!" an old man shouted in a quavering voice, trembling at the sight of Shmulevitch hammering his butcher blows in the direction of Moshe Wolf's bowed head.

"Come on, take out the Scroll. We can't stay here all day!" came an urgent voice.

"I will not allow the Scroll to be taken from the Ark as long as he stays in the synagogue," Shmulevitch shouted. He planted his enormous body in front of the Ark.

Moshe Wolf lifted his head. There was violence in the air. A few of the congregation were preparing to storm the pulpit and drag Shmulevitch away from the Ark. Without a word he took the praying shawl off his shoulders, folded it, put it into the bag, and walked toward the door of the synagogue.

"Moshe Wolf, don't go!"

"What difference does it make where a Jew prays? The Heavenly Father is everywhere," Moshe Wolf said to those who tried to restrain him from leaving.

"Jews, I forbid you to buy in his store!" Shmulevitch shouted. "A Jew who takes a Christian daughter-in-law in his house and keeps a baptized grandchild can't be trusted to keep a kosher store.

392

God forbid, he will sell you unclean food on the Passover! I declare your store unclean for Jews!" he shouted after Moshe Wolf. "Your store is *trefe*. I'll make a complaint against you!"

"What is he? A rabbi? Who is he to decide that Moshe Wolf's store isn't kosher?" a voice demanded.

"If you don't like it you can go out after him!" Shmulevitch thundered. "I don't need such worshipers in my synagogue! It's my *shul*! I built it!"

"Then you can keep it! Come on, brothers, let's go! This isn't a *shul*; it's an annex for Shmulevitch's poultry business." One of Moshe Wolf's supporters stalked out, a few others following.

Moshe Wolf walked slowly into the flat.

"What's the matter, Pa? Why are you home so soon?" Nat asked.

"I came too late. The services were over," Moshe Wolf answered. He put on his prayer shawl and swayed back and forth at the kitchen table, the prayer book in his hand.

The following day was Palm Sunday. Mary washed and dressed little Nat and walked with him to the church on Second Avenue.

It was between masses. The church was oppressively hot from the crowds of worshipers and the many lights burning in the large candelabras. She knelt near the door. The child had learned to keep still when he was in church; he put his finger to his lips, an imitation of his mother's gesture when she wanted him to make no noise.

Mary's eyes sought out the wooden crucifix which hung near the ceiling, half hidden in the thick shadows. Gradually her eyes became accustomed to the dimness and she was able to discern the figure of Christ.

The early spring light shone through the red and blue stained windows. The soft illumination fell on the face of the crucified figure. There was a deep stillness in the church, as though the body of one just dead lay there. The sacred statues which stood about the church were draped in mourning crepe. Only the hanging wooden figure on the cross was undraped; it seemed to dominate and hover over the others.

Mary knelt and prayed for a long time. Her heart was heavy with indecision. Should she heed Nathan and make up with

393

Irving? Besides, how would Irving receive her offer? Maybe he had already lost all love for her and their child. She knew how stubborn he was; let him get an obsession into his head and it couldn't be driven out of him. He had convinced himself that they were all against him. Mary, too. And now that his mother was with him, he would be completely under her influence. He had surely lost any feeling for Mary. He had swept all feelings for her and the child out of his heart and had determined to make the separation permanent. She would simply be made a fool of if she should go to see him. He would insult her—or his mother would; she had hated her from the very beginning. What would he think of her if she came groveling? She'd lose what dignity she had left in his eyes. They might even show her the door. How could she risk it?

No, she'd rather scrub floors, or work at home on "Davidow-sky's bundles" than face that kind of insult.

But what of Moshe Wolf and Nathan? How could they get along without Irving's help! And the Passover was coming, too, the sacred Jewish holiday. How would Moshe Wolf be able to manage without his wife's help? She herself wouldn't be able to help him. The ritual for the holiday was so complicated and so important to them that if she should touch the dishes or the special Passover foods, she would only make things worse.

But it was more than the need to prepare for the holiday or the worry about providing for Nathan and his father that troubled her. It was something deeper, something that kept her awake and tossing about half the night. She knew the pangs that cut like a sharp knife into Moshe Wolfe's heart each time he looked at little Nat. She sensed and felt in all its acuteness the life-and-death struggle which was going on between the Jew and the father in the heart of the old man.

She stood in awe of his veneration for his ancient traditions and his staunch faith. And she was frightened by the almost visible struggle going on in him between the knowledge of the long martyrdom of his people and the natural longing to open up his heart to his grandson—his own flesh and blood. She honored him for his strength and loved him for his humanity. Since she had begun to live so close to him and had observed all the doubts and uncertainties in his reactions to her, and especially to the child, she had come to realize what his faith and the faith of his fathers

394

meant to the Jew. It sometimes seemed to her that Moshe Wolf was not one individual Jew—he was all Jews; the long Jewish generations stretched behind him in an endless line. They were part of him, within him, and his struggle to keep the faith was the struggle of all Israel. And at the same time he was struggling against the generations to give his grandchild a place in his heart. He was risking everything—his religion, all his moral values, and his portion in the life hereafter. He was risking everything for his deep, human love.

Her awareness of the vastness of the love within him made her almost worship him. In the face of the victory which his human feelings were winning over his religious scruples, her own religious convictions began to weaken.

"Maybe it was wrong to have the baby baptized.... The generations have to go on ... and Irving is the only one ..." she thought to herself, half in fright, as she knelt before the figure of Jesus. But what of the salvation of her child's soul? Dear God, could she have left him in the dark forest of unbelief? Could she doom him to the wild beasts waiting to devour the unbaptized? Could she condemn her child to the eternal tortures of Gehenna— as Father McKee had told her—no, as her own conscience had told her?... But what of Moshe Wolf, and Nat! And all the millions of good and kind people who were at the other side of the doors of the Church? Were they, too, condemned to Gehenna and doomed to eternal destruction? She could not believe it. Jesus, who loved everyone and who suffered for everyone, would show His mercy toward Moshe Wolf and toward Nat and toward all the other millions of good and kind people, whatever their religion. And surely the kind Jesus would extend His grace toward her child even if she returned him to his Jewish roots. Had not Jesus Himself been a Jew, and the Mother, and all the holy Apostles?

She suddenly realized what her thoughts really meant. She wanted to abandon Jesus. She would never again be with Jesus. She would be going over to another faith; she would be abandoning the Church. She started in fright. "No, dear Jesus, I love You with my whole heart! Do not punish me! I will not take my child away from You. I want my child to worship You as I worship You. Always! Forever!"

"Mama, Mama, why are you crying?" little Nat said, tugging at her arm.

"I'm not crying. I'm happy, darling, because we have Jesus, our Savior. Love Him all your life. It is so sweet to love Him." She made him kneel beside her and lift his hands to the crucifix.

"Come, darling, pray to Jesus for your daddy to come back so that we can all live together with Grandpa. Here, darling, say after me: 'Dear Jesus, let us all be together; Daddy and Mother, and my grandpa, and my grandma, and my uncle Nat—all the family, and let us all love each other. And please be merciful to us, just as You're merciful to all Your creatures. And forgive us our sins as we forgive . . .'"

"I know the words, Mama. I know them. Shall I tell you?"

"Tell Jesus, darling. He wants to hear them. Say them for Jesus . . . there above you. . . ."

The child huddled close to her and his young voice rose clear. "Our father . . ."

When Mary got back to 48th Street, the store was closed. She felt a sudden alarm; this was Sunday—the store was closed only on Saturday, the Jewish Sabbath. She ran upstairs, dragging little Nat after her. Moshe Wolf was lying in bed, his face turned to the wall. Nat stood helplessly near the bed on his unsteady legs, murmuring, "Papa, Papa. . . ."

"Nat, what is it?"

"I don't know," Nat answered. "All night he tossed around and moaned, and wouldn't tell me what was bothering him. This morning he couldn't get up. I'm so frightened. If only my mother were here."

"Did you call a doctor?" Mary began; for the moment she forgot how impossible that would be for him.

"Please, Mary, run down and telephone to Dr. Chazanowitch. I know he'll come over right away."

"All right. Just watch out for Nat. I'll be right back."

She hurried to the corner store and called Doctor Chazanowitch on the phone. Then she ran up First Avenue, signaled the first taxi she saw, and gave the driver her Riverside Drive address.

In the lobby of the large apartment house she looked curiously at the heavy, ornate Spanish furniture and the artificial ferns which decorated the lobby. It was all so familiar to her and yet so strange. The elevator man recognized her.

"Oh, it's Mrs. Davidowsky. Welcome home."

"Is my husband upstairs?"

"I think so."

"And my mother-in-law?"

"I didn't notice them come down."

She rang the apartment bell and Irving came to the door. Without a word she brushed past him, Irving following her.

Deborah was seated at the kitchen table. She stared belligerently at Mary.

"Mrs. Davidowsky, your husband needs you!"

"What is it? What's happened?" Deborah suppressed the harshness that sprang to her lips; instead her voice was frightened and confused.

"He's sick. I'm afraid it's serious. You've got to come with me at once." Mary took Deborah's arm.

Deborah did not notice the gesture. Only one thought filled her. Moshe Wolf was ill. All she thought of and knew was that something had happened to her husband and that he was alone with their crippled and helpless son.

"The stubborn fool!" she wailed. "He has to wait till he's sick to send for me! He couldn't send for me before. . . . Where's my shawl? Give me my shawl." She took it from the chair on which it lay. "What are you standing there for?"—she turned to Irving—"Come on!"

Only then did Mary turn toward him.

"Irving!"

"Mary!"

She fell into his arms and wept.

"Don't cry. Everything will be all right. Please don't cry. Where's the baby?"

"He's with Nat."

"What are you standing there for? Come on! Hurry!" Deborah called from the door.

Irving stood still in indecision.

"Shall I go, too?" he asked Mary.

"Yes, darling. Come. He wants you."

"Did he tell you that?"

"I know it." They went out together.

When they reached 48th Street, they found Dr. Chazanowitch at the sick man's bed. "Who ever heard of such a thing!" he

399

grumbled. "If a woman quarrels with her husband before Passover, what else can she expect? A pious Jew like Moshe Wolf and no wife to prepare the *seder* for him! Naturally, he got a heart attack. You should be ashamed of yourself, Deborah!"

"Let me go to him! Moshe Wolf, my husband!" she began to wail. "Why didn't you call me before? I was only waiting for you to call me."

"Deborah, if you want a *seder* in the house for the Passover, then keep him in bed. No quarreling, do you hear? Give him these pills regularly; he'll be all right. Remember, Deborah. . . ." the doctor shook a warning finger.

"Yes, Doctor, I hear you. I'll do everything you tell me. Just save my husband, my dear husband. Moshe Wolf, have pity on me, have pity on your children."

"No wailing, Deborah; nothing but quiet. He must have quiet."

"Yes, Doctor. Yes, Doctor."

While Dr. Chazanowitch talked to Deborah, Moshe Wolf kept his gaze on Irving, who stood with Mary beside the bed. He looked long and solemnly at his son's face. His expression softened. He seemed to be asking something. At last his lips moved and he said in a low voice: "Is this my son Irving?"

"Yes, Pa, it's Irving," Nat said soothingly. "He's here. He's come back." He raised his hand and pushed Irving closer to the bed. "Go to him," he said.

Irving bent over the bed. "Papa," he said, the tears streaming down his cheeks.

"My son," the old man stammered, his eyes still searching Irving's face.

"That's enough, that's enough!" Dr. Chazanowitch interrupted. "Later, later. Now remember, Deborah, he's got to be kept quiet. No excitement."

"Yes, dear Doctor."

"All the rest of you go in the other room. I'll be there in a minute. He's got to have absolute rest."

Deborah sat by the bed and held her handkerchief to her eyes. Dr. Chazanowitch left her there with a parting warning: "Remember, no arguing."

When he came into the other room Irving had little Nat in his arms. The child was squealing with excitement; Mary was trying to quiet him. Nat was seated on the couch.

"It's a heart attack," Dr. Chazanowitch said. "How bad it is, I don't know yet. We'll have to wait to see. He'll have to stay in bed and have complete rest. He needs a nurse. And no more work for him."

"He didn't need to work all the time! You know that, Doctor," Irving said tearfully. "He didn't have to keep up that damn store. And he didn't have to stay in this tenement. He could have had anything he wanted, more than he wanted. It isn't my fault."

CHAPTER NINETEEN

MOSHE WOLF fought hard for his life. Mary and Irving, afraid to leave the house, walked about on tiptoe. Deborah sat by the bed and wept. "Moshe Wolf, have pity on your wife, on your children. . . ." Bitter words of self-reproach burst from her lips. "It's all my fault! I left him alone with a crippled boy to take care of. . . ."

"Deborah, what did I tell you?" Dr. Chazanowitch warned. "When he gets better you can cry. In the meantime, quiet . . . quiet. . . ."

"Doctor," Irving begged. "You can have everything I've got, only see that Pa gets better."

Dr. Chazanowitch looked at him scornfully. "Do you think you can make your father better with your stinking money? Your money made him sick."

Mary rushed to the rescue. "That isn't what he meant, Doctor. He meant for you to call a specialist, if you think it would help."

"I was already thinking of it," Dr. Chazanowitch grumbled. "We'll see about it tomorrow. In the meanwhile there's nothing to do but pray to God—if you believe in that idiocy."

"I believe in that idiocy," Mary said coldly.

"Like him. . . ." The doctor gestured toward Nathan, who sat quietly staring into space, his face a mask of tragedy.

Later in the night, as the family sat aimlessly about, the doctor came out of the sick man's room. There was a smile on his face.

"All right, Deborah," he said. "You can have your Passover *seder*. It's all right. You can all get some sleep now."

In the morning when Dr. Chazanowitch returned, he found them all rested and refreshed. Moshe Wolf lay quietly in bed, his gaze fixed on his sons.

He spoke softly to Nat. "Talk to him, my son," he said. "And listen to him, Irving. It's for your good."

"Yes, Pa."

"And listen to what your wife tells you, Irving. She's a good wife. . . ."

Dr. Chazanowitch came back in the afternoon. The family was seated in the kitchen, Nat and Irving in the midst of a heated discussion.

"I leave it to you, Doctor," Irving pleaded. "Let him tell me what he wants me to do. What do you want me to do?"—he turned to Nat. "What do you and Pa want me to do? And you, Mary? Do you want me to give up the factory, and wind up the business? If that's what you want me to do, I'm willing. It's true I wanted to make money, but not for myself. I wanted it for you, for all of you. Ever since I was a kid I've wanted to get the family out of this damned poverty. Was that a crime? Is that why you threw me out, like a leper, and refused to let me help you?"

"But at whose expense did you want to do all that?" Nat insisted. "You wanted to give us security at the expense of people who sweat for a living, at the expense of maintaining a factory that's a fire trap. You wanted to give us security at the expense of smuggling out work from your own factory to get it made up at starvation wages in tenement flats! Did you think that we—or Mary, who knows what poverty means—could be happy in a situation like that?"

"I can't help that. I'm only one individual; I can't change the whole system. I've got to do what my competitors do. I'm not any worse than they are. I do what I can. I stood out against the association; I won't stand for a lockout in my shop. I told it to them right to their faces."

"You mean that you didn't side with them on the lockout?"

"No. But what's the difference! What do you want me to do? The garment industry's not the only business a man can make a living in. And if you don't want me to have a factory, all right, I'm ready to sell the business and go in for something else."

"It isn't a question of what business a man's in. If your intentions are good, and you have a decent attitude toward people, you can be honest in any business. I don't see why you have to give up the factory. The garment industry is growing to be one of the most important businesses in the country; you have a chance to take the lead in establishing new conditions. America still needs pioneers."

"Just tell me what all of you want me to do; tell me what'll satisfy you." Irving demanded. "Shall I keep the business or give it up?"

"Stay in the business. You say you're opposed to the association's lockout policy. Then go to the union and be the first to come to an agreement with them. Give the other manufacturers an example to follow. And there's got to be an end to the 'Davidowsky bundles.' "

"Okay, I'll go further than that. I'm ready to go into partnership with my employees. I'll make a co-operative out of the firm."

"There's no need for that. Just be honest with your workers. You know very well that the union is the only protection the workers have against the greed of the employers—as well as against their own greed to become little bosses on their own."

"All right, Nat. I'm satisfied to do my part. Tomorrow I'll go to the union and get things fixed. Anyway I'll have to do some pioneering—whether I want to or not. When the association finds out that I'm agreeing to a closed shop, they'll try to drive me out of the industry. Believe me, it'll take plenty of pioneer spirit to hold on. All right, Nat, are you satisfied now?"

"Sure, I'm satisfied. I'm more than satisfied. I'm proud of you. I'm proud to have a brother like you."

"And what about you, Mary?"

"I'm proud, too, Irving."

"Well, the only thing now is to see if Pa is satisfied. After all, I'm dealing with a bunch of millionaires here! Did you ever hear anything like it? I beg them to let me help them and they refuse—unless I meet their conditions!"

"You leave your father to Nat," Mary said. "He'll fix everything."

"Don't I know it? I've known it ever since we were kids. Whatever Nat did was all right; whatever I did was wrong."

"Well, you had Ma on your side. I could never be as close to her as you were." The brothers looked at each other and suddenly exploded into happy laughter.

Dr. Chazanowitch broke into the conversation. "Listen, you mule," he said. "It's time you went back to Columbia and started your studies again."

"Not now, Doctor. Didn't you hear what Irving said? The manufacturers are getting ready to stage a lockout."

"What have you got to do with that? The union won't let you talk for them, anyhow; they threw you out once! That's your socialist freedom of speech."

"And what about you anarchists? Are you any better? Would you let me say anything I wanted?"

"As for instance?"

"You know. About religion . . . that real brotherly love can only come through faith. That there can be no social justice without faith in God."

"And you mean to say that that's what you want to talk about? Do you want my advice, you mule? What you ought to be is a rabbi, or a minister, or a priest. Not a labor leader."

"And I tell you, Doctor, that it's only the religious man who can be a real labor leader. A real labor leader must consider his work as a service to God."

"Why don't you write a book about it instead of making speeches?"

"That's what I'd like to do. But how will I manage it?"

"What do you mean?" the doctor asked, glancing at Irving.

"You can have everything you need, Nat. You know that perfectly well," Irving said earnestly.

"No, Irving. You'll have enough to do to provide for Ma and Pa. I've got to find the means some other way. As soon as it's known that I'm being supported by you, I'll be poison to the very ones I want my ideas to reach."

"But, Nat," Irving broke in, "all my life, ever since I was a kid, I've been waiting for the day when I'd have money, so that I could fix some sort of a trust fund for you. It's the honest truth, it was on your account I wanted to make money. I wanted to make up for everything that you've been robbed of."

"Believe me, I appreciate it, Irving," Nat said, "but I can't accept it."

"Why not? Why can't one brother help another?"

"That may be right, but how could I take money that comes from everything I've been fighting against as unjust?"

"You idiot," the doctor broke in. "Do you think anybody else's money is any cleaner? All the money in the world comes from 'bundles' in one way or another. It's the system that's to blame, not Irving."

Nat was silent. Mary got up from her chair and walked up to him. "If there's no one else to take care of you, Nat," she said, "I'll be here. I'll take care of you."

"No, you belong to Irving and the boy."

"Not if there's no one to take care of you."

"What do you all want of me?" Nat suddenly burst out. There was a thin foam at the edges of his lips. "Don't you see what you're all doing? You want to steal the only thing that's left to me. How can the workers—the people I'm trying to reach—have any confidence in me when they find out that I'm dependent for my very existence on my brother—a manufacturer! The workers are jealous, and resentful of anyone who doesn't share their lot!" He grew calmer. "And believe me they've got plenty to be jealous about after the way you've treated them."

There was a minute of awkward silence.

"But how will you manage? How will you be in a position to do anything for them?" Irving said at last.

"I'll try to get some sort of a job, something that's up to my physical possibilities," Nat said. "The best thing would be if I could give a series of talks in a labor auditorium or a place like that, and teach the workers some of the things they ought to know. I have so much to tell them, there are so many things I'd like to show them—" He seemed to be carried away.

"There's one thing you won't talk me out of, Nat," said Mary. "If you won't live with us, then at least promise me that you'll live near us. I'll find a room for you and someone to take care of you."

"You'll all have to move from here anyway," Irving said. "They're tearing the building down. The neighborhood's getting fashionable; they're going to put up some high-class apartment houses. The whole block's been sold to some realty company. There'll be no place for us here any more."

"You see, we'll have to find a new place anyway for your father and mother," said Mary.

"I'll work it out," said Nat. "Don't worry about me."

Decisions and adjustments seemed to move along so quickly that Mary could hardly conceal her bewilderment. Only yesterday

404

a wide abyss yawned between son and father—one would have imagined it could never be bridged—and suddenly, like a miracle, here they were all together, united in a strong family bond. She couldn't believe that it was real. There was one bitter drop in her cup of happiness—the thought of her own family. She envied this Jewish family. If only she could be reconciled with her own. "How strange," she thought to herself. "Here they were fighting each other tooth and nail, and the moment some common disaster happens, they forget all their differences and bitterness. They weep in each other's arms and they forgive each other. But with us the feud goes on to the death. No mercy, no forgiveness! And we call ourselves Christians!"

Irving and Mary wanted to take Moshe Wolf to their house at once, but Dr. Chazanowitch was opposed to any immediate change. "He's much improved," the doctor said, "but for the while he mustn't be moved from bed."

Besides, Moshe Wolf wouldn't hear of holding the Passover services anywhere but on 48th Street. As a result Deborah had no choice but to accept Mary's help; it would be too much to take care of Moshe Wolf and attend to the holiday preparations as well. Then she had promised the doctor to spare Moshe Wolf any excitement and she was afraid to say anything that might create argument. If she as much as ventured a word of protest, her sons would remind her—"Ma, remember Papa is sick." So she had to make peace with the *shikse*.

What could she do? She would have to recognize the inevitable. Any hope of separating Irving and Mary was gone. Rachel was engaged to someone else, and that old fool of a husband of hers had taken Mary and the child to his heart and made peace with them. She would have to accept Mary and even get used to the baby—as a matter of fact the child, with his friendly ways, was already beginning to worm himself into her affections. After all— Irving's child! She began to look at him with different eyes.

The peace and quiet that had descended on the Davidowsky household gave Mary a new feeling of security. She watched her mother-in-law anxiously, carefully following her instructions about scrubbing the pots and pans to insure their ritual cleanliness, attending to the Passover purchases and making the house spick-and-span for the holiday.

405

She went home to the Riverside Drive apartment each night with Irving, but each day she was at 48th Street helping Nat and lending a hand in the household chores.

Dr. Chazanowitch came in to see Moshe Wolf a couple of times each day. It was as though the doctor had set himself the task of making sure that this Passover celebration—the first in a long time with the entire family reunited—would go off with Moshe Wolf at the patriarchal seat at the table's head. The festive table was set in the large room, whose windows looked out to the street. The table was pushed up to the bed where Moshe Wolf lay in state.

Deborah took the holiday linen table cloth out of the chest where she kept it locked up. It was already threadbare in spots; she had had it ever since she was a bride. She put it on the table, set the massive candlesticks on it, and lit the candles.

Mary watched her as she put the flat cakes of unleavened bread on the table, covered them with a white cloth, placed the wine beakers about and the brightly polished Passover carafe, another memento of her early married life. In the middle of the table she placed the special copper beaker, its outside surface ornately etched, for the Prophet Elijah. On a dish she placed the Passover symbols—the roasted shankbone and the hard-boiled egg, symbol of sacrifice, and the bitter herbs and almond paste. She took the old Haggadas from the cupboard and placed them around the table.

The careful arrangements communicated a feeling of awe—almost fright—to Mary. She saw and felt the profound mystery of the symbolism of all these preparations. It seemed to her that everything, even the tiniest detail, was surrounded with such meaningful tradition, and was so sacred and holy, that it all must have come down from those ancient days when Christ walked the earth—in Jerusalem. This was how the table must have been set at the Last Supper, in a poor home—just like this one. She was in terror lest she might make some of these holy things unclean by the mere touch of her hand.

The men put on their skullcaps. Moshe Wolf wore his prayer shawl over his shoulders. Dr. Chazanowitch, who had kept his promise to join them for the evening, also wore a skullcap; Deborah wouldn't let him sit at the table without it.

Little Nat sat near Mary. He was scrubbed and clean, and

dressed in a new sailor suit. Mary had worried about putting a hat on him; Jews, she knew, kept their heads covered during any religious services, but maybe she would be committing some breach of the religious ritual by putting a hat on this Christian child's head. She took the chance. She wanted him to be a Jewish child on this Passover evening, no different from any of the others. She put a skullcap on him, and even combed his hair so that the little side locks hung in front of his ears—as she had seen Jewish mothers do on occasions like this.

Moshe Wolf raised the wine cup in his hand. He glanced around the table to see that everything was in order. His gaze halted at little Nat. He saw him in the Jewish skullcap and with his glowing Jewish eyes; there was no difference between him and the countless Jewish children sitting around Passove~ tables all over the world, waiting to play their long-awaited part in the Passover service—the asking of the traditional Four Questions. But Moshe Wolfe knew that that bliss was denied him; and he could not restrain a heavy sigh.

"If he were only a Jew, he could ask the Four Questions," Deborah burst out. She spoke in Yiddish so that the *shikse* should not understand.

"Deborah," Dr. Chazanowitch said sternly, and put a warning finger to his lips.

"All right, all right. I didn't say anything." She put her own hand over her mouth. "But my heart is breaking. I can't help it."

"Foolish woman!" Moshe Wolf said, with a faint smile on his lips. "They're still young; they can have a Jewish child, too."

Dr. Chazanowitch chuckled. "A Christian child for the Christian God and a Jewish child for the Jewish God. What about some for themselves . . . ?"

Propped up against the pillows, Moshe Wolf took the wine cup in his hand and recited the grace with the traditional cantillation. Then, as though he wanted to ease any strain which his wife's outburst might have caused, he took the cup which he had blessed and handed it to Mary so that she and the child might sip from it.

"It's all right. If there's any sin, then it's on my conscience," he said to Deborah in Yiddish.

Later, while he recited aloud the narrative of the exodus from Egypt, he began to make his own comments on the printed text, according to the custom, so that those at the table might more clearly understand the meaning and the symbolism of the ritual. "Slaves were we unto Pharaoh in Egypt ..." he recited from the Haggada, then wandered off into his own dissertation. "The Jew cannot be a slave," he began in Yiddish. "The Jew is a free man. He labors because of God's curse on Adam—'with the sweat of thy brow shalt thou eat thy bread.' Labor is the curse that God put on man—but only to earn his bread, which is to say, his livelihood. When a man labors not for a livelihood but to accumulate wealth, then he is a slave. Therefore it is that God granted us the Sabbath. For it is by the Sabbath that we know we are not work animals, born to eat and to labor; we are men. It is the Sabbath which is man's goal—not labor, but the rest which he earns from his labor. It was because the Jews made the Sabbath holy to God that they were redeemed from slavery in Egypt. It was by the Sabbath that they proclaimed that they were not slaves but free men...."

Dr. Chazanowitch interrupted Moshe Wolf's exposition. "Enough, Moshe Wolf. Enough explaining. You can tell us all about it another time. You're not strong enough now. Deborah, bring the gefüllte fish to the table; we've had enough of the Haggada for one night."

"He can't stand a single bit of Jewish learning," Moshe Wolf complained in good humor. "Nathan, tell them in English what I just said. Let them understand, too." He pointed to Mary and the child.

Irving knew for whom his father's remarks had been intended. He smiled. "It's all right, Pa," he said. "Everything's all right."

CHAPTER TWENTY

"WHAT ABOUT your family? Have you found out where they are?" Irving asked Mary as they sat in the living room after they returned home.

Mary was silent for a moment.

"My mother's dead. And Grandma, too."

He went over to her and kissed her softly. "Did you see the others?"

"No, I couldn't find out where they live."

"Then how do you know about your mother and your grandmother?"

"The priest at St. Boniface's told me. He read the funeral services over my grandmother—then later over my mother."

"It's tragic," Irving said sorrowfully. "Especially now when everything is working out so well. And you don't know where the others live?"

"I couldn't find out. I went to the street where I saw Sylvie and Jimmy last; they aren't there any more. To tell the truth, the only one I care about is Sylvie. She's had the whole burden on her shoulders... and she's so young." Mary's eyes filled with tears.

"Don't cry, darling. We'll find them."

"I don't want to see the others. You know why."

"Yes, darling," Irving comforted her. "I know how bad it was. But now you have your own child. It's your duty to be happy with him and make him happy."

"Yes, Irving, you're right. I'll give him everything that I never had."

"And the things I didn't have," Irving added.

"Let's be good to him. Let's be good to one another. Why can't we be like your father! Ever since I was a child, when I saw the way your father devoted himself to Nathan—as though he wanted to make up to him for all his misfortune—I used to cry! I used to be jealous of Nat. I wanted to be crippled like him, and then maybe my father would act to me the way your father did to Nat. I longed for love—because I never had it! That's the reason I fell in love with Nat. I have to tell it to you, Irving—I was in love with Nat first!"

"Yes, I know."

"And you know that I still love him!"

"Yes, I know."

"But really, really! You know I really love him."

"Yes, darling, I know."

"And you still want me?"

"Yes, with all my heart."

"Why?"

"Because I know that you love me, too."

"Oh, Irving darling." She threw her arms around him and kissed him. "I'm so ashamed! And I wanted to leave you!"

"Mary, darling, it doesn't make any difference that I know. The point is, does Nat know?"

"Yes, I told him."

"When?"

"Just a few days ago."

Irving was silent.

"What are you thinking about?" Mary asked.

"Now I understand why he doesn't want to live with us, or even near us. Now I understand why he doesn't want to take any help from me."

"Yes, now I see it, too. Oh, what a fool I was to tell him!"

"He'll get over it, Mary. He'll understand. But we've got to do something about your own family; about Sylvie."

"She's the only one of the family I think about. I'm afraid for her. . . ."

"Don't worry, darling," Irving said comfortingly. "I'll find her, even if I have to turn the city inside out."

His first move was to go with Mary to call on the old priest, Father Mahoney, at St. Boniface's. Father Mahoney was friendly and ready to help. He kept his folded hands tucked in the broad sleeves of his black cassock. His face, for all his years, was firm and even ruddy, the face of a man accustomed to spending his time in the open. He didn't ask Mary any questions about her marriage; he seemed interested only in helping her.

"As I told you before, Mrs. Davidowsky," he said, "the only way I can suggest for you to find them is to look in the saloons between here and 23rd Street around First Avenue." The priest's voice was sympathetic. "It's sad, but that's the way it is. It looks to me as though McCarthy has gone from bad to worse since Mrs. McCarthy died. I've asked of all the churches in the neighborhood, but none of them know anything of him. It must be bad with McCarthy if he's abandoned the Church. I know the way you feel," the priest put his hand on Mary's shoulder, "but that's the way it is. When a man loses his way to the Church, he finds his way to the saloon. It's too bad. Whatever else he was, McCarthy was always a good Catholic."

"Why do you think we'll find him in this neighborhood?" Irving asked.

"When you get used to the East River, you can never move away from it. The McCarthy's always lived around the river."

Irving took the priest's advice and went from saloon to saloon, making inquiries. In a saloon on First Avenue near 30th Street he found what he was looking for.

"You mean that old drunk, Patrick McCarthy? Sure, his daughter comes in rushing the growler for him. Try that house near the stables up the block. That's where he lives."

Leaving Mary to wait on the street, Irving went to the house the saloonkeeper had indicated, on 30th Street, hard by the river. Most of its flats stood empty, the broken windows covered with boards. Only the upper floor was occupied; the stairs leading to it were narrow and half collapsed.

From an open door on the landing an old woman emerged.

"Who're you looking for?" she mumbled, brushing the matted white hair away from her vacant eyes.

"Patrick McCarthy."

"Down there." She pointed to the far end of the hall and retreated inside, banging the door after her.

There was an overpowering stench of decay and putrefaction from the dank room as Irving opened the door. McCarthy, in carpet slippers and undershirt and frayed pants, stood at the stove boiling some coffee. He didn't notice Irving come in. Irving looked around and shuddered at what he saw. The walls were

411

peeling; large strips of mildewed, damp paper hung down from them. The bed was a heap of dirty blankets. In a corner of the room he saw an opened bundle of cut material near a sewing machine. A shudder shook him.

A wooden board covered the lower half of the broken window; strips of wrapping paper covered the cracks in the upper half. The sink was piled with dirty dishes and pans. Empty bottles were strewn all about on the floor.

"Who are you? What do you want?" McCarthy growled when he became aware of Irving's presence.

"I'm Irving Davidowsky, Mary's husband."

"What are you doing here, you Jew bastard! Get out of this house!"

"Where is Sylvie?"

"What business is it of yours? Do you want to ruin her the way you ruined her sister?"

"Listen, McCarthy. You can't live in a hole like this, and Sylvie can't live in a place like this. She's a young girl. You've got to get out of here. I'll help you."

"Who wants your help, you Jew bastard! I told you to get out of here!" McCarthy's face flushed and his eyes glared.

"You can't make a slave out of Sylvie! I can see what you're making her do." Irving gestured to the bundle near the sewing machine.

"Are you going to tell me what I can do with my own daughter, you Jew bastard?" McCarthy picked up a pan from the stove and made a threatening motion with it. "Get out of this house!"

"Father!" It was Mary; she stood at the door; she had followed Irving and climbed the stairs after him.

"You too! You Jewish whore!"

"If you weren't a sick man I'd kill you for that." Irving went up to McCarthy and pulled the pan out of his hand. "You're sick. I'll see that you get into a hospital for alcoholics; that's where you belong. Come on, Mary, there's nothing to do here." He took Mary's arm and helped her down the stairs.

"We'll have to get Father Mahoney. He's the only one who can help. He always knew how to handle him," Mary said, sobbing.

"I'll go and get him. You wait here for Sylvia. She'll listen to you sooner than she will to me. But be sure to wait down here on

the street. Why did you come up after me? I told you to wait for
me."

"I wanted to see him. Just once. I didn't know, I didn't realize,
how bad he was."

"He's sick. He doesn't know what he's doing or saying. That's
the way all alcoholics are. He's out of his mind; he's not responsible for anything. Please promise you'll wait here."

"I promise. I don't want to see him any more. I don't want to
see him." Her voice shook.

"Father Mahoney," Irving said when he told the old priest
what they had found, "I'm ready to do anything I can to help him.
It's terrible to see what he's doing to his daughter—just what
he did to his wife. He's got to be taken to a sanitorium. I'll pay
whatever's necessary. But please do what you can. Sylvie will
come to live with us—or she can go to any place you recommend.
I'm willing to see that she gets a chance. I'll pay for everything.
You're the only one that can handle him, Father Mahoney. If
you won't help us, we'll have to get the police in. You can't
imagine how they're living."

"I knew it, I knew it. He must have reached the gutter if he's
gone so far as to abandon the Church," the priest said, putting on
his overcoat and hat.

They reached the place to find Mary and Sylvie on the sidewalk in front of the house waiting for them. Sylvie was tall and
thin, like her father. Her dress was shabby; on her stockingless
feet she wore old and dilapidated shoes. Her pale face was long
and thin, the cheeks sunken.

"What could I do?" she began to weep when she saw the
priest and Irving. "After Mama died, he began to drink more
than ever. Every evening we had to go and carry him home. And
then in the morning he wasn't able to move out of bed. They threw
him out of his job, with a week's pay. He didn't stop drinking as
long as the money held out. Then Jimmy left the house. At first
he used to come to visit us once in a while, then he disappeared
entirely. We got a letter from him from somewhere in Illinois.
Then we were dispossessed, and somebody told Papa that we
could get cheap rent here, so we moved here. There was nothing
I could do. I had to get bundles to sew in the house the way Mama
used to do; I couldn't go out to work; Papa couldn't be left
alone. He's afraid to be left alone, especially when he's sober.

And he made me get him liquor every morning. He said he'd die without it. And every time he gets drunk he gets his gall bladder attack. The charities refused to help him because he drank up the money they gave him. They wanted him to go to a hospital, but he wouldn't go. What could I do? I had to stay with him. There's no one else to take care of him."

"It's all my fault! It's all my fault! All the time I was living in luxury they were starving. . . ." Mary moaned.

"It wasn't your fault," Irving comforted her. "You wanted to help him, but he wouldn't listen to you. It was no different with my father. It isn't our fault, no, it's the fault of all the hatred and prejudice and superstition they brought with them from the old country!"

"Let me go up to him. You all stay here," Father Mahoney said.

"I'll go with you, Father," Sylvia begged. "I have to take this up to him." She took a bottle from under the shawl she was wearing over her shoulders. "He'll die without it!"

The priest took the bottle from her. "I'll take it up to him. He's not to see you any more. He's got to learn that he can't count on you any more; otherwise he'll hold you in his clutches forever. You take her home with you, Mrs. Davidowsky. And you wait for me here," he said to Irving. "I'll come down as soon as I can."

When the priest returned, he seemed to be a changed man. His face was tired and wan, his shoulders were bowed as though they were loaded with a heavy burden. He was mopping his perspiring face with his handkerchief.

"He took it like a good Catholic. Come, Mr. Davidowsky. We'll have to make arrangements to get him out of here. He can't stay here alone."

It was late in the evening when Irving got home, tired and worn out. Mary was waiting up for him.

"Everything's arranged," he told her. "They took him to Bellevue for the night. Tomorrow he'll be sent to a permanent sanitorium. He didn't make any protest; Father Mahoney must have worked some sort of magic on him. He even let me help him down the stairs. He never even once called me 'Jew bastard.'"

"Oh, darling, I was so ashamed! Now you know what my father was like!"

414

"Ashamed of what? When two people love each other they have to share everything, joy as well as sorrow. There's a greater bond in common suffering than in common joy."

"Oh, Irving, I love you so much!"

"Do you know what upset me most? The sewing machine and the bundle of homework I saw there. My God, to think that that's the way the clothes are made for American women to wear! I tell you, it nearly killed me. You and Pa and Nat should have despised me long ago, the moment I started handing out the bundles. I felt like a criminal when I saw the stuff. Believe me, from now on I'm going to fight the rotten contractor system in the industry, even if I've got to risk everything I own." Irving's eyes glowed with fervor.

"Oh, Irving, darling!" Mary put her arms about him and pressed herself convulsively to him. "It wasn't only your fault. It was mine, too. That's what sent me back to 48th Street..."

"Where is Sylvie?"

"She's sleeping like a child. I made her take a hot bath and eat a little something, and I put her in Nat's room. They're both fast asleep."

"I'll watch out for her now. I'll make up to her for all the trouble she's had," Irving said firmly. "The trouble she's had from everyone, from your father, and from 'Davidowsky's bundles' too."

CHAPTER TWENTY-ONE

I T WAS not stubbornness that made Nathan refuse all offers of
help; he was convinced that there was nothing else for him
to do.

The leaf on the tree strains toward the sun's light. The roots
of the tree know where the spring of nourishment is to be found,
and they fight their way past rocks and barriers so that their
mouths may find the breast of mother earth. Nat knew what he
needed. What if he did accept his brother's help? Money might
buy another's hands to serve him and wait on him; but money
could not buy the will and the desire which should move those
hands. It was only love which could extend to him willing hands
—his father's—or Mary's—love.

But his father was a sick man; he would need the help of others
himself. And Mary's love, newly awakened to him in his hour of
need, he had rejected. Not rejected—turned it back where it belonged—to his brother.

Now, left dangling over the abyss of his helplessness, his regret and longing came back to him. He tried with all the strength
of his moral convictions to check his yearning for Mary from
passing over into forbidden bounds—but his longing was like
a hungry mouth evading all barriers and straining to the breast of
love. Again and again he asked himself: "Why should I be denied
the solace which God or destiny has sent to comfort and repay
me for my pain?"

Every individual, no matter how mean or inadequate, is the
center of his own universe, the one for whom all other things
exist. Nathan was unable to allow his acceptance of his fate to
stifle his natural feelings. His desperate need broke through the
bonds he sought to impose on it. "The hands which I need are
Mary's; I have a right to them, for they are part of my life. She
is a part of me. I have a right to her." For all his efforts Nathan
416

could not completely deaden his normal and healthy desires. In spite of himself they would find culmination.

The physical sexual act is not the sole expression of love; it is one of love's manifestations and experiences, but not the chief one. If it were, man would have accepted it as the highest expression of spiritual satisfaction and human worth and would guard its sanctity so jealously that it would be transformed into a holy rite—instead of regarding it as unclean, as an animal convulsion over which he has no control. Love, the highest gift of God to man, has manifold ways for its expression and fulfillment—stronger, deeper, and richer than its mere physical realization. Man's noblest feeling is too vast and too sacred to be so limited and enchained.

With Moshe Wolf no longer able to help him, Nathan lay in bed in the small room for hours at a time, patiently waiting for someone to come and help him dress. Patience became his other nature. He divided his personality into two parts. The Nathan who lay helpless on the bed was pure thought and feeling. Everything that happened seemed to be unreal and somehow fantastic; the soul within the motionless body on the bed soared on the wings of desire and imagination. In that half-world, fantasy and reality mingled and became one, and no boundaries stood in their way to divide them. The other personality took over only when Nathan, dressed and attended to, sat in his wheel chair. The chair became an organic part of his body; it took the place of his limbs. It permitted him to move about. In his chair he felt an equality with all men. Now that he was compelled to spend long hours of the day in bed, he fled from the real world into the interior world of unfulfilled yearnings and desires which he imagined he had long conquered and thrust out of his life.

In the short time that Mary had been in the house and had helped him in the ordered round of his day, his longing had taken on new intensity. He lay waiting all morning for the miracle of her presence to manifest itself. But even before she came, as though in a dream, as in that first day she had returned, he could feel again on his body the cool touch of her fingers, like hungry lips, drawing out of the pores of his skin his hidden yearning for her and communicating her own yearning for him. The feelings were sinful, forbidden, taboo—but for that very reason they were all the sweeter.

He fought against his sinful thoughts. Sometimes he could prevail against them, but most of the time he yielded to their insistence. Then he would feel himself damned in body and soul—until his faith in God would come to him, like a protecting angel, and guard him with its wings from the terrors of the night.

His faith in God and his surrender to the Divine Will was his guardian and his protector in the terrifying darkness. It was only his faith that could save him from the uncleanness of his thoughts; it was the filter through which his confused thoughts about Mary were purified. They lifted his desire for her into a world of eternal longing, a refuge and a sanctuary from the physical and moral torment which was his portion in the world of reality.

His mother, the only one left to help him, did what she could to win his trust; she tried hard to take Moshe Wolf's place. With the realization of what it meant to him to be deprived of his father's help, a deep love for him had awakened in her heart. She had seen Nathan's paralysis as something decreed by heaven—she had been callous to it because she was powerless against it. But her heart had bled for him, and if she had been distant from him it was as much Nathan's fault as her own. He had sensed, with the sharpened instincts of the cripple, her coldness toward him, and with the stubbornness of the cripple he had retreated from her, had refused to allow her near him. When, as often happened, Moshe Wolf was so occupied in the store that he was unable to come upstairs and instead his mother came to dress him, Nat petulantly refused. He convinced himself that he felt a definite physical aversion to the touch of her hands.

"I don't need you, Ma! I'll wait until Pa comes up," he used to say, and turn his head away from her.

"I won't eat you up, God forbid," she would answer. "Can't you stand your own mother!" She could not help feeling a bitter resentment at his shrinking from her, and she had paid him back in the same coin. "Oh, dear God in heaven, why did you visit this punishment on me?" Gradually the enmity between mother and son had increased.

Now that Moshe Wolf was sick, she tried in every way she could to find again the love and tenderness she had felt for Nat before the illness had struck him down. But he rebuffed her each time she tried to help him.

"But who else will take care of you? Your father is sick and he can do nothing for you," she said to him one morning.

"Don't worry, Ma. There'll be somebody. It'll be all right."

"Why do you stay in bed this way? Let me dress you."

"No, no, I'm all right," and he turned his face away.

Was it her fault that he did not sense in her touch the delicate pity and tender comfort that he felt in his father's fingers?

"But you'll have to lie in bed all day like this! There's no one else to do anything for you." Tears of mortification came to her eyes.

Moshe Wolf could hear what was going on from his bed in the other room. "Deborah," he called in his weak voice, "leave him alone...."

Nat began to feel a wave of pity for his mother. He knew that he was being unjust toward her, and that he was equally guilty with her in the alienation that had taken place between them; no, more—he was willing to take all the blame on himself! But it was too late now. There was nothing else he could have done. And now there was this new and uncontrollable sense of shame which had come over him; maybe it was the consequence of the long alienation between mother and son—but whatever it was, he rebelled against the very thought of having his mother's eyes see his naked body or her hands touch his naked flesh. His refusal to allow her to attend to him sent her off into a flood of tears.

"I am a stranger to my own son," she complained bitterly.

"What nonsense are you talking?" Moshe Wolf answered. "There's no sense in making things worse than they are."

For Nathan nothing was left but to brood over his lot. He compared himself to a hunted creature with a pursuing lion hot on its heels. For a moment he might find refuge in some hidden path, but then the beast would be pouncing on him again to devour him. It was only his profound faith which interposed its sheltering wings to save him from eternal destruction. "God has not forgotten me. He has allotted a purpose for me. It is not I who am the master of my fate; I am only its custodian, and it is my task to be of service to God and man. Since God has made me dependent on others, then He will not deprive me of the power to find that other who might help me. And if the good will of that other can only be earned through love, then surely He will implant in that other the love of a father for me. There are no strangers before God; all men are fathers and sons."

Moshe Wolf had become so much better that Dr. Chazanowitch allowed him to leave his bed, but he had not yet given permission to move him to the new apartment which Irving and Mary had rented for them near their own home, and where Nathan was also to stay until he could arrange his future.

Moshe Wolf, however, simply found it impossible to imagine leaving 48th Street. How could he leave the store and the customers among whom he had spent so many years? Had not God placed him in the store so that he might provide each day's food for the poor people of the block? How could he leave them? Even though most of the old customers had moved away, the block still held Moshe Wolf bound fast with strong chains.

He was glad that Dr. Chazanowitch would not consent to his immediate transfer to the new apartment. He was still too weak for that, the doctor said; it would be safer to wait. But each day he reminded the sick man—"Well, Moshe Wolf, it's getting to be time for you to start packing up. In a week or two you'll be able to say good-by to this neighborhood for good."

"In a week or two? So quickly? There are so many things to attend to before I can leave."

"What, for instance?"

"Well, first I have to wind up the affairs of the store. I've still got merchandise."

"That's all been taken care of without you," Deborah commented. "Irving took care of all the bills, and the goods he sent away to the hospital—to Bellevue, where Nathan was. The Doctor advised him."

"And nobody asked me about it?"

"That's also something for you to worry about! Maybe we should have carried you down to the store in the bed so that you could attend to everything?" Deborah said ironically.

"If he had at least given away some of the things to the poor neighbors."

"So we did that without you. Nat told Irving, and Irving did it," Deborah said.

"Then I'm satisfied," Moshe Wolf said. "Well, then, we're through with the store. Dear God," he added with a sigh.

"What are you sighing for? Maybe you're sorry!"

"Why shouldn't I sigh? Of course I'm sorry. So many years ... so many years seeing that the poor neighbors had some food...."

"Let someone else do it from now on. They'll be smarter than you. They won't give the store away for nothing, the way you did...."

"And do you think that will be good? It's a pity for the poor people..."

"Let others show pity. You've done your share. More than enough."

Moshe Wolf didn't answer, but later in the day he said to Nat: "Before I move away I'd like to go once more to the prayer house on Norfolk Street, to my Hasidim. It's so long since I've been there."

"I don't know if the doctor would allow you, Pa. You'd better wait till you're altogether better."

"But when I move away from here, I'll never have a chance to go down there...."

"Yes, you will, Pa. You can go down in a taxi."

"All the way to Norfolk Street?"

"Sure."

Moshe Wolf lapsed into silence.

"Just the same," he said after a while, "before I move out of the neighborhood I'd like to go down there and say good-by to them. After all, so many years..."

"Don't worry, Pa. I'll talk to Irving about it."

"Yes, my son. Talk to Irving. Thank you, my son."

It had grown warm outdoors. A bright sun was shining. The summer had come on quickly—in the typical Manhattan way—leaving the spring lost somewhere along the road.

Since the days were so pleasant, Dr. Chazanowitch permitted Moshe Wolf to spend some time outdoors, on a chair on the sidewalk. They both sat—father and son—in front of the closed store and let the sun's warmth descend on them. Moshe Wolf gazed up and down the block, as though he were seeing it for the first and the last time. He hardly recognized the familiar street. Half the block was in the process of being rebuilt. There was the sound of hammering, and the confusion of construction going on.

At one end of the block a roof was being pulled down. Enormous trucks rumbled by, laden with lumber and bricks. At the East River end of the block Harry Greenstock's house had been entirely demolished. The lot on which it stood, and the yard in which 48th Street had planted its gardens and where Long Anthony, Zelig's horse, had pastured on Sundays, was now blocked by a high fence which hid the river from the street.

"They've blocked off the river!" Moshe Wolf said in astonishment. "The road to the river is blocked."

"Yes, Pa. They're going to build a big apartment house there. The river will belong to the people who live in the house now."

"And I thought a river was free, that it belonged to everybody."

"The river is still free, Pa. It's only the entrance to it that's blocked."

"What's the good of the river if the people can't get to it?" Moshe Wolf murmured. "Without the river 48th Street won't be the same. It's too bad. A shame."

From his shop window across the street Heimowitz saw father and son quietly talking together. He had read in his Yiddish newspaper the account of how Irving Davidowsky was the first of the manufacturers to settle with the union and to give up the contract system and the bundles. And he had read the articles which praised and held him up as an example to other manufacturers; all that must have been Nathan's doing, Heimowitz had decided, and he had made peace with Nathan in his own thoughts, as well as with Moshe Wolf. After all, Nathan had accomplished something really important. . . .

Now, seeing Moshe Wolf downstairs on the street for the first time since his illness, he got up from his sewing machine, left the store, and crossed the street. How could a man do less? Especially when he had heard that they were moving from the block.

"I rejoice to see you well again, and you too, Nat." Heimowitz held out his hand. "That was a good job you did with your brother. I read about it in the papers."

"I didn't do it. My brother did it, out of his own good heart," Nat replied.

"Whichever way it was . . . what's the difference? As long as Davidowsky's bundles are gone for good. . . . Well, when are we going to see you around in our ranks again?"

"I don't know that they're so eager to have me in your ranks."

"What are you talking about? While the strike's on, they need everybody...."

"You don't mean to say they'll let me talk to the strikers? They threw me out as a spy...."

"A spy! You know very well that as long as Irving wallowed in those bundles, the mud covered you, too. But now, as long as he's behaving the way he is and was the first one to settle with the union and give an example... well, who can have any objection?"

"You've done enough, my son," Moshe Wolf interrupted. "You've made speeches, you've shouted your lungs out, and for nothing! They chased you away. Now you've got to start to do things for yourself."

"Pa, you said you wanted to go down to your Hasidic prayer house to pray with your own people. Well, the workers are my people. I want to pray with them."

Moshe Wolf was silent.

"That's an answer for you, Moshe Wolf!" Heimowitz chuckled. "So you're moving away, eh? You're not the only one. We're all moving. We've all been given notice—Melamed, Tony the Italian, Zelig the junk dealer, even Choleva, and the pigeons. They've served a notice on me, too. All the poor people are being thrown out of the block. Tammany's moving out. They're tearing down the buildings and they're getting ready to put up big apartment houses for the rich. The Republicans are moving in. You see the way they've blocked the river."

"Yes, we saw," Moshe Wolf answered sorrowfully. "It's a shame, especially on account of the synagogue."

"You mean Shmulevitch's *shul?*"

"Yes, Shmulevitch's."

Heimowitz laughed sarcastically, showing a mouthful of yellow teeth.

"What's there to laugh at? It's our own congregation, after all."

"No more! It's not your congregation any more. The congregation has already moved away from here. It isn't even Shmulevitch's congregation any more."

"What do you mean?"

"Haven't you heard about it? There'll be a moving picture theater there instead of a *shul*. While Shmulevitch was throwing you out, it was already sold for a theater. They say that Shmule-

423

vitch bought it himself from the bank, after he let the mortgage go by default."

"And what'll he do about his kosher poultry business?"

"That's gone, too. Now he's in the real estate business. That's where the money is, ever since the boom started."

"Then there's nothing more for me to do here," said Moshe Wolf with a sigh. "Now it's time to move. But one thing more. What'll happen to poor Melamed if they put him out of his flat and there are no more bundles to take in? What will he do? Who'll look out for him?"

"Don't worry, Moshe Wolf. Melamed had luck. His wife got a touch of consumption—she started to spit blood—and the charities are sending them to the South to a sanitorium. And they'll take care of the children, too."

Moshe Wolf sighed. "It's time for me to pack up my belongings and move on," he said. "Only it's a shame to leave the East River. Tell me, my son, in the neighborhood where we're going, is there an East River there, too?"

"Sure, Pa, the Hudson River. You'll be right near the Hudson River."

"Hudson?" Moshe Wolf looked doubtful, and then made a contemptuous motion with his hand. "What kind of a river is that! How can you compare it? Over here, the river is here and the houses are here"—Moshe Wolf held his hands close together to illustrate his meaning. "But there—where are the houses, and where's the Hudson?" He looked up triumphantly, the point made. "Anyway, it's time to go. Deborah!" he called.

"I'm coming. I'm coming," came Deborah's voice; she came out and helped him into the flat.

When Moshe Wolf had gone inside, Heimowitz turned to Nat.

"There's something I want to tell you," he said. "Ever since I heard that your father was sick, I've been thinking about you."

"About me?" Nat said. "I thought you were through with me after our last talk. Remember?"

"Yes, I remember. That was a lot of foolishness. What's past is past. Now things are different. Irving's turned out to be a good boy; he gave up those cursed bundles, and he was the first to settle with the union. And if he's all right with the union, he's all right with me. Besides, who doesn't know that you're the one

424

that's responsible? But I want to talk about something else; about you. I've only been waiting for the chance."

"What is it?"

"This is what it is. Now that your father's sick and can't take care of you, and as long as you don't want to go to live with Irving..."

"Who told you that?"

"Nobody has to put a finger in my mouth. I know you won't go to live with him, and I know you won't take his money."

Nat stared at him in astonishment. "Who told you that?" he repeated.

"I know; I know! And I know, too, that what you need you can't get from Irving or from his money."

Nat was silent.

"No, Nat," Heimowitz continued. "What you need, none of them can give you and their money can't buy. What you need is another Moshe Wolf, another father, do you understand? Maybe the best thing would be for you to move in with me. Anyway, I've got to find a new place. I was thinking maybe I'd move down on the East Side, among our own people, do you understand? I could take care of you; I could watch out for you; I could never be like your father, but I—I could be some help." Heimowitz pulled out a handkerchief and mopped his face.

Nathan looked at him. It was as though he had never really seen him before. In his tired eyes was a new softness, as though they had been washed in tears, and they looked at him with such timidity and love that Nat had to struggle to hold back his own tears.

"But why, why, Heimowitz?" he stammered at last. "Why should you burden yourself with me?"

"Because you're a human being and I'm a human being. What else? You need help and I can give it to you. Isn't that enough? And after all we're not strangers. We've been close to each other for years. We went to meetings together and we made speeches togther—and we'll do it again."

"And I suppose if I make speeches about God, you won't have anything to do with me again!" Nat laughed nervously to hide the tremor in his voice.

"All right, so it was a mistake! You're not going to hold it against me all my life," Heimowitz grumbled in embarrassment.

425

"What does a man do if his son believes in nonsense? He lets him talk it out. And especially when he sees that the nonsense isn't so useless after all—that it even helps a bit." He was silent for a moment. "After all, the ideals we have are the same; isn't that the way it is? I have no wife, my children are far away, they don't need me and I don't need them. Why shouldn't you come to live with me? I'll help you the way I used to; it'll be something for me to do. I'll have a friend around, someone in the house to talk to, to do something for. After all, a man isn't an animal."

"How will we manage together? What'll we live on?" Nat asked. He could hardly get the words out for the lump in his throat.

"Something! What do we care! That's nothing to worry about. First of all, I've still got my shop. Did you think I was going to be a banker and live on my dividends? Besides, something will turn up for you, too. If not today, then tomorrow. Do you think they can get along without you now, while the union is having such a fight on its hands? What is the difference—union or no union? The workers need you and they'll want you back. Don't worry. Something will turn up. Besides, how much do we need after all? We're not going to any dances ... and certainly not to the opera...."

"Maybe we'll go to the opera, Heimowitz," Nat said, laughing happily. "I like the opera."

"All right, so I'll take you to the opera.... What choice have I got? If I have to put up with your bourgeois nonsense, your religion, and God, and all that foolishness, then I'll have to put up with the opera, too. Opera! What can I do? Well, Nat, what do you say?"

"What I say, Heimowitz, is that you're caught in that nonsense yourself."

"What nonsense?" .

"The bourgeois nonsense about God."

"Me?"

"Sure, Heimowitz. You."

Yes, Nat thought, Heimowitz, too. He was the symbol of the masses; he had the virtues of the masses as well as their intolerance. Their religious intolerance was only a result of their sufferings. Heimowitz's protest against God was an outcry against social injustice and against the poverty which destroyed the workers' lives. It was in reality a cry against all of society. Break down the iron wall of society's indifference, and they would find their way to God. Was it not to the breaking down of that iron wall that he had dedicated his own life?

Heimowitz helped him off the wheel chair and into the house. Yes, Nat thought, Heimowitz would be his limbs. He would be the other half of himself—as his father had been. What else was he waiting for? Why should he not accept? The labor movement would use him; they would find something for him to do. They wanted him among them; they needed him. Was it not the labor movement which was the wife, the beloved, with whom he had sought to unite his life, the justification for his tortured existence?

When Nat told his father, Moshe Wolf fell into a brooding silence. Then he said: "And what about Irving? I thought that now..." He did not finish. Instead he said: "Maybe you're right. After all, he's a God-fearing man. Yes, it's good. You always wanted to be with the people. May God bless you, my son," and Moshe Wolf closed his eyes.

CHAPTER TWENTY-TWO

IN MOSHE WOLF'S voice was a new softness and contentment. "Deborah," he said, "before we move away from here
for good, I'd like once more to spend the Sabbath at my old
Hasidic prayer house downtown, with my old friends and kinsmen. Who knows if I'll ever see them again?"

"But with your sick heart—where will you stay over Friday
night?"

"I'll stay at Shmuel Chaim's, where else—the same as before.
He still has the dairy store on Norfolk Street, across the street
from the prayer house. You'll take me there on Friday afternoon,
and on Saturday night, when the Sabbath is over, you can come
for me."

"But Moshe Wolf, God forbid, it's a risk for your health. . . ."

"To pray on the Sabbath with the friends of my young days?
No, Deborah, it's not a risk. Our holy writings declare that if
one sets out on a journey to perform a good deed, no harm can
come to him."

"And what will the doctor say? Will Dr. Chazanowitch allow it?"

"Foolish woman, who says he's got to know anything about it?
Naturally, a stubborn unbeliever like him would say no."

Deborah yielded. Early on Friday, when Nat was away from
the house, she packed some night clothes for Moshe Wolf, together with his prayer shawl, and took a taxi—"a fortune of
Irving's hard-earned money," she complained—and took him
down to Shmuel Chaim's flat on the floor above his kosher dairy
store.

"Malke, my crown, my jewel," she said to Shmuel Chaim's
wife, "I have brought you a guest for the Sabbath. He took it into
his head that he had to come down once more, at least before we
move uptown, near my son."

428

"You understand, Shmuel Chaim," Moshe Wolf said. "I had to come. I had to be with all of you once more before we move away. Who knows when...? You understand me, Shmuel Chaim."

"Of course I understand you, Moshe Wolf. Why shouldn't I understand?" Shmuel Chaim was a small, thin man with a long graying beard. "It's been a wonder to me that you stayed away so long."

Moshe Wolf sighed. Yes, it had been a long time, but there had been reason enough. So many things had happened, so many things.

"Don't worry, Deborah. We'll take care of him," Malke said cheerfully. "We'll take care of him."

"If God wills," Deborah sighed devoutly, "I'll come for him tomorrow night, when the Sabbath is over."

The Hasidic prayer house on Norfolk Street was located on the upper floor of a two-story building across the street from Shmuel Chaim's store, in a long, low-ceilinged hall, with white-washed walls. It was only on Friday evenings and Saturdays that the congregation had the use of the hall; during the weekdays and on Sundays it was rented out to lodges, societies, clubs, and the like for their regular meetings. Flags and banners and emblems were stacked in a corner of the room. Photographs of club functionaries hung on the walls. In the afternoons the hall served as the office of an East Side marriage broker, and in the mornings an old-world rabbi sat at a desk advising the clients who came to consult him on matters of ritual or domestic problems. On the few evenings when no lodge meetings were scheduled, the room was let out for various purposes—sometimes to a dancing teacher giving lessons to members of a young people's club, or to a radical group for lectures on socialism given by a well-known lecturer.

But always on Friday evenings the hall became a sanctuary for the spirit. Shmuel Chaim, who was sexton and "treasurer" of the Hasidic group, would come up to the hall early in the afternoon. He would clear the hall of the reminders of its weekday uses and sweep the floor, sprinkling it with sawdust for cleanliness. From the corner behind a protecting curtain, where it had reposed all week, he would bring out the small Ark of the Law and place it against the east wall. The Scroll, which he kept at home between Sabbaths so that it might be safe from the contamination of the weekday goings-on in the room, he would bring over from his flat, carefully wrapped in a prayer shawl, and place it in the Ark. Malke, his wife, would polish the heavy brass candlesticks and Shmuel Chaim would set them on the altar.

As dusk began to descend, the devout assembled, as in the town of their younger days, gathered around their rabbi, breathing in the glow which shone forth from the saintly presence, the earthly symbol of the Messiah himself. Now, too, they stood in their shiny and worn caftans, skullcaps on their heads. They stood there, these remnants of a devouter Israel, in an East Side hall, yet transported to the rare spheres where the holy Sabbath reigned. The candles flickered at the altar. The Scroll reposed in its Ark. At the eastern wall stood Reb Leibush, messenger of their rabbi far away in the old world, and Shmuel Chaim chanted the ancient, familiar Sabbath eve greeting—"Come, my friend, to greet the Bride, to give welcome unto the Sabbath."

Outside in the street was the modern Babylonia, where store windows were bright with electric light. Raucous gramophones split the air with chants and popular tunes. Both sides of the street were lined with pushcarts, with flaring kerosene torches lighting up the piles of goods—shirts, dresses, corsets, shoes, remnants of woolens and silks, bankrupt stock and fire-damaged merchandise. There were pushcarts piled high with pots and pans, hardware, dishes, and glass. Old Jews stood about, strings of suspenders and belts and neckties over their shoulders. Women stood in front of barrels of herrings and pickled cucumbers, peppers, and tomatoes.

The noise and confusion mounted skyward—peddlers calling out their wares, altercations, shrieks of playing children. Over all rose the glare of the flaming torches and the red glow of burning crates, garbage, and sweepings, the bonfires built by the children in the middle of the gutters. The flames of sound flared and leaped up like the flames of the bonfires. "Women, women, hurry, hurry! Corsets, underwear!" And from an open window a woman's harried voice calling "Jimmie, Jimmie!"

In the prayer house, above the babel of noise, stood the small group of the devout, rocking back and forth in devotion, held together by the vision they saw behind their closed eyes. They were dancing on green fields, going forth with their rabbi to

430

greet the Sabbath, bathing their souls in the fragrant scents of the trees and flowers. It was good to worship among the trees and wild grasses, to hear the song of adoration each blade of grass and each leaf sang to the Eternal, the Creator of all things. The blades of grass sang their songs of praise without any other thought; they sought no reward. They sang their song of praise out of serene joy.

So they too sang. They sought no reward. They asked for nothing from the Creator of all things; they sought only to unite in the joy that streamed out of the holy Sabbath. Sabbath was a Queen, the Queen Sabbath, the eternal spirit of peace. No, Sabbath was more than Queen; Sabbath was the Bride, the eternal Bride, arrayed in her shining garments so that the saints and sages and virtuous might greet her. They beheld her with the eyes of the soul. A rain of mercy came floating from the clouds, and they saw her walking forth, her feet naked, her body clad in shimmering raiment, haloed by stars, the Sabbath crown on her head, her face covered with a black veil, in mourning for Israel in exile. They saw her coming toward them, and they stretched out their arms to her in adoration. Their hearts melted in longing and their lips sang—"Come, my friend, to greet the Bride, to give welcome unto the Sabbath!"

When the services were over, the congregants gathered together for learning and discourse. They were waiting to hear from the lips of Reb Leibush words of saintliness and devotion to quicken their souls and hearten them through the week of toil in the cursed sweatshops of their exile. Reb Leibush was delicate and fragile-looking. An ethereal quality shone out from his long pale face; it seemed as though any moment he would be wafted on the wings of pure spirit to some higher sphere. He was tall and gaunt. His wise rabbinical forehead rose high on an enormous head entirely disproportionate to his fragile body. His pale yellow beard was so scanty that each particular hair seemed to have been set carefully into the flesh by a parsimonious hand. His watery blue eyes either gazed timidly to the side or were downcast. During his devotions he swayed with such unexpected dexterity that at one moment the upper part of his body would be parallel to the floor and at the next he would be bent down so that his head almost touched his toes. His words could almost be seen

431

rising past the bones and sinews of his gaunt throat before they escaped from his lips.

Reb Leibush ordinarily was a silent man, hardly ever saying a word until, between the meals on the Sabbath, he would expound the Torah, or on these Friday nights when he would discourse on the mystic books of the Kabbala to quench the spiritual thirst of the devout followers of his rabbi.

How had this rare plant of the ecstatic East been transplanted to the cold shores of America? The truth was that Reb Leibush had come to the New World on a mission from the Hasidic Court in the old country to the rabbi's devout followers in America, so as to hold them fast to the rabbinical grace and at the same time raise enough money to publish the writings of the rabbi's grandfather, the founder of the Hasidic dynasty. The war that had broken out in Europe after he left had prevented his return. The wealthy Hasidim in the New World had fobbed him off with modest gifts of money; they had moved away from the East Side; now they lived in the elegant districts farther uptown. Only the poorest of the poor were left in the East Side prayer house, the artisans and laborers who spent their weeks in factories and shops. It was these who had taken the rabbi's representative to their souls; they squeezed enough pennies out of their meager wages to provide for him in the home of an orthodox kinsman.

All week Reb Leibush wandered about as though he were in a pagan wilderness. In the house where he lived, there were only women and children, with their constant noise and tumult and squabbling. Sewing machines rattled and creaked all day. During the day the bed on which he slept was folded up and kept behind a curtain in a corner; he had no place to sit in comfort and reflect. He spent most of his time in a small synagogue near by, where the sexton permitted him to sit at the table and pore over the holy volumes.

The week days were long and weary and lonely. But on Friday night his Sabbath of pure joy began. After the Friday evening prayer services he did not hurry to go home; there was no one for him to go home to. Some of the congregation, too, were alone and lonely; they had left wives and children behind them in the old country; they lived with strangers; they, too, were in no hurry to depart from the intimate and familiar atmosphere of the prayer house. Even those with families preferred to remain until late in the night. Shmuel Chaim had brought a carafe of Sabbath wine and two Sabbath loaves which his wife, Malke, had prepared; there were a few pieces of savory fish, too. Shmuel Chaim dragged out a table and set it before the altar, covered it with a white cloth, and put on the loaves and the fish. Reb Leibush sat at the head of the table and pronounced the benediction.

What does the devout man need to be joyous? A loaf of bread and words of wisdom from his rabbi. Reb Leibush had already recounted some of the rabbi's precious words—they would be remembered over and over and would bring solace to weary hearts during the long week in the shop. Now he was preparing to ascend to higher spheres. His eyes were closed behind his hands, and he was swaying like a blade of wheat in the fields. His body trembled with awe and terror at the majesty of the words he uttered. It was not on the Torah he was discoursing now; he was telling of the mysteries of the Zohar.

"It is written that God said unto Moses—Thou shalt cleave unto the Lord thy God. But how shall man, made of uncleanness and sunk in the sin of the world, laboring in the sweat of his brow—how shall he cleave unto God, may His name be blessed, whose majesty man cannot conceive? Therefore is it that God created the Zaddik, the saint. For the saint is he on whom the foundation of the world rests. He is God's vessel, who brings man close to Him and holds him embraced in His spirit. And therefore does the pious Hasid seek to unite with his Zaddik, become one with him, and purify himself of all other desires. Through the Hasid's love to the Zaddik he is one with him, and through the Zaddik's love to God, may His name be blessed, we may be united with Him in the highest holiness."

Reb Leibush paused. He closed his eyes and stood motionless. Even the hairs of his thin beard were still. About his pale face there was an otherworldly glow which smoothed out the aged folds and wrinkles, and made it younger and of an unearthly beauty.

"Come, let us unite with the Zaddik!" The words came from his lips in a whisper of ecstasy.

An even deeper silence descended on the room. The worshipers around the table stopped their pious swaying and, like the speaker, sat motionless. Some of them covered their eyes with their hands.

433

Others bent forward and sat with closed eyes, transported to distant worlds. The otherworldly glow that shone from the face of Reb Leibush seemed to radiate from their faces too, smoothing away all mundane cares and bathing them in a strange effulgence. The candles flickered in the holders; so tremulous was the silence that the soft spluttering of the melting wax could be heard. Shadows gathered in the corners of the room, as though the Sabbath candles had driven them there, like evil spirits, far from the worshipers who sat immobile in the Sabbath holiness, transported into limitless spheres. Gone were the shops, and factories, and all the alien world. Even the clamorous street disappeared, together with the glaring electric lights which gleamed through the windows, and all the hubbub and noise and confusion. They were in a world where there was only grace and beneficence, only joy and rejoicing. There they would find the Zaddik, the holy flame, like an angel of Heaven, who was compounded only of love for God. And they were one with him through the love which he had set aglow in their hearts, and they could feel it flaming up in them, filling them with unaccustomed strength. Now the flame flared higher; they were bound together in one unity; together they were united with the Zaddik to Holiness itself, to the spirit of grace and holiness of which they were now a part.

Moshe Wolf sat among them. He had lost all awareness of self. The threads that tied him to the world of sorrows were all severed. He was not Moshe Wolf the storekeeper, the troubled father, with a Christian daughter-in-law and a Christian grandchild. That was another Moshe Wolf, the man of yesterday and tomorrow, with whom he had nothing to do. This Moshe Wolf, sitting at the table among his fellow pietists and Hasidim, holding his hands over his eyes and projecting himself into worlds of purity and grace, was a free soul, a Sabbath soul, living only in the ecstasy of the Sabbath. He was pure ecstasy, for he was part of the Ineffable. He had discarded all cares; he was living in the world from which he once had come, in the world of eternal joy and goodness to which he longed to return.

"Great Zaddik on whose sanctity the foundations of the world are built!" Reb Leibush murmured. He shuddered as though a wind were passing over him.

"Zaddik of goodness!" the congregants around the table murmured, trembling and swaying.

Again there was silence, a breathless stillness.

"Prayer and God, may His name be blessed, are one. Through prayer man is bound to God. Open up your hearts and let the Blessed One enter into you through prayer."

The congregants moaned and swayed, moaned and swayed.

"And now," Reb Leibush intoned, "now we enter into the highest stage of ineffable bliss. Through union with the Zaddik we are united with the Holy One...."

Reb Leibush swayed like a lone tree in a field. A moan escaped his lips. "The pillar of the world, Zaddik is his name. He bears the sorrow of the world. The woes of the son of man penetrate into his heart; for he is the heart of the world. And just as the heart feels the pain of the flesh, so does the Zaddik feel the pain of the world. He is the true Zaddik, the great Zaddik, he is Messiah the King. He suffers with us and for us. Well has it been said, the souls of the lesser Zaddikim fly about the world and when they see the sons of men who are oppressed in suffering, and when they see how the wicked of the world lengthen the exile of the righteous, then they hasten to bear the news to Messiah the King. And the Messiah goes into a palace in Paradise which is known as the Palace of the Sons of the Shepherds. And the Messiah enters and takes unto himself all the pain and suffering which oppresses Israel. For if he did not lighten the sufferings of Israel, then no man in the world would be able to bear the pain of the sins which have been committed against the Torah. For when the Jews were in their own land, the Zohar tells us, they lightened their sufferings and their misfortunes through the sacrifices which they brought into the Temple. But now the Messiah carries the burden of man's sufferings, as it is written—'he was wounded for our transgressions, he was bruised for our iniquities; the chastisement of our peace was upon him; and with his stripes we are healed.'"

Reb Leibush was again silent, as though he was brooding over his words.

"And there is a *midrash* which tells that the Messiah lies stretched out on a couch in Paradise and from his eyes pour rivers of tears over the sufferings of the world. And the prophet Elijah sits by him and wipes away his tears and comforts him and says to him—'Do not weep, my son, for soon God will open His heart of grace.'"

From here and there among the congregants came moans that seemed to be torn out of their hearts over the sufferings of the Messiah. The voice of Reb Leibush became joyous as though he were seeking to exorcise the sadness.

"Today is the Sabbath, and the Sabbath is pure joy, for it stems from the highest heights and the deepest springs of eternal truth. Sabbath is the substance and the achievement. For the Sabbath is rest and rest is joy. And joy can be achieved only through the highest virtue, which is love; in love is the Sabbath, and the Messiah, and the Mantle of Grace. 'Let me be faint with love for God as a man is faint with love for his beloved," sang the sainted rabbi. 'I am faint with love,' sang Solomon the great king. And the Zohar declares that in one of the hidden corners of heaven there is a palace which is known as the Palace of Love. There gather the secret things, the most secret of the secret. There the pure souls gather and God is among them and they unite with him, through his kiss of love. And when man purifies himself of all uncleanness and unites with God, not for gain but because he is faint with love for God, then he is worthy to share the reward of Moses the Patriarch—to sit with God in the Palace of Love and to partake of the ecstasy of God's kiss."

All the night Moshe Wolf lay on the iron cot which Malke had prepared for him. His mind and heart were full with the words he had heard from Reb Leibush's lips. If only he could earn the grace to be with God in the Palace of Love which Reb Leibush had described. If only he could earn the grace—if but for the moment of the winking of an eye—to be there, with all of the holy Zaddikim, and to expire with love for God. He could see the Palace before his very eyes. There were no walls, no ceiling. There was only an expanse of space, roofed over with blue clouds. And all around were green pastures, the same fields he remembered from his old home, the green pastures near the stream and the forest in Lenschiz, where the peat fields began. And above them were tall birch trees, and lambs pastured on the field—as David the shepherd had sung : He maketh me to lie down in green pastures. And there, among the green fields, was the Palace of the Shepherds, and the children of Abraham, Isaac, and Jacob, who were shepherds, and Moses, and David; and the Messiah, King of Messiahs, lay on a golden couch. He was sick, sick with love

436

for the world, sick with the desire to save it, sick because of the sufferings which he had taken unto himself. And the prophet Elijah sat beside him and wiped his tears away and comforted him. And around the Messiah were gathered all of the Zaddikim, and they were faint with love for God and with yearning for him. They stretched out their arms and cried, "My soul yearns unto God," just as he himself was faint with love for God and yearning to bring his soul under the wings of the divine grace and hide under it, like a dove that hides its head between its sheltering wings. . . .

But how could he aspire to taste that divine joy and ecstasy! Even the very thought was a sin, a pride and a haughtiness of the spirit. What had he done in his life? How had he spent his days?

Moshe Wolf summoned the book of his life before his memory. He had labored all day in a store, devoting his days to trade and vanity of spirit. "Ah, the black days," he moaned. "Never time to pray to God in dignity and peace!" True, here and there he had done a slight service for others, given a poor man food on credit, overlooked a debt, forgotten a reckoning, helped where he could, made no difference between Jew and Gentile. . . . But what grace, what virtue was there in all of this? After all, a man has not a heart of stone. . . . He had a son, a cripple, on his hands; and, yes, he had tried to be good to him. Should he seek reward for that? Was it not his debt? "Like as a father pitieth his children." Had not the Psalmist sung the words? He had not wanted to profit from another's toil; even now he did not want to profit. God knew how heavy it was for him to accept his son's charity. But was this a virtue because of which his portion should be Paradise? And had he not taken a Gentile daughter-in-law into his house, befriended her, eaten the food she prepared? What, did he think that this too would be overlooked and forgotten?

He felt a surge of strength. He would not let himself be drawn into the pit of Gehenna from whose depths the destroying angels were stretching forth their arms to draw him in. No, dear God, You are the father of all mercifulness! You know that there was nothing else I could do. You Yourself commanded that we be merciful to all Your creation. No, it will not be counted against me for a sin. God will show His compassion. . . . But surely I have not earned Paradise.

The tortured thoughts haunted him through the night. Several times it came to him that he was defiling the Sabbath; Sabbath was joy, and melancholy on the Sabbath was a great sin; he must not tarnish the ecstasy of the Sabbath. But his heart was heavy, as though a mountain of sorrows had piled on him. He tried to crawl out from under it, but he stumbled and fell, then found his footing, and stumbled and found himself again. "God, have mercy on me. I have no one but You."

His heart felt lighter. He saw now that everything was right. So was it destined to be; so should it be. Nathan, too, would find his way. He had Heimowitz now; Heimowitz would watch out for him, like a father. And, who knew, if he, Moshe Wolf, were no longer here, Deborah would open her heart to him. After all, a mother—and who can love a child more than a mother? And there would be Irving, too. Whatever had happened, Irving had always been a good son and a good brother. They would see to him, they would watch over him. . . .

"And who presumes to say that Moshe Wolf, a poor grocer, must be in the Palace of Righteousness with the Zaddikim? What deeds of virtue have I performed to earn so great a portion? And why should I not be content in the humblest palace among the humble people, or even outside, at the window, and listen to the pleasant songs of yearning which the Zaddikim within sing to the Lord of all things? Let them only permit me to stand at the window and listen to the songs of longing and desire."

He remembered the words of the Sabbath song—"Prepare the Sabbath feast for the worshipers." See! The Zaddikim were expiring with longing for the effulgence of God, for the love of God. . . .

And, in his sleep, Moshe Wolf joined them, to expire with them, in longing . . . and in love. . . .

THE END

438